NH

LABOR RELATIONS AND PUBLIC POLICY SERIES

NO. 22

EMPLOYEE RELATIONS AND REGULATION IN THE '80s

Proceedings of a Conference
Sponsored by the Industrial Research Unit and
the Labor Relations Council, The Wharton School,
University of Pennsylvania

Edited by
HERBERT R. NORTHRUP
and
RICHARD L. ROWAN

Professors of Industry and
Director and Codirector, respectively,
Industrial Research Unit

REVIEW COPY

INDUSTRIAL RESEARCH UNIT
The Wharton School, Vance Hall/CS
University of Pennsylvania
Philadelphia, Pennsylvania 19104
U.S.A.

331.0973
E552

Copyright © 1982 by the Trustees of the University of Pennsylvania
Library of Congress Catalog Number 81-84823
Manufactured in the United States of America
ISBN: 0-89546-035-1
ISSN: 0075-7470

June 11, 1981

Nancy and I are very happy to extend our
congratulations and warm personal greetings
as the students, faculty, administrators,
and patrons of Wharton School gather to
commemorate the one hundredth anniversary
of this, the nation's first school of
business.

Over the past century, you and your pre-
decessors have established an institution
of high academic integrity and innovative
spirit. Wharton School espouses so effectively the ideals that are the strengths
of this nation's economic system.

You have our best wishes and, again, our
congratulations.

Sincerely,

Ronald Reagan

University Libraries
Carnegie Mellon University
Pittsburgh, Pennsylvania 15213

Foreword

This volume was planned as part of the celebration of the one hundredth anniversary of the Wharton School of the University of Pennsylvania. It also marks the sixtieth anniversary of the Industrial Research Unit and the thirty-fifth anniversary of the Labor Relations Council of the Wharton School. The articles compiled here were presented at a conference held in Philadelphia on June 11 and 12, 1981, the topic of which was "Employee Relations and Regulation in the '80s." Papers delivered at the conference have been supplemented with contributions by other authorities in the respective fields.

The Industrial Research Unit was established as the Industrial Research Department of the Wharton School in 1921, the same time that the Wharton Graduate Division was first established. Its purpose was to undertake "the conduct of systematic research on important social and economic problems of industry for which competence has been gained by persistent specialization." Under the direction of Professors Joseph H. Willits and Anne Bezanson, the Industrial Research Department won an international reputation for its pioneering studies in industrial relations; its analyses of the problems and economics of the coal, textile, hosiery, upholstery, and other industries; its entrepreneurial histories; and later, for its research in price history, labor migration and mobility, manpower economics, and productivity. The publications of the Industrial Research Department were issued in series of major works, small reports, and a number of special series.

The Industrial Research Department was originally envisioned as a permanent staff of researchers, to be supplemented when appropriate by members of the teaching faculty of other Wharton departments, and by graduate students and assistants. The Industrial Research Department's publications were produced by a virtual who's who of that period's contributors to labor, personnel, and industrial management studies: C. Canby Balderston, Anne Bezanson, Ewan Clague, J. Frederick Dewhurst, Robert R. Nathan, Gladys L. Palmer, George W. Taylor, Waldo Fisher, Alfred H. Williams, and Joseph H. Willits.

World War II scattered the Industrial Research Department's personnel, and many went on to other pursuits. As economic and business knowledge advanced and became more specialized, and as research funded through government and foundation grants became more accessible, research tended to be done more easily within the teaching departments. Moreover, in the post-World War II period, the University was extremely short of funds. Accordingly, a decision was made in 1953 to transfer the Industrial Research Department to the Department of Industry, and to transfer, also on a permanent basis, four persons to the Department of Industry: the late Dr. Gladys L. Palmer, who was appointed research professor of industry; two research associates, the late Miss Miriam Hussey and Mrs. Marjorie Denison; and Miss Elsa Klemp, statistician. The name of the organization was changed to the Industrial Research Unit and Dr. Palmer was named its director.

Under the direction of Dr. Palmer, the Industrial Research Unit continued as an effective research organization. Dr. Palmer pushed forward with her studies of labor mobility, aided by a substantial grant from the Rockefeller Foundation, as well as grants from other sources. In addition, the Unit continued to perform funded research in the other basic areas in which it had gained expertise, particularly in industry problems and industrial relations. Upon Dr. Palmer's retirement in 1965, the Unit was practically dissolved.

In January 1964, Professor Herbert R. Northrup succeeded Dr. George W. Taylor as chairman of the Department of Industry. The Industrial Research Unit was then largely concerned with final details of the last Rockefeller Foundation grant and with the publication of Dr. Palmer's last book, *The Reluctant Job Changer*. With the need for more of the department's attention to be placed on research, and with opportunities for research available, the Industrial Research Unit was seen as capable of fulfilling its long-time role to the advantage of all. Accordingly, a decision to revive it was made and approved by the Dean of the Wharton School, and Professor Northrup assumed the directorship.

A temporary home was found and segments of the library were brought together. Mrs. Denison and Miss Klemp were assigned to the Unit to assist in research, in particular, to develop background materials on Black labor market problems, since discussions were beginning with the Ford Foundation on financing a major effort in this area. "Seed funds" were sought and obtained from industry to support faculty research and the development of research proposals. By the summer of 1968, the Unit again had become an active, vital organization contributing to knowledge in its traditional areas of competence: industrial relations, labor market, and industry studies. The contemporary publications of the Unit are listed on the back cover of this book.

The Labor Relations Council of the Wharton School was established in 1946 and, except for a one-year interval, its programs have been an integral part of the school's program. Dr. George W. Taylor served as its chairman until 1968, when Dr. Herbert R. Northrup succeeded him. Through the Council, a close cooperation has been maintained over the years between the faculty of the Industry Department and executives of the member companies. In the monthly seminars, which are attended by faculty and company members of the Council, many subjects of mutual interest have been discussed. The roster of guest speakers is an impressive one. The monthly seminars have been the heart of the Labor Relations Council, but we believe that other parts of the program have been very important.

Council funds have been used primarily to sponsor research by faculty members and graduate students in the field of labor-management relations. The results have been made available frequently in the form of articles in numerous journals. The Council has also issued publications under its own auspices. They include the monograph series on Industry-Wide Collective Bargaining, published in 1948, the Labor Arbitration Series, published in 1952, the book entitled *New Concepts in Wage Determination,* published by the McGraw-Hill Book Company in 1957, and the volume, *The Negro and Employment Opportunity,* published by the Bureau of Industrial Relations at the University of Michigan.

There is a third facet of Council activities. Whenever it has seemed that some particular problem of national importance might be clarified by public discussion, the Council has conducted public conferences. For example, in November 1960, at the beginning of what seemed to be a period of economic growth and adjustment to technological change, a conference was held on "Industrial Relations in the 1960s—Problems and Prospects." Holding another public conference was not given serious consideration until early in 1964 when it became apparent that the most critical and perplexing issue of employer-employee relations had become the provision of equal job opportunities. It seemed not only timely, but urgently necessary, to bring together a group of outstanding people whose experience eminently qualified them to discuss not only the nature of the problem but also the ways and means of resolving it. As a result, a public conference on "Equal Opportunity—The Job Aspect" was held on November 13, 1964.

In November 1971, a conference was held commemorating the fiftieth anniversary of the Industrial Research Unit and the twenty-fifth anniversary of the Labor Relations Council. This conference was planned around the important theme, "Collective Bargaining: Survival in the '70s?" and it brought together representatives from industry, unions, government, and academia. The keynote speaker for this conference was The Honorable James D. Hodgson, Secretary of Labor. Given the issues currently before us, the June 1981 conference was an obvious need.

Throughout the history of the Industrial Research Unit and the Labor Relations Council, emphasis has been placed on "the conduct of systematic research on important social and economic problems of industry." Interest in national labor problems was extended to the international field following a sabbatical leave that Professor Rowan took at Cambridge University in England in 1972. The fascinating complex of problems requiring analysis and the varied interest of faculty and students provide both a never-ending source of questions to be answered, as well as questioners desiring to find answers, and this should ensure a future that is as interesting, and hopefully, as constructive as the past.

The arrangements for the conference were made by Mrs. Margaret E. Doyle in her usual competent manner and good spirit. The staff of the Industrial Research Unit, including Professor Janice Bellace, Lois Rappaport, Dr. Betty Slowinski, Christian Schneider, Richard Henriques, Duncan Campbell, Steven Geovanis, Philip Miscimarra, Mario Gobbo, Nicoletta Camerini, David and Philip Northrup, Thomas Ward, Theresa Diss, Mary Jane Welsh, Mary Kiely, and Cathy Crawford, performed the innumerable tasks so important to the smooth functioning of any conference. Cheryl DellaPenna and Patricia Dornbusch provided excellent editorial assistance. The greatest debt, of course, is owed to the conference participants, who came to the University to express their ideas in an open forum.

RICHARD L. ROWAN, *Professor of Industry*
and Codirector
Industrial Research Unit
The Wharton School
University of Pennsylvania

Philadelphia
November 1981

Table of Contents

PART I

EMPLOYEE RELATIONS, REGULATION, AND TODAY'S NEEDS

A. Some Overall Considerations

ያ33ӏ
い.ら.

Employee Relations and World Competition---
The View of a Chief Executive

David M. Roderick[†]

Marc Connolly, a famous playwright from my hometown of Pittsburgh, once remarked that "everything nailed down is coming loose."

If business, labor, academic, and government leaders are to cope effectively with the present and the future, then I suggest that we must recognize that much of what used to be "nailed down" in Western industrial nations has certainly come loose over the past fifteen years.

The circumstances which govern corporate decision making are never static, particularly in a global marketplace. It is a serious mistake for those who manage businesses or lead labor unions to believe that proven strategies in one generation will apply comfortably in another. Today's problems will not yield to yesterday's answers.

We in American industry are at a crossroads in our industrial history—one that requires us to rethink how we do business, and how the groups which are a part of the industrial equation relate to one another. It is reflected in the loss of our competitive strength in the world market, evidenced by a declining U.S. share of world industrial production. The concerned parties—business, government, and labor—must thoughtfully reexamine their identities and purposes and . . . act accordingly.

To understand the magnitude of the problem, one need only look at what has happened here in our own marketplace. My industry provides ample illustration of the problem. In steel, we have seen the demise of once healthy companies—Alan Wood, Youngstown Sheet & Tube, and Wisconsin Steel—and of a Bethlehem Steel plant near Pittsburgh and portions of plants at Johnstown, Pennsylvania and Lackawanna, New York. These and other plant and facility closings in recent years cut American steel capacity by almost seven million tons and directly affected over 35,000 workers. Although some of this capacity has been restored through installation of new facilities at

---

† David M. Roderick is Chairman and Chief Executive Officer of the United States Steel Corporation.

some plants, this problem was created by an onslaught from competitor companies in other societies organized much differently than our own.

We are experiencing tough competition from the European Economic Community (EEC) countries. In March 1981, Canadian imports unaffected by Trigger Price enforcement represented over 25 percent—one-fourth—of the total imports of steel mill products for that month, and only 35,000 tons less than imports from Japan.

Another source of competition, even less known to most Americans, is perhaps more troublesome—newly industrialized countries such as Brazil, Taiwan, South Korea, Venezuela, and Mexico are pouring good products into our consumer markets, often in violation of our trade laws.

Because of their state-supported capital formation, labor intensity, and subsidized pricing, these countries can offer steel at price discounts no private employer anywhere in the world can match over the long run. The impact of such disparity is profound! Ask people from the communities where our facilities had to be closed.

Our largest steel customer, the auto industry, is also beleaguered by more sophisticated international labor and industry combines. U.S. automakers are as concerned with exports as with imports, and when competition is rigorous, they should be able to move in both markets.

Domestic automakers, caught by the Organization of Petroleum Exporting Countries (OPEC) cartel, were soon out of phase when the marketplace changed to small, fuel-efficient cars. Now customers are thinking small, and the automakers have responded with a massive capital-spending program to meet the challenge. And with the exception of Chrysler, that risk is being undertaken with private funds. Coupled with their regulatory burden and their labor cost commitment, the automakers are in a fight for their very economic survival—and millions of Americans are in it with them.

Both General Motors (GM) and Ford are making huge capital commitments to the future of the industry in order to meet the challenges of the world marketplace. GM's $40 billion program for 1980 to 1984 is the largest capital commitment ever made by an American manufacturing company. But financial commitment by management alone will not save the industry. It requires the understanding and commitment of all the parties involved—management, government, consumers, and certainly labor.

Steel and autos are but two of the industries facing strong competition from other societies. For all practical purposes, the television and textile industries have been lost to foreign makers. Zenith held out longer than other domestic makers. Remember when Harley-Davidson was the king of the road? Now we have Hondas, Yamahas, and Suzukis—bikes of excellent quality. We have lost most of the shoe industry to Taiwan, Korea, and Italy. The tire companies are struggling because of technological changes in radial tires introduced by a French tiremaker. And the American semiconductor industry is bracing for battle with its Japanese counterpart.

We are losing ground in the world marketplace because we have regrettably forfeited our leadership position while taking on one another.

Labor and government and management have fought for domestic ascendancy and for a bigger piece of the economic pie, and have only succeeded in allowing competitors in the global market to grab a larger share virtually uncontested.

Last year we were fifth among all nations in per capita gross national product (GNP). Now we are tenth. Still not a crisis, but one in the making. At the turn of the century the United States had just taken over first place from the British. In any given year since, the difference in growth has been small, but continuing over eighty years, it has given Great Britain a per capita GNP one-half that of ours.

Today's battlefield is world trade. We must shake off the mind-set competing under terms and conditions developed when our own domestic economy· was preeminent and face up to the changed circumstances.

None of us is fault-free.

The historic thrusts of business, labor, and government have been to get the most for their perceived constituencies—whether stockholder, union member, or citizen voter—often at the expense of one another. Business too often concentrated on short-term results to the detriment of longer-term considerations.

Labor for its part has come to the bargaining table for four decades now with essentially two demands: more pay and more benefits in return for less output and less quality, and it is suicide not to face the fact that there are obvious limits to that overreach.

Government has used business to correct social ills and to help finance political objectives through taxes. Consider the experience of my corporation. Since U.S. Steel began operations in 1901, it has paid out approximately $13 billion in taxes; yet in the same period, the stockholders have received only a little more than half that amount— about $7 billion—as a return on their investment.

If the United States is to compete in this global market, industry, labor, and government must recognize the interests of each other. All of us can remain advocates for our constituencies, but only if we become much more effective and sophisticated in balancing the needs and concerns of all the groups who expect to draw down on our GNP; and we cannot continue to resolve differences in this arena by refusing to produce GNP.

The only way American industry can compete in the market today is by producing quality products at lower costs.

Improved quality requires an atmosphere conducive to technological innovation. This means significant capital for research and development (R&D) and the implementation of that R&D. During 1980, patent applications filed by U.S. inventors rose by 2.8 percent. Foreign patent filings in the U.S. registered an increase of 7.4 percent last year—triple our rate. You will draw the inevitable conclusion.

Management must make a commitment to excellence through increased attention to quality, the addition of technical support staff, and the expansion and improvement of production facilities.

The current effort by government to improve capital formation is late but welcome. The administration's economic recovery program is critical to the needs of American industry if we are to rebound in the marketplace.

The effectiveness of all these efforts will finally require the worker to put his or her effort and attitude into the equation. Attitude determines quality as much as tools and technology. Much is made of the Japanese worker's almost religious devotion to the workplace. I have never been one to believe that duplicating Japanese culture here would be either possible or desirable. We are our own people, and we have always managed to produce in the crunch—"money players," in baseball parlance. But there is ample evidence that too many of us have grown casual in our attitude toward a fine product. Workmanship requires commitment from the chief executive officer to the shop floor.

Any labor union leader worth his salt will continue to stand for his membership. He can stand between the worker and the abuse of authority. He can be a force in insuring the safety and dignity of the worker. He can bargain for a fair share. But he must stand for quality, performance, and productivity as well!

Consumers expect quality; management must plan and invest for it; labor must do its part to deliver it. The class-struggle rhetoric of the first half of the century is out of date. Workers are consumers, too!

We can meet the challenge if labor and management join in a common commitment. American industry will do its share. In U.S. Steel we have closed obsolete and nonprofitable plants and facilities. We are converting idle and excess raw material reserves to cash. We are entering into joint ventures to enhance our capital strength. With that new capital we are investing in new plants and equipment at the fastest rate in the American steel industry. We are upgrading our product mix, reorganizing our own lines, and bringing our company back to full strength.

Labor unions, particularly in the heavy and mature industries, will have to accept some of the risk. Recent figures from the Bureau of Labor Statistics reflect that the consumer price index (CPI) increased 175 percent from 1961 to 1980, while the average hourly earnings of production employees in the steel industry rose 270 percent during the same period, and total hourly employment costs increased a staggering 363 percent. That cannot continue!

There are several areas where I believe labor must take a closer look at itself.

First, the unions must look at uncapped cost-of-living allowances (COLA) and their affect on job-producing capital and product costs. As COLA increases are generated, price increases follow and are passed right back to that same consumer-worker who bargained for the increase to start with. Other consumer-Americans, not represented in powerful labor unions, tend to turn to products where costs are not inflated by COLA. There are many foreign cars to be seen in American factory parking lots! The present COLA formulas greatly outpace the actual rises in the CPI.

Secondly, the unions must review their position regarding work practices. Work practices have built up in many industries over the years in response to varying economic, social, and convenience issues. Many of these practices have not only outlived the purposes for which they were designed, but now pull squarely against job security.

Japanese firms are making increased use of industrial robots. Their 75,000 units now account for 70 percent of the world total. Our 20,000 robot units put the United States in the all-too-familiar second-place spot. Yet there is reluctance on the part of many unions to the introduction of this technology. Industry must bargain with unions about the introduction of new technology and its impact. The survival of the enterprise, however, depends upon the rapid introduction of cost-effective new technology—not its opposition.

In the final analysis, we do not vote for a standard of living. We cannot ratify a labor agreement that will insure us a standard of living.

The standard of living must be earned in the mines and the shops and in the marketplace through capital formation, by investment in tools, by safe working conditions, and good leadership culminating in output per man-hour. Those labor relationships which come to grips with this truth will prosper no matter what political system they are contained within, and if we continue to abuse our political freedom by temporizing with marketplace realities, our economy will continue to flounder.

It has been the unique contribution of American society to demonstrate to the world that man's condition is improvable, but some of us had begun to believe that economic improvement was inevitable. Our society is going through a period of adjustment in which we will have to deflate our exaggerated ideas of the American role in the world and perhaps even the American capability at home. We have been deluded with an inflation of promises and an inflation of hopes in the myth of American supremacy, and all that will have to be deflated because it is beyond our means. Our national economic policy must shift from stimulating consumption to stimulation of capital formation and investment. Collective bargaining must focus on efficiency and productivity, if our society and if the American workman and the unions who represent him expect to satisfy their aspirations for wages, pensions, and other benefits. If there is a "new breed," it must appreciate that job enrichment, job satisfaction, and leisure time are a luxury for the productive only. In most economies short of productive capital, people toil simply to endure.

As leaders in government, labor, and industry grapple with wage and price decisions, candor will be required. The wage earner who sells his labor to the company is the same consumer who must buy it back in the marketplace. In both roles, he is the primary beneficiary of investor savings, capital formation, and productivity. When we compromise those elements, we may call the result inflation, or stagflation, or recession, but the real deception is to promise, or to be promised, that we can, over the long term, consume more than we produce. In steel we are working with the proposition that improved productivity is the best guarantor of economic progress.

We need a new accommodation among government, labor, and business that recognizes reality and responds to a changed world marketplace.

One response to a new business climate a century ago was the founding of Wharton. Many things nailed down between 1881 and 1981 have come loose, only to find new relevance in different settings.

If new circumstances teach new duties, then certainly they can lead to new opportunities and a resurgent American economy.

8331
v.5.

9 - 15

Employee Relations Innovations
for the 1980s

Howard H. Kehrl[†]

My purpose this morning is to describe several innovations in employee relations at General Motors (GM). I will discuss some of the
factors which have led to these innovations and the results which we
have seen thus far. But before getting into specifics on this, let me
take a moment to set the stage—not only for this topic—but perhaps
for the entire conference.

Since my experience lies within the automotive industry and that
industry has been a prime object of much regulation in the past, I will
speak from an automotive frame of reference. The critical dimensions of what some people refer to as "The Domestic Auto Industry
Problem" have been well-documented in the President's Task Force
Report published in April.

That report affirms and extends similar findings published by former Secretary Goldschmidt this past winter, and I might add, con-
firms many independent analyses made before that time. I am sure
you are familiar with those analyses and the prescriptions offered for
the rejuvenation of the automotive industry. My purpose is not to debate the policy implications of these reports, but to discuss changes in
the human factors which can help the domestic industry become more
competitive in the changing global environment.

As we look down the road, it is clear that the domestic automotive
industry will be assuming new shapes and new dimensions in every
area. One of the key elements in the changing shape of this industry
is a more effective use of human resources. We often hear that "people are our most important resource," and things of that sort. In
those cases in which it has not already been done, that cliché
must be converted to reality, because all organizations must be expected to improve their effectiveness if they are to stay in the race
for leadership.

And, make no mistake about it, really effective organizations must

---

† Howard H. Kehrl is Vice Chairman of the General Motors Corporation.

9

excel in every area—in R & D, in technology, in financial affairs, and in manufacturing. None of these has the highest priority—they all have equal priority.

But the human dimension is still largely untapped, and human potential can become the deciding margin of difference in the years ahead. To realize the benefits of the human potential within the organization requires a period of readjustment and a willingness to accept the risks arising from change. That we need to make major improvements on this score hardly needs elaboration. As you may recall, the so-called Harbour Report prepared for the Department of Transportation last winter cited the potential of human productivity in its comparison of domestic and Japanese automakers.

In a more recent report, Harbour, along with William Abernathy and Jay Henn from Harvard, issued a new study of productivity and cost advantages. If I may quote from that report, the authors state:

> The problem is a people problem rather than an investment problem. Although there is a costly wage differential favoring the Japanese, an equally important cost penalty stems from the manner in which U.S. management and labor policies have involved employees in their tasks.

> It will take years to close this cost gap because it involves human and institutional relations with a long history of adversarial proceedings.

As far back as 1960, management theoretician Douglas McGregor insisted that individuals and organizations *can* integrate personal and corporate objectives within the work environment. More recently, in his book, *Theory Z*, William Ouchi has come to similar conclusions and has proposed a specific model which would integrate some features of Japanese management systems into the U.S. corporate environment. Ouchi makes a strong case for focusing on the human side of business for productivity growth. To reach maximum potential, he cites a need for an entirely new philosophy of management, and new structures to carry out those intentions.

There is abundant good sense in the conclusions reached by all of these authors. It is now time—indeed, it is past time—that we listened to and acted on their advice.

At General Motors, we have been doing just that for more than a decade. We are working hard to involve our employees in the business, and where useful, we have recast numerous business structures to better utilize our human potential. Although we do not have a single model or formula which can be recited, we are convinced that innovations in employee relations are beginning to pay dividends— and I will cite a few examples later in these remarks.

All of our efforts proceed from a basic belief that imagination, ingenuity, and self-respect are distributed widely—not narrowly—in any organization. We know that most employees want more than just a job to come to—that most of our people want to become more involved, more effective, and more satisfied during the time they are on the job. And we know that just a 60 percent performance from employees will not achieve our goals for the future of General Motors. These things we think we understand—but effectiveness depends on more than mere understanding. It depends on willingness to adopt new ways of looking at the relationship between people and work.

There are no easy answers to this issue, but at General Motors, we began by looking at our management philosophy and the structures which implement those fundamentals. We are now into a second decade of experience with these innovations. As you might imagine, our original goals have become clarified as we gain experience, and we continue to invent as we go along.

Since the 1960s, socioeconomic and political forces have converged to forge new industrial relations movements throughout the world. These movements have taken many forms and many names—industrial democracy, codetermination, and in Japan, the Spirit of Wa, which means roughly, unity, kinship, or oneness.

At General Motors, we use the term "quality of worklife" (QWL) as an umbrella title for a wide range of activities and structures which include organizational development, union-management cooperation, employee participation groups, new plant design committees, and many others.

As we use the term QWL at General Motors, we are speaking of both a *goal* and a *process*. As a goal, we are seeking an organization that is a more satisfying place in which to work—where people gain a greater degree of personal dignity and self-worth from their contributions. As a process, QWL is a philosophy of management, a means by which people can create and sustain an environment which simultaneously meets business, human, and social objectives.

I realize that these definitions may not lead to perfect clarity, but I assure you that quality of worklife is not soft management. Creating and maintaining organizational systems which require increased involvement and commitment is often difficult and frustrating. But we are convinced that such systems can be sustained and can offer superior results for the organization and the employees within that organization.

One thing that makes QWL so demanding is that we know all too little about organizational forms that will harmonize changing human values with changing business needs. This is complicated further because organizations tend to change more slowly than the people in them. For one thing, employees in today's organizations—and even more certainly in tomorrow's—are already equipped by education and experience to perform more effectively than ever before. When it comes to readiness for change, there is clear evidence that many employees are already more flexible than existing institutions—and that includes the companies which employ them and the unions which represent them.

Too often, those on the management side shrink from more open, sharing styles of leadership because they fear loss of control. In too many cases, they have resisted change because of organizational inertia, or because they are not prepared to assume new role identities within the changed social structure.

Some in positions of leadership within union organizations have been equally reluctant to press for democratization on the plant floor because they, too, fear loss of role identity. . . because of uncertainty about their representative function within the enterprise. These are difficult problems—and, for the most part, we still are looking for workable solutions to the questions they pose.

Despite this gap in information, we cannot sit idly while waiting to be struck by perfect understanding. And so we have moved ahead to experiment with new organizational structures and more participative relationships . . . and in some cases, these changes have led us into uncharted waters.

At General Motors, we have been fortunate to have the benefit of concerned, involved union leadership. In many cases, unions representing employees have been a positive force, and both nationally and locally, joint QWL committees have helped implement change at many locations. We have found that the *support* of the local bargaining unit is not enough—they must be *involved* if maximum results are to be obtained.

Quality of worklife is not a single program—not something that can be turned on and off. Neither can it be packaged and moved from place to place. Once launched, a QWL effort must be continually reinforced—individual ideas will change, and what does not work at first trial can be replaced with a different approach. It is follow-up that makes ideas like QWL part of the corporate woodwork.

QWL is not limited to job enrichment, nor to productivity gains, nor to better quality. Nevertheless, all of these may become natural by-products of an effective QWL process. These, then, are some of the definitional dimensions of these innovative efforts—the question is, do they really work?

Let me say that we think they do pay off, but the results come mostly over the long haul. Because QWL is intended to alter fundamental relationships in the industrial environment, changes are likely to be evolutionary. Management simply cannot demand a dead dragon every week as evidence that the innovations are having the desired effect. It goes deeper than that, and it takes longer than that. But we have had some very satisfying experiences at a number of GM units. Let me mention a few of these.

About four years ago, the Chevrolet division initiated a major restructuring of the top-level functions at a diversified manufacturing complex. Within this complex are eight different plants, and each is now organized into a plant team. This permits an administrative organization at the top to concentrate on more strategic issues, since day-to-day operating responsibility has been shifted downward to the plant level.

To extend this philosophy into the plant organization, some 109 hourly work units were identified. In about half of these, we have set up employee participation circles similar to quality circles used at many organizations. It is already apparent that as these circles gain maturity, they take on many responsibilities which have been typically performed by supervision at most locations.

So far, we have been able to document major reductions in absenteeism, scrap rates, and repair costs in those units that have adopted the new organizational structure and philosophy. For the same time period of measurement, discipline cases were reduced from nineteen cases to just four, and grievances dropped from sixty-five to only nine. In all, it has been a significant turnaround at this one location.

I mentioned that QWL takes many forms and many titles at General Motors. Another example is the creation of product teams. The management at our Inland Division, recognized that they were becoming noncompetitive at one point because of bulky, outdated organizational structures and systems. Things just could not get done as fast as was needed.

After an initial examination, it became evident that decisions made at top levels could, and should, be moved downward. But rather than simply talk about delegation, this division created eleven product teams, each having individual identity and leadership.

The eleven units achieve organizational integration through temporary assignment of staff people to serve as financial or personnel advisors and through periodic reporting to a so-called "Board of Directors"—which is the newly-defined role for the general manager and his staff. The division also created a joint union-management QWL committee which operates at the plant level. These joint committees have helped introduce quality circles and employee participation in day-to-day decision making far more widely than ever before. The entire system is bonded together by common aims, mutual interests, and integrated business structures. This division has been using the product team concept for many years . . . what they have developed is unusual, but it is effective.

More recently, our Buick Motor Division made plans for a new product which was to be built in a renovated foundry. The philosophic goals and structure of this new work unit were jointly designed by a core group of union and management people.

The plant, which now employs about 500 people, is structured around autonomous, self-managing work units. Within each unit there is a single job classification—quality operator. Compensation is based on job knowledge—the more jobs people learn, the more they can earn. Symbols of differentiated status have all but been eliminated. There are no time clocks, no privileged parking spots, and no shop rules. In short, it is an open rather than a closed industrial society.

The Buick experiment has been remarkably effective. Since the new product was launched last fall, production quality of their product has remained extremely high—better than 99 percent to specifications. Short-term, controllable absenteeism at this one facility is less than half the rate for all of the Buick division. One grievance has been filed, and that was settled at the lowest level of responsibility.

The important thing to remember is that the most recent Buick experiment was made possible only because of earlier groundwork laid by union-management cooperation which began some five years before on a division-wide basis.

I have briefly described three innovative employee relations systems now functioning at General Motors. I should stress that there are about ninety-five QWL projects involving both union and management within General Motors at this time. In addition, there are many other QWL projects working which involve only salaried activities at General Motors.

The variety of structures being used within General Motors is quite striking, and includes such things as: business teams, parallel planning structures, structured employee training in problem solving, and at one location, a committee which works to increase organizational competitiveness, thus improving the job security of employees. Each of these structures is tailored to the situation and to the potential which exists at that location. All of these innovative structures, whether large or small in scope, are designed to improve business performance by transcending traditional boundaries and attitudes, involving people in their work, and enhancing satisfaction from the job.

I have pointed out that we are learning even as we move ahead. The innovations we have implemented are working well in some cases, not so well in others. As you might expect, we see cycles of improvement and regression. But we are convinced that some things remain constant and should be maintained. For example, there probably is no one best way to design an effective organization. We are convinced that people support that which they help create. And it is evident that existing organizational structures can impede rather than enhance effectiveness. So, we keep innovating, we keep learning, and we keep improving.

Let me close by saying that innovative employee relations is hard work. It involves some significant risks, you cannot always prove direct benefits resulting from change, and there is a good deal that we do not know about the process itself. Despite these cautions, organizations which want to remain viable in the future must get on with the search for a better way to manage their human potential. Above all else, the organization which wants to lead in the future must not become a prisoner of its own inertia—it must get on with the task—it must get on with the search.

8331
v.5.

The American Workplace—
New Winds A-Blowing

James D. Hodgson[†]

I found that in Japan, a speaker always begins his remarks with an apology. Today, an apology is exactly what my situation calls for.

When I strayed into the dubious domain of diplomacy nearly a decade ago, I did so at a cost. I had to sacrifice keeping current on developments in that first love of my corporate life—employee relations. So at the outset today, I must apologize for my inability to bring you anything like an informed discourse on the present state of this always fascinating function. I must seek other pastures in which to graze.

What to do? Well, since I can no longer provide insights of intimacy, I must substitute the perspective of distance. When one loses touch with the nitty gritty, about all that remains is the lofty perch. While the view from that perch may be broad, it can also be fuzzy. So if in what follows a little fuzz creeps in around the edges, I beg to be excused.

What I want to do today is this. Let us step back and take a sweeping look over the 1970s. Let us see if we can identify the important developments that hit the American workplace in those years. Then let us analyze the significance of these developments and see what they may mean for the future—particularly for the future of employee relations.

When identifying causal elements in any situation, one is tempted to range over a whole spectrum of influences. But today, I have decided to sharpen my focus and zero in on just four—four of what I call "new winds a-blowing" in the American workplace. These winds, as I see them, (or should I say "feel" them?) will have a telling impact on our work and our lives in the years to come. Someone once called the oboe an "ill wind that no one blows good." I am afraid that several workplace winds of the 1970s were oboe-type ill winds, blowing no good for American industry.

[†] James D. Hodgson, former Secretary of Labor, is United States Ambassador to Japan.

Before trotting out my chosen four for your consideration, I want to mention briefly a couple of others I weighed for possible inclusion but ultimately relegated to second rank.

The first of these also-rans was the *decline of unionism and union influence in America.* I find a mixed bag here. You will recall that as we entered the 1970s, inflation even then seemed to be a problem. Wage-push pressure was seen as its cause. As the main architect of that pressure, organized labor was tagged as the villain.

A decade passed and what a change! Today the inflation bogey is more than ever with us, but this time demand-pull is its source, and *government,* not labor, is the villain of fashion. So perhaps one decline we can say the unions have suffered is a decline in villainy.

But let us remember—as the 1970s got underway, unions had big-league firepower—power formidably evident on both the political and the bargaining fronts. During the early part of the decade, union-sponsored regulatory measures sailed through state and federal legislatures in abundance. Union bargainers in those years consistently extracted gains for American workers in real (not just dollar) income.

But as the decade ended what did we see? One after another union power play attempt in the Congress was shot down in flames. Negotiated wage gains could not even keep pace with price and tax increases. And today when Americans are asked whether they respect the American labor movement, only 13 percent answer "yes."

So a case can be made that the American union movement came upon conspicuously hard times in the 1970s. In my view, however, the case is not yet strong enough for labor's detractors to take too much comfort. For one thing, *all* American institutions, not just labor, suffered a loss of respect in the eyes of the public during the 1970s. Union bargaining and political power may have been crippled, but they are by no means shattered. Thus, the recent misfortunes of America's union movement warrant notice, but they are insufficiently conclusive for me to rank this phenomenon among my top four.

Among other workplace influences during the decade, a second near miss was the reputed *decline of our American work ethic.* Both texts and tabloids have trumpeted the passing of this vestige of our Protestant heritage. Certainly, fragments of evidence can be scraped together to build a case for it. Absenteeism has shot up. Indifferent working attitudes are now often blamed on something called "alienation." And certainly, the moral factor skidded as a source of working motivation in America.

Yet one does not have to stretch objectivity very far to uncover an opposite side of the coin. For instance, a greater portion of American adults now hold jobs than ever before in history. The number of moonlighters—holders of two and three jobs—also zoomed upward during the last decade. And now we are beginning to note a tendency among workers to postpone retirement. These trends hardly reflect the posture of a nation that has lost its zest for work.

Clearly, the *nature* of our work motivation in this country has changed, but the *residual strength* of it is still in question. Accordingly, I am going to keep the jury out for a time before I write off a healthy work ethic as a lost American-workplace asset.

Now, having disposed of these two also-ran factors, let me introduce you to the select circle—the Hodgson Gang of Four. A twofold criterion provided a basis for their selection. First, they came strongly to the fore during the 1970s, producing telling impact both in and beyond the American workplace; and second, their impact was of such magnitude as to assure persisting effect far into the future.

Here, then, are my first two:

Number one: A *massive shift occurred in the size and composition of the American work force.* In the 1970s, a drama of demography was enacted in our workplace. First, the post-war baby boom disgorged its copious issue en masse into America's shops and offices. In just one year, 1978, America's labor force increased by an unheard of three million workers.

Also, another phenomenon. New roles and rights for women transformed them from a transitional to a permanent component of our national work force. Of the twenty-three million new jobholders in the 1970s, more than half—in fact, well over twelve million—were women.

Total new job entrants during the 1970s vastly exceeded those in the 1960s. They will vastly exceed those in the upcoming 1980s when we will see a drop to far less than a million new job entrants a year.

Now number two: *Government regulation of the workplace escalated* from nit-picking to nut-cracking levels. First came the benighted Occupational Safety and Health Act (OSHA). Then came "Equal Employment Opportunity (EEO) quotas" and later, legislated extensions of retirement age. The Employee Retirement Income Security Act (ERISA) and an array of other acronyms came along to spell new and noxious interdiction of the workplace by the feds. Clearly, the 1970s gave us regulatory headaches for which no aspirin exists. And despite all, they will remain.

In industry, employee relations practitioners live daily with the two forces I have just mentioned. Their impact on the workplace is direct and discernible.

The third and fourth forces of my selection, however, are at once less immediately evident and yet far more telling in their ultimate impact. At least that is my view of them. I want to discuss each of them in some detail.

Number three: *International competition* has become an enormous fallout from our now interdependent economic world. The results descended upon the American workplace to create everything from monumental chaos in some sectors to manifest opportunity in others. (With one in seven American jobs dependent on exports today, we must not forget the pluses of foreign trade.)

Foreign competitors have, however, shown a positive genius for seeking out the soft spots in America's industrial armor. Those soft spots include several industries where a kind of togetherness—a togetherness sometimes induced by industry-wide union bargaining—had often seemed to protect them from competitive realities. In the 1970s, some of our industries suddenly found themselves with out-of-line wage levels and spotty productivity. They were ripe for picking and many of them got plucked. So now, unfortunately, the effect of these ravages is being written in gallons of corporate red ink and reflected in swelling unemployment rolls.

Perhaps the real mystery in all this is why we Americans did not see it coming. Could it be that we felt we were beyond the reach of foreign challenges? When the crunch came, however, we found yet again that Darwinian principles still operate in the economic world. Survival is still the acid test.

So now, bruised and bleeding a bit, we Americans regroup to counterattack. We trust that our nation's fundamental genius, i.e., its ability to adapt to meet the changing needs of time, has not deserted us. Here is one observer at least who is certain it has not.

And now the time has come for me to introduce the final factor on my list. Number four will surprise no one.

A precipitous *decline in productivity* was the most distressing phenomenon to hit the American work place in the 1970s. Coupled with rising international competition, this decline produced a double disaster. American industry lost ground both absolutely and relatively.

At home, the decade started with our industrial machine regularly clicking off 3 percent annual productivity growth rates. It ended with a year of no growth. Zero. When compared with other nations, our picture is even more bleak. Just a generation ago, one American worker produced four and one half times as much as did one Japanese. Today, the ratio is down to one and one fourth. Since 1960, Japanese productivity has soared ahead at a rate almost four times that prevailing in this country. The crossover point looms menacingly just ahead.

So today, American productivity *is bad:* but why is that important? I see the answer this way. In any society of stagnant productivity, life becomes a zero-sum game. In a zero-sum world *you* can only improve *your* lot at *my* expense and vice versa. A zero-sum world does not exactly reflect *my* view of what America has promised its citizens throughout history.

How did we get into this mess? Why did productivity improvement in America first slow and then come to a stuttering halt? A cluster of reasons exists. You know them, but let's tick them off:

1. America, this most modern of modern nations, quit modernizing. We stopped putting the necessary dollars into new plants and equipment. Why, I wonder, did we believe that with American industrial facilities averaging eleven years in age, we could compete with Japan's six year average?

2. American research budgets have taken a clipping. They were cut by a third during the 1970s. Our flow of new technology thinned to a trickle. Productivity was the casualty.

3. The 1970s brought us an energy crisis. Suddenly we had to spend more for it and use less of it. It may not be widely understood, but the productivity of a nation has been shown to be almost directly proportionate to its use of energy. Yet in the 1970s, America had to cut back.

4. The flood of new entrants that descended on the American workplace in the 1970s were just that—new. They presented industry with all the problems of newness, and in numbers difficult to assimilate readily. So again—productivity suffered.

5. The size of one of our better productivity sectors—manufacturing—has been shrinking. It lost a third of its slice of American jobs in ten years. Today, only one American job in five is still in the manufacturing sector. Meanwhile, service work, perhaps our *least* productive sector, took off and zoomed upward. The Bureau of Labor Statistics (BLS) tells us that 72 percent of working Americans are now in low-productivity service jobs.

Now I am sorry if this list seems to run on and on, but hold tight, we have not quite come to the end.

6.   A sixth reason for our productivity slowdown is harder to define. A whole new set of negative and profoundly skeptical citizen attitudes burst on the American scene during the 1970s. We know that it is hard to sell a skeptic on the rewards of hard work and efficiency.

7.   Finally, we must return to my item number two—government regulation. A governmental regulation may raise a barrier, may add a cost, or may delay an effort, but it can produce nothing. Out in my California homeland, for instance, a power plant was constructed in the early 1960s. It then required *five* government permits and took six years to build. An almost identical plant in the same location was started in the mid-1970s. This second plant now requires *eighty-three* permits and will take eleven-plus years to build. Enough said.

Now in this lengthy recounting, I have cited as productivity drawbacks a number of things that are clearly *good*, things assuredly good for America. Clean air, worker safety, lots of personal service, jobs for new entrants, the saving of energy. . .these things are all incontestably worthwhile.

So the situation adds up like this: productivity in America suffered because all these many factors I have listed occurred *simultaneously*. They all hit us smack in the decade of the 1970s. Over the years, this enterprise economy of ours has proven itself to be so vigorous and creative that probably it could have absorbed two or three of these factors at once with little trouble. But in the 1970s, too many were piled one atop the other. Something had to give. What gave was our one-time industrial pride and glory . . . our record of constantly-improving productivity. Our past productivity performance record had given this nation the most affluent society in the world. But we now must face reality. We in America are no longer the most affluent of peoples. We have sunk to about number nine in the world and are headed still further downward.

So now I have identified briefly four vital forces that hit the American workplace in the 1970s. What about the 1980s? What do these past developments signal for the employee relations function in the years ahead?

To me, each of the four factors presents highly tangible implications. Taken together they add up to a new challenge for employee relations practitioners. Near my conclusion of these remarks I will say more about that challenge.

Now, one by one, let us return and analyze some implications. First, what will be the future fallout of what I have called the "Drama of Demography" that hit our workplace in the 1970s?

Dick Cyert, president of Carnegie Mellon University, has figures to show that for every three new entrants to the American work force in the 1970s, there will be but one in the 1980s. The huge bulge of new twenty-year-olds that went to work during the past decade will now move into their thirties. As they do, pluses of maturity and experience will replace the newness minuses of past years. With more than normal confidence, by the late 1980s we can predict the following:

1. Several sectoral *labor shortages* will crop up as competition for the limited inflow of new entrants develops.
2. Work force *productivity will improve* as the cumulative effect of added years of working experience is reflected in better performance.
3. The general *unemployment* levels that prevailed in the 1970s will drop by a couple of percentage points. (The young always constitute a disproportionate share of those out of work and there will be fewer young.)
4. The diverse and often fuzzy *aspirations* that have characterized what we call the "now generation" will soon start to reflect a more *settled pattern*. Family formation and long-term career objectives will become more prominent motive forces.

Every executive will be faced with these and related changes as this unique age group "hump" moves implacably upward in age through the work force during the ensuing forty years.

Though I cannot take time to develop the point here, I am convinced that planners and managers should pay sharply increased attention to demographic patterns. With demography, the data are both evident and available. The downstream results are both identifiable and predictable. Yet too often, the subject is largely ignored.

With the recent trend toward inflicting government regulations on the workplace en masse, a number of other implications have become equally evident. First, it is clear that we must all shake off the last vestiges of passivity that have too often marked industry's past posture on this subject. Industry must resolutely move in and participate in regulatory policy formulation. We must show we know our

way around in both legislative and executive branch levels of government. Courage will often be needed for resistance to faulty prescriptions and bureaucratic excesses.

Yet I think the climate in the 1980s may shift to a point where
"working with" regulatory bureaucrats rather than merely damning
them from a distance may pay off in ways that have not been rewarding in the past. I sense at least a whisper suggesting a move away
from the past "knee-jerk" bureaucratic pursuit of adversaryism for
its own sake. Should this happen, we may then find we can go beyond
industry's rather plaintive "get government off our backs" stance of
today, and instead, find ways to *work with* sympathetic elements of
government to create policies that will turn our whole economic picture around.

Now let us move on to the implications of our current era of international competition. To me, they are so overwhelmingly evident,
they hardly need remarking. But until recently, American industry's
response has been largely lax or late. From this new competitive reality there is no place for American industry to hide, nor is there any
future in protectionism. We have only one recourse—to match the
zeal and efficiency of other competing societies. We did it spectacular-
ly for the first three quarters of this century. We will do it again. But
something else is of interest here. It seems to me that if the employee
relations function really wants to be an effective part of modern management, it must reach out and play a substantial role in meeting
this challenge. As just a minor example, when you make compensation surveys of your competitors, do you include examination of the
labor costs of *foreign* competition? That might be a good place to start.

Clearly, we now live in a new economic age. While *political* borders
may still exist, *economic* borders are practically a thing of the past.
Do we realize that today one product of every six produced anywhere
in the world crosses a political border on the way to market? By the
end of the decade, the ratio will be down to one in four.

In our new global economy, a company that fails to stay competitive worldwide can find itself run out of business in five years. Helping an enterprise stay competitive thus becomes a major employee relations responsibility.

And now let us return to that most distressing of subjects—America's stagnant productivity. The negative implications of our woes
here are obvious. What may not be so obvious is the opportunity it
offers—the opportunity that the nation's need for productivity improvement provides employee relations people. In my view, no managerial function is in a better position to make a major contribution

in meeting this challenge than employee relations. What do I have in mind? This:

Simplifications are troublesome, but a major goal of employee relations practitioners in past years has been this: they sought to help make their respective organizations and the jobs within those organizations more *attractive*. My suggestion today is that we all now proceed to redirect our energies. Let us substitute the word "productive" for "attractive." Thus, the new focus would become "to help make our organizations and their jobs more *productive*."

Some may demur and ask. . ."doesn't making a job attractive like we have done in the past, also make it more productive?" My answer . . ."sometimes yes, sometimes only maybe, or even, at times no." I urge that we work to eliminate the "maybes" and "nos."

I guess the time has come for me to talk a bit about Japan. When I decamped across the Pacific in the mid-1970s and took a firsthand look at Japanese industry, especially at its personnel practices, I could not believe what I saw. My reaction was much like that of G. K. Chesterton. . . ."I have seen the truth" he once said, "and I can tell you, it doesn't make sense!"

What I saw in Japan was a nation that had taken all the things that I thought were guaranteed to *discourage* worker initiative, and used them to create a superbly motivated work force.

Look at them. Job promotion—in Japan it is unrelated to ability; wage levels—they are unrelated to performance; job security—it is unrelated to competence. Are not these things patently absurd? Not in Japan. They are not because they are a product of the unique Japanese culture. In Japan, for instance, you do not lose your job if you perform poorly, rather you lose *face*. And to the Japanese, loss of *face* is ten times more crushing than a mere job loss.

America now finds itself looking wistfully across the ocean toward Japan. We wonder what we can learn from that flourishing economy to regenerate our own. I believe we are looking in the right place, but mostly, looking for the wrong things.

For nearly three years in the mid-1970s I watched a parade of American industrialists and academicians stream into Tokyo questing for the Holy Grail of that nation's productivity secret. Most of them went away shaking their heads sadly. The problem was that they looked solely at Japanese managerial techniques and personnel practices. If there is one thing I believe I have learned, it is that the success of a technique or practice depends on its cultural base. What works in one culture, say one like Japan, where *harmony* is society's greatest value, will surely run into trouble in an avowedly *adversary* culture like ours.

Can we learn anything, then, from the Japanese? I think we can. To do so we should raise our sights and look beyond Japanese personnel and managerial practices. Instead, let us examine Japan's *priorities*. Here we will strike it rich—at least, we will if we sincerely want to learn something.

What priorities do I have in mind? Let me start our inquiry this way: would not it indeed be remarkable if the major institutions of our nation—business, government, labor, education, et al.—would get together with broad agreement to work in harmony toward a single, shared priority objective? In Japan, they have done just that. In Japan, their human progress proceeds directly from a consensus on one thing—the need for a constantly expanding economy. Equally important is an associated corollary objective . . . . one of specific interest to you as employee relations people.

The Japanese industrial world agrees that the *human* resource is industry's *number one* resource. They give it top priority attention. In contrast to our country where manpower is treated as the *most flexible* of our industrial resources, Japan treats it as the *least flexible*.

So Japan couples a top priority for economic growth with a top priority for the human side of industrial enterprise. If cultural barriers prevent us from adopting their techniques, we can at least move toward accepting their priorities. I hope we do.

My concluding message is this: developments of the 1970s point to one thing. Today the industrial ballgame is being played in a vastly widened arena. If I have one profound worry, it is that those of us holding managerial roles in American industry may continue to pursue our present internally focused courses. If we do, we will likely find ourselves merely becoming better and better at less and less. If instead we redirect this nation's enormous abilities and resources, and focus our efforts on how the game is now being played, we can end up playing it better than anyone.

So to me, America's choice today, my choice and your choice, lies between comfortable continuity, and ultimate irrelevance, on one hand; or change and success on the other. That change will involve our restoring our productivity, and that success depends on our becoming internationally competitive.

Now what does all this mean to America's employee relations practitioners? To me it means they would do well to broaden their efforts if they want their enterprises to survive and prosper. In so doing, they will do more than merely help their own organizations, they will help put America back on the high road to better productivity. They will help enable us all to escape from our present demeaning zero-sum quagmire.

When you come to think of it, if we expect to outflank the bogs of our now stagnant productivity, many American minds must be changed. Many personal values must be revised. New and more positive attitudes must be nourished. Open communication must flower. Intergroup cooperation must be gained. Industrial leaders must both share and inspire. Workers must be both reassured and challenged.

Now just who in American industry can fill the role of catalyst to see that these things get done? Today, I suggest it is you. As America's employee relations practitioners, you are the ones who can do it best. Here is a proper "turf" for modern employee relations work. I urge you to seize that turf—seize it and occupy it well.

In my view, the employee relations function in America is ready and ripe for new worlds to conquer. Further, I believe it is pregnant with creative possibilities for improving industrial productivity and challenging foreign competition. When you boil it down, a basic focus of industry's productivity problem today centers on the relationship between the worker and his work, and that, my friends, is *exactly* your world. It is a world still worth conquering. As the kids say, I hope you "go for it!"

8331
U. S.

The Beginning of the Industrial Relations Renaissance: Can Management Adjust to the New Requirements?

Virgil B. Day[†]

A former president of the United States once said: "Every time we learn to make ends meet, someone moves the ends."

The symptoms of our current economic problems have been growing more apparent in the last decade. In the 1950s and 60s, for example, our national productivity increased at an average rate slightly above 2.5 percent a year, which was below that experienced by our rising competitors such as Germany and Japan, but still adequate to help most families and businesses experience real economic progress despite surges of inflation and ebbs of recession. In the 1970s, however, the productivity gains began to drop off to only 1 percent a year, and in the past three years, productivity has actually been declining on an annual basis. This is a scenario for disaster.

The meaning of this relative decline in productivity for working people is not just hypothetical bad news. While their pay has gone up substantially over the past decade—just about doubling for the average worker—inflation and taxes have negated any real advances in their standard of living. Primarily, this is because productivity in our country has not been the offset to inflation that it was formerly. Over the long run, increases in productivity have given us the basic, real advances in our standard of living. Too few recognize the other side of the coin: declining productivity means declining standards of living.

Like the "increase" in workers' pay, the after-taxes profits of business over the last decade are similarly illusory. Reginald Jones, the former chief executive of General Electric, has explained it this way: "When statisticians looking for reality remove the effects of inflation—first removing the effects of under-depreciation and illusory inventory profits and then deflating the remaining dollars by means of the consumer price index to find their true purchasing power—it turns out that corporate profits did not triple in the past decade.

---

† Virgil B. Day is a Partner with Vedder, Price, Kaufman, Kammholz & Day.

Rather, they actually declined by 12%." Thus, inflation and falling productivity are enemies of us all.

Just to make things more difficult, we live in a world where foreign competitors are seeking to undercut us in our domestic markets, offering lower price or higher quality just as we are seeking to win with our products in the other world markets. With limited exceptions, the reality is that there are no longer truly domestic markets for most goods, but only world markets, attracting world competition. In this new ball game, it is fatal to fall behind. We are working harder to make ends meet; but every time we learn to make ends meet, someone moves the ends.

Our predicament is clear—how to survive economically as individuals and as a nation during the next five, ten, or twenty years and maintain or enhance the standard of living that we have today. The alternative is a progressively smaller economic pie with more and more people fighting for smaller and smaller slices. This was not the predicament facing our country one hundred years ago in the beginnings of American industrial expansion.

Inflation is a monster, and there are many would-be St. Georges in the field eager to slay the beast. But we are going to be devoured by another more terrifying dragon if we do not solve the productivity problem. Inflation, after all, rises and falls in part due to poor productivity. But poor productivity can doom us forever—no exit, no escape.

Strangely, much of our performance in the industrial relations sector has tended to ignore or temporize with the problems of inflation and productivity. The recent record is generally too short on progress and too long on pusillanimous avoidance of fundamental issues. Of course, industrial relations results can only be achieved where there is a will on the part of top management to show the way and address critical problems.

A recent Op-Ed column of the *New York Times* suggested productivity is just a propaganda program to satisfy the materialistic rich and that "doing one's thing" is more important. That may be right for the writer, if that's where his "head is at," but the theory that "small is good, smaller is better, smallest is best" is a recipe for economic disaster in a growing population. Why are we having problems with an estimated ten to fourteen million illegal aliens? Did we force them to come to share in an abundant life? Did they come here only to do their own thing, or did they seek an environment where productivity produces rewards that can be shared by all?

So let us take a hard look at industrial relations and personnel policy in a time of great needs and, let us hope, of great opportunity. This is the focus of our chief executives in industry as they look at the very demanding scenario of the next twelve months, the next twenty-four months, and the next five years. They want results. They want to reappraise the fundamentals, to seek some long-range answers, rather than the quick fixes of yesterday.

Thoughtful chief executives are asking two things:

A) How do we get the needed revitalization of human resources to reverse the productivity challenge that is giving us unacceptable and noncompetitive costs; and

B) How do we cope with the government's remaining as an unwelcome partner in our business, with its costly intrusion into employer-employee relationships, and its counterproductive overregulation?

Are there any easy answers? Are the problems of an overregulated workplace going to disappear, for example, now that we have a new administration in Washington? I do not think that is a good scenario to suggest to a thoughtful and knowledgeable chief executive looking at these questions. As my friend George Shultz has said, "Hope is a great companion, but a lousy guide."

To be sure, there has been a suspension of the "midnight regulations" issued in the waning moments of the Carter administration, including some of the proposed revisions of the equal opportunity rules administered by the Office of Federal Contract Compliance Programs (OFCCP), some of the Occupational Safety and Health Administration (OSHA) rules pertaining to walk-around pay, some regulations effectively barring federal contractors from paying membership dues for employees in private clubs that allegedly discriminate, and regulations revising the enforcement of the Davis-Bacon Act.

The new administration's effort to determine whether such regulations, and other regulations presently in force, meet the goal of achieving "less burdensome and more rational federal rules" is helpful in avoiding some of the excesses in government regulation instituted during the last administration and earlier administrations, both Democratic and Republican. It is doubtful, however, as you will hear, whether there will be a reversal of the fundamental basics mandated by Congress with respect to pensions, equal employment opportunity, health and safety, wages, government contracts, or labor-management relations. We will still be living with a highly regulated workplace as contrasted with many of our foreign competitors.

The costs of regulation are not to be ignored. A study for the Busi-

ness Roundtable of compliance costs for forty-eight major companies
for 1977 shows that they paid out $2.6 billion over and above what
good corporate citizens would have spent on environmental protection, employee health and safety, and other matters, if six government agencies had not intervened. And this extra cost for all
businesses has been estimated at 100 billion dollars.

The critical nature of the productivity issue and its companion
issue of government overregulation is illustrated in the economic
business and political news every week. While the auto and steel industries have had a good share of the attention, it is clear to corporate
executives that the problems that face these industries are endemic
to the entire economy. Few have been fortunate enough to escape
from the need to accomplish change in the effectiveness of their enterprises if they are going to survive and prosper.

I suggest that what must come about is a change of such magnitude
in current practices that, if we are successful, the historians of the
next century will look back to 1981 as the start of an *American industrial relations renaissance.*

I.   Federal Legislation and the Regulatory Process

Some forty years ago, a shortsighted law professor said: "The corporation will prevail over its many problems because—no soul to
damn, no ass to kick." Not a very accurate prediction.

A recent chart prepared by a personnel officer shows federal
regulations that have impacted on the way we manage human resources in the United States, along with what has happened in other
areas of public policy, including tax laws and protection of the
environment.

None of you will be surprised to learn that this chart shows the inevitable interrelationship between a vast growth in government regulation and the decline of productivity. There are obviously other factors that have to be recognized, including dilution of management
rights and effectiveness within the factory, and the decline of the
work ethic. Nevertheless, the impact of government regulation has
been significant, and it is worthy of attention if we are to recover the
productivity we need to stay competitive in the world marketplace.
We see competitors from all over the world—good, aggressive competitors who are not equally shackled by government—competing
with us in almost every segment of our domestic markets.

The overregulation of American society is in great contrast to the
governmental climate enjoyed in Japan. The Japanese do not often
resort to lawyers or courts and there are said to be only 11,900

lawyers in a country of 116 million people. To put this in perspective, Japan has at least thirty-four certified flower arranging teachers for every lawyer there.

In looking at the legislator's role in the regulated capitalist economy of this country, a more perceptive law professor has suggested that if Hammurabi had been responsible for the existence of the modern body of regulations in the United States, he would not have proudly proclaimed "I established law and justice in the land" but would have preferred to have his regulations published anonymously!

II. Identifying the Problems

The search for the answers ranges from the simple to the sublime. It includes exotic explanations for how we got into our current difficulties.

Alvin Toffler, author of *Future Shock* and *The Third Wave,* has observed that our industrial society is changing rapidly and predicts that it will be replaced by a "third wave society" which will be characterized by high technology, dispersion of people, high demand for cognitive skills, and a merging of work and home. This intriguing view suggests that these changes will affect the industrialized belt of North America, Western Europe, Russia, Japan, and Australia. Lifestyles can be expected to change and our education systems, which have been training people to work in an industrialized society, will have to start training for more self-sufficiency. Hard-nosed skeptics, however, discount this view as a priority for the next five years and say, "Fascinating, but we are going to be sunk by the 'second wave' unless we learn how to manage our ship better now. We are taking in water, and we had better get back to the fundamentals like stopping the leaks of productivity and recognizing what is essential if we are going to survive in this second wave."

There is thus new emphasis on the old fundamentals of productivity. As G. G. Michaelson, senior vice president of Macy's, keeps emphasizing, "We have to understand that people really do make the difference and that we have to find ways to let people work more imaginatively and creatively, with fewer people doing better work." And Professor Michael Beer, lecturer in organizational behavior at the Harvard Business School, agrees: "The most successful foreign companies have demonstrated that, over a long period of time, industry is built as much on the commitment and involvement of its workers as on the shrewd investment of capital." It sounds simple, but is it? How do we make this a reality in our own organizations?

The trend in the last few decades has been for the government to attempt to legislate layers upon layers of requirements that must prevail in the workplace, and a zealous, inventive bureaucracy has expanded many of these far beyond the original congressional intent. The results, to say the least, have been somewhat uninspiring, as we look at the record in these areas—OSHA, Equal Employment Opportunity (EEO), the Employee Retirement Income Security Act (ERISA), the Age Discrimination and Employment Act (ADEA), the Rehabilitation Act, the Vietnam Veterans' Act, the Labor Management Relations Act (LMRA), Wage-Hour, Equal Pay, and in the future, thanks to the recent 5 to 4 Supreme Court decision in *Gunther,* this will include the comparable work concept (price tag: $60 to $150 billion).

Is the governmental involvement in our business going to go away, will it continue unabated, or is it going to be more reasonable and less excessive in unwarranted demands which are costly and counterproductive for our economy? The answer, unfortunately, is not optimistic, as I have indicated. Whatever improvement occurs in government administration and interpretation from the standpoint of common sense and good judgment can be offset as private plaintiffs and public interest groups go instead to the courts for help. The new "third force" that has grown up, i.e., the activist organizations and the public interest advocates, will continue to be determined to resolve in the courts their views of what social justice demands. These constituency groups have become known as "third party attorney generals" and are an effective force as an alternative to government involvement. Thus, Weldon Rougeau, the former head of the OFCCP, has predicted that there will be little effective change in the EEO policies established under his leadership in the Department of Labor because, as he states, "if there is a backing off from the full implementation of these policies, the constituency groups can be expected to take the battle to the courts." Rougeau also points out that there are several hundred cases in the OFCCP pipeline now emerging against targeted industries. He might also have pointed out that, thanks to the 1977 Judiciary Act, President Carter appointed more federal judges during his single term than any other president in history. These judges have lifetime tenure, and many would be called "liberal" by any definition.

This brings us to another reason why the personnel or human relations function is in the spotlight, aside from economic exigencies and the role of federal bureaucrats. With increasing frequency, our employees may find an activist individual or organization to represent them if they do not think that decisions that affect them in the workplace are up to date; and sex discrimination issues are just one example. In addition, boards of directors are increasingly concerned about their liability and exposure. As a consequence, they have necessarily become more interested in evaluating what is going on in operating areas in their own "cost-benefit" analysis. Legal fees and big-ticket vulnerability do not appeal to them. They want to be sure, absolutely sure, that you are complying with your fiduciary responsibilities as far as pension fund investment is concerned, because they may be held accountable. In today's world they want to have a defensible position in terms of corporate social responsibility. The activist role of boards of directors in management "oversight" is going to be increasingly prevalent, I predict. This is a marvelous advantage in terms of getting your proposals to the attention of key people on the board. But they had better be sound, because the board wants to be responsible only for sound policies. Human resources planning is moving up in importance as the problems of business intensify. And ultimately, it all adds up to a question of productivity: how can management motivate workers in such a way that the drain on productivity caused by worker dissatisfaction, government regulation, and costly litigation is superseded by a committed and involved work force?

III. Productivity

Cancer specialists talk of the Big C as being the major target in health research. In our economy, the target is the Big P—Productivity. As I have noted, productivity among U.S. businesses fell in 1980, marking the third consecutive year of decline. One bright spot was that productivity among manufacturers began a sharp increase in the last quarter of 1980.

The dismal productivity picture was a growing problem for the last part of the 1970s because many of our economic decisions in this country since World War II were based on an assumption of a continuing level of increasing productivity throughout the economy of approximately 3 percent. The continuing downward spiral worries economists and businessmen, because when productivity lags and wages rise, the labor cost of producing a unit of output obviously goes up, and this puts pressure on businesses to raise prices. Thus, unit labor costs rose at a 10.9 percent adjusted rate in the fourth quarter for the nonfarm business sector and were over 10 percent higher in 1980 than in 1979, according to the Labor Department's productivity report. Three successive years of productivity decline have had a highly detrimental effect on our cost competitiveness in world markets, and a continued trend could be devastating.

We can hope that some of the productivity loss attributable to over-regulation by government will be cured, but unquestionably only a small part of the productivity problem lies within the jurisdiction of the *government*—the major portion is clearly within the jurisdiction of the *private* sector, as we know to our distress. There have been efforts to change the productivity of workers, and fortunately, many are success stories. But we have some vivid illustrations in Japan, Germany, and elsewhere of better ways to approach the problems of individual worker productivity, and of group productivity as well. The Japanese worker goes to his job armed with a guaranteed life-time job, a bonus based on productivity and corporate profitability, and a wage rate that attaches to him as an individual and not to the particular job that he happens to be doing. This will not fit many of our organizations, perhaps, but there must be a better way for us, too!

Knowledgeable management has already taken some steps to prepare plans to meet changes in work force demographics, changes in employee attitudes and expectations, changes in union perceptions and priorities, and to bring about a fundamental change in what government, employees, and the public regard as socially acceptable solutions that are effective.

Whatever government does to stimulate (or retard) productivity, we have to look to the required internal changes in our businesses, including possible major changes in the incentive structures facing labor and management, and we must position our measurement of the economic health of companies on the long haul rather than on the short-range measurement of current profits.

IV.   Wage Costs

The basic role of "total labor costs in inflation" is a top issue for 1981 and beyond. More and more, analysts are fearful that an annual rise of at least 10 percent in wage and benefit levels is so firmly built into the economy that it will set an essential floor under our inflation for years to come. This view is not shared by some economic advisors who have the ear of the new administration, including Mr. Alan Greenspan, who argues that while unionized workers in certain lead industries do better than the rate of inflation, the overall fall in real wages for employees throughout the economy minimizes the wage factor as a principal element in inflation.

An eloquent statement to the contrary has been made by the chief economist for Kidder, Peabody and Company. "A license to steal" is his term for the formulas written into union contracts in auto, steel, and other major industries for basic pay increases in excess of productivity, coupled with automatic additional increases whenever prices go up. He takes the pessimistic view that unless something of a major remedial nature occurs, the country could face its greatest crisis since 1930-31, one that could trigger another worldwide depression.

It is clear that as a matter of ideology the president and the current administration are strongly against any form of direct government intervention to restrain wages or prices through an incomes policy. George Shultz, the chairman of the administration's Economic Policy Committee, is against guidelines or any other form of wage or price control, and is for not helping those institutions that refuse to recognize the realities of a government effort to establish an economic environment consistent with declining inflation. Mr. Shultz believes the government should say to business and labor, "You're free to set any prices or wages you want, but we're going to stick with our policy. If you price yourself out of the market, that's your problem." Mr. Shultz takes the position that industries like auto and steel, where the wages and benefits far outdistance other industries, have to find ways out of the bind they have gotten themselves into. If they come to the administration for help on imports or industrial revitalization, he says the White House should take into account the degree to which these industries have acted to moderate their jumps in labor costs. Whatever the political reality of such a position, all agree that the persistence of wage increases at the threshold of the double-digit range is the most stubborn factor the Reagan administration must face in its fight against inflation.

Already in 1981, a 10.5 percent pay increase is in place for oil workers under union contracts negotiated a year ago after a ten-week strike. And the can companies have settled on a basis that seems comparable with last year's steelworker contracts. The second coal settlement is not anything but bad news in terms of potential impact elsewhere on both costs and productivity improvement. This is not a new and different beginning for 1981 bargaining developments. What is new is that more companies are saying, "Not for me—my situation demands a settlement in line with *our* business realities."

V. The Bargaining Scene

The biggest news on the labor scene is, of course, the Chrysler agreement, which the general public views as simply an emergency arrangement to save jobs. It is certainly that, but it is also much, much more.

Indeed, Chrysler has gotten a break. By March it was paying each worker $3 an hour less than the contract originally required. By the contract's expiration in 1982, it is estimated that Chrysler will be paying $5 an hour less, about $17 an hour in labor costs compared to $22 at Ford and General Motors. But as the wage costs in Japan are even less, a short-term scenario is predictable. Ford and General Motors are going to have to get some reasonable equivalent of the Chrysler settlement. On the union side, there obviously will need to be a quid pro quo. In addition to all the other special arrangements made at Chrysler, a key ingredient was a profit sharing system. There seems to be no question that that is the price of accommodation with the major auto companies by the United Automobile, Aerospace and Agricultural Implement Workers of America (UAW). The question is whether a profit sharing scheme will be implemented in such a way as to enhance productivity.

But let us go beyond the auto industry. If General Motors and Ford push for Chrysler-like breaks on labor costs, will this stop in the auto industry? The answer is probably no, because the logic does not stop in the auto industry. The logic extends to steel and to many other industries, particularly those that have been affected by the high-cost spillover effects of the steel and auto patterns.

Ideologists in the labor movement agree that concessions to keep Chrysler operating were necessary, but they stress that important breakthroughs besides profit sharing were made in "workplace democracy," including worker participation in the corporate decision-making process (that is, union representation on the company's board of directors), financial disclosures by management, procedures relating to the ratio of supervisors to workers, limitations on plant closings, and outside sourcing. This latter issue, outside sourcing, is an essential part of management control for most companies; and it relates to productivity.

There is an extraneous factor that complicates the perspective. Construction industry settlements have gone wild over the past two years, rising to the largest increases in nine years despite the high unemployment rate among construction workers. There is a major increase in the trend to pick nonunion contractors when efficient labor utilization can be obtained over and beyond the modest concessions to improved work practices that can be negotiated with many construction unions. What the construction unions have apparently failed to realize is that the major customers, faced with intense problems of their own to become more competitive, will finally decide that they have no choice but to go nonunion whenever they can in implementing the enormous capital investments that they have on the line now, or planned, in order to improve productivity.

All of this is taking place as cost-push factors continue to be a major aspect of our total economic problem. The Labor Department report on major collective bargaining settlements for 1980 indicated that the first-year contracts covering one thousand or more workers contained wage increases that averaged 9.5 percent compared with 7.5 percent in 1979. But as you professionals all know, first-year wage increases give only a partial measure of labor costs for the more than three million unionized workers who negotiated new contracts, including the highly controversial wage practice called COLA, or cost of living adjustments. Last year, COLAs added 2.6 percent to the rise in wages, down from 3.0 percent the year before, because of the modest drop in the rate of inflation. But those of you bargaining contracts this year and next may expect to receive even more vigorous demands for COLA arrangements in your contracts.

For the historians among you, let me recall that the COLA concept was invented by a chief executive of General Motors, Charlie Wilson, while he was in the hospital, and was immediately embraced by Emil Mazey of the UAW and Jim Matles of the United Electrical, Radio and Machine Workers (UE), both of whom are militant and astute left-wing union leaders. In defense of the concept, it proposed a "more rational approach to negotiations" by assuring a permanent COLA arrangement plus an annual productivity factor to guarantee increases in real income at a time when national annual productivity increases of at least 2 percent were regarded as a sure thing. Privately, the proposal had two objectives: to avoid or limit collective bargaining in its more turbulent sense and to avoid strikes. It succeeded in both, to a certain degree. Yet today, auto wages and benefits are 60 percent above the national average, and there are 80,000 workers on indefinite layoff at General Motors. Strikes have occurred in 1964, 1967, 1970, 1973, and 1976, while the 1979 negotiations were described by an auto negotiator as one more exercise in "backing down aggressively." A strike-free settlement resulted. General Motors and Ford have stated they can no longer live with it, and with government help, Chrysler does not have to anymore.

VI.   The Need to Revise Obsolete Labor Relations Practices

A harsh observer has recently suggested that employee relations people should come up regularly before a psychiatrist—at least those who have been negotiating our union contracts over the past decade. And perhaps it would not be a bad idea to reevaluate some of the concepts and practices that have let us coast along believing we have achieved "maturity" in labor relations. But we have also achieved rigidities in labor cost structure, ignored the realities of declining productivity, forced patterns on companies where they did not fit, and undergirded inflation by building in unrealistic unit labor costs, which have contributed to our basic competitive problems.

We are all familiar with these and many of us have been present at their creation: the labor contracts providing for an annual improvement factor of 3 percent, the cost-of-living adjustments attempting to protect real wages against the erosion of inflation (but unfortunately being a generating source of inflation themselves), the employer-pay-all plans for medical costs which eliminated the incentives for cost control, and the extravagant new fringes in pension and other benefits, so that total benefit payments in the past decade have risen from around 20 percent of payroll to well over a third for most companies. The most grievous sin of all, in my judgment, has been the incorporation of these new features in so-called "patterns" which, sometimes with the willing acquiescence of employers, have been enforced on all companies bargaining with a particular union, such as the steelworkers, the auto workers, and others.

About a year ago, the witty and perceptive Arnold Weber put it this way: "Adherence to comprehensive bargaining structures has meant the uniform application to the lame and the swift alike. This pincer effect has hastened the shut-down of marginal steel mills and fabricating plants, provoked extensive surgery by the major rubber companies and helped to tighten the noose around Chrysler. As in other areas of economic behavior, adherence to past wisdom in labor relations often results in current folly. Additional casualties undoubtedly will be incurred in these blue collar redoubts." Dr. Weber was correct—they have occurred.

Fortunately, those industrial relations practioners who have seen their psychiatrists, or their chief executive, have started to reverse these unwelcome trends. Pattern bargaining no longer seems so attractive as the easy and comfortable way out.

VII.   New Union Initiatives

Labor experts have been too hasty in announcing the decline and fall of the American labor movement. These experts tend to say that there is little evidence that labor has developed innovative plans to confront its enemies and address its problems. The truth is that the enemy has changed and the problems are different for the unions. The current leadership is wise enough to accept these realities. They are engaged in a massive effort to regain their political clout, which they intend to exhibit in 1982 bi-elections, where they believe their money and manpower will again be the winning ingredient along with social issues.

The new enemy is failure to help create and maintain jobs. Lester Thurow, the economist from the Massachusetts Institute of Technology, has said that the world economy and manufacturing methods are changing so drastically that the old union methods of winning support of workers, such as raising wages, no longer have much relevance. Unions must find ways to help companies improve productivity if American manufacturing is to remain competitive with foreign manufacturing. But unions can do this and still win membership support on issues of industrial justice within the plant and support of collective bargaining, a major force in our economy, as the coal miners and even the baseball players would testify.

The problem for both labor and management is that few new initiatives from either side have characterized their relationships over the past decade at least, and collective bargaining has been marked in too many cases by the dominant position of the union, as in the auto industry. But the results of over-generous settlements have finally forced the parties to a day of reckoning.

The labor leaders I know are familiar with the problem, but point out that management will have to create the climate of understanding that will make possible settlements that are in accord with the realities.

VIII.   Better Labor-Management Relations

It is easy to engage in woolly profundities about labor-management cooperation. I do not hesitate to suggest that, given the current scenario, reasonable cooperation is a "must," and I note that some substantial progress is underway. This is not to say that political infighting will not continue and may intensify on certain social issues on which management and union leaders have agreed to disagree.

Fortunately, a lot of activity is occurring on both the national and the enterprise fronts. I think these developments are positive and need not diminish the vigor of the parties in areas where they must disagree. The labor movement and the business community are completely in agreement about supporting measures that will produce a bigger economic pie in America, then arguing over the best distribution of it. They both reject and will be vigorously opposed to the "smaller is better" philosophy, so they are natural allies in terms of much of the basic philosophy underlying our system.

Let me give three or four quick examples:

1.   In order to restore communication between the leaders of organized labor and of the business community, the informal National Labor-Management Committee has been reinstituted, headed by Lane Kirkland on the union side and Cliff Garvin of Exxon on the management side, with an agenda devoted to key economic issues, but not to specific collective bargaining problems. The purpose is to restore effective communication as to what each side thinks is in the best interest of the American economy. Whether this produces consensus on approach to issues such as inflation and tax policy, it is likely to produce mutual understanding, respect, and perhaps better ideas.

2.   There are some interesting efforts in legislative cooperation underway. The ERISA law is a very complex law, primarily passed to reflect the views of labor unions about guarantees of pension rights. It contains a number of unworkable provisions, including a contingent insurance liability system that could have bankrupted many multi-employer plans set up by unions. A somewhat extraordinary industry coalition was put together last year to assist the unions in obtaining the necessary corrections to the multi-employer insurance act. A similar coalition is at work today, consisting of employer organizations and a wide range of union organizations, working to obtain passage of a similar bill covering single employers' plans and also correcting the improvident provisions of the ERISA as originally passed.

3.   On the operating front, unions and business groups are getting together to heal the divisiveness in their industries or companies and attempting to work out rational and cost-effective solutions to their problems. For example, the "quality of work life" movement has begun to expand even to the skilled crafts. A new labor-management pact between the bricklayers' union and the organization representing masonry contractors has announced the creation of a joint organization for improving all aspects of their industry, including collective bargaining. The bricklayers' union said that the venture was a recognition of the fact that labor and management were at "a dangerous crossroads that could lead either to greater cooperation or to growing hostility detrimental to both sides." This follows upon the prior action of the auto workers and the steel workers to develop common programs with management to build productivity and worker satisfaction. Similarly, the communication workers and American Telephone & Telegraph (AT&T) are formulating plans to put a simi-

lar system into effect in white-collar jobs in the Bell System.

4. A number in this audience are encouraging unions to take their initial experimental steps into this new water, while being sensitive to the political repercussions with the membership.

But all the news is not good in terms of new ways to be helpful to the enterprise. For example, the graphic arts union says profit-sharing plans are basically intended to trade wages for investment in a failing enterprise. Stock-sharing and particularly employee-stock ownership plans (ESOP), were roundly condemned in this union's recent bargaining conference. It was asserted that, generally, stock is offered in a company so that a plant can continue to operate; that workers have no say in operations, their earnings are tied up; and that "this is no way to guarantee future security of the members."

It is going to be hard to change attitudes, but if some of you old-timers remember back to the hostile attitudes of the unions in the post-World War II era, miracles were accomplished under very difficult conditions. As someone once said, "The truth will out even in an affidavit."

IX. New Technology

Microprocessor and information processing technology are poised for new breakthroughs in both factory and office. At the present time we have only about 800 robots at installations in this country, while over 8,000 robots are employed in the automated factories of Japan. This new technology will be coming into play with the gradual introduction of robots into difficult assembly jobs in the interests of both quality, productivity, and safety.

The acceptance or nonacceptance of change of this nature will affect the timing, payback, and cost-effectiveness of new technology investments and applications. Obviously, it will require extensive human relations planning as well as redesign of the structure of work.

A French author, M. Jacques Servan-Schreiber, in a book entitled *The World Challenge* has made some exaggerated claims about the impact on industrial society by microchip technology, but certainly it will have a place in factory automation.

X. Should We Copy Japan?

Since 1950, Japan's annual productivity growth rate has been four times that of the United States and twice that of major European nations. Their success has been phenomenal, and partly in desperation, many in American management are undertaking a major effort to import management techniques made in Japan. These efforts, most of them favorable in contrast to the prior efforts to improve productivity, include stock and cash bonus plans, the suggestion box, and superficial labor-management committee efforts that seem to have only marginal impact. This has resulted in much literature which states, in effect, that we should copy Japan.

My conviction, like that of Mr. Hodgson, one of the few people who really understands Japan, is that successful programs will have to be tailor-made to the realities of each individual company. I am also convinced that the rethinking of America's productivity is going to depend in large part on how successful we are in giving employees more responsibility for their work and more influence in the organization.

XI.   What to Do

First, the core *political* problem is to get the federal government back in place where it is part of the solution and not part of the problem. Fortunately, the current administration is intent on putting the federal establishment on a diet and in shrinking the overregulation of business activity that cannot be justified on a cost-benefit basis. In terms of specific regulations, this will require the participation and the input of the business community in order to provide the empirical data to justify the shrinking of excessive regulation.

The core *operating* problem is planning to create an environment for effective management of human resources. In too many businesses, this really has not been done in depth. While the process of human resource planning is practiced by all in one form or another, it really needs to be a major part of the strategic plan of the business. The external environment and the key business strategies should both be examined in preparing the plans for human resource management. You are all familiar with your own business strategies, but it is essential to comprehend the external environment in order to identify critical factors on which plans are to be based and necessary changes considered.

A third key area for attention, I suspect, is enhanced communication effectiveness in several areas:

  a)   as a tool in employee participation;
  b)   as an adjunct to needed "economic education"; and
  c)   in relation to public issues and government decisions.

Time will not permit my developing this theme, but the need for qualitative improvement in our management communications in these three areas is quite serious. Just communicating is not enough. As one critic said about one corporation's efforts: "They have a message even a pigeon wouldn't carry."

And in the area of economic education, do not be lulled to repose by the theory that the conservative trend has taken over in the nation, and that the job is completed. As George Gilder remarks in his excellent book, *Wealth and Poverty*, a mere rejection of the socialist vision is not enough. The economics of the business must be related to the fortunes of the participants in the business, in addition to making the case for the market economy. The only weapon against bad ideas is better ideas. Profits and the role of the profit system are still a point of contention. One wit has put it this way: "Profits are now viewed the way sex used to be. Everybody thinks there is more of it then there really is—and that somebody else is getting most of it."

The need for communication in relation to public issues and government decisions is going to be increasingly important. In most businesses, the responsibility for speaking out on industrial relations issues will be vested in industrial relations management. So this is a new and broader aspect of the professionalism that will be required in this functional area.

Finally, there must be genuine emphasis on improvement in all areas of employee selection, training, and promotion, including recruitment, career charting, performance appraisal, testing, and compensation. My impression is that a "renaissance" is already under way in the practice of these fundamentals of personnel administration.

XII. Summing Up

The problem of regaining our competitive strengths at home and abroad must be a top priority for the 1980s.

The challenge was recently illustrated by this candid remark by Shin Koo Huh, president of an electronics concern planning to open the first Korean plant in the United States. A reporter for the *New York Times* asked:

"Will the management of the plant be Korean or American?"

The answer was: "In the beginning we think that the five or six top managers at the plant will be Korean, but except for the plant manager, the chief engineer and the chief financial officer, there is nothing that Koreans can do better than Americans. Eventually maybe all the employees could be American. About 50 people from Korea will come initially, to train the American employees, especially in quality control."

You managers should regard this as "the most unkindest cut of all." *Eventually,* it seems, our management can come up to Korean standards. Meanwhile, they will outperform us in our markets.

"They should live so long!" as we say in New York. But we do have a catch-up game to play. A major effort must be made, led by top management, based upon a major strategic plan for the business, which will help to start working on the required changes. Fortunately, a lot of preliminary success has been achieved, and major U.S. industry is working hard to move forward on a total attack on the problem areas. Productivity is starting to move up sharply—judging by early results in 1981. The beginnings of an industrial relations renaissance are already under way.

What does this mean for you? It is really a time of opportunity for the hot personnel professional.

The *challenge* is bigger—the *job* is bigger. The *need* will be for "a man of all seasons." This will result over the short and long pull in raising the sights of corporate management in terms of the talent and the performance required for key personnel jobs. Business is now seeking the "superstars" for personnel chiefs.

Also, the talent requirements will change. An experienced observer has predicted that "no longer can one person be the complete industrial relations expert." There will be a need to have a supplemental team of experts—truly professional problem-solvers—in areas ranging from behavioral research to government relations matters.

I wish you luck. And in terms of the philosophy to attempt the changes now required for success in the world of the 1980s, may I commend to you what I call Day's Law on Problem Solving: "lunatics always win over paralytics."

PART I

B. Union and Management Views

Employee Relations and Regulation—
A Union Viewpoint

Elmer Chatak[†]

I. Introduction

As much as we as a nation should be concerned about excessive red tape and unnecessary government regulation, we must fear the current attack on the nation's regulatory framework being led by overzealous and misdirected *deregulators*.

When I speak of these deregulators I am referring to those who have jumped on an out-of-control bandwagon that is indiscriminately rolling over essential government protections.

Members of this gang are leaving a paper trail of Op-Ed pieces, full-page ads, and biased studies that rivals the *Federal Register* in volume, and at the same time, they are doing little to help us reach the inseparable goals of an *equitable, healthy, safe,* and *productive* workplace.

As much as workers are also concerned about overregulation, they will not condone a wholesale attack on measures that, over the last few decades, have improved their quality of life.

And as easy as it is for management to make broad overgeneralizations about "overregulation," it must not. If management endorses the gutting of affirmative action programs, fair labor standards, and health, safety, and environmental protections, it will undermine the progress being made toward greater productivity. This move toward greater productivity, in many cases, is the result of regulations themselves and is also a result of a new era of labor-management cooperation that is also being threatened by the actions of the deregulators.

II. Certain Standards are Based on Real Needs

There are certain minimum standards of economic equity, health, safety, and environmental quality. Efforts to weaken protections below these standards will not be tolerated by the American worker.

These standards are not the result of some philosophical discus-

---

[†] Elmer Chatak is Secretary-Treasurer of the Industrial Union Department of the AFL-CIO.

49

sion. These standards do not come from some hypothetical academic pursuit. These standards are *not* based on this quarter's profits.

Instead, these standards are based on actual needs and on the real risks that workers and their families take daily both on the job and in their communities.

I have worked in the steel mills of Pennsylvania and can tell you what substandard health and safety protections mean in terms of real human suffering. I have seen too many cases where workers have been permanently disabled because management tried to save a few cents here, and a few cents there, on safety equipment. I know what happens to a man and his family when he is forced to retire early because of an illness that results from years of exposure to unsafe chemicals and production processes.

Here in Pennsylvania, on the other side of the state where I grew up, few people who are old enough to remember will forget the Donora disaster. In 1948, the wind shifted in town and poisonous gases from a zinc reduction plant and a steel mill combined and were trapped in the atmosphere. Within a day, twenty residents had died and over half of the town became ill.

In every area from the minimum wage to affirmative action, regulations have arisen to correct real abuses and respond to real needs.

III. The Market Alone Cannot Meet These Standards

Yet, the new administration and a large portion of the business community are obsessed with the notion of an unregulated market allowed to roam free. But the record is clear. The market has not, and will not, protect workers' health and safety if left to its own devices.

I believe the term for this type of market failure is called "negative externalities." Instead of paying for safety equipment or pollution control devices, the owner lets the workers and members of the community pay some of his costs with their health. Well, at the heart of our system of free enterprise is the concept that you have to pay your own way. You cannot make someone else pay your costs while you reap the benefits.

The question then becomes, "How do we get business to pay all the costs of production?"

I am not an economist by training and have to admit I am somewhat confused by all the talk in Washington these days. It seems that when it comes to things like taxes, business wants government intervention in the form of incentives—to get them to do what they should be doing. Yet proponents of deregulation claim that if we would just get government out of the way, business would do things voluntarily.

I think it is clear that without government intervention in the market, what must be done, will not be done. Regulation must be a permanent feature of the American economy.

IV. Regulation and Productivity

Unfortunately, there is a growing lobby in this country which refuses to recognize the need for regulation, or for other reasons, is intent on repealing many essential regulatory protections . One of its key arguments is that regulation lowers productivity. In fact, in many cases the opposite is true.

As much as everyone seems to have their favorite Occupational Safety and Health Administration (OSHA) story about this or that silly regulation, the overall facts are that OSHA works, not just for workers, but for management. In the ten years that OSHA has been in existence, in just one industry alone—manufacturing—job-related injuries and illnesses have fallen by almost 25 percent. Occupationally related deaths have dropped by almost one-half.

I do not need to tell management experts what these lower rates can mean for productivity. A healthy work force is a more productive work force.

Also, regulation is opening up new markets for industry and encouraging new, cost-cutting technology. The National Academy of Sciences reports that between 1971 and 1976, over 650,000 workers were employed in the pollution control industry. And since then, the number of new jobs and workers in the field has continued to grow.

Also, when corporations are forced to redesign products or manufacturing processes to meet health, safety, or environmental goals, more efficient and more productive solutions often result. For example:

—At a Kaiser Steel pipe mill in Fontana, California, workers were getting bad cuts from an old saw. A new saw, required by safety regulations, not only protects the workers but is also reducing the wear and tear on the tools.

—The textile industry, which for so long has fought regulations requiring filters to clear cotton dust out of the air, has found that after installing these filters, productivity and profits are up.

—General Motors knows how regulations can *cut* costs. When it was forced to control pollution, its engineers designed new boilers

that monitor emissions and set air-to-fuel ratios that provide
cleaner air and lower energy bills.

—Steel mills, railroads, chemical plants, and a host of other manufacturing plants are finding that by complying with regulations,
they are recycling and reusing materials they used to just throw
away. And they are finding it is not only socially desirable, but
profitable.

We must identify those aspects of regulation that contribute to the
nation's productivity. Let us not throw the proverbial baby out with
the bath water.

V. Overregulation is a Problem

Of course, I do not mean to say that all regulations are a good thing.
As I mentioned earlier, the labor movement is itself familiar with
regulations that do not work or take too long to work. It is currently
not unusual for it to take *years* to put a stop to serious health threats
in the workplace.

For example, workers at a lead smelting plant in Omaha, Nebraska, were suffering from headaches, dizziness, and highly abnormal
blood counts. The culprit?— massive lead poisoning. The employees,
in 1971, filed one of the first complaints under the then new Occupational Health and Safety Act. OSHA proposed a $600 fine and a sixty-
day abatement period.

The complaint was only the beginning of a series of hearings and
appeals that seemed to go on forever. All in all, the process took *five
years* before the fine was finally levied and the abatement period begun. In the meantime, the hazard to the workers' health had continued unchecked.

The labor movement is also well aware of overregulation. The Taft-
Hartley and Landrum-Griffin Acts severely restrict workers' rights
to organize and bargain collectively (though I guess I should not expect Mobil Oil or any other corporate opponent of regulation to take
up our cause in their war on regulation).

VI. Business Has Historically Sought to Deregulate Selectively

In fact, this point underscores an important truth about the current
rampage of the deregulators. Their attack is selectively focused on
those regulations that benefit consumers, workers, and the general
public. They have a blind spot when it comes to the millions of regulations and hundreds of thousands of federal workers protecting man-

agement's interests. Historically, business has worked either to control regulatory agencies or to abolish them.

Most of the largest regulatory agencies in Washington were created to curb corporate anticompetitive activity that drove prices *up* and drove productivity from competitive innovation *down*. The Federal Communications Commission, the Industrial Communication Council, the Federal Trade Commission, the Consumers' Advisory Board, the Federal Energy Regulatory Commission, and the Maritime Commission were started to curb corporate abuse in the marketplace.

In their early years, many of these agencies fell prey to the very industries they were supposed to regulate. More and more, these agencies served to protect the larger businesses already established in a particular field. And, not surprisingly, there were few complaints from big business.

Ironically, the most vocal opponent of certain efforts at deregulation has been the business community. The most vehement objections to deregulating the airline industry came not from those awful bureaucrats in Washington, but from the nation's largest airlines. Now the trucking industry is battling efforts to deregulate that particular industry.

The business community's current attack on regulation comes at a time when regulators again have begun to regulate more and more with the public's interest in mind. Agencies like OSHA, the Environmental Protection Agency, the Consumer Product Safety Commission, and a revitalized Federal Trade Commission (which are the most often mentioned objects of business complaints) are also those agencies that have the greatest responsibility for curbing corporate abuse for the common good.

It is not unexpected that once again, the business community is trying to regulate the regulator's impact.

VII. The Reagan Administration is no Exception to this Practice

The first few months of the Reagan administration are a good example of how the deregulators are going about their attack on the nation's regulatory framework in a very selective way.

At the top of the Reagan administration's chopping block are OSHA standards, Environmental Protection Agency air quality standards, and an attempt to gut the Consumer Product Safety Commission.

On the other hand, there seems to be very little concern to clear up the thicket of regulation involved in taxes, rebates, subsidies, credits,

market barriers, and other special concessions made by the government to corporations. There rarely is a complaint about these difficult-
to-administer programs, and there appears to be little effort to repeal
them.

VIII. Deregulators are Undermining Labor-Management
Relations and Productivity

The remaining question is what will the impact of the current deregulation fad be on employee relations? Leading from this question
we must ask, "What in turn will the impact be on the nation's economic health?"

Underneath all the economic theory and stacked cost-benefit
analysis, the American worker perceives that he or she is the ultimate target of the current drive to deregulate. And in many instances, I believe he or she is right.

The risks the business community is running are great. At a time
when our European and Japanese economic rivals have shown us
that cooperation is the only way, the American business community
is about to declare war on its workers and make any cooperation between worker and management at any time in the near future difficult, if not impossible.

The American work force is becoming increasingly better edu-
cated. Workers understand carcinogens. They know the implications
of faulty equipment design. They see the links between the plant
floor and the hospital bed.

In states all across the country, workers have organized occupational health and safety committees to monitor business. In twenty
states, workers and environmentalists are developing a coalition
called OSHA/Environmental Network to fight any future encroach-
ment on laws that protect the workplace, the air, or the water.

In my travels around the country, I have found the one unifying
issue among all workers—black and white, skilled and unskilled,
blue-collar and white-collar—is *health and safety on the job*. It is one
issue that every worker understands and that every worker is willing
to organize for.

The health and safety interests of America's working men and
women are currently on a collision course with the lobbying objectives of the deregulators. Yet, all that either side can hope to achieve
after a prolonged period of conflict is more complicated and unworkable regulations that will result from a slugfest in the Congress, in
the state capitols, in the courts, and in the streets. This ensuing brawl
can only serve to sidetrack both labor and management from the real
issues involved in improving productivity.

IX. Labor is Willing to Work with Management on Reasonable Regulatory Reform

The labor movement again is not taking the position of "Regulations— Love Them or Leave Them." The AFL-CIO and labor bodies throughout the country are ready to work with business to create regulations that are clear, that are competently and efficiently administered, and that achieve their purpose. There are also many areas where labor and management can work together to change those regulations that are vague and waste the energies of both labor and management.

Yet if the campaign against deregulation is used to achieve unrelated political objectives or if the business-backed deregulation movement places profits before protection, there will be no room to work together.

X. Conclusion

A misdirected attack on regulation, one that focuses on the very guarantees workers are willing to fight for, cannot enhance employee-management relations or productivity. If any major regulatory reform is to succeed, it must be carefully thought out and it must be a cooperative effort of both labor and management. The stated purpose of the deregulation movement, of improving the nation's economic health, will prove elusive if a blanket condemnation of regulation is pursued. The inseparable goals of an *equitable, healthy, safe,* and *productive* workplace will be unobtainable unless the deregulators are themselves regulated.

8220
8331
U.S.

Managerial Control of Regulation in the '80s

Douglas H. Soutar[†]

My remarks will not address a particular regulation or industry, which is an approach compatible with government's changed emphasis in recent years from the regulation of specific industries to a focus on national problems such as environment, equal rights, energy, pensions, public lands, etc., although our interest here today is in those regulations which affect the workplace. Of course, we are all acutely aware of the Niagara of regulations during the past twenty years, which has reached the point at which major changes are required.

Based on recent surveys, it would appear that regulations are here to stay and that most businessmen not only acquiesce in this but also say most regulations are necessary. There are conservative business spokesmen who feel, and organizations which take the position, that industry should not acquiesce in retaining existing regulations or in contemplating new ones, much less in cooperating in their administration. On the assumption that the management majority is correct, then we had better prepare to make the best of our current regulatory atmosphere.

Despite acceptance of this need for regulations, management, like the public, expresses a strong desire to overhaul the present regulatory system—if it can be called a system. Presumably, this would be sponsored by the Reagan administration. Such overhaul should address the six most basic regulatory problems, recently identified by a 1980 Conference Board report as follows:

1) Overlap and conflict among agencies on regulatory subjects;
2) Overextension of the agency mandate, frequently through a concern with means as well as goals, leading agencies to dictate how goals will be met;
3) Unilateral and retroactive rulemaking and overregulation without regard to costs or efficiency;
4) Adversary attitudes toward business;

---

† Douglas H. Soutar is Vice President of Industrial Relations and Personnel for ASARCO, Inc.

5) Delays in exercising mandated authority;
6) Duplicative and unnecessary reporting requirements.

The end result should be better *management* of the regulatory process; specific *goals* with adjustable features; greater *flexibility*, including more reliance on expertise and counsel of the regulatees; and an improved congressional *oversight* mechanism.

An unexpected end result of this overhaul may be less progress toward *consolidation* of regulatory functions and less *specificity* than management would hope for because Congress, much as in our organizations such as the Business Roundtable, at times finds it impracticable to speak "with one voice" because of the many conflicting interests represented, and must solve problems on a consensus basis. Thus, having in mind some of the vague language we in management circles compromise upon, our criticisms of Congress ought to be tempered a bit.

To give the Carter administration its due, its later phases generated several undertakings in response to public outcries against regulatory excesses, including interagency task forces, bills in Congress, and an executive order requiring assessment of regulatory impact.

Assuming the best case, i.e., that the Reagan administration will, in due course, be able to substantially improve the regulatory process, what can employers do to lessen its impact? A review of the available literature and unwritten history of employer efforts in this regard leads to the oft-warranted conclusion that "what's past is prologue." Management *has been* adapting to the increasing impact of regulations to the point where primary emphasis can now be placed on the perfection of efforts previously tried or still underway.

A broad-brush approach to this subject requires attention to the many laws, agencies, and types of regulations with which we contend in managing the workplace.

Some of these employment laws are:

Wage-Hour (Fair Labor Standards Act—FLSA), Davis-Bacon, Walsh Healey Public Contracts Act, Service Contract Act of 1965, Labor-Management Relations Act (LMRA), Employee Retirement Income Security Act (ERISA), Age Discrimination and Employment Act (ADEA), Health Maintenance Organizations, Social Security, Occupational Safety and Health Act (OSHA), Mine Safety and Health Act (MSHA), Environmental Protection Agency (EPA), Equal Employment Opportunity Commission (EEOC), Equal Pay Act, Office of Federal Contract Compliance Program (OFCCP), Handicap, Vietnam Veterans', Apprenticeship and Training.

Most of us have discovered that an important cornerstone in constructing a plan to manage government regulations is the need to structure our organizations to fit the task. Management has added specialists to staff— or developed them from within— to deal with the specifics of regulations, to identify the prospects of future ones, and to innovate methods of preempting them when possible.

Thus, a whole new breed of employees and executives has been added to payrolls. Passing by the highly-debatable subject *of the need* for such regulations, and the popular issue of the extent of management's social responsibilities over and above its need to produce profits, all will admit that payroll and related costs have skyrocketed as a result, substantially jeopardizing our productivity and competitive positions at home and abroad. The challenge to management inherent in restructuring its organizations to adapt to changing regulatory patterns, particularly in the human resources field, remains one of the most urgent challenges facing it in the 1980s.

Another critical choice and challenge facing management in its planning for accommodation to regulations is a resolution of its posture vis-à-vis *participation in a "partnership"* relationship with government. The precedent of cooperation between foreign governments and industry, widely touted lately, must heavily influence this choice.

Many of the new staff in our organizations deal directly with regulatory agencies to provide assistance in the form of research, advice, and cooperation when requested, although all too often, management has complained that such assistance is rarely requested, and that it is, more often than not, rejected. The expressed hope behind such partnership efforts is to enhance management credibility, improve and expedite standard-setting, avoid overlaps and duplication with other agencies, standardize and simplify reporting, and generally assist agencies in attaining more effective administration. (I refer you to the *1980 National Industrial Conference Board Report,* No. 769, Chapter 4, for a variety of specific examples.)

When employers feel little need or enthusiasm for such participation, they often pursue other tactics. For example, management has frequently complained of an inability to cooperate in such fashion with the OSHA, the EPA, the EEOC, and the OFCCP, thus being forced to plan a policy evidenced by adversary proceedings at almost every administrative and legal step, all the way to the United States Supreme Court.

I am sure that effective managerial control of regulation means different things to each of you. To some of you, the most important and effective step in controlling regulation is to anticipate and influence the legislative process before the enactment of the *legislation* that would give rise to the regulations themselves. To others, the most important role in the managerial control of regulations would be to get involved early on in any rulemaking processes and try to influence the scope and substance of the *regulation* itself. To still others, I suspect that deep down you have come to the unhappy conclusion that the best way to control the regulatory process is through the courts, as I just noted. I might say at this point that after the past four frustrating and trying years, I can certainly empathize with this view, but also hope that it is a transitory and declining one. Finally, managerial control of regulations means disseminating the information and making and implementing the necessary decisions to enable your company to comply in the most effective and efficient manner with the regulations themselves. A corollary to this latter concept would be the processes taken—be they corrective or legal—in response to allegations of noncompliance by the government.

It will come as no surprise to you that my view is that effective managerial control of regulation includes—indeed mandates—action in all of the foregoing processes. To merely react to citations or notices of noncompliances from government agencies—though perhaps a necessary part of the managerial function at times—is nevertheless more the absence of control than the presence. Similarly, the mere act of resorting to litigation upon the final promulgation of a regulation is more an indication of a lack of managerial control than of its presence. Clearly, the concept requires hands-on participation from the very beginning of the legislative and regulatory processes to the day-to-day attempts to comply with—and perhaps ultimately change—the final regulations. The failure to stay involved at all levels is indeed the abdication of managerial control.

The effective implementation of these processes requires contacts and communication with the legislative staffs on Capitol Hill, with the regulators themselves—from the very top to the middle level bureaucrat—with officials in other government agencies such as the Office of Management and Budget and, of course, particularly in the industrial relations area, with the various union officials.

Many of management's dealings with regulators involve unions in one fashion or another. Their role was indeed singularly noticeable in the Carter administration, and though I suspect a more even balance in this administration, their input and views will certainly not be ignored. As representatives of employees in our organizations, they have the right by law to interject into many such proceedings, and management must be structured to deal constructively, when possible, with union hierarchies. Effective interface with labor is frequently of substantial and even critical importance in the planning of regulatory preemption. It can be accomplished on an individual company level, or through multiple bargaining units, or by utilizing specialized associations of employers.

Another facet of union interface, recommended by top regulators such as former Secretaries of Labor Dunlop and Marshal, is a tripartite approach to the development of regulations, rules, and standards. Fortunately, or unfortunately, depending upon your view of this approach, it has been little used. At least during the Carter administration, this could well be because labor felt its position, particularly at the Department of Labor and at the National Labor Relations Board (NLRB), was such that any help was considered about as necessary as an appendix, and that the most effective regulatory method was to "hold management's feet to the fire." Perhaps this administration will show further interest in the tripartite approach; I understand that Thorne Auchter, the new assistant secretary for the OSHA, has so indicated, with heavy emphasis on a joint labor-management model which could provide a strong recommendation for the agency's final proposals. The recent report of the National Air Quality Commission apparently was partially a result of tripartite compromise, but as is the case with so many governmental commissions and advisory councils of this sort, the results, democratic as they may be, are more often counterproductive from management's view.

While we do not have the time to thoroughly document what various employers have done, or plan to do, in their efforts at managing regulation, a general review of some experiences will be helpful in illustration. A caveat will help in our perspective, namely, that it is often difficult to pin down the factual difference and define the line between an employer's formal planning on the one hand and mere reaction on the other.

1. Although we do not yet know the final outcome, the experience with which I am most familiar, and one that covers the entire range of what I have been talking about, involves the OSHA lead standard. Putting aside, for the purposes of my talk today, our efforts on the legislative front—though there were many on our part however inadequate they ultimately proved to be—my company was involved intimately in the early stages of attempting to obtain a lead standard that we could live with and one that would adequately protect the health of our workers. We participated at great

length in all of the rule-making proceedings, including the proffering of testimony by very senior company officers. We supplied mountains of information to the agency. We worked closely with other companies and trade associations, and we attempted to maintain a dialogue with the United Steelworkers of America.

Well, as most of you probably know, despite all the efforts on our part, we were very unsuccessful in persuading the agency of the correctness of our views and were forced to resort to the courts. After losing at the court of appeals, we filed a petition for certiorari. While awaiting action on that petition, another opportunity presented itself to us with the election of President Reagan.

I could not possibly delineate in the short time I have today the scope of our efforts to bring to the attention of the new administration our concerns and problems with the OSHA lead standard. Suffice it to say that through constant communications with individuals in the vice president's office, the Office of Management, and the Department of Labor, as well as in the Department of Commerce and elsewhere, we succeeded in getting the administration's attention. As I indicated previously, we do not know whether we will ultimately be successful in our attempts, but the administration has asked the Supreme Court to remand the matter back to the agency for reconsideration.

2. As you all know, several other regulations have been postponed or withdrawn since the new administration took over. And, as with the lead standard, some of them might have met the same fate regardless of the activities of various companies and trade associations. After some rather lengthy communications with the new administration, primarily by the Chamber of Commerce, OSHA postponed or withdrew its walk-around pay requirement and its hearing conservation standard. I might add that just ten days ago or so, OSHA gave the walk-around pay rule its final burial.

Through the efforts of the chemical industry, the American Industrial Health Council, and other associations and industries, OSHA has also withdrawn or postponed regulations involving its carcinogen policy and its labeling standard. The efforts to get relief from regulations at agencies other than OSHA have to date been less productive. Nevertheless, to date, regulations increasing the minimum salary levels for exempt employees under the minimum wage laws, as well as the private club regulations under the OFCCP, have been put on hold. The efforts by many continue, and I am sanguine that satisfactory results will come to those making the greatest efforts on the greatest number of fronts. Some of the most conspicuous efforts involve attempts to obtain legislative or regulatory changes in the EEOC-OFCCP field, the Black Lung Act, the Longshoremen and Harbor Worker's Act, and the Davis-Bacon Act.

3. Perhaps the most familiar story is that of the rubber industry's handling of the *vinyl chloride* proceeding before OSHA, and more particularly by B.F. Goodrich. What at first appeared to be insurmountable turned out to be manageable and practicable cost-wise. This industry has funded considerable ongoing research and education on a variety of fronts, and appears to have weathered the storm quite well.

4. The asbestos industry, in which ASARCO is a major factor, although heavily regulated, has established several associations to aid in preventing more stringent standards. These engage in research and dissemination of information regarding *real* health hazards and the monitoring of proposed government actions.

I am sure you are aware of similar activities in your own and other industries designed to either avoid regulation or make it more effective. One of high visibility is the American Industrial Health Council funded largely by the chemical industry to impact OSHA's proposed carcinogenic regulations. In the area of occupational health, independent studies conducted prior to those of government have been at times successful in providing ammunition to ward off or soften regulations which might result from the skewing of government's own studies.

Thus, Monsanto's 1980 study of dioxin found no relation between employee exposure and cause of deaths. Likewise, chemical companies' studies of acrylonitrile's effects, and self-imposed regulatory actions, may well have resulted in a more reasonable OSHA standard—at least it is the first of OSHA's health standards not to be challenged in court!

Another well-publicized example of this type is the chemical industry's success in placing before the public the facts of its saccharine study showing the ludicrous number (800) of bottles of soda pop a consumer would have to drink to equal the comparable dosages fed to animals in the government's study of carcinogenic effects. Congress thereafter passed the Saccharine Study and Labeling Act, thus prohibiting the Food and Drug Administration (FDA) from banning saccharine for an extended period. In this same vein of study and research, self-enlightened planning by management now *mandates* such attention to the health implications of its *investment decisions*.

5. Another phase of planning and management involves *greater employee participation* in those workplace problems susceptible to government regulation. This can be manifested in collective bargaining contracts and joint labor-management committees thereunder, or in nonunion versions of the latter. During World War II, thousands of such joint committees sprang up as a result of government promotion through the War Production Board, but they almost all disappeared during the intervening years with a few exceptions, such as those at Armour, Kaiser, and American Motors, and they have not been heard from recently. During the past half dozen years, new versions have appeared in steel, auto, construction, and other industries, including a fair number set up on a regional basis.

In some countries, such as Sweden, joint committees are established by law for all employers with over fifty employees, and they are dominated by labor. They have veto power over a variety of management decisions in the area of safety and health. It is doubtful that any Yankee enthusiasm for such measures would extend to these lengths!

6. A popular subject on the programs of workplace-oriented seminars lately is that of *plant closing and relocation*. The threat of federal legislation has spawned accelerated attention to management's planning on this subject, both in relation to collective bargaining and to open shop operations. Task forces and subcommittees have been established by employer associations to study the problem, and there is a good deal of coordination among them. Further, mechanisms are already in place in numerous collective bargaining agreements and company policies. Publicizing of these efforts and other evidence of management's sincere attention to the problem may well head off such legislation in this administration.

7. The same can be said for the threat of a federal privacy law to cover employees, now fairly common in several states in varying degrees. Management has done a thorough job in researching and studying this problem. Enlightened application of these recommendations, again, could obviate the necessity for federal intervention.

8. A lesser-known but meaty area for heading off regulation is one of which you may be less aware, namely, "unfair dismissal" growing out of alleged personal misconduct or incompetence. The United States stands almost alone in not providing statutory protection against unfair dismissal, excepting of course in the area of employment discrimination. The extent of American manage-

ment's planning and preparation on this subject is meager, its protection lying primarily in sophisticated administration of collective bargaining contracts as well as in less circumscribed workplaces. The recent container settlement with the Steelworkers et al. contained a "Justice and dignity on the job" provision which keeps suspended or discharged employees on the job until their grievance is settled or arbitrated.

9. Again, with particular attention being given to the international scene, management is spending a great deal of time in planning for warding off or accommodating possible laws and regulations on the subject of:

—Application of International Labor Organization (ILO) conventions and resolutions to U.S. labor and the employees of multinational corporations elsewhere.

—"Guidelines" and "Codes of Conduct," already promulgated, or soon to be, by the Organization for Economic Cooperation and Development (OECD), the ILO, the United Nations (UN); the European Economic Community's (EEC) "Vredeling proposal."

—So-called "international bargaining," loudly trumpeted by the International Trade Secretariats in Europe, which may yet be a real threat to management's traditional bargaining role.

10. It seems increasingly popular to include, under my subject heading, planning by employers to manage the full thrust of the National Labor Relations Act (NLRA) and other laws and regulations which impact more forcefully on union shops than upon the more usual open shops. I am sure we need not detail here the many innovative programs at work across the land.

One might consider the J.P. Stevens type of game plan as a pragmatic example, and certainly one not to be considered *sui generis*. Also includable under this subtitle could be the very real regulation of employers by the collective bargaining agreement itself, and by its grievance and arbitration procedures, both in turn increasingly regulated by the government.

Unquestionably, the leading example of self-help and long-range planning under this heading is the effort of the so-called Labor Law Reform Study Group, originally begun in late 1965 by a small group of industrial relations executives and their attorneys, to correct the maladministration of the National Labor Relations Act (NLRA) by the Board, both through legislation and a program of highly effective activity in the courts. Out of its efforts eventually arose, at least in important part, the Construction Users' Anti-Inflation Roundtable, the Washington Pension Group, and the

Business Roundtable. Quite an accomplishment, and a milestone in our nation's labor-management history.

11. Another potential statute and regulation, probably not as current in your thinking, lies in the area of so-called "Emergency Disputes"—a most popular subject in some years past, and probably far from dead. Management can claim some gold stars here for its extensive planning, research, and activities in warding off legislation, which could have included compulsory arbitration and binding "recommendations." Such mechanisms have invaded public sector legislation requiring additional activity by the private sector both to inhibit such growth and to avoid the spillover effect.

12. A vast field for additional regulation lies in the field of *unemployment compensation and workers' compensation*. Much planning and successful preemption by management have occurred here, yet the threat of more onerous legislation has hovered ominously over our heads during the past four years. Now is not the time for relaxation, despite new political balances. In particular, the work of the United Breweries of America (UBA), a specialized employer organization in this field, is notable.

13. If there exists a "success story" extant in the management of EEO's regulations, it is a closely guarded secret. From unrealistic mandatory quotas in the construction industry through "consent decrees" with substantial "back-pay" liabilities, past the latest round in the saga of pregnancy-related disabilities at *Newport News Shipbuilding*, to the current "equal pay for *comparable worth* issue," this area is a battleground strewn with failed policy planning, "modified regulations" that enhanced dispute, adversary confrontations, and bitter antagonisms, including the backlash of *Bakke* & *Weber*.

If we had to select one subject that lends itself to regulatory overhaul, EEO is certainly near the head of the list, although the administration of Chair Eleanor Holmes Norton at the EEOC has accomplished much in alleviating some of these problems.

14. This review of various areas for management's management of regulations would be incomplete without reference to a federal "incomes policy," which the administration decries. Nevertheless, a continuation of employee compensation practices geared in some degree to the past regulations of such agencies should be firmly considered—just in case.

We would be remiss in considering the parameters of my title today if adequate attention was not paid to *selection of the talent* necessary to properly and equitably administer laws and regulations. Industry, particularly large industry, has spent much time—mostly volunteer—on this vital activity but has far to go in perfecting its act. A great deal of attention is required in the future, at all government and industry levels.

As a result of last November's election results, we appear to have taken *the most basic step of all* in management's efforts to live productively with onerous regulation, and that is help to "throw those other rascals out" and put in a new team to overhaul the ailing machinery.

In summary, I hope that you will perceive and appreciate the many employer efforts, more often than not unpublicized and unsung, to head off at the pass, and exercise practical and effective managerial control of and accommodation to, undesirable regulation.

There is no question that our bureaucrats have been taking away from management much of its key decision making. If management does not set up adequate countermeasures, then it will lose more and more of its decision-making powers, not to mention its ability to innovate and create, and the traditional responsibilities it is hired to discharge. Failing this, we risk becoming mere papershufflers and processors in a nationally planned and socialistic society.

PART II

FEDERAL AGENCY REGULATION

A. Administration and Congressional Views

Transportation Regulation

Drew Lewis[†]

Ronald Reagan's landslide victory last November was a clear call for change—not only in leadership, but in direction.

—A call for change in government spending policies that have produced chronic deficits and a near trillion-dollar national debt.

—A call for change in tax policies that have discouraged saving and favored consumption; policies that restrain capital formation and shrink real income.

—A call for change in federal subsidy programs that reward inefficiency while penalizing innovation and initiative.

—A call for change in the flood of government regulation that has been costing the country an estimated $100 billion a year.

To turn it all around—to achieve real economic recovery—we must get government off the backs of the American people and American business. We must renew public confidence in our country and in the free enterprise system. And, if we are to restore lost jobs, create new ones, and build bigger markets for U.S. products, we must make American industry competitive again.

Until we get the economy under control and bring inflation and interest rates down—goals that President Reagan's budget and tax programs will achieve—we are not going to have a thriving automotive industry, housing industry, or a vibrant economy in any consumer durables. In terms of our meeting here at Wharton, I sense a growing awareness on the part of both management and labor that they must live together, and that the vitality of the great American industrial machine depends on their appreciation for each other's needs and problems.

For example, Conrail's fourteen largest labor unions have offered to take $200 million in future wage concessions, and Amtrak management has begun a 25 percent reduction of its white-collar force. Our current efforts to assist Conrail and Amtrak, to at least reduce their drain on the federal treasury, depend ultimately on the participation of labor in the final solutions.

---

† The Honorable Drew Lewis is Secretary of Transportation.

Amtrak has labor obligations which must be modified to some extent. We believe, however, that the $735 million budget the administration has accepted for Amtrak is sufficient to keep most of the trains running (actually more trains than can be justified) and for Amtrak to work out its labor situation.

In view of their historic labor obligations, it has been difficult for Conrail or Amtrak to achieve employment economies. At the same time, America's taxpayers have been subsidizing Conrail to the tune of nearly $1 million a day, and picking up $35 for everyone who travels by Amtrak.

To get the government off the hook while protecting rail freight service for the Northeast, we proposed a three-point plan that would relieve Conrail of its high overhead costs. That plan involves, first, labor reform; second, a transfer of commuter operations to passenger-oriented agencies; and third, a greater sharing of terminal costs with other railroads.

We are saying, in other words, let us not allow our social obligations to labor and to commuters to get in the way of efficient rail freight operations. I believe it is far better to replace the present labor protection package with a $400 million federally-funded labor relief measure, and to pay interim subsidies where necessary to support commuter operations, than to allow these liabilities to continue to drag Conrail down.

Earlier this week, we worked out an agreement with key leaders in the Senate, which has the support of the full Senate and is designed to transfer Conrail to the private sector. By the timetable worked out under that agreement, Conrail will not be put on the market for at least a year.

Under this plan, Conrail can be put up for sale after June 1, 1982, but only in one piece. If the railroad is not sold in the next six months, one of two things can happen: if Conrail has become profitable by December 1982, it can still be sold only as a single entity; but if it has not become profitable by then it will be made available in various "packages" to different buyers. After August 1, 1983, Conrail properties will be sold intact or in pieces. We believe this is a workable plan and a reasonable timetable, and we are confident that we can work with the members of the House to achieve all of our fundamental objectives in a single legislative package.

Personally, I believe that the sooner we can clear away the obstacles and convey Conrail to the private sector the better it will be for the shippers who depend on rail freight service in the Northeast, for the taxpayers who have been paying heavily to support it, and for the future of railroad employees. Our dual goal is to protect and improve rail freight service in this region, and to get the government out of the railroad business—and those objectives, in my judgment, go hand in hand.

The shift from "business as usual" in Washington is also bringing major changes in our attitude toward government regulations. During the 1970s, government spending for the major regulatory agencies *quadrupled*; the number of pages published in the *Federal Register* (which reports regulations) nearly tripled; and the listings in the *Code of Federal Regulations* doubled. At the same time, prices soared and productivity growth declined.

Some regulation—for safety, for example— is necessary. But over-regulation is the arch-enemy of private enterprise. It stifles innovation, discourages investment, increases labor costs, and reduces competition. It leads to higher prices and, in the end, it is always the consumer who pays. We almost overregulated the auto industry into an early grave.

Not that government regulations were solely responsible for the downturn in auto industry fortunes—certain of the safety regulations and the fuel economy regulations, at least for a time, were helpful; but in a lot of areas we reached the point of diminishing returns. The benefits simply did not justify the costs. Why, for example, should we insist that every car and truck meet the pollution standards required for operation at 5,000-foot altitudes, when relatively few of our vehicles will ever be driven at those altitudes? Why do we mandate a bumper standard that adds weight to the car, and raises the repair cost for high-speed accidents while only marginally reducing the costs of repairing damages incurred at "walking speeds?"

In all, we have identified thirty-four auto regulations to be relaxed, modified, or reconsidered. We estimate these actions alone will save the industry $1.3 billion in capital costs, without giving away anything important in the health and safety areas. We estimate the savings to consumers at about $9 billion over the next five years, or about $150 on each new car or truck.

We are not through. Assorted other standards and regulations are under review, including a new look we are taking at crashworthiness standards. Generally, we take the view that government is best that regulates least. So there will be no more regulation for the sake of regulation. And reducing the burden of regulation, I am confident, will lower the cost of doing business, bring down the price of products, and enable U.S. manufacturers to be more competitive.

Finally, as I said earlier, the new directions President Reagan is taking in his economic policies are designed to restore American confidence in the private sector as the primary engine of economic growth and progress. In calling for a "new beginning" for the American economy, the president is calling for a return to "first principles"—those tried-and-true doctrines of thrift, self-reliance, and personal determination that are both our heritage and our best hope for the future. In calling for a return to the pioneering spirit that gave our country its character and our people the incentive to work and to build, the president is reminding us that what once made our country great can make it still greater.

We are not so far removed from our heritage that we cannot appreciate what those virtues of personal enterprise and rugged individualism have meant to our country and can mean for our future. It is time again to dream the American Dream, which has always been the possible dream—never the "impossible" dream. With confidence in our country and with faith in free enterprise, I am sure we can restore the American economy to full health and vitality.

75-9

8220
U.S.

We Can Work It Out

Orrin G. Hatch[†]

One of the biggest problems we have in government is making sure we are not feeding today's masses with yesterday's fish. Agencies and programs designed a quarter of a century ago or more, to solve problems then critical, may not always be able to deal with second- and third-generation issues. Keeping our institutions—both public and private—current and responsive to present problems not thinkable twenty years ago takes real effort. Today, we face an unprecedented rate of inflation accompanied with a drop in productivity and a growing polarization between our governmental and business institutions. As Professor Chandler has noted, "Why is it in the United States, that government and business have often appeared as adversaries?"[1] In coming to grips with the problem, there are two central questions to be asked: one, how do we eliminate conflict and establish a working partnership between our business and governmental institutions for the benefit of the nation; and two, how do we provide for a continuous renewal of our business and governmental institutions?

Turning to the first point, it seems that both business and government should take the initiative in trying to understand and define each other's role. "What is needed is an understanding in both business and government that these institutions are merely a means to an end in our society. Neither is ordained by Holy Writ. Both have to show that they are doing what society wishes, not just what they themselves might wish."[2]

In many instances, we have seen the rising conflict and what we end up with are programs "grounded in vindictiveness rather than practicality, and all the while enormous amounts of energy are being put into adversarial politicking that could more properly be used to resolve the nation's real problems."[3]

For example: over the past decade, we have seen an escalation of the struggle between our business institutions attempting to survive on the one hand and government institutions constantly thwarting them with more regulations and statutes on the other. This struggle

---

[†] The Honorable Orrin G. Hatch, Senator from Utah, is Chairman of the Senate Committee on Labor and Human Resources.

75

is most dramatically played out in the employment arena and it is manifested by strained employee relations.

Because a conflict-laden atmosphere exists in the workplace, created by the plethora of regulations, is it any wonder our productivity rate is as low as it is? Employers find themselves preoccupied with constant litigation, compliance reviews, audits by state and federal agencies, employee grievances, and other all *too* exhaustive due process procedures.

It is important to examine how this situation developed and what business can do about it generally. More specifically, what can Congress through its oversight responsibilities do to solve the problem? Let us turn specifically to the statutes and regulations on equal employment opportunities since they have the greatest potential to create tension in the workplace, exhaustive regulatory review, and actual dollar losses in conciliation agreements, consent decrees, and litigation.

Since the passage of the 1964 Civil Rights Act, there has been a mushrooming of bodies of regulations, statutes (the General Accounting Office reported 87 as of 1978), and executive orders designed to implement that act. In many instances, we have seen the regulating agencies—the Equal Employment Opportunity Commission (EEOC) and the Office of Federal Contract Compliance Programs (OFCCP)—promulgate more restrictive and demanding regulations with little challenge from the business community and Congress, since challenging the regulations could cause one to be perceived as being against civil rights. The result, however, has been to give the regulatory agencies a very shallow understanding of how each felt and license to continue without challenge. In short, by our silence and lack of candor we were part of the problem which has created the current chaotic state of affairs in the American workplace.

We started out in the early 1960s with a general belief that the best way to correct race discrimination was to establish strong enforcement procedures, then go out, find the violators and punish them. We were concerned about the blatant discrimination then existing, and we were eager to eradicate it once and for all. In keeping with the dynamics of any institution, individuals in the administrating agencies quickly became more concerned about maintaining the program for its own sake, and success was measured not by advances against discrimination but rather by how much bigger the program was and how much more power it had accumulated. As is possible with any bureaucracy, the process becomes more important than the results. All of us who have worked in large organizations know how institutions very quickly lose sight of the problem which they were created to resolve—that is, they lose sight of their mission.

It does not take a wizard of organizational behavior to know that organizations must renew their missions periodically if they are to maintain their vitality. This is true especially in the arena of the free enterprise system, where competition forces constant scrutiny of direction. If a business slacks off in trying to build a better mouse-trap, a strong reminder will be provided by the ads of its competitors. The question, then, is how to provide for the constant renewal of governmental institutions when there is no competition for the service they were created to provide. Or, to put it bluntly, when you are the only show in town, and no one is watching, then you do not have to change your act.

Fortunately, our system of government does provide our government agencies with a mechanism to review their missions, reexamine their goals, objectives, work programs, and budgets in relation to that mission, and to demonstrate their stewardships to the American public—congressional oversight. Unfortunately, few agencies view that as an opportunity for self-renewal. They often see it as at least an inconvenience, if not an outright invasion of their domain. But neither has Congress always assumed its responsibility to demand accountability from our public institutions. At times, the attitudes have been to not upset the special interest groups and bureaucrats whose self-survival instincts are to protect their turf—right or wrong. We have seen congressional committees skim over their reviews of agencies without asking critical questions with the attitude of "Let's see what we gave them this year and increase it 20 percent because they cannot get their work done for lack of funds." It is much easier to be "nice" and be liked than to ask the hard questions crucial in accountability and efficiency. This becomes the critical and valuable part of congressional oversight responsibilities, for it is here that Congress can be of service to an agency in renewing its mission and giving its leadership new vitality.

Congressional oversight can serve as the point at which federal agencies come before Congress and report to the public how effectively they have carried out their congressional mandate. The agency has the opportunity to recommend to Congress why changes are needed in order that it may continue to carry out its mandates under current national conditions rather than when it was originally established.

Through oversight hearings, the public would be well served. Aside from informing it how its tax dollars are being used, the agency can report progress in solving the problems for which it was established.

If agencies are aware that thorough oversight responsibilities will be carried out by Congress, they will be more careful in carrying out their mandate and assume greater responsibility for management of the agency. Recently the Senate Labor and Human Resources Committee made an agency aware of how poorly it was managing its program. Though it made administrators uncomfortable, the problems were aired and the net result will be that the administrators will be more responsible and effective.

While it is easy to place blame on governmental agencies for governmental inefficiency, Congress must also bear its share of the blame if it fails to carry out its oversight responsibilities in a thorough and forthright fashion. This means it must ask the difficult questions which will lead to greater efficiency and productivity rather than shying away from them simply because they may generate conflict. An agency's performance must be evaluated using established management principles. That is, agency directors should be required to defend their work program and budget based upon the goals and objectives they have established to accomplish their mission as mandated by Congress. Too frequently, administrators tell congressional committees the reason they have not done an effective job is because they need more money. The problem is they cannot define what constitutes effectiveness or what is the unit of productivity. Seldom do they report to Congress how this budget reflects their objectives. And what are they doing with the budget they have?

The Senate Labor and Human Resources Committee is now getting under way in discharging its oversight responsibilities. The committee is resolved to review the various governmental agencies for which it has oversight responsibility thoroughly and objectively. It will not be satisfied with answers which are shallow and meaningless. Its recent set of hearings should serve notice to other agencies that the commitee plans to ask simple but difficult questions of administrators, such as: How do you measure success? Does your budget reflect your priorities? What is your unit of productivity? Do you understand your congressional mandate and do your agency goals reflect that mandate? What do you plan to accomplish and when?

Programs due for early review are those which are having a burdensome effect in employee relations. This includes the OFCCP, the EEOC, the Occupational Safety and Health Administration (OSHA), and the Employee Retirement Income Security Act (ERISA). Executive Order 11246 regulations promulgated by the OFCCP will be reviewed in the immediate future.

Summary

Because we live in a society that is constantly changing, we must periodically assess our governmental institutions to make sure they are responding to current problems rather than maintaining old programs for their own sakes. Thomas Jefferson said it well:

> I am not an advocate for frequent changes in laws and constitutions. But laws and institutions must go hand in hand with the progress of the human mind. As that becomes more developed, more enlightened, as new discoveries are made, new truths discovered, and manners and opinions change, with the change of circumstances, institutions must advance also to keep pace with the times.

If we are to bring productivity and freedom back to the American workplace, it means that both business and government must be more assertive in solving problems. That may mean challenging regulations when they go against the grain of our moral principles of fair play. By our acquiescence and silence we have created a fantasy world in which we have led the government regulators to believe that they were doing the right thing. Our problems are too grave for us to remain silent. If we care about our government, we must be critics—but loving critics—who will ask the tough questions but will also be there with a helping hand.

The avenues to renew our governmental institutions do exist. The only ingredients needed are our will and creativity.

NOTES

1. Alfred D. Chandler, Jr., The Adversaries, *Harvard Business Review*, Vol. 57, (November-December 1979), p. 88.

2. Irving S. Shapiro, The Process, *Harvard Business Review*, Vol. 57, (November-December 1979), p. 98.

3. *Ibid.*, p. 99.

PART II

B. The NLRB

A View of the
National Labor Relations Board
in the '80s

John H. Fanning[†]

Today's topic is federal agency regulation in the '80s, and as my part of today's discussion I have been asked to give you a chairman's view of the National Labor Relations Board (NLRB) in the coming decade.

Preliminarily, it should be noted that the NLRB is not a regulatory agency in the normally accepted sense. We do not regulate pricing structure in a particular industry, the marketing of securities, the granting of licenses, etc. We do not inject ourselves into problem areas in labor-management relations. All of what we do is triggered by the filing of an election petition or unfair labor practice charge by an interested private party. Although we do not solicit business, people are coming to us in increasing numbers, so, in that sense at least, we must be doing something right, but the basic point is that we function in a fashion much more aptly described as an adjudicatory rather than a regulatory one.

The statute I and my colleagues have been asked to administer was adopted to meet two needs: to enhance bargaining power, and, in that, the dignity of the individual employee in relation to his or her employer, and thereby to promote industrial peace. To implement these purposes, the National Labor Relations Act recognizes the right of an individual employee who so chooses to join with other employees to bargain collectively or otherwise act for mutual aid or protection. The act prohibits employers and labor organizations from coercing or discriminating against those employees in the exercise of this right. It also encourages the practice and procedure of collective bargaining as the foundation of the national labor policy.

In July, the Board will begin its forty-seventh year, and I think that during the years the act has been in effect, the congressional pol-

---

[†] John H. Fanning has been a Member of the National Labor Relations Board since 1957, and Chairman of the Board since April 1977.

icy on collective bargaining has come to be accepted in large measure. Some 150,000 collective bargaining agreements exist in the United States and, on the whole, there is a faithful adherence to them by the parties. But despite this level of acceptance of collective bargaining, there is still some defiance of the congressional policy, and therefore, the act has been the subject of criticism throughout its history. This is not surprising in view of the controversial and dynamic nature of labor relations. The statute represents compromise and accommodation of many conflicting interests, and contending forces continue to seek to modify the statute in their behalf. But, criticism and debate, if expressed in good faith in the light of past experience and current needs, is valuable in identifying problems and encouraging solution of the problems. No system is perfect, but I submit that this one has worked well and has, to a substantial degree, achieved the goals for which it was enacted.

In the period since its adoption, many employees in many industries have come to work under collective bargaining agreements which have improved their living standards and have given some stability to labor relations and some certainty to employer and employees alike as to their financial conditions and economic opportunities. The act has minimized the costly social consequences of completely unregulated organizational activity while permitting parties to a bargaining relationship to retain their economic weapons and reach agreements based upon their own compromises. It has proved adaptable to problems of wartime and peacetime economies and the organizational drives of competing labor organizations. I think the basic system of regulation it establishes will prove adequate to the needs of the '80s. I see certain problems and challenges ahead, however, which are both administrative and substantive in nature.

When I spoke here in 1971 at the Wharton conference on collective bargaining in the '70s, I emphasized the substantial administrative problem facing the Board in handling the constantly increasing caseload. The problem continues today.

The Board's first annual report, which covered a ten-month fiscal year ending June 30, 1936, showed that the Board received 1,068 cases that year. The last published annual report for fiscal year ending September 30, 1979, shows the case intake to have been 54,907 cases. The preliminary and as yet unverified figures for fiscal year 1980 indicate a filing of more than 57,000 cases, about 13,000 representation cases and 44,000-plus unfair labor practice cases.

To meet the sustained increase in caseload, the Board has tried, with some success, to improve its management techniques and increase its efficiency. It has, in the last decade, managed to handle about a 75 percent increase in caseload with only about a 34 percent increase in staff. It has always followed a policy of encouraging the settlement of cases, and maintains a high settlement rate—for several years now, in excess of 80 percent of merit cases. The Office of the General Counsel, which has general supervision of the Board's regional offices where cases are filed and investigated, has established a case-management system which has removed backlogs and decreased the time for processing unfair labor practice charges, despite the increase in total case intake. Under this system, the standard time for investigating and determining the merits of an unfair labor practice charge is thirty days, and the time for implementing the merit determination—that is, issuing complaint or a dismissal letter or negotiating a settlement—is an additional fifteen days. The Office of Personnel Management, the Office of Management and Budget, the former head of the General Accounting Office, Elmer Staats, and an independent task force composed of representatives of management, labor, and the academic community, at one time or another in the last few years, all have designated the system an exemplary practice in federal productivity.

Thus far, the agency has managed to handle its workload. For fiscal year 1980, it issued a record number of decisions despite federal restrictions severely limiting the hiring of staff and despite a vacancy among Board members for almost eight months of the year, and two vacancies for another two months. This year, we have had only three Board members since January.

I am concerned, however, as to whether the Board can continue to carry out its statutory responsibilities in a reasonably prompt way when a larger number of cases are filed each year and the agency's budget and personnel resources are being reduced.

One of the agency's serious problems is the shortage of administrative law judges (ALJs). In an effort to attract more applicants for these positions the Board has decentralized the geographic locations of offices of the administrative law judges, and has opened a New York office and an Atlanta office in addition to the Washington and San Francisco offices. The decentralization has been fairly successful in attracting a number of current ALJs who would not have become ALJs but for the decentralization, and currently, we are investigating the feasibility of additional offices.

But despite this and numerous other attempts to make judging for the Board a more attractive job, we have been unable to employ the necessary number of ALJs. I suspect that the most important deterrent to our recruitment efforts is the fact that labor practitioners are financially so much better off working in the private sector. The agency has absolutely no control over this. But it is a matter which extends well beyond the recruitment of administrative law judges and, as I see it, the disparity between federal and private remuneration and the prevailing fashion of placing blame upon the government employee for all complexities and dissatisfactions with government will increase the difficulty of hiring the best employees and of retaining experienced and qualified workers. And, in that connection, I will only repeat here what I wrote a few weeks ago in response to an inquiry from Congressman Ford. There is no doubt in my mind that the federal government is on the brink of a brain drain because of current pay policy.

Recently, public suggestions have been made purporting to help solve the Board's administrative problems. Sometimes these proposals are offered with the lurking implication that the Board is remiss in performing its duties and the Board members lack the competence or experience needed to administer the act. At other times, the proposals, in the guise of increasing efficiency, seek to influence statutory policy, and suggest that the Board solve its caseload problem by ceasing to exercise its authority in certain types of cases.

Regardless of the spirit in which they are offered, these proposals will be debated, and their merits should be given sober consideration.

One of the proposals being made would have the Board reexamine its discretionary standards for asserting jurisdiction. As you know, the Board's statutory jurisdiction is broad, extending to all enterprises which affect interstate commerce, subject only to the rule of *de minimis*. In the 1950s, however, the Board developed certain standards to aid in determining when it would exercise its jurisdiction. These standards are in part based upon an employer's amount of business, expressed in terms of annual dollar minimums. The Board's authority to decline jurisdiction upon a discretionary basis was approved by the 1959 amendments to the act, but the amendments provided that the Board should not decline to assert jurisdiction in any labor dispute over which it would assert jurisdiction under the standards prevailing at that time.

Some proponents of the proposal to reexamine the discretionary standards suggest that the Board raise the minimum dollar amounts of the standards to compensate for inflation. The proposal has superficial appeal because we all are aware of the impact of inflation upon dollar amounts, and it may be that some change in the standards is advisable. But, a decision to make a change involves more than the mathematical exercise of adjusting jurisdiction figures to account for inflation. There is little doubt in my mind—I was on the Board at the time and am familiar with the legislative history of the provision—that the 1959 amendments froze the Board's jurisdictional standards so that they cannot be changed without statutory amendment. Also, it must be noted that significant labor disputes with extensive consequences may arise in small business operations, requiring some formal means of resolution. Further, there is a need for equitable application of the act to competing employers whatever their size, and a need to protect employees whether they work in large or small businesses. In any event, if a change is to be made in the standards, it must be made not on the basis of some speculation as to how many cases can be cut from the Board's caseload, but on the basis of empirical data as to what percentage of employers will be covered by the new standards and what percentage of employees will be protected. A change in jurisdictional standards is not merely a matter of reducing caseload; it affects the way the protections and restraints of the act will be applied.

Another approach to reducing the Board's caseload is a proposal that the Board decline to assert jurisdiction in cases where grievance/arbitration machinery is available under a bargaining contract, even where the dispute has not been submitted to the contract machinery. As you know, for a number of years the Board followed a deferral policy as announced in the *Collyer* case.[1] More recently, in 1977, the Board limited the deferral policy to refusal to bargain cases involving an interpretation of the bargaining contract, and excluded coercion and discrimination cases from deferral.[2] The Board members who constituted the majority which adopted the deferral policy are no longer on the Board, so a question of whether the Board should follow the policy may have to be considered anew. I have never agreed with this deferral policy, and in various decisions have stated why I consider it inappropriate to leave the determination of cases involving statutory violations to private contract machinery.

But apart from my individual views on the subject, calls for increased deferral, in part because of the impact it would have on caseload, like calls for expanded jurisdictional standards, would seem to require a statistical analysis of just how significant a reduction the policy would achieve. Although it is true that any reduction in caseload is better than none, the nature of the deferral debate is such that it at least implicates fundamental statutory policies concerning individual employee rights and, to that extent, arguing for a heightened use of deferrals because of what that will do to caseload without indicating with greater precision what exactly it will do to caseload does not strike me as the most persuasive way to state the case.

A different plan that has been advanced for relieving the pressure of work at the Board level would limit review of the decisions of the administrative law judges. Under this plan, the Board would adopt a certiorari-type review of unfair labor practice cases, exercising its discretion in granting review. This plan, which would require legislative authority, has certain advantages I think. Under discretionary review, the Board could eliminate review of routine cases and those turning on factual and credibility resolutions, giving its attention to all substantial legal issues, and yet maintaining a single statutory policy by reversing and modifying administrative law judges' decisions that are contrary to Board precedent. The plan would not affect court review of unfair labor practice cases, as the circuit courts of appeal would consider enforcement of Board orders, whether issued directly by the Board itself or inferentially by denial of review of an administrative law judge's decision. In my judgment, Board review of administrative law judges' decisions on a discretionary basis is preferable to review of administrative law judges' decisions by various federal district courts, a plan which also has been suggested. Review of unfair labor practice cases by separate courts—and there are, I believe, well over 500 district court judges—could result in disintegration of a national labor relations policy. Moreover, I question whether court review of cases would be faster or cheaper than Board review. Currently, the median time for district court dispositions of cases going to trial in the District of Columbia is fourteen months,[3] a median which in part is the product of the expanded use of magistrates in pretrial matters and of the nature of pretrial itself in the district courts, which is broader in scope than would be the case with Board proceedings.

It may be that the most potent way to cut the inflow of cases would be more effective enforcement of the act, and legislative action to take the profit out of unfair labor practices. The Board's authority to correct unfair labor practices is remedial only, and although we constantly try to devise more individual and adequate remedies, restoring the *status quo ante* does not always fully remedy the violation that is found. A remedial order by the Board often costs a respondent no more than legal fees. Postings of notice and orders to bargain carry no money assessments.

I have long felt that the collective bargaining process would be encouraged and bad faith bargaining deterred if some remedy were available to compensate employees for benefits which might have flowed from collective bargaining if the respondent had fulfilled the bargaining obligation instead of defying it. I have always doubted the Board's present authority to order such a remedy, however, as my vote in the *Ex-Cello*[4] decision indicates.

In addition to administrative problems confronting the Board in the '80s, legal problems undoubtedly will be presented concerning interpretation of substantive provisions of the act. At this time, the Board has before it questions as to the impact and application of three recent Supreme Court cases: the *Detroit Edison* case,[5] the *Yeshiva University* case,[6] and the *Longshoremen's* case.[7] The questions in these cases grow out of social and economic developments of the times as reflected in labor-management relations, and they may herald the type of problems the Board will have to resolve in the coming years.

Detroit Edison involved the duty of an employer to furnish relevant information to the bargaining representative about a testing program, and the effect upon the bargaining duty of the need to preserve the secrecy of the test questions and answers and the need to protect the employees' privilege to maintain the confidentiality of their test scores. The extent of the duty to furnish information is obviously a significant issue with the increasing use of testing by management to determine the aptitude, competence, honesty, and psychological characteristics of employees, with the growing awareness of management's need to document disciplinary action in order to protect itself from charges of arbitrary action, with the greater emphasis upon the bargaining representative's duty of fair representation to individual employees, and with the recognition of privacy rights of employees. Indeed, if there should be a substantial relaxing of governmental regulations concerning occupational safety and health and civil rights of employees, as some have suggested, the duty to furnish information may become even more important as bargaining machinery will be called upon to resolve disputes over demands for the furnishing of information perceived to be pertinent.

The *Yeshiva University* case considered the employee status of certain university faculty members and concluded that they were managerial in view of the role they played in policy making for the university. As the organization of white-collar and professional employees progresses, application of the *Yeshiva* decision to other employees will be required. Teachers, nurses, and other professional groups have special organizational interests. They are concerned not only with traditional terms and conditions of employment but with the way in which their skills are used, and with professional development and goals as well. They have experienced a different type of relationship with management from that of production workers, having routinely supplied management with their independent professional judgment. Questions will arise about the extent to which these groups are covered by the act and how the collective bargaining system meets their special interests.

The *Longshoremen's* case presented the issue of whether provisions of a collective bargaining agreement, which were adopted in response to the recent practice of using containers in the shipping industry, were violative of the so-called "hot cargo" restrictions of the act. Containerization in the shipping industry is but one of the innovations of accelerated technology affecting management-labor relations today. The automation of many job functions and the computerization of record-keeping has resulted in the elimination of jobs, the combining of functions of different job classifications, and the blurring of traditional unit boundaries. These changes in industrial practices raise questions for the Board on unit clarification, the extent of the duty to bargain about technological advances, and the competing jurisdictional claims of unions.

Other developments in industry and the general economy are also placing some strain upon the collective bargaining process that may be revealed in issues coming to the Board. In an attempt to solve the problems of absenteeism and thievery in plants and to increase productivity, management is seeking to negotiate efficiency standards, to tighten job rules, and to adopt innovative means of weeding out less desirable employees. In an attempt to meet job security and lifestyle needs of workers, labor is seeking to negotiate layoff allowances, job relocation expenses, housing financing, day care service, and programs for employee development and retraining. Such negotiations may test the limits of the subject matter of bargaining and the definition of conditions of employment.

Manifestations of employee interest in political matters that affect their economic situations are also appearing in the workplace more frequently. Literature is distributed concerning political candidates and issues of particular concern to employees, and work stoppages occur in support of certain legislation or in protest of government acts. This conduct may challenge the boundaries of protected activity.

These are some of the matters that I anticipate will demand the Board's attention in the years immediately ahead. Certainly, problems will arise in a democratic system of regulation which attempts to accommodate diverse interests. Tensions will exist between the rights of the individual and minority groups and the rights of the majority; between individual and collective action; between managerial and property rights of the employer and organizational and bargaining rights of the employee; between union institutional interests and the rights of individual union members and dissident groups. And inevitably, there will be disagreement as to how competing interests should be balanced. No matter how the Board may strike the balance, the losing side will be dissatisfied and observers will criticize. To the extent, however, that the Board can promptly determine representational questions and clarify bargaining obligations, and to the extent that it can achieve the confidence of the public as an agency where a reasonable and fair resolution of problems can be obtained, the Board will fulfill its role of reducing industrial strife and regulating labor-management relations so that industry can move forward to the advantage of management and labor and, because of that, the nation.

NOTES

1. Collyer Insulated Wire, 192 N.L.R.B 837 (1971).

2. *See* General American Transportation Corporation, 228 N.L.R.B 808 (1977) and Roy Robinson, Inc. D/B/A Roy Robinson Chevrolet, 228 N.L.R.B 828 (1977).

3. Director of the Administrative Office of the United States Courts, 1980 Annual Report.

4. Ex-Cell-O Corporation, 185 N.L.R.B 107 (1970).

5. Detroit Edison Co. v. NLRB, 440 U.S. 301 (1979).

6. NLRB v. Yeshiva University, 444 U.S. 672 (1980).

7. NLRB v. International Longshoremen's Association, 447 U.S. 490 (1980).

Future Shock

Edward B. Miller[†]

No one could help but regard this as a prestigious event if he or she looked at the program. Some of the ablest people in the whole field are participating, and I feel very much honored to be in such distinguished company.

High among those distinguished people, certainly, is John H. Fanning, a man who well deserves the respect of all of us, whether or not we agree with his views and philosophy with respect to a proper interpretation of the National Labor Relations Act (NLRA). He is a dedicated, hard-working man with a very long history of putting up with the barrage of criticism, internal and external, that goes with the job of being a member, and particularly a chairman, of the National Labor Relations Board (NLRB). Believe me, I know whereof I speak. In the Baron Munchausen jargon, I vas dere, Charlie. John, God bless you, and I thank you for all the help you gave me when I was in the shoes you are now filling.

The message I want to bring to you today, however, probably will not be one which John will agree with—for a number of reasons, the chief of which may well be that he has simply been there too long to be able to accept what I am going to say.

The Board has done a creditable job—I have said so repeatedly, and as those of you who have read the monograph I wrote at Herbert Northrup's request know, I have said it in a publication, which, surprisingly to me, has been rather widely read. But my message to you today is that the Board, if it is to survive beyond, or even very far into, the 1980s, needs to make major changes in its *modus operandi*.

I do not think John Fanning thinks so. Nor do his current colleagues, so far as I can tell, although Member Zimmerman is new enough at the job that I think he may have some willingness to face up to the need for change.

Howard Jenkins not only does not think so, but he has said that he regards it as "unseemly" for former Board officials like Guy Farmer,

† Edward B. Miller is Managing Partner at Pope, Ballard, Shepard & Fowle, Chicago, Illinois, and was Chairman of the National Labor Relations Board from 1970 to 1975.

Pete Nash, John Irving, and myself to make critical remarks about the Board and to suggest changes in its current ways of operating. He has company in that regard, as you know. Lane Kirkland of the AFL-CIO also apparently joins Howard in wishing we would all take a Trappist-like vow of silence. Lane, of course, uses the *ad hominem* approach—rather than debate the merits of our criticism, he would dismiss the criticism on the theory that all management lawyers are prostitutes, and anything we say is said just to please our clientele or to attempt to attract new clients. Lane ought to know better. Guy Farmer called me the day after Kirkland's blast made the papers, and asked me if I had ever had even one client come to me because of a speech I had given. He said he never had. Neither have I.

But then, Lane Kirkland is, I think, one of the promulgators and perhaps even one of the authors of another myth—the current union party line to the effect that labor relations have never been as bad as they are now because employers and their lawyers and consultants are suddenly all hard-nosed, ruthless brigands who are out to destroy unions by fair means or foul. It amazes me that that bit of fiction has seemingly been received with acceptance in the press and even in the industrial relations community among people who, by their own experience, know better. In the last few years we have had less time lost in labor disputes than at any other time in our history. The percentage of hours lost to strikes in both 1979 and 1980 was far lower than the average for the last half of the decade of the '60s and the last half of the '50s. We have seen significant cooperative, mutually devised innovations, such as the experimental negotiation approach in the steel industry, and the neutrality pledges agreed to by the huge auto industry.

What Lane really means, of course, is that unions are losing more and more elections—elections, by the way, in which 90 percent of the losses are in situations where there is not even an accusation, much less a finding, of employer misconduct. But then, nobody likes to blame himself or his own organization for failure. It is so much easier to blame it on evil employers, evil consultants, and on the Board's election timetables—which, on the whole, are almost the best they have ever been. I hate to admit it, but the Fanning Board's election timetable looks as good as the Miller Board's. And, indeed, the timetable for regional director decisions in election cases—and the regions make the decisions in approximately 97 percent of the cases in which a decision is required—has been shortened from forty-six days when I was chairman to nineteen days in 1979.

Well—enough exploding of some of the new mythology. Let us talk about the future of the Board.

We are in a time of change. We are reappraising the enormous, incredibly expensive, regulatory apparatus that our federal government has become. I do not know whether this mood of a need for a new beginning will last, but there can be no gainsaying that it is here now.

What does that mean for the NLRB? It means, first of all, the end of a long era when the Board could count on ever-increasing budgets. When John Fanning came to the Board, the Board's budget for his first year as a member was less than $15 million. It increased every year thereafter, and last year it was over $100 million. The Reagan administration is asking for yet another increase for the next fiscal year.

Did it increase when I was there? You bet it did, though one year we shook up the bureaucracy by not spending as much as had been appropriated, and returned a nice wad of money to the federal treasury.

But those days of the availability of ever-increasing funds are over—at least for the foreseeable future.

Thus far, the reaction of the Board has been a typical bureaucratic response. Anytime you cut, or threaten to cut, an agency's budget, any good bureaucrat has an immediate, almost involuntary, knee-jerk response—"tell 'em we're going to cut where it will hurt the public the most." This is an old Washington game—if you are regulating air travel and someone threatens to cut your budget, do not sit down and try to figure out how many less file clerks you could manage with—instead, project a huge cut in the number of inspectors and investigators you will have, and project huge resulting increases in the probability of fatal air crashes.

So, too, the Board. When the Board's requested budget was cut, the Board responded by projecting that it would develop a larger backlog of undecided, unprocessed cases.

That is the traditional response. What lies beneath it is the unspoken premise that the Board will keep right on doing what it has been doing in the same old way at the same old stand. And, of course, if you project that, it is fairly accurate to say that less money will result in a proportionately larger backlog. Not quite accurate, you see, because I suspect the Board ignores the real world that exists out in the regions. Regional Directors and their staffs have developed, over the years, some pretty good work habits, and some pride in their efficient handling of cases. They are not going to let a somewhat leaner staff louse up their record. They will have to work a little harder, and they may not quite maintain it, but my guess is they will not slip as badly as the figures that the Board's budget-figure manipulators may pull out of their computers may show. Also—let us be frank—the Board and its regions have a lot of good people, and a very large number of them put in a good day's work—maybe not as long a day as John Fanning puts in, but a good day's work. But we all know that a lot of them do not over exert themselves, and there is always some slack. There is nothing like a little budget crunch to take up some of that slack.

But, with some modifications for those practical factors, it is doubtless true that the Board's simplistic approach of less money, more backlog, can and will become a self-fulfilling prophecy. It will also, if it slides that way, be the beginning of the end for the NLRB.

Remember the Equal Employment Opportunity Commission (EEOC)? In its floundering years, it allowed its backlog to build, even despite ever-increasing budgets. I remember the presentations at budget hearings when I was in Washington, D.C. The EEOC would ask for more money so it could decrease the rate of increase in its backlog. I always thought that was wonderful bureaucratic gobbledygook. But the Congress got sick of it. And had it not been for Eleanor Norton's willingness to take a new and fresh look at how that agency ought to try to get its job done, we all know that Congress was right on the verge of either abolishing it or cutting its budget so far that it would have been virtually inoperative. Some of us who represent respondents in EEOC proceedings did not always agree with Eleanor's views—but she made the EEOC a viable agency. I suppose that now I am not only a disloyal Board official but also a Republican of dubious credentials. So be it.

Well, you may ask, what should the NLRB do to continue as a viable agency in a time when it cannot realistically expect ever-increasing budgets? I have some answers. I suspect John will not like them, but I have some answers.

There are a lot of things that can be done administratively. I will just list a few—administration is a dull chore, at least to me—and I cannot imagine that this audience has much interest in that kind of minutiae. But here are a few items that would save lots of dollars.

One—immediately and totally decentralize the law judges. Get them out of Washington and San Francisco and put them out in the regions where the cases are. And require each of them to dispose of thirty-five cases a year by settlement and/or decision or be fired. To help them achieve that, permit and encourage bench decisions. Encourage pretrial conferences and institute limited discovery. But then require thirty-five cases each. Just like that. No exceptions. No excuses.

Two—require all parties filing objections to elections to deliver to the regional office either affidavits or witnesses to support their objections within three working days of filing the objections.

Three—decentralize all the enforcement of Board decisions in courts of appeal to the Board offices closest to the respective courts of appeal. If an attorney in the region specializes in appellate cases, require a minimum of fifteen briefs a year (the average now is about five). Farm out appellate briefs and arguments to private attorneys on a fixed price per brief basis, say $5,000 per typical brief. That is *substantially* less than present per brief costs.

There are a few suggested changes. Radical, debatable changes, every one. Tough, too. Some employees would quit. So? Hire new ones—the Board gets a hundred times more applications per year than it has vacancies.

None of that fits the old mold. The old mold, and the one in vogue when I was there, was—more cases? Then, more people. And still more money—ask for even more so as to improve quality by training programs, details from Washington to the field, and from the field to Washington. Nothing wrong with any of that when the mood of the country was to expand and try to improve existing regulation. But that is not the new mold. So administrative change—tough, stringent change—is needed to meet the requirements of a new age. Change that will not just build a bigger backlog.

So much for administration. A similar fresh approach is needed to the whole concept of labor regulation. If the money is not there for the old-style regulation, then where should the available money be put? That is the question the Board and the Congress need to think about. Obvious, is it not? But there is not a single, solitary sign that this obvious message has been heard by the General Counsel or the three present members of the Board.

It has been heard, though, by some of their experienced staff.

A lawyer in one of the regions with whom I was chatting off the record a few weeks ago understood one rather basic thing quite well. I asked him, "Think the budget cuts will hurt you?" He smiled. "Hell," he said, "we'll be okay. We'll just stop issuing the bullshit complaints."

There is one plain truth, simply put, Doc Penello had been preaching for years, in his speeches and in his opinions, that General Counsel should stop squandering money on processing miniscule borderline complaints. Stick to the basics, Doc said. But nobody listened. It is time to listen now.

Another staffer—a very able, very experienced gent who heads up the Office of Representation Appeals—Burt Subrin—had some advice for the Board, too. "Make some rules on appropriate units," Burt said in an excellent article in the February issue of the *CCH Labor Law Journal*. That's not a quote. This is:

> In this day of ever-burgeoning caseload and concurrently more strin- gent budget limitations, the Board cannot afford the luxury of litigat- ing anew the boundaries of the playing field for each collective bargain- ing game.

That is well put. It is advice that a number of scholars have given the Board over the years. Nobody listened. I tried to interest my col- leagues in some rule making when I was there. Nobody listened. The Board members have not shown any interest, as far as I can see, in listening seriously to Burt Subrin, either. But is it not obvious that it is time to listen now?

Another Board careerist—an administrative law judge (ALJ)— wrote to me after I had given a speech along these general lines in Seattle a month or two ago. He said:

> It is a bit of irony that your April 9 address as reprinted on page 54 of the May 18 issue of Labor Law Reporter is followed at page 59 with the announcement that the number of Board administrative law judges has now reached 111.

> There appears to be no willingness to recognize that the Board's in- creasing caseload is symptomatic of substantive and procedural prob- lems which cannot be resolved by throwing more money and judges at them.

That same judge wrote an article for publication. His article shows that he sees the need for some new approach. He says that, by rule change, the Board can and should:

1) mandate pre-complaint settlement negotiations;

2) mandate pleading with particularity in both complaint and answer;

3) authorize issuance by the chief administrative law judge of broad pretrial orders, providing for early pretrial conference, pretrial identification of witnesses, and pretrial exchange of witness statements and other non- impeaching documents; and

4) authorize limited pretrial discovery for good cause shown.

In addition, the Board, under its rulemaking authority, can and should:

1) adopt a policy under which final decisions of the courts of appeals are to be considered controlling by the Board until reversed by the Supreme Court; and

2) adopt a deferral policy, compatible with the traditional notion that the proper role of courts in the administration of justice is to avoid reconsidering issues already litigated, under which appropriate deference is given to the decision-making authority committed by the parties to the arbitral process and by the Congress to other federal agencies.

To that last paragraph, especially as one of the authors of *Collyer*, I say "Amen, brother." And as a believer in the fruitlessness of having two, three, and even more agencies dealing with such subject matters as employment discrimination, workers compensation, and safety at the workplace, I also say "Amen, brother."

But so far, those three holdover appointees at 1717 Pennsylvania have not got this message either. They continue to stifle *Collyer* and chip away at *Spielberg*. They stretch the law to find the filing of an unemployment compensation claim to be concerted activity, although almost all workers' compensation laws already prohibit retaliation against an employee who files a comp claim. And although the General Counsel explored the possibility of an accord with the EEOC on processing cases involving both NLRA and Title VII issues, when no agreement was reached the Board apparently gave no further thought to simply deferring to the EEOC's jurisdiction in cases where race or sex discrimination is the central or primary issue.

They are not listening to the loud, clear message. They are stuck in the old patterns, and do not see the need for change. Program a larger backlog, they say.

I suggest it is time they took some initiative. The ones I have talked about so far could all be done administratively. But the Board could also urge the administration to support some legislation which would enable the Board to concentrate its resources in areas where regulation is needed the most. It could suggest to the administration, for example, some more realistic jurisdictional standards which reflect the inflation which has occurred since the present standards were set.

It could suggest modifications of the law which would reduce regulation in areas of marginal significance.

A case came down the other day involving U.S. Steel,[1] an employer which has probably one of the most stable, most sophisticated relationships with its unions—particularly with the United Steelworkers'—of any employer I can think of. U.S. Steel had taken pictures of a big demonstration, at a plant entrance, by the Union's Women's Committee. The Women's Committee had invited the media to come and cover the event and had published its own photo of the demonstration on the front page of one of the union's publications. Not a hint of union animus in the record.

"Bad, bad"—found the Board. Serious 8(a)(1). Overruled one of its ALJs to get to that result. Can you believe it? Program a larger backlog, but spend, I would estimate (and I won't be far off) $5,000 of your money and mine to investigate, try, have heard, and review exceptions on that kind of regulation.

Sure—John Fanning may tell you that is how he and his colleagues read and interpreted the statute, and I understand the argument that, if that is how you read it, then that is how you have to apply it, no matter what the philosophy of the party in power may be.

But it does suggest to me the need for the Board—and it may have to be a Board under new leadership—to take some legislative initiatives. If the money that will be available to the Board over the next several years has to be carefully husbanded so that it can be devoted only to the areas in serious need of regulation, then how can the statute be amended so that this kind of marginal regulation will not eat away at the available funds?

Some of you may have seen my Seattle speech, where I suggested some revisions of the law which would restrict the Board's jurisdiction to regulate mature relationships, like those, for example, of U.S. Steel and the Steelworkers. In that *U.S. Steel* case, the Board said, "Nor does the fact that Respondent and the Union enjoyed a long bargaining history or the absence of animus by Respondent justify a conclusion that no remedy is warranted." Perhaps not, in the present state of the law. But do not such facts from a policy point of view suggest not only that no remedy is warranted but that no regulation of such relationships is warranted?

I have no pride of authorship in the specific suggestions I offered in Seattle to get the Board out of some unnecessary areas. They may well be full of bugs and problems. But certainly someone can figure out appropriate and acceptable legislation which would accomplish the purpose of getting the Board out of some of the less significant, indeed marginal, areas of its present regulatory sphere.

I would not be too surprised if a group of sophisticated management and union representatives, meeting perhaps under the aegis of the Board, could not agree on at least some approaches or directions which would be mutually acceptable. Both management and labor have a stake in effective regulation of significant areas. But there are areas of the Board's regulation of both unions and employers which must be regarded by both as of tangential value, at best. And both have an interest in seeing that limited funds be put to the most important uses.

I will not test your patience with further detail. I have neither the time nor the inclination—nor do I think you have—to explore today all the potential avenues to getting back to basics— back to the kind of federal regulation of labor relations that should have the highest priority, and modifying or eliminating the frills, the esoteric, the superfluous, the least cost effective—a word we may tire of, but one which is of prime importance today.

The message I want to convey to you—and, if it be possible, to John and his present and future colleagues—is that initiatives are sorely needed. To someone like John or Howard it is not easy to abandon, even temporarily, one's beliefs in expansive regulation.

But I value the Board and its history too much—and I know they do—to want to see it fail and die. If the present approach of "If we can't have the money we want, we're just going to build a bigger backlog" is allowed to continue, its slow but certain demise is exactly what I foresee.

Future Shock was a book which told us how the world was passing some of us by because things were changing too fast for some who were too steeped in the ways of the past. I hope the Board and its administrators will not be immobilized by a severe case of Future Shock, but instead I hope they may provide the leadership and initiatives we need in these ever-so-rapidly changing 1980s.

NOTES

1. United States Steel Corporation, 255 N.L.R.B. No. 164 (May 7, 1981).

PART II

C. Other Agencies

105-13

8223 U.S.

Occupational Safety and Health Administration

Bruce W. Karrh[†]

When President Nixon signed into law the Occupational Safety and Health Act (OSHA) on December 29, 1970, he hailed it as landmark legislation representing "The American System at its best: Democrats, Republicans, the House, the Senate, the White House, business, labor, all cooperating in a common goal—the savings of lives, the avoiding of injuries, making the places of work for 55 million Americans safer and more pleasant places."[1] There is no doubt that this act, which authorized the establishment of a government agency to administer and enforce safety and health standards and an institute to conduct scientific research on occupational health matters, *was* landmark legislation.

Through this act, a national commitment was made to assure "so far as possible every working man and woman in the nation safe and healthful working conditions."[2] Some may argue that such legislation was not needed, but there is no doubt that such a national commitment was timely. Safety statistics showed a steady reduction in the number of work-related injuries from World War I to the 1960s, but during the latter half of that decade, the injury rate stabilized and then began to rise. A determination to halt this rise and a means of doing so was clearly needed. Congress, representing the people, saw the Occupational Safety and Health Administration (OSHA) as the mechanism that would reverse the trend and bring about significant gains in worker health and safety.

This conference offers a unique and important opportunity to examine how well the act, and the agency it created, have met their intended goal of assuring safe and healthful workplaces for the some 100 million people working in the United States today. Let us examine the on-the-job injury rate of the '70s to see if the agency has reduced injury incidence, and then discuss some of the problems industry has encountered with the agency. Finally, I want to focus on OSHA in the '80s and what the agency can do to carry out its mis-

† Bruce W. Karrh is Corporate Medical Director for E.I. du Pont de Nemours & Company, Inc.

105

sion more effectively . . . a mission that we at Du Pont endorse wholeheartedly.

But, before I begin I want to set two things straight. First, I am here to analyze and to offer constructive criticism. Secondly, I recognize that there is no magic solution for improving the intricate system that monitors occupational safety and health in this country.

The occupational safety and health scene is played out on a complex stage. There are many props—scientific knowledge, technology, industrial budgets, hazardous materials, the 1970 OSH Act—around which the players—the regulators, the labor unions, the corporations, the workers, the press, the public, the medical experts, and the courts—must act. And the lead role, as far as Du Pont is concerned, is carried out by corporate management. It is the responsibility of the men and women who manage this nation's chemical plants, oil refineries, hospitals, papermills, and other private sector operations to ensure that safe and healthful working conditions exist in all workplaces. I will come back to this later.

Not only is the occupational safety and health stage a complex one upon which many actors perform, but all the characters and props are of critical importance. If we want to make a better play, we will have to work with what we have . . . and what we have is basically good. OSHA has the potential to contribute to significant improvements in the health and safety performance of American industry and many of the occupational safety and health regulations in existence today are clearly desirable. And corporate management, for the most part, is determined to prove that with the assistance and guidance of government, it *can* reduce on-the-job injury incidence and provide each and every person in the U.S. labor force with a safe and healthful working environment.

Do we need to improve the quality of the occupational safety and health play? Yes. The numbers alone argue in favor of changing the nation's approach to occupational safety and health. United States Bureau of Labor statistics covering the period from 1972 to 1979 show that private-sector injury and illness rates declined slightly overall between 1972 and 1975 and have been rising slightly since.[3] A close examination of the mix within the overall rates shows real cause for concern: while less serious illnesses and accidents have declined, there has been a sharp increase in serious injuries.[4] It is an understatement to say that the number of serious occupational injuries *should not* increase under a federal program aimed at improving workplace safety. Why have OSHA's efforts not been more successful?

Many critics have cited the OSH Act as the cause. I just do not believe that this is true. While the act is less than a perfect piece of legislation, many of the changes needed to turn OSHA into an effective catalyst for reducing occupational illness and injury can be accomplished without revising the act. I believe that most of the problems OSHA has encountered are the direct result of how the agency's administrators have chosen to *interpret* the act.

Let me give you two examples of how the way in which the act has been interpreted has created conditions that not only have prevented its successful implementation, but have at best delayed progress toward its goals, and at worst, created counterproductive schisms between the agency, industry, and workers. The two areas I will discuss are: (1) standards development and (2) enforcement.

The OSH Act directed the secretary of labor to make any national consensus standard a mandatory occupational safety and health standard, unless he determined that the standard would not result in improved safety and health.[5] Many, if not most, of the consensus standards were developed by voluntary associations as guides for manufacturers; they were never intended to carry the force of law. Much of the criticism OSHA has received up to now has been the result of these standards being made mandatory in the absence of careful analyses as to how they would contribute to improved worker protection.

The national consensus standards and existing federal standards which were made into law have been supplemented by a handful of new permanent health standards. These occupational safety and health standards are, for the most part, detailed, specification-oriented standards. Few would argue that OSHA should not identify health hazards and set the performance levels that industry must meet, but what in the past engendered resentment and frustration on the part of industry and prevented the development of the most effective, but least expensive, ways to protect worker health was the agency's determination to specify *how* safety and health goals should be met. Industry was given the cookbook and there was no incentive to come up with a better recipe. Such an approach has obviously stifled innovation. In addition, technology-based regulations not only handcuff industry's valuable occupational safety and health resources, but they also handcuff OSHA's resources. When designing such regulations, the agency has to spend its own limited time, money, and manpower on the minutiae of industrial engineering, management science, and applied chemical research, instead of concentrating on the desired outcome.

During the past decade, and especially in recent years, OSHA has developed standards without considering the costs they will impose on industry. The agency has interpreted its mandate to provide "medical criteria which will assure insofar as practicable that no employee will suffer diminished health, functional capacity, or life expectancy as a result of his work experience"[6] as meaning that all risks in the workplace must be eliminated at any cost. Consequently, many standards have been issued which either carry extremely high price tags due to their detailed requirements,[7] or lack price tags altogether because cost analyses were never conducted.

I realize that no dollar value can be assigned realistically to an individual's life or limbs, but since occupational safety and health resources are finite, it is of critical importance that an assessment of the benefits to be incurred by mandating costly standards be made *prior* to the issuance of such standards. Such cost/risk/benefit assessments are made by society all the time in areas that affect our everyday life: automobile design, police protection, pollution control. Obviously, when business is forced to deal with health and safety problems in ineffective yet expensive ways, valuable resources that could be directed more usefully are wasted.

Not only have cost/risk/benefit analyses been lacking, but so have analyses of the need for new standards based on sound, scientific data. Far too often, the data upon which OSHA has based regulatory decisions have been challenged by the medical community, academia, industry, or even other government experts, and in many instances, OSHA's data have been discredited.

This happened when OSHA was trying to regulate worker exposure to beryllium. In 1978, a group of highly acclaimed toxicologists and epidemiologists charged that data from the government-sponsored studies cited by OSHA as evidence that beryllium was carcinogenic in humans had been compiled carelessly and grossly misinterpreted. Although the carcinogenicity of beryllium is still in question, the National Institute for Occupational Safety and Health (NIOSH) has conceded that there were flaws in the studies.[8]

Another, highly publicized example of controversial data being cited by OSHA in support of its policies was the so-called "cancer estimates." At OSHA's request, a group of government scientists conducted an analysis of the incidence of occupational cancer in the United States. The group concluded that "occupationally-related cancers comprise a substantial and increasing fraction of total cancer incidence" and that such cancers "may comprise as much as 20 percent or more of total cancer mortality in forthcoming decades."[9]

These "estimates" were released just in time to get them into the record of the hearings on the OSHA cancer policy. The estimates have been severely criticized by scholars both in the United States and abroad as lacking in scientific soundness.

A final point on OSHA's approach to development of standards during the past decade: the agency has used its rule-making power to intrude into matters traditionally reserved for the collective bargaining provisions of the National Labor Relations Act. Two such examples are OSHA's recently withdrawn walkaround pay regulation and its rule on access to medical and exposure records. Both rules gave unions virtually unchecked rights in areas that were formerly handled by involved parties under the time-tested collective bargaining process.

Before I focus on how OSHA can turn some of these negatives into positives, I want to say a few words about the enforcement strategy the agency has followed during the past decade. To put it bluntly, I believe enforcement at all levels has not been carried out in a constructive manner. Although a large field organization devoted exclusively to enforcement exists, this organization has been spread too thinly in its effort to ascertain whether all firms are complying with safety and health standards. Inspectors have not been free to concentrate on those employers whose track records in safety and health have been poor.

Not only has there been a lack of concentration on businesses with poor occupational safety and health records, but there has been a lack of focus on the most serious, and most numerous, preventable injuries and illnesses. One only needs to look at the numbers to see that this is true. The National Safety Council's statistics for all industry show that the incidence rates for cases involving days away from work and deaths have been increasing since 1975.[10]

I believe this indicates two things: firstly, that no thoughtful targeting has been taking place; secondly, that the inspection approach just is not detecting the real safety and health problems. The conclusion of the final report of the Interagency Task Force on Workplace Safety and Health is worthy of attention. The task force concluded that enforcement by inspection is estimated, with present standards, to possess a potential for preventing perhaps 25 percent of workplace accidents by itself, since most injuries involve the behavior of management and workers as well, and some hazards are transient and will not be seen during an inspection.[11]

Finally, it is unfortunate that the agency's enforcement arm has played the policeman's role of citing and fining. Constructive guidance as to how to ameliorate problems has not been offered. Incentives for encouraging initiatives by employers and employees to make their workplaces more safe and healthful have been lacking. Section (2)(B)4 of the OSH Act, which directed OSHA to achieve its goal "by building upon advances already made through employer and employee initiative for providing safe and healthful working conditions,"[12] has been ignored.

The long-term future of OSHA—whether it will be able to fulfill its charge and be a positive force in protecting the health and safety of American working men and women—will be determined in the next four years. Without a doubt, the agency has the potential to fulfill its mission and help improve the safety and health performance of American industry. But it can achieve its potential only if it develops properly managed programs and takes a cooperative, and not adversarial, attitude toward American industry.

But, the responsibility of turning OSHA into an effective force in occupational safety and health by no means resides only with the agency. Industry *must* show that an OSHA which is cooperative and fair with all parties can and will produce results. Industry, drawing upon its own safety and health experience, has to come up with thoughtful, constructive suggestions of how it, with the assistance and guidance of OSHA, can fulfill the congressional mandate of providing our nation's workers with safe and healthful workplaces.

Workers, business, and government should develop intelligent, well-managed programs which have the common goal of reducing injury and illness. These programs should also measure program and personnel performance, focus on unacceptable risks and high injury-rate workplaces, and further encourage employers to establish effective safety and health programs. But, as I said before, the group that should be ultimately responsible for seeing that this goal is reached is corporate management. For in the final analysis, management determines whether safety standards are adhered to, whether health hazards are controlled, whether workers are trained to perform their jobs safely, whether equipment is in good shape, whether safety budgets are adequate . . . in short, whether workplaces are safe and healthful. But, I have been asked to talk about OSHA, not management, so let me offer some suggestions as to how the agency can function more effectively. The changes I will suggest can be divided into three categories: agency administration and personnel, standards development, and enforcement.

With respect to administration and personnel, the agency needs to define a clear policy for how reduction of injury and illness should be achieved. It also must establish policy control and a clear line of authority over the field organization. Performance evaluations and auditing systems should be designed to measure the success personnel and programs have in reducing injuries and illnesses in the worksites under the jurisdiction of each OSHA manager. From statements attributed to the new OSHA chief, Thorne Auchter, I understand that this is being done. The solicitor's office should provide leadership in the development of innovative approaches to improve safety and health performance. "Flexibility" and "creativity" should become the agency's watchwords.

With respect to standards, OSHA should adopt performance standards which focus on the results industry must achieve to protect the health and safety of workers. Wherever possible, industry should be allowed to come up with the best means of meeting safety and health standards. Cost/risk/benefit analyses of all proposed standards should be made. To do this, OSHA will have to conduct careful analyses of all available scientific data pertaining to industrial hazards. In addition, priorities, based on the severity of hazards and the number of workers exposed, should be set as to which standards will be developed. And industry should be consulted early in the process of developing standards. Management is in the best position to ascertain whether a proposed standard can be successfully implemented and complied with, once promulgated.

The agency should continue to review existing occupational safety and health standards to see if they serve a real worker protection need. Let me add the caveat, however, that I believe it would be a mistake for OSHA to move too quickly to correct the agency's excesses of the past, and in its desire to reduce regulatory red tape, eliminate necessary regulations. The evidence to date indicates that careful consideration has been given to all recent modifications and withdrawals of regulations.

A whole new approach to enforcement is needed. OSHA inspectors should discard their police uniforms and replace them with the garb of expert safety and health advisors. The consultative role of OSHA must be emphasized. Moreover, the agency should study various consultation and training methods to encourage employers to develop their own safety and health programs. First-instance citations for other than imminent danger situations should be eliminated, and the agency should invoke the general duty clause only in those situations that "are causing or likely to cause death or serious physical harm."[13]

The agency has to recognize the limitations of its resources and develop programs that will encourage voluntary enforcement and a targeting mechanism that will allow the agency to concentrate its enforcement activity on companies and industries with high injury rates. I understand that such a targeting mechanism is being developed by OSHA and will be completed within six months. Thorne Auchter has indicated that the new targeting strategy will focus on identifying hazardous workplaces on a site-by-site basis, regardless of whether an establishment is within an industry statistically recognized as "high-hazard."[14]

Let me now close on a positive note. I realize that criticizing the state of the art can be counterproductive. Recognizing the need for change and taking steps to effect change is the beginning of the solution. It is obvious that if we are to improve the quality of the occupational safety and health play and upgrade the role of one of the key actors, OSHA, all the players must join together. One way to do this is to hold a national, presidential occupational safety and health conference. At the request of the president, occupational safety and health experts in the United States could meet to address current occupational safety and health problems and assist OSHA in long-term planning.

I am confident that change will occur. It has got to, if we are to meet the challenge of inproving this country's occupational safety and health performance. Management, with the assistance of an effective OSHA, can do the job.

NOTES

1. "President signs job safety measure," *The Washington Post*, December 30, 1970.

2. Occupational Safety and Health Act of 1970, Public Law 91-596, 91st Congress, S. 2193, December 29, 1970, Sec. 2(b), p. 1.

3. *Chartbook on Occupational Injuries and Illnesses* U.S. Department of Labor, Bureau of Labor Statistics, 1972-1978 (Bulletin Nos. 1830, 1874, 1932, 1981, 2019, 2047, 2078; *Occupational Injuries and Illnesses in 1979: Summary* U.S. Department of Labor, Bureau of Labor Statistics, Summary No. 2097.

4. *Ibid.*

5. Occupational Safety and Health Act of 1970, Sec. 6(a), p. 4.

6. *Ibid.*, Sec. 2(b)(7), p. 1.

7. "Occupational Exposure to Lead Standard," *Federal Register*, November 14, 1978 (section on compliance costs), pp. 52982-52985.

8. "Devasting Attack on NIOSH Beryllium Study Levelled by Co-author," *Occupational Health and Safety Letter*, Vol. 10, No. 23 (December 8, 1980), p. 2.

9. "Estimates of the Fraction of Cancer in the United States Related to Occupational Factors," Report of The National Cancer Institute, The National Institute of Environmental Health Sciences, and The National Institute for Occupational Safety and Health, September 15, 1978, p. 24.

10. *Accident Facts* (Chicago: National Safety Council Press, 1976).

11. "Making Prevention Pay," Final Report of the Interagency Task Force on Workplace Safety and Health (Exposure Draft), December 14, 1978.

12. Occupational Safety and Health Act of 1970, Sec. 2(b)(4), p. 1.

13. *Ibid.*, Sec. 5(a)(1), p. 4.

14. *Occupational Safety and Health Reporter* (Bureau of National Affairs, Inc.), May 28, 1981, p. 1569.

Equal Employment Agencies

8220
9170 U.S.

Kenneth C. McGuiness[†]

In considering federal agency regulation in the '80s from the standpoint of the equal employment agencies, the threshold question is "What will the Reagan administration do first?" The answer is speculative and the policies and events that will follow are even more so, but the initial step may signal what to expect later.

Regulatory restraint is obviously high on the president's priority list and we have already seen that this administration is one that establishes and maintains priorities. The most important formal policy step in reducing the burden of regulations that have been announced thus far was the president's issuance, on February 17, 1981, of Executive Order (E.O.) No. 12291. There, the "General Requirements" pertaining to regulations were stated as:

> Sec. 2...
> (a) Administrative decisions shall be based on adequate information concerning the need for and consequences of proposed government action;
> (b) Regulatory action shall not be undertaken unless the potential benefits to society for the regulation outweigh the potential costs to society;
> (c) Regulatory objectives shall be chosen to maximize the net benefits to society;
> (d) Among alternative approaches to any given regulatory objective, the alternative involving the least net cost to society shall be chosen; and
> (e) Agencies shall set regulatory priorities with the aim of maximizing the aggregate net benefits to society, taking into account the condition of the particular industries affected by regulations, the condition of the national economy, and other regulatory actions contemplated for the future.

This seems to be a clear directive that regulatory action is not to be undertaken unless the potential benefits to society outweigh the potential costs; that regulatory objectives must maximize the net benefits to society; and that the methods used to achieve objectives must be the most cost-efficient legally available.

---

† Kenneth C. McGuiness is Senior Partner, McGuiness & Williams, Washington, D.C., and President of the Equal Employment Advisory Council.

To assure that this directive is followed, E.O. 12291 provides that for each "major rule" proposed, agencies must first prepare a Regulatory Impact Analysis (RIA) setting forth a description of the potential costs and benefits of the proposed rule and a determination of its potential net benefits. The analysis also must include a description of alternative approaches which might substantially achieve the regulatory goals at a lower cost, and a brief explanation of the legal reasons why such alternatives could not be adopted. Agencies are required to make their preliminary and final analyses available to the public.

The director of the Office of Management and Budget (OMB) and the Presidential Task Force on Regulatory Relief, chaired by Vice President Bush, are given authority to order that a proposed or existing rule be treated as a "major rule," to prepare uniform standards for measuring costs and benefits, and to consult with agencies in the preparation of RIAs. The director and the task force also have authority to state their approval or disapproval of the analyses on the administrative record and to require the agencies to respond to these views before taking final action.

The executive order states that it is not intended to create any rights or benefits that are enforceable by a party to litigation against the United States or any agency. The order does provide, however, that the analyses and determinations of costs and benefits are to be included in the agency record for purposes of judicial review. As explained in a Department of Justice legal memorandum analyzing the executive order, the effect of this provision is to preclude direct judicial review of an agency's compliance with the order. But, because the analyses will become part of the agency record for purposes of review, courts will be able to consider it in determining whether the agency action under review is consistent with relevant statutes.

The new order applies directly to the Department of Labor (DOL). Its application to the Equal Employment Opportunity Commission (EEOC) is less certain. The order is ambiguous as to EEOC coverage, but, from a practical standpoint, it seems likely that the OMB will find a way to insist that the agency conform to the order. The outcome of a court test of the issue is not as predictable, however.

The foregoing are the policies that are supposed to apply. What has actually happened? The short answer is, "To date, nothing." EEOC activity in the regulatory area has been minimal, probably because of the two vacancies on the commission and the uncertainty as to the new chair. Formal action at the DOL and the Office of Federal Contract Compliance Programs (OFCCP) has likewise been minimal, although withdrawal of the "Club Dues" regulations was welcomed by employers. None of this activity would qualify as a "major rule" requiring use of the E.O. 12291 procedures.

Consequently, I would identify the most significant development concerning regulations affecting Equal Employment Opportunity (EEO) agencies at this time as the Department of Labor's current proposal—which is not yet formalized—to amend the E.O. 11246 regulations that are enforced by the OFCCP. The DOL's actions in the next few weeks in this area could have a profound effect on government contractors for an extended period. I would, therefore, like to spend most of my allotted time discussing the background and status of the DOL proposal.

On December 30, 1980, the Carter administration, as a part of its avalanche of "midnight" regulations, issued in final form major changes in the regulations implementing E.O. 11246. This executive order deals with nondiscrimination in employment by federal government contractors. These changes, which were to become effective on January 27, 1981, would finalize, without substantial modifications, proposals issued a year earlier. The new administration has postponed the effective date of the amendments twice, the current date being June 29, 1981.

Immediately following the original January 28th postponement, little was heard from the Department of Labor about changes in the executive order program. Generally it was felt that, with primary administration emphasis on economic matters, such changes had low priority, but many interest groups were working on recommendations for amendments to the regulations or on revisions to E.O. 11246 itself. As it turned out, by early March, the OFCCP staff had persuaded the new solicitor, Tim Ryan, that prompt action was necessary and that changes should be made by amending the regulations.

The proposals that resulted were developed by the OFCCP staff with very little input from outside sources. They remained a closely guarded secret until late April when Secretary Donovan announced that a series of briefings to discuss tentative proposals would be held for various interest groups. But, the briefings turned out to include more explanation of decisions already reached than of ideas for discussion. Details of the proposals, which are too lengthy to be discussed here, can be found in the *BNA Daily Labor Report* of May 14, 1981.

Some of the department's recommendations are responsive to genuine concerns which have arisen under E.O. 11246. Abbreviated affirmative action plans for small contractors, consolidated plans for multiple small establishments, deletion of certain certification requirements, and abandonment of a proposed preliminary administrative enforcement procedure are examples of welcome changes.

Other recommendations seem certain to draw severe criticism from constituent groups and labor organizations without generating a significant improvement in E.O. 11246 enforcement. Raising the jurisdictional thresholds for executive order coverage and for preparing EEO-1 forms and AAPs is one example. The AFL-CIO already has criticized the department for suggesting withdrawal of privileges to participate in conciliation discussions, which were given to unions by the Carter "midnight" regulations. (The administration reportedly is now leaning toward acceding to the AFL-CIO position.) In general, however, the proposals amount to little more than "tinkering" with the existing program—significant issues such as the legality of back pay as an executive order remedy and standards for determining labor market "availability" of women and minorities are to be deferred to a later date.

It is clear that Solicitor Ryan strongly favors amending the regulations at once. His conclusion seems based on the belief that President Carter's last minute action forced immediate consideration of major issues. While one possibility is to withdraw the proposals and go back to the old regulations until the new administration can make a complete analysis of the issues, Solicitor Ryan appears to feel that this is not desirable because "momentum" for changes would be lost. Intermixed with this is an obviously strong desire to demonstrate that the Reagan administration wants to make regulation of business generally "more manageable." Other contributing factors are the belief that failure to amend the regulations would result in Alameda- county type lawsuits (*Legal Aid Society of Alameda County v. Brennan*, 381 F. Supp. 125, 608 F.2d 1319 (9th Cir. 1979)) to force amendments and, perhaps, an over-reading of a Justice Department instruction that the agencies not leave the suspended regulations "hanging."

Many employer representatives, on the other hand, think that the proposals do little more than make minor adjustments to a flawed program while accepting its conceptual basis, including, at least for the present, back pay as a remedy. They feel that employers would be better off to live with the present program for a few more months than to go through another temporary change, a problem that has plagued industry for years, with the promise of still further changes in the indefinite future. Of particular concern is the fact that proposals to change the jurisdictional thresholds for monitoring contractors have been tried in the past and then withdrawn because of the depth of opposition by protected groups. It therefore seems certain that the proposals will arouse a storm of protest likely to discourage more significant improvements at a later date.

The Equal Employment Advisory Council (EEAC) is one of the groups that believes the department's proposals are ill-advised. In a letter to Secretary Donovan last week, the council pointed out that the problems raised by the proposals can be avoided and that the existing regulatory difficulties are not an inescapable consequence of a desirable social program. The program can be remedied without sacrificing its uniformly supported objective—equal opportunity and equal job mobility. It can be harmonized with the administration's general economic and regulatory program, but these improvements will require a reorientation of its theoretical and regulatory basis. Unnecessary paperwork and bureaucratic duplication must be eliminated. An emphasis on training and on assisting minorities and women in achieving the requisite skills to take advantage of job opportunities should replace the current preoccupation with setting unrealistic goals. It is the EEAC's view that these objectives can best be obtained by issuance of a new executive order, supplemented by new regulations which would assure its accurate implementation.

Such a step would be advantageous from several perspectives. First, a new executive order is the most effective solution to the current duplication between the EEOC and the OFCCP. The latter should become an affirmative action agency, and collection of back pay and other forms of compensatory relief should be left to the EEOC. Such an arrangement of responsibility would avoid costly duplication of effort by both the government and contractors. It could not be challenged on the basis that it constitutes an arbitrary reinterpretation of the existing order, a challenge which could be raised if this differentiation were attempted through regulations. Congress has charged the EEOC with the task of devising remedies to alleviate unlawful employment discrimination. It has never delegated to the Department of Labor any comparable authority.

Second, the Reagan administration could foster job mobility by allowing contractors to establish voluntary training programs designed to equip minorities and women with skills that are required either by the contractor conducting the program or by other employers in the community. Unlike the current "linkage" program, which is a component of the department's proposals and requires extensive government involvement, this approach could be used without government funding and with minimal monitoring responsibilities.

Moreover, the encouragement of contractor-sponsored training programs in a new executive order would address the primary impediment to equal employment opportunity for women and minorities, namely, the absence of marketable skills. It also would partially fill the void created by recent reductions in Comprehensive Employment and Training Act (CETA) programs, and would be consistent with Assistant Secretary Angrisani's proposals for redirecting the Employment Training Administration. Since contractors can be expected to tailor the training programs to their own skill requirements, there is little danger that individuals would be equipped with skills for which there is no demand.

Third, regulations implementing an executive order based on these principles would ensure effective management of the program. The agency's focus would not be on searching for past discrimination but on creating true job mobility for minorities and women. Voluntary compliance could be encouraged by providing exemptions from recordkeeping requirements and compliance reviews. In the EEAC's view, this alone would be sufficient but, in the alternative, tax relief or other incentives for contractors with a demonstrated commitment to affirmative action might be used to reduce the costs to all concerned.

Also, there no longer would be a need to excuse contractors from the program's requirements by raising the jurisdictional thresholds. Instead, reporting requirements could vary according to contractor size so that small contractors would not be burdened unnecessarily by paperwork requirements that are meaningless for their small work forces. Similarly, repeated annual reviews of the same contractors, solely because of the number of people they employ, could be avoided by devising a targeting system designed to review contractors on a "worst-first" basis. By utilizing proven auditing techniques in conducting compliance reviews, and by adopting a flexible approach to statistical requirements, more effective use of the agency's budget could be obtained. In 1980, the OFCCP spent $31.8 million or 62 percent of its budget on compliance reviews in which there was no finding of discrimination.

Finally, one of the most valuable attributes of a new executive order would be the opportunity it afforded the administration to announce a program in a positive rather than in a negative light—a program that truly would meet the needs of minorities and women—the development of marketable skills which match actual job openings. If the foregoing suggestions were to be incorporated into a new order, it could be presented as a new and innovative approach to affirmative action. It could outline a program based on incentives for voluntary compliance designed to enhance the skills of women and minorities, thereby opening up employment opportunities not previously available to them. In addition, the program could be portrayed as yet another example of the administration's ongoing effort to eliminate bureaucratic duplication and inefficiency and substantially reduce the paperwork burden imposed on the public.

Although, as indicated earlier, the Department of Labor proposals for amending the regulations are not "major rules" and therefore E.O. 12291 does not apply, they are currently being reviewed by the OMB. The OMB review is important because the amendments, in effect, give implicit approval to a program whose potential benefits do not outweigh its costs, whose objectives do not maximize the net benefits to minorities, women, and society generally, and whose methods are not the most cost-efficient legally available. In other words, the amendments will continue a program that does not conform to Reagan administration policy on regulatory change.

Issuance of a new executive order, on the other hand, would permit modifications that would reflect both the Reagan policy and constructive changes. Secretary Donovan has stated on several occasions that he has not yet made up his mind as to whether a new executive order would be more desirable than amended regulations. Also, this question still seems to be open at both the OMB and the White House.

As indicated before, the way in which it is answered will have long-range implications. If the decision is made to amend the current regulations, the resulting outcry from labor and civil rights groups is very likely to delay further changes indefinitely. Because the OFCCP will continue to duplicate the EEOC's function of remedying past discrimination, a major part of the OFCCP's budget will be diverted to this activity and its affirmative action efforts seriously diluted. Back pay will continue to be an issue, with extensive litigation the result.

On the other hand, if the decision is made to issue a new executive order, the current regulations will remain in effect for a limited period while the specifics are being developed. But when the order issues, it could well retain the best features of the present program while incorporating some of the ideas outlined above. If so, it could usher in new affirmative concepts that would benefit minorities, women, and employers while reducing the role of government—a role that has been proven to be ineffective.

PART III

INTERNATIONAL REGULATION
OF
EMPLOYEE RELATIONS

A. Intergovernmental

125 — 30

44²⁰ 833¹
5140
6190

International Codes of Conduct
and Corporate Behavior

George B. McCullough[†]

I plan to cover three topics. First, I would like to review the history of guidelines for multinational enterprises (MNEs), or what are more commonly called international codes of conduct. Then I would like to talk about two of the codes that I think have had the greatest impact on multinational enterprises and, finally, about where these various codes might be heading.

The first of these codes of conduct was actually adopted by the International Chamber of Commerce (ICC). It may seem strange that codes of conduct for MNEs were actually begun by a business organization; however, the leaders of the ICC were fairly farsighted. They could see that various codes were being developed and would undoubtedly be promulgated by many international organizations. Consequently, a resolution was developed by the ICC in 1969 and adopted in 1972 under the title *Guidelines for International Investment*. The objective of the ICC was to preempt some of the international agencies by developing a code of conduct for international business which would embody certain underlying principles that hopefully would be incorporated into any codes ultimately adopted by international bodies. In fact, this is exactly what happened.

The first international agency to adopt a so-called code of conduct for MNEs was the Organization for Economic Cooperation and Development (OECD). As you know, the OECD is a government-to-government agency comprising twenty-one industrial nations. When it adopted its *Declaration on International Investments and Multinational Enterprises*, it did indeed inculcate the same concepts that had been established in the ICC code. I might add that the OECD, in working on its guidelines, did solicit input from both business and labor unions through two appendatory agencies known as the Business and Industry Advisory Committee (BIAC) and the Trade Union Advisory Committee (TUAC). It was through BIAC, using the ICC

[†] George B. McCullough is Vice President of the Exxon Corporation.

Guidelines for International Investment as a model, that certain underlying precepts were incorporated into the OECD's code. The four principles adopted by the OECD that came out of the ICC code were:

—recognition of multinational enterprises as a "positive force" in world trade;
—a guaranteed free flow of capital between nations with the right to remit profits;
—equal treatment with national companies under national law; and
—a code that would be voluntary in nature.

The OECD adopted its *Declaration on International Investments and Multinational Enterprises* in 1976, and it was later ratified by all OECD members except one. It covers all companies operating in more than one OECD country; and it has a series of sections, including one on employment and industrial relations.

This particular section is prefaced by a so-called "chapeau" clause that modifies all of the items within the section. The chapeau clause ensures the primacy of local law and practices over the guidelines in cases in which they might be construed differently.

There are nine articles in the section on employment and industrial relations covering the following specific items:

—The right of employees to be represented and to engage in constructive negotiations on employment conditions and on procedures to resolve issues.
—The provision of representatives of the employees with the facilities needed to assist in the development of effective collective bargaining.
—The provision of employee representatives with information enabling them to gain a true and fair view of the performance of the entity or the enterprise as a whole.
—The observation of standards of employment and industrial relations not less favorable than those observed by comparable employers in host countries.
—The utilization, training, and development of members of the local work force in cooperation with their employee representatives, and, where appropriate, government authorities.
—The provision of reasonable notice to employee representatives and, where appropriate, government authorities of changes in operations that will have major effects on their employees'

livelihoods and cooperation with employee representatives and governments to minimize adverse effects on employees to the extent practicable.

—The avoidance of discrimination in employment practices.

—The prohibition of threatening employee representatives of a transfer of operations in order to influence negotiations or to hinder the right to organize.

—The right of employee representatives to conduct negotiations on collective bargaining or labor-management relations with representatives of management who are authorized to take decisions on the matter under negotiations.

This particular code stayed in effect for three years with no changes. In 1979, however, the guidelines were reviewed in depth by a Committee on International Investments and Multinational Enterprises, commonly referred to as the CIIME.

The CIIME spent about a year investigating the guidelines, including several meetings with both the TUAC and the BIAC. The BIAC's position was that the code had met its objectives and, therefore, no changes need be made.

The TUAC brought before the CIIME about twenty individual cases in which it was claimed that multinational companies had violated the code. It is important to note that all of the so-called violations were applicable to the industrial relations section of the guidelines.

In addition, the TUAC, using these so-called violations as a basis of the need for change, suggested a number of changes they would like to see made in the guidelines. First of all, they recommended that the status of the code be changed from voluntary to mandatory, and that individual OECD countries be obliged to police multinational companies operating within their nation and to impose penalties in the event of guideline violations.

Also, the TUAC requested that the OECD set up some form of judicial review procedure to adjudicate individual violations by multinational companies. The TUAC also proposed that the guidelines include a requirement that bargaining be moved to the central headquarters of a multinational company whenever local management does not "effectively" respond to union demands.

They requested that safety and health standards be established and included as a part of the OECD guidelines and, by ignoring extraterritoriality, the TUAC also recommended that the guidelines be applicable to developing countries, as well as to those in the OECD.

The TUAC recommended substantial requirements for disclosure to unions by multinational enterprises. It is a likely coincidence that these disclosure requirements, which were rejected by the OECD, were subsequently introduced into the European Community (EC) under the provision now known as the Vredeling proposal.

As a result of the investigation by the CIIME, and the subsequent review by the OECD itself, no substantive changes were made in the guidelines. One change was effected, however—the movement of strikebreakers across country boundaries was prohibited. This change was prompted by one of the cases cited by the TUAC in its investigation process. This was the so-called Hertz case, in which, during a strike against Hertz in Denmark, a number of Hertz employees from other European nations were moved to Denmark, where operations were continued during the strike.

I would be derelict if I did not add one footnote. Although the OECD adopted the guidelines virtually unchanged with the exception that I noted earlier, the staff of the CIIME put out a report which clearly favored many of the actions proposed by the TUAC. When the guidelines are again reviewed by the OECD, I think that we in business should be very cautious that this bias on the part of the CIIME staff does not get translated into proposals that may be difficult to change at the OECD ministerial level.

The second major code of conduct in effect today is that of the International Labor Organization (ILO), the *Tripartite Declaration of Principles Concerning Multinational Enterprises and Social Policy.*

The development of the ILO code began with a tripartite working group in 1972; however, the declaration was not adopted until 1977. The delay was caused by the demands of employers that any "code of conduct" be based on factual data.

It is interesting to note that the ILO is the only body that developed substantial studies to serve as the basis for their code of conduct. The ILO published two studies that reviewed the impact multinational enterprises in the metalworking and petroleum industries had on social policy in both developed and developing countries. The studies clearly recognized the value of multinational investment in both developed and developing countries and put to rest, in a very factual basis, many of the charges and allegations that had been made by trade unions and others that multinational companies operate in an irresponsible manner. These studies, in fact, pointed out that in many countries, particularly lesser-developed nations, multinational enterprises were a major force for social reform.

The ILO *Declaration of Principles* is not far different from the

OECD *Declaration on International Investments*. It includes the same basic principles outlined by the ICC in its earlier guidelines: it recognizes multinational enterprises as a positive force; it guarantees the free flow of capital; it calls for equal treatment with national companies under national law; and the codes are voluntary. Unlike the other codes, however, the ILO's code did define multinational enterprises, and it defined them in a manner that is advantageous for American MNEs. MNEs are defined as enterprises from the private sector, from the public sector, or mixed companies—those capitalized from both the private and public sectors. The advantage of this, of course, is that government-owned companies are considered multinational enterprises in terms of being measured against these so-called codes of conduct.

Like the OECD, the ILO set up a mechanism by which the codes should be reviewed periodically. Last September, the codes were reviewed by a Tripartite Subcommittee of the governing body, which in turn recommended that no changes be made to the code at that particular time.

One last thing about the ILO *Declaration of Principles*. As you know, the ILO is a tripartite organization and, therefore, there is direct input by both workers and employers. I would like to read from Article 1 of the *Tripartite Declaration of Principles*, because I think it indicates the influence that employers can have in these international bodies when they are organized effectively and have a direct input.

> Multinational enterprises play an important part in the economies of most countries and in international economic relations. This is of increasing interest to governments as well as to employers and workers and their respective organizations. Through international direct investment and other means, such enterprises bring substantial benefits to home and host countries by contributing to the more efficient utilization of capital, technology and labor. Within the framework of development policy established by governments, they can also make an important contribution to the promotion of economic and social welfare, to the improvement of living standards and the satisfaction of basic needs, to creation of employment opportunities, both directly and indirectly, and to the enjoyment of basic human rights, including freedom of association throughout the world.

It is indeed gratifying to see that such a document put out by the ILO begins with that particular set of sentences.

I would like to conclude by talking about what might be the outlook for codes of conduct in the future. Though the OECD code is due to have a midterm progress report in 1982, and is due for a complete revision in 1984, there is no question that the TUAC will make demands in the following areas: to make the codes mandatory; to use the CIIME as a board of arbitration; to establish an international OSHA; to incorporate the Vredeling proposal into the code; and to demand multinational collective bargaining. At the ILO, worker delegates are likely to make the same demands as the TUAC. At the United Nations, international trade unions will unquestionably make the same demands as are made to the OECD and the ILO. In addition, Less Developed Countries (LDCs) will make much more stringent demands on restrictions covering investments, remittances, and transborder data flows.

For those who follow the international scene, it is easy to see that trade unions have their act together. They know their objectives, they are well coordinated, and they act in concert among all the international organizations. Consequently, one sees the same proposals in the OECD, the ILO, the United Nations, the EC, and among legislatures in various countries.

To end on an optimistic note, however, I also see the employers beginning to get their act together. The BIAC was effective in 1979 in countering the TUAC recommendations to the OECD guidelines. The ILO code was strongly impacted by employer representation—both in drafting the initial language and in the interim review. After an almost fatal delay, the Union of Industries of the European Community (UNICE), supported by the United States as well as European employer groups, is working to defeat or to mitigate the effects of the Vredeling proposal in the EC.

There is no question in my mind that trade unions will continue to bring pressure to change these various codes in order to further restrict the ability of multinational companies to manage their enterprises in the host countries. Our job as employers is to refute groundless charges and to influence these international bodies to become a force for positive change rather than to promulgate restrictive legislation.

It is in the self-interest of every U.S. business organization that operates outside of the United States to follow these matters closely and to support those organizations and those individuals who are working to maintain the basic principles, developed back in 1969, that underlie the ICC Code of Conduct and which were subsequently embodied into the codes of various international organizations.

131-6/

8220
8331   W. Germany

Codetermination: Wave of the Future?

Harry R. Gudenberg[†]

Codetermination—its future and its implications—presents one with an opportunity to do some crystal-balling, and as anyone who has studied the field of labor relations can tell, it is similar to picking the winning baseball team for the World Series in March. Like baseball, prediction generally requires a look at the past and the present, so today, I will sketch out where codetermination has been, where it is today, and where we may see it going.

Historically, codetermination, or industrial democracy as it is referred to, was born in Germany. Germany has the oldest and most notable system of codetermination in the world. The first attempt to establish works councils began in 1920 with laws that provided employees rights on social security and personnel matters.

After World War II, the Law of May 1951 established codetermination for employees in mining and steel producing industries. It was amended by a supplementary act of 1967. This legislation required that supervisory boards of corporations belonging to these particular industries comprise shareholders and employees on an equal basis. So, for example, if a board has eleven members, five are appointed by the trade unions. The elected members of the supervisory board must then agree upon the last neutral member (the eleventh) in order to break a tie vote and to make board decisions possible in the case of a deadlock.

In 1952, the Industrial Constitutions Act came into effect for industries other than mining and steel. This law provided the legal basis for employee representation through works councils and one third of the membership on supervisory boards.

Often overlooked when codetermination is discussed is the fact that the works council system in Germany is the basic labor relations system. The works councils are the body politic that in Germany gives workers—not unions directly—a voice in decision making through representation on plant-level councils dealing with many items we historically consider part of collective bargaining. These

---

[†] Harry R. Gudenberg is Vice President of the International Telephone and Telegraph Corporation.

councils are elected by employees at the plant and have broad rights of consultation on working conditions, layoffs, local personnel policies, and so on.

Unions in Germany negotiate national economic and working condition settlements across the economy, for local application. The power base at the local level rests with the works councils more than with the unions that wield major political power across the country.

In Germany, corporate law provides for a two-tier management system. The superivsory board is, to a certain extent, similar to the U.S. board of directors. It appoints the management board and must approve major top management decisions. It does not take part in the actual operation of the company.

In 1972, a new industrial constitutions act came into effect, replacing the 1952 act. It expanded the legal basis for works councils and employee rights to codetermination, consultation, and information. The works councils' powers and scope of activities were greatly increased by this law. Both unions and employers generally support the works council system.

The 1972 act outlines nine main subjects, and they are:

—Responsibilities of the works council;
—Functions of trade unions and employers' associations;
—Constitution and election of the works council;
—Rules prescribed for the conduct of business by the works council;
—Works council assembly;
—Responsibilities of the plant and other assemblies;
—Codetermination rights of the works council in social, personnel, and economic decisions of the firm;
—Rights of individual employees;
—Grievance procedures.

Please note that the emphasis is on the works council.

Four years later, in July of 1976, the West German legislature passed a compromise act which today has given new thrust to codetermination, and which is the focal point of much attention whenever codetermination is discussed. This law applies to all companies with more than 2,000 employees. It is a compromise between, on the one hand, the 1951 parity representation for the coal and steel industries, which still exists and was sought by the trade unions for all industry and supported by the Social Democratic Party and, on the other hand, what was acceptable to their coalition partners, the Free Democrats. Certain groups of employers challenged the constitutionality of the 1976 law, but its validity has been upheld in court.

The law provides that supervisory boards will be composed of twelve, sixteen, or twenty members, depending on the size of the enterprise of which:

—half are shareholder representatives
—the other half comprise one senior executive representing the employees, two or three union representatives, and the remainder employee representatives.

The chairman and the deputy of the supervisory board are elected by a two-thirds majority vote of the members.

In case such a majority is not obtained, a second election takes place in which the stockholder representatives elect the chairman and the employee and union representatives elect the vice chairman.

Except for the appointment of the chairman and vice chairman, all supervisory board decisions require a simple majority. In case of a tie vote, the chairman has two votes and can break a tie. It was the extra vote that was the legal reasoning behind the constitutionality of this statute in the opinion of the German Supreme Court.

All representatives of the supervisory board have the same rights and responsibilities, which are to:

—appoint members of the management board;
—review the performance of the management board;
—examine the company books and records and approve the balance sheet;
—be informed of all major plans for investment, rationalization, and so on that can have a major impact on company liquidity and profitability (and in practice approves them). This is naturally the key area of impact.

This then is the historical basis of codetermination in Germany; its footings are steeped in sixty years of history, and it is an ingrained part of the political, social, and cultural policy and philosophy of Germany. Management, unions, employees, works councils, and supervisory boards have established roles—but those roles have been and are being threatened by this new process.

Today, difficulties have arisen in companies' abilities to plan and discuss competitive issues or critical personnel transactions in board meetings, for information that was once contemplative now has a high likelihood of becoming public.

Another threat arose last summer when a major steel company covered by the 1951 act announced plans to reorganize its corporate structure and merge its steel operations into its pipe-making subsidiary. From a business standpoint, the move made sense.

Steel production used to be one of the firm's chief pillars, but years of crisis in that industry have diminished the mill's role to where now, in effect, it is little more than a supplier of the metal for the pipes division. Organizational streamlining and a merger of the two, management contended, would have saved some $28 million a year.

The reorganization would make the company no longer a "steel producer," however, and thus the company would no longer be subject to the jurisdiction of the 1951 codetermination act.

Political factors intervened and early this year a bill was introduced and passed in April which provides that any company no longer subject to the 1951 act because of reorganization or a change in its production program will have to retain the parity management system for six years after it has been restructured.

These difficulties with codetermination, among others, have affected the once harmonious labor relations atmosphere in Germany, but Germany is not the only country with codetermination. Simpler forms of it are found in Norway, Denmark, Sweden, Austria, France, Luxembourg, and the Netherlands.

Proposals for various forms of codetermination have also existed in England under the Labour government, for example the so-called "Bullock Commission Report," and they currently exist before the European Community.

Against this framework, let us look briefly at the attention that codetermination has received in the United States. As you are aware, the United Automobile, Aerospace and Agricultural Implement Workers of American (UAW) has been on the leading edge of this issue in the United States, and when the Chrysler Corporation was faced with financial chaos, and our Congress agreed to give this corporation loan guarantees, the UAW, as a condition for such assistance, was forced to agree to sizable wage and benefit reductions. Among concessions received by the UAW for these actions was an agreement to the appointment of Douglas Fraser, president of the UAW, to the Chrysler board. Not surprisingly, the company has nothing but praise for Fraser's contributions to the board, although some union officials seem somewhat more reluctant to express any opinion as to the value of Fraser's participation on the board to the UAW.

Similarly, the American Motors Corporation agreed to give the UAW a seat on its board if the U.S. government would approve the legality of such a seat. Under the Carter administration, the Department of Labor gave an opinion that union representation on U.S. boards of directors does not violate U.S. labor laws. The U.S. Department of Justice has, however, ruled that union representation on more than one company board in the same industry may violate the antitrust laws.

American labor law and antitrust law never contemplated the problems of a union official's presence on a company board of directors, particularly when that union official was an officer of a union that was the legal bargaining agent for the employees of the company in question. It would seem that such board membership represents a violation of the spirit, if not the letter, of the National Labor Relations Act, which clearly contemplates that the management and labor partners should be completely independent of one another—something not really possible when a union president is both a board member and the titular head of the union bargaining agent.

What naturally can follow is for the UAW to request an appointment of someone other than a current UAW officer—for instance, a former officer or officer of another union, to the board.

The legal troubles of the UAW codetermination push, however, may not be over. Court cases may still challenge Chrysler's acceptance of union board members. As you can well imagine, this issue is also receiving much attention among lawyers representing boards of directors.

Where other automotive manufacturers will stand on this issue remains to be seen.

As I said earlier, codetermination involves much more than the appointment of a worker or union official to the board of directors of a company. To be effective from a union point of view, codetermination also involves joint union-management responsibility for hiring, layoffs, plant reductions or closings, appointment of supervision and at least lower management, production, and the plants in which products are produced.

The real codetermination issue, however, is the difference in the political, social, and philosophical environments in various countries. United States unions operate under U.S. laws—not anyone else's, and if—mind you—if codetermination is to occur here it should occur within a prescribed set of rules in keeping with our system, not on an ad hoc crisis basis.

Today, in Germany, unions are unhappy with the codetermination system. They continue to want full parity codetermination in all industries and are critically concerned with any attempt to dismantle that system as is in process in the mining and steel industries. The president of Germany's largest union believes that dismantling the codetermination law is a blatant danger to social peace. Also at issue is the fact that Germany is now in a period of economic downturn, with less employment and higher inflation resulting in more concern with decisions that affect workers and the workplace. Within that economic framework, debate and discussion of alternative business actions now require consultation at supervisory board levels with unions and employees.

As examples of this, an automotive company wanted to invest several million dollars in plants outside Germany to augment production of its German subsidiary. Labor, at the locations it selected, was cheaper than in Germany. Union members on the German subsidiary's supervisory board got wind of the plan and insisted on an equivalent investment in Germany. The result was the elimination of savings to the company.

Another example: a building concern told its employers' federation, during recent wage negotiations, that it cannot afford even the modest 4 percent wage increase subsequently agreed to with the union. Union representatives on the company's supervisory board disputed the claim and forced the company to go along with the 4 percent increase, even at risk to the company.

Certainly, companies can no longer rely on the consensus that has generally made labor relations so much smoother in Germany than in other nations for the last thirty years. How much of this results from codetermination, how much results from the economic conditions, and how much results from a change of philosophy is difficult to assess. What is predictable is that codetermination will be around and will continue to be a subject of uncertainty, but also of interesting discussion. It clearly warrants watching and it requires understanding, both in Europe and in the United States.

Responding Effectively to International Pressures

Robert W. Copp[†]

In commenting upon how multinational employers can respond effectively to international pressures concerning their employee relations, let me try to identify and summarize the major sources and the general nature of these pressures, most of which will be familiar to you.

For those of us involved in development and administration of employee relations policy, national and international trade union organizations probably represent the major source of criticism or pressure concerning labor and social affairs in multinational companies. For nearly twenty-five years now, some of the larger international trade union secretariats, like the International Metalworkers' Federation, have been active in developing and publicizing their views about multinational corporations.

Especially in some of the industrialized market economy countries during the past fifteen years or more, there has been a perceptible influence of national and international trade union officials on policies of national host governments and, in turn, on their participation in intergovernmental organizations. In some cases, trade union officials themselves, active in social democratic politics and in the Socialist International, have achieved leadership of, or at least important positions in, their governments.

Spearheaded by these trade union officials, the critics of multinationals have embraced, in addition, representatives of organized religious bodies, especially those of a Christian persuasion, consumer-interest groups, ad hoc university student and faculty groups, and both elective and appointed officials of national and local governments as well as of intergovernmental bodies.

This galaxy of the sources of pressures on multinationals has resulted in emphasis on several significant employee relations questions, which we might summarize quickly: (1) frequent, but not always consistent, positions about deployment of investments by multinationals, including plant expansion or plant closings and

---

[†] Robert W. Copp is Overseas Liaison Manager for the Ford Motor Company.

137

sourcing for manufacturing components for their products; (2) persistent and increasing pressures for development of formal arrangements for consultations between trade union officials and management representatives at the transnational regional and global level, extending to topics or functions traditionally regarded as responsibilities of management; (3) more intensive demands for the extension of employee participation in management decision making, including employee representation on boards of directors and in other organs for management decision making; (4) broadened collective representation of employees to include supervisors and managers; and (5) an enhanced interest in topics related to occupational safety and health.

And, finally, we should note one rather unique pressure setting—criticism of private business investment and activity in the Republic of South Africa. Here, the critics of multinational enterprises extend their concerns beyond labor and social affairs and some of them insist that investors actually withdraw in order to put pressure on the government of South Africa to abandon its policy of legal segregation of the races and to move toward political power sharing by black Africans and those of mixed race (colored).

Having looked briefly at the sources and nature of some of the more important pressures on the managements of multinational enterprises, what are some ways in which management might respond? It is useful to consider this question in two ways: the process or method of response, on the one hand, and some of the principles that ought to govern employer response on the other hand.

In terms of method or process, it is important, first of all, that we employers know and appreciate the institutions and personalities that formulate and press the labor and social issues with which we must deal. By now, most large multinational employers have allocated time and staff resources to this objective, and during the decade of the 1970s employers began to achieve a level of appreciation and information exchange that allowed them reasonably to match the already developed activities of some of the critics, especially several of the larger and well-established international trade union secretariats. Probably the most significant development that assisted employers in this objective of knowing and appreciating was the establishment of the Multinational Research Advisory Group (MRAG) in the Industrial Research Unit of the Wharton School. No other activity has matched this not-for-profit MRAG in the thoroughness, relevance, consistency, and scholarship of its reporting and its analysis of developments in international industrial relations.

This need for analysis and interpretation of developments, supported by the MRAG's research and publications, is a second aspect of employer response. What were, until a few years ago, issues and pressures largely left to employee relations specialists in management have become—increasingly and pressingly—questions of real concern to general management, including chief executive officers. This means that we employee relations specialists have had to develop and refine our techniques for analysis and presentation of industrial relations issues, to hone our ability to forecast more accurately, and to learn how to relate employee relations issues to the broader goals of our respective firms.

This appreciation by management of institutions and issues presumably should lead to some kind of employer action. Two features characterize this action by most large multinational employers in industrialized market economy countries.

First, such employers have usually found it more effective to respond to governmental initiatives at both national and international levels through established business or employer organizations rather than through their positions as individual companies. This joint approach has both advantages and disadvantages. On the positive side, an agreed position among employers clearly carries more weight, especially among intergovernmental bodies involved in attempts to regulate multinational employers' behavior through guidelines or declarations of principles. On the other hand, reaching those agreed positions among employers is often a tedious and sometimes frustrating task, especially in the United States where we employers have less experience in working through business and employer associations than do our colleagues in western Europe, for example.

The other feature is related to the first. Because of the commitment of Western employers to a competitive and free-enterprise system of economic organization, they tend to want to pursue their respective firms' objectives independently and to put their own positions before governmental bodies to assure maximum support for their respective objectives. In this situation, the need for an exchange of information among employers still remains in order to assure a reasonable degree of consistency among the positions that they are pursuing. This is the more important feature because intergovernmental bodies—and, even more, international trade union organizations—do not distinguish clearly among individual enterprises' various actions; rather, they tend to impute to all multinational enterprises the behavior or action that characterizes only one or a few enterprises.

Finally, let me suggest three broad principles that generally ought to govern how managements of multinational companies respond to external pressures about labor and social affairs questions.

Firstly, our stewardship as managers assumes that we will, to the maximum feasible extent, maintain (or preserve) a degree of unhindered flexibility that will allow the management to manage the enterprise. Our critics put the rhetorical tag of "management prerogatives" on this principle. But, prerogatives or not, the array of attempts to regulate employer action in just the field of employee relations goes far beyond what is reasonably necessary or socially required. A good illustration of this attempted intervention is the 1980 draft proposal by the staff of the International Labor Office for an international instrument about promotion of collective bargaining—a proposal aggressively supported by both national and international trade union bodies. Another current illustration is the October 1980 proposal by the Commission of the European Communities for a directive about informing and consulting employees of undertakings with a complex structure, in particular, transnational firms.

Secondly, we should support and pursue voluntary, rather than mandatory, responses that are characteristic of our commitment to an economic system based on free private enterprise. The proponents of regulation of employee relations, of course, press for mandatory instruments—thus the "directive" from the European Communities or the pressed-for convention instead of recommendations from the International Labor Organization. There are some effective, working examples of voluntary instruments and we employers should continue to cite them: the Organization for Economic Cooperation and Development's (OECD) *Guidelines for Multinational Enterprises* (1976), the International Labor Organization's (ILO) *Tripartite Declaration of Principles Concerning Multinational Enterprises and Social Policy* (1977), and the principles about employee relations in South Africa developed in 1976 and 1977 under the leadership of the Reverend Leon H. Sullivan and monitored by the staff and task groups of the International Council for Equality of Opportunity Principles, Incorporated.

And, finally, a principle about equal treatment. The entities of a multinational enterprise are, after all, national companies organized and operating under the laws and norms of host countries. Especially with respect to their employee relations—probably the most indigenously oriented of management responsibilities—it is hard to see why these national subsidiary companies should be subject to regulations different from those applicable to domestic firms. The so far unsuccessful efforts by the United Nations Commission on Transnational Corporations to agree on a definition of a transnational corporation (or multinational enterprise) suggest that whatever uniqueness is claimed about multinational enterprises is more the result of emotion than of careful study and analysis. One almost wonders whether international trade union bodies, in order to justify themselves to their constituent national trade unions, have not attempted to fabricate an employer adversary at an international level.

However reasoned our arguments about not needing unique treatment or regulation of employee relations in multinational enterprises, the prognosis for the decade of the '80s is continued controversy over the role and behavior of multinational enterprises. The actors and the issues are not likely to be significantly different from those during the '70s, and the methods and principles that characterized employer response in the '70s should remain relevant for the '80s.

PART III

B. Union-Management

Management Response to Multinational Union Pressures: The IUF, Unilever in South Africa, and Coca-Cola in Guatemala

Herbert R. Northrup and Richard L. Rowan[†]

8321
8310
8331
4420

Introduction

Multinational collective bargaining is an idea much discussed, but one that has almost never been effectuated. Widely divergent national labor legislation and customs, opposition of employers to opening up another level of expense and strike-risk, fear on the part of national union officials that bargaining beyond national boundaries would force them to cede authority to international organizations, and employee disinterest all militate against the internationalization of collective bargaining.[1] Faced with the fact that any direct bargaining role is unlikely to be found for them in the near future, the international labor movement, and particularly the coordinating bodies, or so-called "International Trade Union Secretariats" (ITSs)[2] have sought to extend their influence vis-à-vis multinational corporations in several ways. One of the ITSs' approaches is to use international organizations such as the Organization for Economic Cooperation and Development (OECD) or the International Labor Organization (ILO) to promote "guidelines" or codes of behavior for corporations that can encourage corporations to deal with international unions.[3] Another ITS policy is to lobby in the European Community for legislation that would require international union-corporation contacts in Europe and thereby set a pattern for the rest of the world.[4] A third approach involves the ITS's assuming the role of an international social conscience and attempting to pressure the corporation to deal with it to resolve a well-publicized issue of human rights. This article is concerned with the attempts of one of the smaller, but more active union secretariats, the International Union of Food and Allied Work-

† The authors are Professors of Industry and respectively, Director and Codirector of the Industrial Research Unit at the Wharton School, University of Pennsylvania. This article is part of the Industrial Research Unit's ongoing Multinational Industrial Relations Research Project.

ers' Associations (IUF), to utilize the last of these approaches in cases involving Unilever in the Republic of South Africa and the Coca-Cola Company in Guatemala.

The IUF and Unilever 1973-1977

The IUF affiliates national unions in the food, beverage, hotel, catering, and tobacco industries. Organized in 1920, it now has a dues-paying affiliated membership of approximately 1.5 million.[5] This compares with an affiliated membership of 13.5 million for the largest ITS, the International Metalworkers' Federation (IMF).[6] The chief administrative and operating officer of the IUF is the general secretary. Dan Gallin, a native of Poland, and now a Swiss citizen, has held this post since 1970 after serving as acting general secretary for two years and assistant general secretary for the previous eight years. The IUF's headquarters, located in a large old house in a Geneva suburb, is staffed by ten full-time employees, two part-time employees, and one free-lance translator.

Unilever, the world's largest food manufacturing company and the twelfth largest manufacturing company in the world on the 1980 *Fortune* list, is a British-Dutch company, headquartered in London and Rotterdam. In 1979, Unilever had sales of $21.7 billion and 309,000 employees.[7] It has long operated in the Republic of South Africa, where it has a large number of facilities. As the largest food company, Unilever has long been a target of the IUF and other secretariats. Obviously, if this company would agree to deal with the IUF, it would be a tremendous gain for the ITSs.

Formation of a "World Council"

The efforts of the IUF to arrange a contact with Unilever began in 1973 and have continued ever since. In 1973, the IUF and the International Federation of Chemical, Energy and General Workers' Unions (ICEF) jointly established a Unilever World Council. The first meeting occurred in Geneva from June 6 to 8, 1973. These dates corresponded with the opening of an International Labor Organization conference, which the meeting sponsors hoped would "facilitate the participation of some delegates from distant countries."[8] The meeting was preceded by analyses of Unilever businesses and profit positions, number and locations of plants, and personnel and labor relations practices. It appears that the IUF compiled nearly all these data using both reports from affiliated unions and published materials.[9]

The attendance at the June meeting was apparently disappointing. Ten countries were represented, a majority being IUF affiliates, plus three observing delegations. Australian, Canadian, and American delegates, as well as delegates from several other countries, were not present. A "permanent IUF/ICEF Unilever Council" was established, and the first issue of the *Unilever Bulletin* was issued in mimeograph form on June 20, 1973.[10] Most of the conference time was directed to delegates' reporting on conditions in their respective countries. Six issues of the *Unilever Bulletin* had been published by early 1976 and were apparently jointly issued by the ICEF and the IUF. Then in November 1976, the IUF alone began issuing the bulletin in a new format, entitled *Unilever Information* (seven issues had appeared by December 1979). By late 1976, the joint world council had become moribund.

Incidents in Italy and Spain

One matter that was reported to the first world council meeting involved pressure by the IUF to alter Unilever action. In September 1972, a telegram was sent to Unilever's Rotterdam headquarters by the IUF protesting what was considered to be the company's decision to close a small tomato paste factory in Parma, Italy. A Dutch IUF affiliate also expressed its concern to Unilever management.[11]

Unilever claims that its Italian company had decided that tomato paste no longer fitted into its product line and had made arrangements to sell the factory, if a satisfactory buyer could be found to continue the business. While negotiations were in progress with a prospective buyer, a rumor was circulated that the plant would be closed by a property developer. This led to the IUF response. Unilever is still operating the plant.

The second incident involved a union in Spain, where organized labor then operated in the shadow of illegality. On August 10, 1973, the IUF and the ICEF sent a joint circular letter to affiliates in the Netherlands, the United States, Belgium, the United Kingdom, and Germany concerning a strike at a Unilever facility near Madrid in which, pursuant to Spanish law then in effect, five strike leaders had been suspended following a wage dispute. The affiliated unions were requested, "in the name of the IUF/ICEF Unilever Council," to intervene with the managements of their national companies to express their support of the Spanish workers and pressure Unilever to settle the dispute. The affected strikers were reinstated by an agreement reached pursuant to Spanish conciliation procedure prior to the company's receipt of the IUF/ICEF communications.[12]

Second Meeting and U.S. Strike

The Second IUF/ICEF Unilever World Council Meeting was held

in London from March 5 to 6, 1974. On March 15, four United States Unilever (Lever Brothers) plants were struck by the International Chemical Workers Union, an ICEF affiliate. The president of this union attributed in part the "final success" of the strike, settled on March 28, to "effective international cooperation and solidarity." Although there appears to be no factual basis for the claim that the strike length or settlement was affected by any international action, the claims were repeated by a consultant's newsletter as showing "the ability of the international union movement to mobilize and react quickly."[13] This same newsletter also erroneously reported that Unilever management had met with the IUF/ICEF council in Geneva in June 1973. Even the secretariats never claimed that such a meeting occurred; in fact, Dan Gallin, general secretary of the IUF, wrote a letter, reprinted by the newsletter, emphasizing that no such meeting occurred.[14]

On March 28, 1974, *De Tijd*, a Dutch newspaper, reported that a meeting had been held between Unilever-Netherlands and Industriebond of the Dutch Federation of Trade Unions (NVV), which is affiliated with both the IUF and the ICEF.[15] It was further reported "that Unilever had agreed in this meeting not to export goods to the United States during the strike and that the NVV representative, Mr. Van Hattem, communicated this position to Charles Levinson, secretary-general of the ICF." According to the paper, "Levinson said that efforts would now be made to bring pressure on the Unilever in the United Kingdom through the British trade unions." This paper also reported, however, that "a Unilever spokesman pointed out that there could not possibly be any question of conceding to the NVV demands since Unilever Netherlands did not export to the U.S.A. at all."[16]

Actually, no such meeting between Unilever and NVV affiliate representatives occurred. What happened was that a Dutch union official telephoned the company to find out if any products sold by Lever Brothers Company in the United States were now exported from Europe. After receiving an answer in the negative, the Dutch unionists issued a statement of solidarity with the American strikers![17] Nothing in fact resulted, nor was there any overt reaction by British unionists, who were also contacted by Levinson.[18]

IUF Meat Industry Meeting

Besides its participation in the joint world council with the ICEF, the IUF has attempted to coordinate other national union activities involving Unilever, again without noticeable success. Thus,

Fifteen delegates from eight food workers' unions in Belgium, Denmark, France, Germany, the Netherlands, and the United Kingdom, affiliated to the International Union of Food and Allied Workers' Associations (IUF) met in Amsterdam, September 19 to 20, 1975, for an exchange of information and consultations on the growing unemployment in the meat industry.[19]

The meeting was called largely at the instigation of Dutch trade unions, which claimed rationalization was reducing jobs in the Netherlands. IUF General Secretary Dan Gallin was present.

From what we have learned, there was some discussion of attempting to obtain a meeting with Unilever for a multinational committee, but instead the delegates decided first to seek redress for their grievances at the national levels. The plan apparently called for national unions to meet with Unilever personnel concerning Unilever's investment plans in the meat industry, for each union to keep the others informed about results, for a second meeting to occur in early 1976, and for the national unions to seek support for their position regarding the meat industry and employment therein from their respective ministers who represent their countries in the European Parliament.[20]

In December 1975, however, officials of chemical and food affiliates of the French Confédération Française Démocratique du Travail (CFDT), which had representatives at the meat plant workers' conference, wrote the Unilever board in Rotterdam requesting a meeting between the Unilever World Council and the Unilever board to discuss company investment policies and employment guarantees. The secretary of the Unilever board replied that industrial relations issues in France are matters for local management.[21]

Second IUF Meat Industry and IUF/ICEF Working Party Meetings

The second meeting of the IUF meat industry group, originally set for January 1976, was held in Geneva on June 28, 1976. No delegates from the United Kingdom attended, and apparently little was decided. The company meanwhile closed one meat plant in Britain and announced the closing of another. In each case, an agreement was reached beforehand with the affected British unions on closure procedures and severance arrangements. Both plants were closed without any stoppage of work or dispute arising.

Following the meat industry meeting, an IUF/ICEF working party was convened in Geneva from June 29 to 30, 1976. There was the usual discussion of company policies, and a decision was made to continue the *Unilever Bulletin;*[22] but as noted below, the meeting was not well attended, and as already discussed, the IUF now apparently is handling the publication without the ICEF's involvment.

Spanish Unrest and ASTMS Booklet

Unilever, like many companies, has received numerous communications from the secretariats, in this case from both the ICEF and the IUF, during periods of industrial unrest in Spain. In addition, national unions in Britain and the Netherlands have charged the company several times with permitting unhealthy or substandard conditions in Spanish factories, a charge that the company has vigorously refuted. The Association of Scientific, Technical and Managerial Staffs (ASTMS), which is trying to unionize Unilever's British salaried workers, has been especially active in this regard. It has also published a booklet claiming that it is moving toward joint action with Industriebond-NVV on negotiations with Unilever regarding salaried employee conditions.[23] Actually, neither union represents a significant portion of Unilever's salaried work force in the two countries, and there have been no actual attempts for joint action.

IUF/ICEF World Council Meeting and Second U.S. Strike

As noted, an IUF/ICEF World Council working group met in Geneva from June 29 to 30, 1976, but the British and Belgian representatives and all non-Europeans were absent. Representatives from the Dutch, German, Italian, and French unions were present. Apparently, little action resulted, except to consider whether to request Unilever to meet on a multinational basis.

While this meeting was in progress, the International Chemical Workers Union (ICWU) was on strike against four plants of Lever Brothers in the United States after the employees rejected a company offer. This strike began on April 9 and lasted until July 3. The Oil, Chemical and Atomic Workers (OCAW) accepted the same offer at the single plant where it represents Lever Brothers employees, and its members kept working all during the ICWU strike. The OCAW changed its international affiliation in 1976 from the defunct International Federation of Petroleum and Chemical Workers to the ICEF. Nevertheless, an ICEF circular letter was issued criticizing the policies of Lever Brothers and requesting a boycott of the American company's products, most of which are either not produced outside the United States or are known by different brand names in different countries.[24] The ICWU also asked for a boycott in the United States. No noticeable effect resulted either from the ICEF's or from the ICWU's requests. The strike ended with terms so similar to those accepted by the OCAW without a strike that no renegotiation of the latter's agreement was necessary. OCAW disaffiliated from the ICEF in 1980.

1977 World Council Meeting

The IUF/ICEF World Council met in London on July 11, 1977, where it concerned itself primarily with the fate of meat plants that had become marginal in the Netherlands.[25] Unilever had previously submitted proposals to Dutch unions and works councils proposing a reduction in the number of employees and new investment. Attempts of the Dutch unions to obtain support from the British or German unions were met with suggestions from these groups that they negotiate with Unilever under Netherlandic law and institutions. After the world council meeting, the Dutch unions proposed, and Unilever's Dutch Meat Group agreed to, an investigation of the matter by a committee of outside independent experts. The report of the experts, known as the "Janssen Committee," upheld the company's basic contention that two plants were uneconomic and had to be closed.

South Africa

By late 1977, numerous IUF allegations concerning Unilever had failed to produce any meetings with the company. Obviously, if the IUF was to alter Unilever's posture, it needed to discover and to capitalize on a bigger issue. This, the IUF came to believe, was the union-race issue in the Republic of South Africa.

In late 1977, the IUF held an African regional meeting and established an African office. Following this, the Swedish central union federations' (LO and TCO) international committee provided the IUF with funding of 816,000 Swiss francs (about $400,000) per year for six years (1978-84) to develop an "ongoing education program . . . intended for IUF-affiliated unions in Africa, Asia, and Latin America." The funds were provided via the Swedish hotel and restaurant union, Hotell-och Restauranganställdas Förbund, an IUF affiliate.[26]

The IUF has long concentrated a lot of attention on Africa, with special reference to multinationals that operate in South Africa. The 1977 IUF/ICEF World Council Meeting passed resolutions regarding Unilever's alleged failure to recognize black workers' unions in South Africa, although Unilever had publicly expressed a willingness to do so if any such union could evidence the support of the employees involved.[27]

The Swedish unions and the IUF continued their attack on Unilever. On May 6, 1978, a Swedish daily paper, *Aftonbladt,* which is owned by the LO, the Swedish federation of blue-collar workers, stated that the Swedish food workers' union was preparing to challenge Unilever in Sweden over its investments and, specifically, that sit-in demonstrations would occur. Three days earlier, a Netherlands radio commentator, interviewing a person in Sweden, indicated that sympathy strikes would occur in four Swedish Unilever plants.

The journal of the Swedish food workers' union, issued April 25, 1978, contained a cover cartoon and a lead article castigating Unilever for not recognizing the black union at the plant in Boksburg, South Africa; it further urged the employees of Unilever plants to engage in stoppages to protest, stating, "We do not want Sweden to accommodate within its boundaries a company practicing racial discrimination of the worst kind."[28]

Financed by the Swedish unions and fed by a steady stream of propaganda by the IUF to affiliates, the campaign about South Africa against Unilever seemed to generate a sufficient following by the fall of 1978 for the IUF to announce its "Unilever South Africa Action Week" from October 23 to 28, 1978. The IUF clearly hoped that there would be major stoppages and demonstrations throughout Europe and proclaimed beforehand that it was assured of widespread national union support, particularly in Europe. The results, as summarized below, fell far short of these expectations.[29]

1. The Federation of Dutch Trade Unions (FNV) organized a "training meeting," permissible under its collective agreement. About sixty Unilever employee representatives attended the meeting. Various works council meetings were held, and Unilever management took steps to correct false statements published in an FNV pamphlet that was based on IUF distortions. Government ministers in the Dutch Parliament were twice asked about Unilever's policies in South Africa and responded factually.

2. In Germany, the Gewerkschaft Nahrung-Genuss-Gaststätten (NGG) distributed a pamphlet, again based upon IUF-supplied misinformation, and the general secretary of the black union involved addressed the German Unilever Works Council. No overt action occurred, and no notices of the "action week" appeared in the press.

3. In France, the Confédération Française Démocratique du Travail left the initiative to its food and chemical affiliates. They sent a common "open letter" to the management of Unilever-France, which was reported on a back page of the CFDT journal.[30] No stoppages and little or no publicity occurred.

4. There were no reported activities in United Kingdom factories, although the IUF had previously announced that the Trades Union Congress was supporting its activities.[31] In

May 1979, IUF General Secretary Dan Gallin made an unprecedented public attack on three British unions for their failure to support the IUF's action week. Speaking at the annual conference of the General and Municipal Workers' Union (GMWU), he stated that the IUF received "absolutely no support" from the GMWU, the Transport and General Workers' Union, or the United Shop, Distributive and Allied Workers' Union, but rather that these unions had been satisfied by a "meaningless" company statement.[32] British union officials defended their position as consistent with the facts.

5. In Italy, there were some meetings but apparently no work stoppages.

6. Two-hour stoppages occurred among hourly workers and supervisors in two Swedish plants. Salaried employees did not take part in the demonstration.

7. In Denmark, a two-hour stoppage by each of two shifts occurred in one plant, and site-meetings were held in two others. Anti-Unilever propaganda was almost as strong in Denmark as in Sweden.

8. On October 25, a two-hour stoppage occurred in one plant in Finland, a slowdown in another, and a token stoppage of fifteen minutes in a third.

9. The IUF's propaganda generated letters and inquiries to Unilever in many other countries, but no stoppages.

10. From the North American continent, one American and one Canadian union wrote Unilever. No publicity seems to have been generated in the press.

Thus, except for letters from various unions to Unilever's general and various country headquarters, plus the short stoppages in the three Scandinavian countries, the so-called action week seems to have precipitated little action and achieved no significant objective, although it gained the IUF considerable publicity as an active international secretariat.

The IUF and Unilever in the Future

Unilever is proud of its good employee relations in plants around the world. Because these employee relations are based upon careful policies that are clearly communicated to national and local managers, Unilever has earned a good reputation for fair dealings with employees and unions. The attempts of the IUF and some Scandinavian unions to sully that reputation by charging unfair practices at Unilever's Republic of South Africa plants proved unconvincing to the IUF's affiliated unions in nearly all countries because it ran counter to the experience of the officials and members of these unions.

Although Unilever management would no doubt be prompt to act in any matter that might damage its reputation as a good employer, it regards industrial relations problems as ones that should be settled at local or national levels. Unilever has thus not shown any disposition to meet with multinational union groups under the auspices either of an international trade union secretariat or of any other international union organization or committee. It is probable that the national unions in most countries agree with this policy. In December 1980, the IUF convened a meeting in Geneva of unions representing Unilever employees from around the world. Since only twenty-five representatives came, the turnout must have been disappointing to the IUF bureaucracy. The delegates, rather surprisingly, declined to urge a meeting with top Unilever management. Instead, the general resolution adopted at the meeting included the following paragraph:

> At present, the question of meetings between international Unilever management and the IUF does not seem essential. However, successful coordination of regional activities and of recognition campaigns will certainly serve to increase the representativeness of the Unilever Council as well as its strength in the face of national and international management.[33]

The delegates to this IUF Unilever Council of Food Workers' Unions did, however, also decide to establish a permanent council. This not only formalized the fact that the earlier organized IUF/ICEF World Council, long moribund, was in fact buried, but also indicated that the IUF would promote a more active relationship among Unilever union-represented employees. Of particular interest was a resolution endorsing a new black union organizing campaign at the Unilever Boksburg, South Africa plant. Clearly the IUF's future activities in regard to Unilever will continue to stress events in the Republic of South Africa.

IUF and Coca-Cola

Coca-Cola has the largest share of beverage markets in the Western world, manufacturing and distributing not only its famous cola drink but also other carbonated and fruit juice drinks, wines, and foods. In 1979, Coca-Cola had sales of $4.961 billion and 38,635 employees.[34]

The small number of Coca-Cola employees relative to sales results from the company's method of doing business. Coca-Cola bottlers are, for the most part, independent businessmen who operate franchises, buy syrup from the company, do their own bottling, and handle their own labor relations. Coca-Cola management historically takes the position that it has no role in a franchised bottler's employee relations policies and could not interfere with such policies, even if it disagrees with those policies. Coca-Cola management had made it clear to the authors that it had nothing to fear from multinational unions because it was thus insulated from responsibility for labor relations policies.[35] As the Guatemala developments discussed below illustrate, this proved to be a naive contention.

The Rome Dispute

The IUF's first attempt to pressure the Coca-Cola Company occurred in 1971. At that time, the IUF claimed a major victory in allegedly forcing the company to reopen a plant in Rome, a story that the company has emphatically denied.

According to the IUF, the 336 workers at the ARIB bottling plant in Rome struck on October 4, 1971, to protest a plant closure. Subsequently, a meeting was held in Rome by representatives of all Italian labor federations (the Confederazione Generale Italiana del Lavoro, Confederazione Italiana Sindacati Lavoratori, and Unione Italiana del Lavoro), which allegedly agreed not to permit other Coca-Cola plants in Italy to send their products to Rome.

According to the IUF account, the company at first refused to discuss the matter since the plant was closed. Workers occupied the plant until March 1972, when the police forced them out; then, 120 strikers continued to camp on the street around the plant. Under the auspices of the prime minister, an agreement was signed in June 1972 whereby 200 former employees were rehired and the plant "would continue in operation."[36]

The IUF version of this story was summarized in the *New York Times*.[37] It was later discussed by the then vice president of Coca-Cola Europe in answer to a letter from one of the authors:

> As I was involved for some time in the liquidation of ARIB, S.p.A. in Rome, I feel that from the very beginning there has been no failure on our part to communicate to all concerned the facts and figures relevant to the case. The Food Workers' Federation's claim which you quote in your letter represents the very subjective view of that Federation's Secretary, but the facts in which you are interested are, to the best of my knowledge, the following:
>
> (a) After the liquidation of ARIB S.p.A. there has been no direct negotiation between Management and Unions; not that this was feared or considered undesirable but, simply, it was felt that the Liquidator who has been appointed in accordance with local laws was solely qualified to implement the liquidation procedures.

   (b)   When, at a certain point in time, the local authorities offered to intervene, we worked in close contact with them and, as far as we know, they, in turn, did the same with the local Unions.

   (c)   As a result of this co-operation with local authorities we were able to arrive at what we consider a satisfactory solution, i.e.

      (i)   ARIB's liquidation proceedings will be completed and there is no question of re-opening ARIB S.p.A.

      (ii)   A new Bottler will be appointed in the Rome territory as soon as certain—rather complex—local conditions are met. This will be a new bottling operation which is expected to function on a streamlined, economically viable basis.[38]

After this letter was received, we verified that this bottling plant was closed and liquidated, and then a new franchise was granted. The new plant is operating successfully. One reason is that truck operations were subcontracted so that the bottler has very few employees.[39]

Since the Rome incident, the IUF has sent numerous communications to Coca-Cola headquarters involving labor problems in Spain, Kenya, other locations, and particularly in Guatemala. The company until recently did not respond to these communications because of its position that its bottlers are independent and that, therefore, the Coca-Cola Company had no jurisdiction in labor matters. The company does, however, occasionally buy out a franchise that is having difficulty. That is what happened in Rome, but after the plant was closed down there, a new franchise was awarded, and an independent bottler is now in operation, as noted.[40] The pressures generated by the IUF in the Guatemala dispute, however, led to the effective repudiation of Coca-Cola's "we are not involved" stance, and, by reason of its lack of an effective policy, to a deeper involvement with an international trade union secretariat than it might find to be wise in the long run.

The Guatemalan Situation

Guatemala is the wealthiest, strongest, and most populous nation in Central America. It is, however, ruled by a ruthless, right-wing dictator and under seige by even more ruthless communist-Cuban-directed and -supplied revolutionaries who operate out of sparsely populated, neighboring Nicaragua, Mexico, and Honduras, and out of the jungles in Guatemala. The result is a record of alarming violence. And, as often seems the case, liberals and leftists in the West condemn moral and physical atrocities of the right but seem to look away from the at least equally horrible ones of the left.[41]

Amid this violence, a number of Guatemalan labor union officials have been gunned down. Among these were union officials representing, or attempting or purporting to represent, employees of Embotelladora Guatemalteca, the Coca-Cola franchise bottler in Guatemala City. As early as 1976, the IUF saw a role for itself in the situation. The IUF's propaganda grew strident when Manuel Lopez Balán, former general secretary of the bottling employees' union, was murdered, the third in that position to die in eighteen months. (It is noteworthy that the company personnel director was wounded and his chauffeur killed in an assassination attempt. Also murdered was the president of an employers' association.) Much of the IUF criticism was directed against John Trotter, a Texas lawyer who ran the franchise on behalf of a wealthy widow, but the Coca-Cola Company was also severly castigated.[42]

IUF Actions and Company Reactions

The IUF obviously saw the Coca-Cola Guatemalan situation not only as a proper international trade union secretariat mission but also as a significant method of advancing its profile and status. It was able to gain support from church and liberal groups, demanding that Coca-Cola buy the franchise. The National Council of Churches (Protestant), through its Interfaith Center on Corporate Responsibility, took up the cudgels with the IUF and joined a boycott attempt, as did various other religious organizations. Amnesty International also issued a series of highly critical reports, which the IUF circulated in four countries in which boycotts are quite feasible—Sweden, Finland, Australia, and New Zealand.[43] Tremendous publicity was generated for the IUF, but little boycott impact was made except in Sweden.

In Sweden, a four-day boycott occurred in May just prior to the nationwide strike there. No Coca-Cola strike occurred. Unions of food, beverage, and restaurant workers announced that they would not sell, serve, or drink Coca-Cola during the four-day period. Some food vendors and restaurants cooperated, and unions halted Coca-Cola production at Pripps Brewery, the company's licensee there. The managing director of the company's Swedish subsidiary was quoted by the leading American business weekly to have said that "there definitely was a decline in sales" during the boycott period.[44] Although some of the impact in Sweden was lost because it occurred during the unrelated general strike there, the IUF did gain considerable publicity.

In Finland, a much more limited boycott occurred with some, but much less, effect. In New Zealand and Australia, no strikes or boycotts occurred. In New Zealand, there was some agitation by a union at a bottling plant for a one-day demonstration strike, but the workers voted against any stoppage. In New South Wales, Australia, the major union in the bottling facilities passed a resolution calling on Coca-Cola to do something about the Guatemala situation and threatening a 24-hour stoppage if it did not, but no action resulted. In Victoria, Australia, a union official apparently became emotionally involved in the situation and tried to precipitate a stoppage, but in this Australian state also, no overt action occurred. Australian unions did decide not to send any Coca-Cola syrup to Guatemala, which they do not do in any case, but such actions do gain a great deal of publicity. The IUF has also claimed actions in Spain and Mexico, of which we found no record, and the Coca-Cola Company and many of its bottlers received numerous communications from unions around the world, most of which followed the same format and were obviously designed by the IUF.[45]

Buffeted by this publicity, the Coca-Cola Company announced that it would like to arrange for the sale of the Guatemalan franchise to a new concern. The publicity whipped up by the IUF made this difficult, according to the company, but the owners, under pressure, also agreed to sell. Then, at its annual meeting, the then Coca-Cola chairman, J. Paul Austin, announced that the Guatemalan franchise would be sold to a group of mostly Guatemalan investors headed by John Kirby, whom Austin described as "a successful Coca-Cola bottler in Mexico," and one who had "an excellent background of good labor relations."[46] Three months prior to its annual meeting, top company officials had received an IUF delegation, including General Secretary Dan Gallin, and assured the IUF leaders that it was "actively encouraging" the sale of the Guatemalan facility.[47]

The Terms of the Sale

Once the decision was made to force the sale of the franchise, Coca-Cola executives seemed literally to clear their actions with the IUF. The company did the following:

1. It kept the IUF fully informed about the progress of negotiations.[48]
2. The proposed new owner, John I. Kirby, met in New York with the IUF North American representative, Laurent C. Enckell, and U.S. and Guatemalan union officials, and discussed the situation. The head of the union at Kirby's Mexican operation also discussed the Guatemalan situation with him.[49]

3. Kirby sent a letter to Harold T. Circuit, senior vice-president, North Latin American Division, Coca-Cola Export Company, in which he stated, among other things, that his group "acknowledge(s) the right of workers to be associated with a union" and "would expect the workers to form a union associated with U.I.T.A. (I.U.F.)." Gallin and Enckell were marked for copies.[50]

4. Kirby proposed to hire the existing work force on a selective basis, an action which the IUF protested.[51] While negotiations to acquire the franchise continued, so did murders. Another local union official and several members of a rival union were the victims. At this point Kirby withdrew, and the company began a new search for a bottler. Meanwhile, stimulated by the IUF, unions around the world continued to send letters and to make representations about the situation to bottling affiliates of Coca-Cola, as well as to the company's headquarters and offices.[52]

5. A meeting occurred on July 8, 1980, in Geneva, between representatives of the IUF and the Coca-Cola Company in which the company presented its plans for the purchase and operation of the plant by a newly formed consortium known as the Administración e Inversiones de Centro America S.A. On July 14, Gallin set forth his understandings of the particulars of the new operation in a telex to the company. It provided that Coca-Cola would provide the financing, take an equity of 35 percent, appoint a new management team, maintain management control for five years, and guarantee union rights exclusively to the union affiliated with the IUF. (There had been a rival union.)

 Circuit replied by telex to Gallin on August 22, confirming that Gallin's terms were correct except that Coca-Cola would not have any equity in the new company.[53] The Coca-Cola Company further agreed to replace all management personnel associated with the previous owner, to replace security forces, to renegotiate the union agreement on improved terms, to ask the authorities to prevent violence from undermining the agreement, and to give favorable consideration to establishing a fund for the benefit of children of murdered union workers. Twenty-three previously discharged employees were reinstated prior to the sale of the franchise.[54]

6. Ownership of the Guatemalan franchise passed to the new consortium on September 5, 1980. Negotiations for a new labor agreement continued for some time thereafter. Although the

IUF is not directly involved in the negotiations, a company spokesman termed Gallin "helpful" by strongly counseling local union officials to cease agitation and obstruction and to cooperate with the new management.[55] The IUF announced the end of the boycotts as the new management was taking control.[56]

Concluding Remarks

Coca-Cola management seemed both surprised by and unprepared for the controversy in which it became embroiled as a result of the violence in Guatemala and the publicity campaign whipped up by the IUF. At first, management took the position that it was both uninvolved and powerless in a matter affecting one of its franchised bottlers. Then, when the publicity commenced to involve it very much, it changed tactics completely, forced a sale of the franchise, and took over the franchise management. In so doing, it bargained and dealt with the IUF, which had no authority other than that which it assumed for itself.

The Coca-Cola spokesmen deny that the company negotiated with the IUF. According to their version, Coca-Cola management merely kept the IUF informed just as they did religious and other groups that inserted themselves into the Guatemalan situation.[57] The record indicates otherwise. Their agreement with the IUF general secretary and North American representative of the terms under which they would operate appears quite clearly to have gone beyond information exchange and to have involved a form of negotiations. Indeed, it would appear that Coca-Cola's actions legitimized the IUF both as a representative of the Guatemalan bottling plant employees and as an indicator of world opinion. Certainly the IUF general secretary believes this to be the case. He was quoted as saying, "If this isn't a negotiating situation, I don't know what is. Our objectives were exactly what we got."[58] The IUF was thus awarded a status that it had not achieved heretofore and is not likely to achieve soon again unless it becomes embroiled with another company that does not have either clearly considered and well-developed policies or personnel for handling such a difficult situation.

It is thus interesting to contrast the Coca-Cola actions with those of Unilever, which as described herein was the target of a similar IUF campaign over alleged unfair treatment of a black South African union. Unilever refused to meet with the IUF or to consider it as a representative of employees in South Africa or elsewhere. Rather, its management patiently explained to unions representing its employees around the world the facts of the case. The IUF activity cost Unilever a lot of management time and a few short stoppages in plants in three Scandinavian countries. It also generated a lot of publicity, but the IUF neither achieved recognition nor effectuated any change in Unilever's well-considered policies. Perhaps if Coca-Cola had put its Guatemalan franchise in order in the first place instead of hiding behind the franchise relationship and had had policies and personnel to handle such situations beforehand, it could have avoided giving the IUF such a major political victory.

What Coca-Cola's relationship to the IUF will be in the future remains to be determined. Apparently concerned, possibly by other companies which no doubt questioned Coca-Cola's IUF relationship, the company allegedly asked Gallin to confirm in writing that the actions in the Guatemala matter would not be a precedent. On September 12, 1980, Gallin wrote the company emphasizing that the IUF does not intervene in a typical labor dispute and certainly does not attempt to substitute for unions representing employees. The Gallin letter, however, made no statement that the Guatemalan action was not a precedent. Rather, he stated that it demonstrated the IUF's capacity to organize a solidarity action when called upon to do so. He concluded that the IUF and the Coca-Cola Company had now established a good relationship based on fairness and common sense, and that he was pleased that they had agreed to maintain contact when serious confrontation was threatened so such confrontation could be avoided before it could develop further.

It remains to be seen whether the Coca-Cola Company can develop a policy similar to that of Unilever. This means developing programs to counter trouble before it becomes a national or international problem. It also requires effective staff personnel skilled in international labor matters to monitor policies and programs and their operations, and counsel operating personnel and franchise owners about them. Effective policies of this nature preclude a swing to extremes, for example, from a denial of responsibility to taking action in concert with an international trade union secretariat. If after such a reorganization, Coca-Cola desires to extricate itself from its new relationship with the IUF, it may then be equipped to withstand the barrage of critical publicity the IUF would likely attempt to unleash.

NOTES

1. For a detailed survey of the record to date, see Herbert R. Northrup and Richard L. Rowan, *Multinational Collective Bargaining Attempts,* Multinational Industrial Relations Series, No. 6 (Philadelphia: Industrial Research Unit, The Wharton School, University of Pennsylvania, 1979).

2. For a description of these union coordinating and information bodies, to which are affiliated unions in the same industry from various countries, see *ibid.*, Chapter II; and Richard L. Rowan, Herbert R. Northrup, and Rae Ann O'Brien, *Multinational Union Organizations in the Manufacturing Industries*, Multinational Industrial Relations Series No. 7a (Philadelphia: Industrial Research Unit, The Wharton School, University of Pennsylvania, 1980).

3. There is a fundamental dispute as to whether these guidelines require multinational management-union consultations. Unions are pressing the affirmative, but have not generally been supported in such interpretation.

4. A proposed European social directive, called the "Vredeling Initiative" after its author, a former EC official, which is now under consideration, would seemingly require some such contacts.

5. For an analysis of the history, organizational structure, membership, finances, and activities of the IUF, see Rowan, Northrup, and O'Brien, *Multinational Union Organizations,* Chapter IV.

6. *Ibid.,* p. 34.

7. *Fortune,* Vol. 102 (August 11, 1980), pp. 190, 204.

8. Letter announcing joint IUF/ICEF Unilever Council meeting, February 23, 1973, p. 1.

9. The various reports issued to the delegates are on file in the Industrial Research Unit library.

10. Summary of meeting and minutes in Industrial Research Unit (IRU) library.

11. Copy of IUF telgram in IRU library; and interview in London, September 3, 1973.

12. Circular letter and company communications in IRU library.

13. *Industrial Relations-Europe Newsletter,* Vol. II, No. 17 (April 1974), p. 7.

14. *Ibid.,* Vol. II, No. 18 (May 1974), p. 1.

15. Since this date, the Socialist NVV and the Catholic NKV have merged to form the Federation of Dutch Unions (FNV).

16. Translation from *De Tijd,* March 28, 1974.

17. This account is based on several interviews in London, Brussels, and the Netherlands with persons who desire to remain anonymous. In fact, an examination of the product mix and brand names of Lever Brothers, U.S.A., and Unilever, NV, will show different products, brand names, etc.

18. Despite the complete lack of evidence that the ICEF was involved in this situation, the *Wall Street Journal* reported that action by Levinson was crucial. See Richard F. Janssen, "Global Clout: How One Man Helps Unions Match Wits with Multinationals," *Wall Street Journal,* July 17, 1974, p. 1. For a complete analysis of Levinson's unsupportable claims, see Northrup and Rowan, *Multinational Union Organizations* Chapters VI-XI.

19. *IUF News Bulletin,* Vol. 45, No. 11 (1975), p. 3.

20. Interviews with various sources. See also *IUF 18th Congress,* Item IX(a), p. 16.

21. Copies of correspondence in IRU library.

22. *IUF 18th Congress,* Item IX(a), p. 16.

23. Association of Scientific, Technical and Managerial Staffs, "A Charter for Unilever Staff" (London, [March 1976?]). See also "ASTMS in Dutch Union Link,"

Financial Times, March 3, 1976, p. 12. A foreword in the booklet from Industriebond-NVV states that the latter is "the main union representing staff in Unilever Holland" and has "recognition for white collar workers in most plants and subsidiaries." This is simply not correct.

24. ICEF Circular Letter No. 60/76, May 7, 1976, sent to all ICEF affiliates and members of the joint council.

25. Pauline Clark, "European unions concerned over Unilever plans for Britain," *Financial Times,* July 13, 1977, p. 23; "Unilever-Wereldraad wil internationaal overleg met concern," *Financieel Dagblaad,* July 13, 1977.

26. International Union of Food and Allied Workers' Associations, *Meeting of the IUF Executive Committee* (Geneva, 1978), Item 3(e).

27. "Black Unions Score Increasing Gains in South Africa," *Wall Street Journal,* August 29, 1977, p. 6.

28. Mål och medel, April 25, 1978, p. 1. All documents in IRU library.

29. The Industrial Research Unit has a large file of IUF materials from this event and has interviewed company personnel and examined company releases. This summary is based on these documents, plus materials in the public press.

30. *Syndicalisme* (Confédération Française Démocratique du Travail), October 19, 1978, p. 17.

31. In a circular letter dated September 23, 1978, the IUF general secretary's office stated: "The support of the Trades Union Congress in the United Kingdom and the Dutch Workers' Federation (FNV) in the Netherlands—the two countries where Unilever has its headquarters—has been assured for the campaign."

32. Nick Garnett, "European official censures UK unions," *Financial Times,* May 23, 1979, p. 12.

33. Circular Letter, signed by Dan Gallin, general secretary, December 17, 1980, attacking the resolution and program adopted by the Unilever Council of Food Workers' Unions.

34. *Fortune,* Vol. 101 (May 5, 1980), pp. 277-78.

35. Interview with Coca-Cola officials, Atlanta, February 15, 1978.

36. See International Union of Food and Allied Workers' Associations, *17th Congress, Documents of the Secretariat* (Geneva, 1973), Item V(8), pp. 15-16. (Hereafter cited as *IUF 17th Congress.*)

37. Clyde H. Farnsworth, "Big Business Spurs Labor Toward a World Role," *New York Times,* December 16, 1972, pp. 53-54.

38. Letter from S. S. Dolfi, formerly vice-president, Coca-Cola Europe, to the authors, February 23, 1973.

39. S. S. Dolfi, interview in Atlanta, February 15, 1978. Dolfi was then executive assistant to the president.

40. Charles Hodgson, general counsel, Coca-Cola Export Company, telephone interview, December 12, 1975.

41. An analysis of the Guatemala problem will be included in a forthcoming Wharton Industrial Research Unit study covering "The Political, Economic, and Labor Climate in the Central American Republics."

42. See *IUF News Bulletin,* Vol. 46, No. 2 (1976), p. 6; Vol. 47, No. 1 (1977), p. 3; Vol 47, No. 4 (1977), p. 3; Vol 47, No. 6-9 (1977), pp. 3-4; Vol. 47, No. 10-12 (1977), p.

10; Vol. 48, No. 6-7 (1978), pp. 5, 6-7; and Vol 48, No. 8-9 (1978), p. 10. In addition, Dan Gallin, IUF general secretary, authored numerous circular letters and press releases in regard to this situation, which are in the Wharton Industrial Research Unit library files.

43. See *IUF News Bulletin*, Vol. 49, No. 11-12 (1979), p. 4; and Alan Riding, "Strike in Guatemala Brings a Drive Against Coca-Cola," *New York Times*, June 6, 1980, p. A2.

44. "Did Coca-Cola 'negotiate' with international labor?" *Business Week*, November 24, 1980, p. 133.

45. This information is based upon facts developed by correspondents in the countries involved, plus numerous IUF communications and a series of telephone interviews with officials of the Coca-Cola Company.

46. John Juey, "Coca-Cola at Unusual Annual Meeting Reports 8.1% Profit Rise for 1st Quarter," *Wall Street Journal*, May 6, 1980, p. 17.

47. *IUF News Bulletin*, No. 1-2 (1980), p. 4. Besides Gallin, the IUF delegation included U.S. and Guatemalan unionists and Laurent Enckell, North American IUF representative. In a letter to one of the authors, April 15, 1980, Donald R. Greene, Corporation Coordinator, External Affairs Division, Coca-Cola, affirmed that this meeting occurred.

48. IUF Circular Letter, May 12, 1980, signed by Dan Gallin.

49. IUF Circular Letter of U.S. and Canada Affiliates, signed by Laurent C. Enckell.

50. A copy of Kirby's letter to Circuit, showing Gallin and Enckell marked for copies, is attached to the Enckell circular letter, noted in the previous citation. "UITA" is the Spanish acronym for IUF.

51. Gallin's protest to Kirby in a teletype is also attached to the above-noted Enckell circular letter.

52. See IUF Circular Letter, May 31, 1980, signed by Dan Gallin, for particulars of violence and of unions' letters and representations. See also circular letters of June 10, 24, and 30, and July 4, 1980, for further details of both.

53. IUF Circular Letters, July 9 and 28, and August 28, 1980, signed by Dan Gallin, and telephone interview, Coca-Cola Company, November 3, 1980. At the July 8 meeting requested by the company, Sigvard Hystrom, IUF president, and Dan Gallin represented the IUF; Harold T. Circuit and Jarcen Díaz, financial assistant to the executive vice-president, represented the company.

corrections for page 165

54. IUF Circular Letter, July 28, 1980; telephone interview, Coca-Cola Company, November 3, 1980.

55. Telephone interview, November 3, 1980.

56. *IUF News Bulletin*, Vol. 50, No. 9 (1980), p. 2.

57. Telephone interview, November 3, 1980.

58. "Did Coca-Cola 'negotiate' with international labor?" p. 133.

165 - 89

[1981]

The Entertainment Industry: Inroads in Multinational Collective Bargaining *

6358
4420
8321
selected
countries

Philip A. Miscimarra[†]

Although questions concerning multinational collective bargaining have produced considerable confusion for industrial relations scholars over the last several years, there is now a general consensus that actual occurrences have been infrequent, highly irregular, and limited in scope. There have been a few undocumented union claims of multinational bargaining success—findings which have been reiterated without further verification in a number of academic articles[1]—but extensive work by the Wharton School's Industrial Research Unit conclusively demonstrates that real progress in this controversial area has been limited to exchanges of information between some multinational corporations and multinational labor organizations, a few cases of multinational union-management consultation, and negotiations between one international trade secretariat (ITS), the International Transport Workers' Federation (ITF), and a variety of individual shipping companies and associations.[2]

The entertainment industry has proven to be a single significant exception to this pattern of limited success in multinational collective bargaining. Two labor federations in particular, the International Federation of Actors (FIA) and the International Federation of Musicians (FIM), have exhibited a remarkable capacity for conducting a high level of professional, ideologically neutral activity while remaining virtually anonymous outside their industry.[3] This article describes in detail the progress to date made by a number of labor and management organizations in entertainment, the outlook for future multinational collective bargaining activity in the industry, and the obstacles that still have to be surmounted before unqualified success in multinational entertainment union activity can be proclaimed.

---

* Reproduced from *British Journal of Industrial Relations*, Vol. XIX, No. 1 (March 1981).

† Philip A. Miscimarra is a Research Assistant, Multinational and Legal, Industrial Research Unit, The Wharton School, University of Pennsylvania, Philadelphia.

The Structure of Multinational Union Activity in Entertainment

International union activity in entertainment is not a recent phenomenon, for as early as 1926, the now-defunct International Musicians' Union pressured the International Labor Organization (ILO) for a survey of employment conditions in the industry The current structure of multinational labor relations in the arts had its origins in 1948, however, with the founding of the International Federation of Musicians (FIM). Other labor groups that have since become active in the industry include the International Federation of Actors (FIA), the International Federation of Unions of Audio-Visual Workers (FISTAV), and the International Secretariat of Entertainment Trade Unions (ISETU).

The FIM's founding in 1948 came about at an International Conference of Musicians convened by the Swiss Musicians' Union for the purpose of discussing the growing dangers of mechanical music and other forms of technological change in the industry. In the years since its inception, the FIM has cooperated extensively with the FIA in developing working relationships with the ILO, the United Nations Educational, Scientific and Cultural Organization (UNESCO), the International Union for the Protection of Literary and Artistic Works (Berne Union), and the Intergovernmental Committee of the International Convention for the Protection of Performers, Producers of Phonograms and Broadcasting Organizations (Rome Convention). More importantly, the FIM and FIA, collectively referred to as the International Federations of Performers (FFF), have negotiated a number of collective agreements with three employers' organizations—the International Federation of Producers of Phonograms and Videograms (IFPI), the European Broadcasting Union (EBU), and the International Radio and Television Organization (OIRT). (These organizations and their agreements with the FFF are described in the sections below.) As of April 1980, the FIM had thirty-four unions representing 112,771 musicians in thirty-two countries.[5]

The FIA was founded at the Second Congress of European Actors' Organizations held in London from June 16 to 18, 1952. Its close relationship with the FIM stemmed from an International Conference on Television held in April 1954 that was jointly sponsored by the FIA, the FIM, and a third performers' organization, the International Federation of Variety Artists (FIAV) that had also been founded in 1952.[6] In 1974, after several years of only limited activity, the FIAV was fully incorporated into the FIA. At the time of its most recent congress held in Budapest, Hungary, during September 1979, the

FIA represented over 142,768 workers through forty-eight unions in thirty-eight countries.[7]

Both the FIM and FIA have expressed a strong commitment to political neutrality, purporting to represent member unions on a strictly professional level, irrespective of national ideological differences. For this reason, the federations have recruited affiliates from democratic and nondemocratic countries, and they have resisted any activities that do not relate to the professional or legal interests of performers. The FFF federations (and FISTAV) are not officially related to the International Confederation of Free Trade Unions (ICFTU), the communist World Federation of Trade Unions (WFTU), the World Confederation of Labour (WCL), or any other central body.

FISTAV is the youngest multinational labor organization in entertainment, having had its founding congress in London during 1974. Although FISTAV, as a representative of nonperformers in the entertainment industry (audio-visual workers and other technical personnel), is not a formal partner in the FFF, the federation still cooperates to a great degree with the FIM and the FIA on a number of issues. All three organizations routinely participate in each other's congresses, and they have established a Joint Committee for European Affairs in London in order to facilitate communication with the Commission of the European Community (EC). FISTAV's impact to date in the industry has been modest—it is not a party to any of the collective agreements negotiated by the FFF. Its increasing interest in cooperating with the FIM and FIA, however, may ultimately lead to concerted action that would benefit all three groups. FISTAV is currently reported to represent over 200,000 workers via thirty affiliated organizations (including "associate members") in at least nineteen countries.[8]

The fourth, and final, entertainment labor organization is the International Secretariat of Entertainment Trade Unions (ISETU), an international trade secretariat associated with the ICFTU. The ISETU was founded in 1965 at a congress attended by thirty-seven unions representing 486,541 entertainment workers (musicians, actors, and technicians) in seventeen countries. From its inception, the ISETU was opposed by the FIM, the FIA, and the FIAV, which had voiced disapproval of prior ICFTU attempts to establish an ITS in entertainment. The ISETU, for its part, avoided official contact with the FFF because of the federations' acceptance of several affiliates from communist countries.[9] Although the ISETU was moderately successful during its early history, a number of financial and administrative difficulties (including the ICFTU's curtailment of funding after 1974) led to a drastic reduction in the secretariat's activities and in the number of dues-paying affiliates.[10] The ISETU attempted unsuccessfully for many years to become a party to the collective agreements negotiated by the FFF and the EBU, and the secretariat's current status in the entertainment industry appears to be extremely limited. Although the ISETU recently held a congress in Brussels from May 20 to 21, 1980 (the first one since 1974) with financial assistance from the ICFTU,[11] the degree of national trade union support that the secretariat will continue to receive in the future is, at best, uncertain.

At the present time, the FIM and the FIA remain the only two entertainment labor organizations actively engaging in collective bargaining. The FFF's primary concern in this area is technological change within the industry, particularly those advances which make possible the widespread reproduction or transmission of individual performances. The FFF's longstanding policy regarding these developments has been to obtain control over the repeated uses of a performance whenever possible or, alternatively, to obtain remuneration for either the displaced performers or those participating in the exploited performance. The sections below summarize the development, content, and current status of the most significant FFF agreements with a number of employers' organizations in the industry.

FIM-IFPI Agreements

The International Federation of the Phonographic Industry (IFPI) was founded in 1933 to promote and defend the national and international rights of producers of phonograms. In practice this has led to an interest in many legal problems affecting the record industry, especially those connected with copyright. As of 1977, the IFPI represented national groups in twenty-seven countries worldwide and 550 individual companies in sixty-four countries.[12] Soon after the founding of the FIM, the IFPI concluded that the musicians' international federation shared an interest with producers in controlling the use of records in broadcasting. After a number of preliminary points were agreed upon in negotiations on July 10, 1950, and November 4 to 5, 1952, a formal Agreement on the Participation in Broadcasting Revenues was signed on March 11, 1954.

Nature of Agreement on Broadcasting Revenues

The 1954 FIM/IFPI agreement provided that the "FIM or its affiliated associations shall be entitled to receive 25 per cent of the net distributable revenue received by IFPI, its National Groups or members and derived from the broadcasting of its members' records."[13] Five percent of the IFPI payments was to be given to the FIM secretariat, subject to the approval of the national recipient(s). The overall agreement was qualified, however, in four significant ways.

First, the IFPI's financial obligation to pay 25 percent of its broadcasting revenue to musicians applied only to countries of Europe, although "the principle of participation [was] accepted by IFPI as applying to all countries of the world."[14] Second, payments were not to be made in a country unless they were accepted by the country's performing musicians (whether affiliated to the FIM or not) in full discharge of the IFPI's financial liability. Third, implementation was to end in any country where (1) it became legally compulsory to share broadcasting revenue with musicians; (2) national legislation was introduced, enabling musicians to "demand payment in respect of or otherwise exercise control over the broadcasting and public performance of records"; or (3) other private contracts provided musicians with a right to receive payments derived from the broadcasting of records.[15] This provision, designed to prevent the IFPI from being placed in a position of double jeopardy (obliged to pay musicians by both the FIM agreement and national legislation), has caused the FIM agreement to be terminated in every country that has ratified Article 12 of the Rome Convention.[16] Fourth, and finally, the agreement is not binding on IFPI affiliates. Under the IFPI's constitution, affiliated organizations maintain managerial autonomy. The IFPI, therefore, can only issue recommendations to its members. Generally speaking, the nonbinding character of IFPI agreements has not been an obstacle to implementation. The FIM observed in 1963, for example, that "experiences made so far show that the members of IFPI strictly follow the recommendations of their international organization.[17]

Agreement in Practice

The early history of the FIM-IFPI agreement demonstrated that the agreement's nonbinding recommendations were made in good faith. By the spring of 1956 over 800,000 Swiss francs (equivalent at the time to about U.S. $200,000) had been issued to musicians' unions in Germany, Austria, Norway, and Switzerland.[18] The agreement could not be implemented in Italy, the Netherlands, or Ireland, however, and there were also obstacles to its implementation in

France.[19] During 1957, the agreement was terminated in Germany and Norway because of changes in domestic law. A separate agreement had been reached, however, regarding the distribution of IFPI revenue derived from the broadcast of commercial recordings in South Africa. By mid-1962, the 1954 agreement was operative in Austria, Ireland, Italy, the Netherlands, and Switzerland, and the total amount of IFPI payments (since 1954) had exceeded two million Swiss francs.[20]

Limiting the Use of Records

In late 1960, the FIM entered into negotiations with the IFPI in an attempt to limit the secondary use of recordings. By March 1963, five "FIM/IFPI-Principles" were agreed upon which condemned all forms of clandestine recording and discouraged several types of secondary use.[21] Again, these principles only took the form of recommendations to IFPI organizations, but, as in the case of the 1954 agreement, implementation did not pose a problem. Since May 1973, a sixth principle has been agreed upon which asserts that "existing phonograms (recordings made for the purpose of being issued as discs, tapes, cassettes) should not be used for the making of videograms without the permission of the performers who had made the original sound recording."[22]

On January 1, 1977, a Protocol to the 1954 agreement became effective which increased the remuneration payable to performers from 25 to $33^1/_3$ percent of the IFPI's broadcasting revenue.[23] The Protocol also makes the FIA a party to the agreement.[24] Other sections provide that no separate national agreements to implement the 1954 agreement will be made in the future; payments to associations of performers (whether or not affiliated to the FIA or FIM) may not be used for any purposes which are contrary to the IFPI, FIM, or FIA's interests; and in countries where the FIM or the FIA derive revenue from the broadcasting of records and the IFPI does not, the record producers of that country shall be entitled to a $33^1/_3$ percent share of the revenue.

In 1979, Ireland ratified the Rome Convention, thus ending the IFPI agreement in the country. As we have mentioned above, the 1954 agreement automatically ended in every country that ratified the Rome Convention, which provides in part that, if "a phonogram published for commercial purposes . . . is used directly for broadcasting or for any communication to the public, a single equitable remuneration shall be paid by the user to the performers, or to the producers of the phonogram, or to both, subject to domestic law or an agreement between the parties concerned."[25] The FIM retained some influence in the distribution of broadcasting revenue in Rome Convention countries, however, by a 1969 agreement with the IFPI (supplemented during 1978) which still covers the distribution of broadcasting revenue in certain cases.[26]

The FIM/IFPI agreement, as revised by the Protocol, currently operates in Belgium, the Netherlands, and Switzerland, with a special agreement that provides for modified operation in Israel.[27] The FFF and the IFPI have also discussed the possibility of applying the 1954 agreement in Spain. Although one payment in that country was made for the period between May 1, 1977, and June 30, 1978, the agreement's subsequent operation has been complicated by the large number of musicians' unions that have developed under the new democratic Spanish government and by the inability of those unions to agree upon how IFPI payments should be apportioned. Although a joint FFF/IFPI committee met in November 1978 and October 1979 in an attempt to resolve the problems, they were not resolved until July 1980; it is expected that the agreement will soon be fully implemented.[28]

The FFF-EBU Agreements

The European Broadcasting Union (EBU), an employers' organization representing broadcasting companies, was founded in 1950 as the successor to the Union Internationale de Radiodiffusion (International Broadcasting Union). The EBU provides a number of services for its members, including advice regarding copyright legislation, contracts, and technical aspects of broadcasting. As of 1977 the EBU had active members in thirty countries within the European Broadcasting Area (as defined by the International Telecommunications Union) and associate members in at least forty-one other countries.[29] Relations between the FFF and EBU represent the performers' pursuit of many of the same goals described above. There have been several additional issues of FFF concern, however, which are unique to broadcasting. One of the most important has long been the EBU's Eurovision network, which was established in 1954 and which provides for the relay of television programs between European countries.

Boycott and Eurovision Agreement

The principles which became the basis of FFF demands regarding Eurovision were originally formulated at an International Conference on Television, jointly sponsored by the then three performers' organizations, the FIM, the FIA, and the International Federation of Variety Artists (FIAV), which was held in Paris from April 20 to 21, 1954. The participants resolved not to extend any oral or written agreements with television stations after June 15, 1954, if an agreement with the EBU regarding international relays had not been reached.[30] Since FFF representatives did not meet the EBU until October 8 to 9, 1954, the boycott on Eurovision transmissions was implemented.

Subsequent negotiations between the EBU and the FFF were not very fruitful, although the boycott was reported, in early 1956, to be a success: "In eight countries all programmes with the collaboration of performers (musicians, actors and variety artists) that were intended for relay, had to be cancelled."[31] Actually, the boycott appeared to take a toll on both sides. Although a number of EBU transmissions had to be cancelled or altered (at one point, the EBU resorted to television transmissions in which the sound was recorded),[32] FFF representatives were forced to abandon their bargaining objective of limiting the number of Eurovision relays, obtaining only additional remuneration for the individuals whose performances were exploited to a greater extent.

After a total of six two-day meetings between FFF and EBU representatives had been held, a formal "Agreement respecting International Television Relays" (hereafter referred to as the Eurovision Agreement) came into force on February 1, 1957. This agreement provided for the originating broadcasting organizations to make supplementary payments to performers (musicians, actors, choristers, singers, dancers, and variety artists) who participate in Eurovision relays. The agreement did not automatically apply to staff personnel (performers employed by the broadcaster on a long-term basis) nor to international relays which did not utilise the Eurovision network. As in the case of the FIM-IFPI agreement, the Eurovision Agreement was not binding on EBU members but constituted, rather, a recommendation that supplements be paid by broadcasting companies in individual countries.

Implementation of Eurovision Agreement

Although some early problems in applying the Eurovision Agreement led to a meeting of the joint EBU/FFF Committee (provided for under the agreement) in June 1957, television relays by 1959 were reported to be "a well-established cultural factor."[33] By 1966 the Eurovision Agreement's provisions had been incorporated in most European countries into national collective agreements.[34]

In 1967, FFF and EBU representatives negotiated a Supplementary Agreement for a two-year trial period effective January 1, 1968. The basis for this agreement was the performers' desire to eliminate "lump-sum payments" (payments which were not in proportion to the extent of a performance's use). In return for the elimination of both lump-sum payments and the maximum amount of remuneration which had been previously set for relays to broadcasting stations in eight or more countries, the FFF representatives reduced the minimum supplementary payment for a Eurovision relay from 50 percent to 20 percent and agreed to supplements which were "individualized by country" instead of being determined by the number of countries participating in a relay. During the trial period, the FFF noted that the Supplementary Agreement was being applied only to a limited extent, with lump sums still being paid by EBU members in two countries, Italy and the Federal Republic of Germany.[35] As a result, the federations decided to terminate the Supplementary Agreement after December 31, 1970. The EBU, in turn, gave notice that it chose to terminate the original 1957 agreement (which was to replace the Supplementary Agreement) on the same date.

On January 1, 1971, a Revised Eurovision Agreement became effective which retained individual supplements for Eurovision countries but raised the aggregate of all supplements (which would theoretically be applied if every country of Europe participated in a Eurovision relay) from 150 to 192 percent.[36] Supplements for relays that were extended to Eastern European (Intervision) countries were placed at an aggregate of 70 percent. The revised agreement also increased the minimum supplement for a Eurovision relay from 20 to 25 percent; it extended coverage to include directors and choreographers who do not acquire a copyright for which they are remunerated; and, although acknowledging the fundamental principle that EBU organizations were not to pay "lump-sum fees" instead of the recommended supplements, it allowed the existing practices in the Federal Republic of Germany and Italy to continue.

On August 30, 1973, EBU and FFF representatives negotiated a new Eurovision Agreement, which became effective on January 1, 1974. The 1974 agreement, like previous ones, applied to free-lance performers (including directors and choreographers as described above) who are affiliated via their national unions to the FFF. The EBU, however, was to "recommend its members favourably to consider in the light of their national situation, the application of the provisions . . . to performers who are not members of a Union or who are members of a Union not affiliated to one of the Federations."[37] The

1974 agreement again retained supplements for different countries but increased the aggregate (for Eurovision and Intervision countries) from 258 percent to 292 percent of the base fee.[38]

For the last several years, the number of Eurovision broadcasts in which professional performers participated has been steadily declining, undercutting some of the Eurovision Agreement's practical significance. The FIM recently reported, for example, that "in view of the small number of . . . Eurovision broadcasts with professional performers the question of revising the respective supplements [is] no longer a high priority in negotiations with the EBU."[39] The FFF and the EBU, nevertheless, agreed to increase a number of Eurovision country supplements, effective July 1, 1980.[40] The revised supplements per country are presented in Table 1.

TABLE 1

Supplements Provided by the 1974 FFF/EBU Agreement respecting International Television Relays (Eurovision Agreement valid from July 1, 1980)

Country	Supplement (percentage)	Country	Supplement (percentage)
EBU Members in			
Algeria	2-0	Luxembourg	4-0
Austria	5-0	Malta	1-0
Belgium	6-0	Monaco	2-0
Cyprus	1-0	Morocco	2-0
Denmark	5-0	Netherlands	7-0
Finland	4-0	Norway	4-0
France	30-0	Portugal	3-0
Federal Rep. of Germany	40-0	Spain	11-0
Greece	3-0	Sweden	7-0
Iceland	1-0	Switzerland	4-0
Ireland	2-0	Tunisia	1-0
Israel	2-0	Turkey	4-0
Italy	27-5	United Kingdom	40-0
Jordan	2-0	Yugoslavia	6-0
Lebanon	1-0		
Libya	1-0		
Nonmembers of EBU in			
Bulgaria	4-0	Poland	10-0
Czechoslovakia	7-0	Rumania	6-0
East Germany	9-0	USSR	40-0
Hungary	5-0		

Source: FFF/EBU—*Agreement respecting International Television Relays* (Eurovision Agreement valid from July 1, 1980), clauses 13(a) and (b).

The FFF/EBU Eurovision agreement, like the FFF agreement with IFPI, is qualified in a number of ways. It applies only to simultaneous or deferred relays (carrying the "Eurovision" identification) which are offered on a noncommercial (nonprofit) basis by an active or associate EBU member located in the European Broadcasting Area.[41] It may also be terminated after six months' notice either by the FFF or the EBU at the end of any calendar year. These restrictions certainly affect the administration of the Eurovision Agreement in a profound way. They cannot, however, be easily interpreted as evidence that the agreement itself is insignificant, for its twenty-three-year history and the provision for a joint committee to settle points of dispute demonstrate a strong commitment by the EBU and the FFF to cooperate on the international level.

FFF/EBU Basic (Sound Radio) Agreement

One of the EBU's main fears in negotiating the 1957 Eurovision Agreement was that an agreement covering international television relays would lead to similar union claims in the area of sound broadcasting. The 1957 agreement provided, therefore, that it was not to be a precedent for agreements in radio.[42] On this basis, the EBU for several years declined to discuss the international use of radio programs involving performers.[43]

In December 1959 the FIM's executive committee decided to boycott the international relay of sound broadcasts emanating from European music festivals, a move which was also supported by the FIA. The EBU, as a result, finally agreed to negotiate the terms of some uses of recorded sound radio broadcasts.

The FFF/EBU sound radio agreement evolved in two stages. After preliminary negotiations were held in July 1961 and July 1962, the Basic Agreement was drafted in September 1962, embodying a number of general principles to become effective January 1, 1963. The specific terms and conditions of the agreement, however, were set out in a number of rules which were written in February 1964.

The basic agreement broadly defines the scope of issues to be covered as "certain types of international exchanges of sound radio broadcasts."[44] The phrase "certain types of exchanges" has included, in practice, those recorded sound broadcasts which do *not* qualify as direct (live) or deferred international relays under the agreement.[45] Protected performers (musicians, actors, singers, chorus artists, and dance and variety artists) are those who are "engaged at a fee" (freelance) and are not part of an orchestra which receives "subsidies or other payments from a broadcasting organisation of a nature such that they could not continue to exist without them."[46] The Basic Agreement also only relates to performers hired by a broadcasting organization itself, provided that the originating organization is an EBU member located in the European Broadcasting Zone (as defined by the European Broadcasting Convention that was in effect during 1963) and that the use is made by a broadcasting organization (which does not have to be an EBU member) located in the same zone.[47]

The Rules of Implementation for the Basic Agreement, as noted above, were agreed upon by representatives of the EBU and the FFF in February 1964. The most substantive provision, Article 2, sets the following minimum supplements for an individual whose performance is reused according to the terms of the Basic Agreement: 10 percent for one organization; 20 percent for two organizations; and so on up to 50 percent for five organizations.

The Rules of Implementation were originally to take effect on July 1, 1964. A number of difficulties arose, however, in drawing up the Authentic Interpretation of the Rules, which was mandated by the EBU's administrative council. The problems centered upon Clause 6 of the Basic Agreement, which excludes direct and deferred relays from the rules' application, and Clause 8, which asserts that the "status of performers and the uses to which the present Agreement is not expressly applicable shall continue to be subject to national practices or arrangements." According to the FFF, these provisions permitted supplements for simultaneous and deferred relays to be the subject of negotiations at the national level; according to the EBU, Clause 6 demonstrated an FFF commitment to forgo supplements for such relays. Finally, after a joint committee of FFF and EBU representatives met in Zurich in January 1965, it was agreed that, when a broadcasting organization applied the Rules of Implementation for the Basic Agreement, the national unions concerned were not to claim supplements for direct and/or deferred relays. This recommendation (known as the "Zurich Declaration") was not to affect national agreements or practices to the contrary which were already in existence at the time that the Rules came into operation.[48]

Ironically, after the obstacles to the Basic Agreement's implementation were removed in 1965, very few of the agreement's provisions were incorporated into national contracts. In 1970 the FIA reported that the agreement suffered from "either opposition from the broadcasting organisations or lack of interest (or strength) on the part of the unions representing the actors in the countries concerned."[49] In 1979, however, the EBU noted that "a majority of . . . [its] members actively participating in exchanges have adopted the main lines of the Basic Agreement and The Rules . . . ."[50]

The effectiveness of the Basic Agreement has been the subject of discussions between FFF and EBU representatives for over a year; many FIM and FIA affiliates have expressed growing dissatisfaction with the January 1965 "Zurich Declaration," which resolved the controversy surrounding Clauses 6 and 8 by prohibiting national union demands for supplementary payments in respect to direct and deferred relays.[51] At the end of 1979 the FFF notified the EBU that it would formally terminate the Basic Agreement by June 30, 1980, unless agreement could be reached on this issue. The FFF/EBU Joint Committee met from January 31 to February 1, 1980, to discuss the "Zurich Declaration's" abandonment. In May 1980 this was accepted by the EBU, and the FFF's notice of termination was withdrawn. The EBU noted, however, that "abrogation of the Zurich text did not mean that either party abandoned its own interpretation of the Basic Agreement and Rules. The FFF representatives [are] well aware that the EBU will continue to recommend its members to refrain from paying supplements for live and assimilated deferred relays as per Article 6."[52]

FFF/EBU Agreements Regarding Cable and Satellite Transmissions

The FFF and EBU have been engaged for some time in discussions concerning the distribution of radio and television programming via cable systems and satellites. To some degree, each party's position in these areas can be seen as extensions of their philosophies regarding conventional broadcasting—the performers desire redistributive control or supplementary remuneration, and the broadcasters hope to retain a maximum amount of flexibility in determining how and when a performance may be transmitted or rebroadcast. A number of additional problems appear unresolved in each area, however, forestalling the conclusion of final agreements.

The critical issue associated with cable television has centered around the right of companies to transmit programs via cable without acquiring the consent of the performers involved or without paying them supplementary remuneration. Representatives of the EBU and FFF met in August 1975 without reaching agreement on this question, but subsequent discussions have been conducted at meetings of various intergovernmental organizations (e.g., the Intergovernmental Committee of the Rome Convention, the Intergovernmental Copyright Committee of UNESCO, the Berne Union, and the Council of Europe) and at meetings of the EBU/FFF Joint Committee.

The performers have stressed a desire for the cable distribution of individual performances to be subject to the same conditions that apply to regular radio or television broadcasts. Although the EBU has reportedly agreed in principle that remuneration should be paid to performers involved in a cable transmission, this general proposition has yet to be put in written form. Moreover, the EBU appears unwilling to establish formal directives in this area on the multinational level. It recently asserted, for example, that "performers'" demands should receive consideration according to a range of possible systems which obviously vary according to national situations . . . [T]he performers' position will be settled *on the national level* in negotiations between a broadcasting organization, the other rightowners and the cable companies."[53]

FFF/EBU discussions regarding intercontinental television relays via satellite have been held at various times since 1969. The EBU position at that time was that, in view of the limited number of satellite transmissions that involved performers, supplementary payments should be negotiated with the performers involved (or their unions) in each individual case.[54] Both the EBU and the FFF, nevertheless, were involved with UNESCO and the World Intellectual Property Organisation (WIPO) in developing a "Convention Relating to the Distribution of Programme-Carrying Signals Transmitted by Satellite" which was signed by fifteen countries on May 21, 1974.[55]

The interest of the EBU and the FFF in negotiating a collective agreement concerning satellite transmissions has recently been heightened by tentative plans for two test satellites, H-SAT and NORD-SAT, which would provide for the direct reception of satellite transmissions in Europe and Scandinavia, respectively. The FFF and the EBU have held exploratory talks in regard to the H-SAT project, which was sponsored by the European Space Agency (ESA), since September 1978. There have reportedly been "no negotiations whatever between the FFF and EBU"[56] on the subject of NORD-SAT, however, because the two performers' federations are unequivocally opposed to the project, fearing its effect on employment in the Scandinavian entertainment industries. Although H-SAT has been abandoned by the ESA in favor of a new project, L-SAT, there have been no indications that the performers' original concerns regarding the practical and legal ramifications of satellite broadcasting have been eliminated or reduced.

The FFF/EBU experience regarding cable and satellite transmissions, like the other instances of cooperation between the two parties, appears to demonstrate at least a partial commitment to multinational collective bargaining. A number of issues remain to be resolved, however, before formal agreements can be concluded. The FFF at this time appears more willing than the EBU to negotiate certain issues on an international rather than a national level. The EBU's position in this regard may eventually change, though, depending upon the performers' ability to solicit meaningful support from their national affiliates, FISTAV, and the entertainment industry's technical personnel. At the FIM's 1980 congress a resolution to this effect was unanimously adopted, providing that, if adequate protection is not achieved by negotiations or legislation within a reasonable time, a partial or total boycott of satellite transmissions will be implemented by the FIM, the FIA, and the FISTAV "to be continued until the interests of workers represented by those organizations are satisfactorily guaranteed."[57]

The FFF-OIRT Agreement

The International Radio and Television Organization (OIRT) is an association of broadcasting companies that was formed in 1946. It is similar to the EBU in that it deals with administrative, legal, and technical problems common to its members and it has a network (called "Intervision") which provides for the international relay of television programs.[58] As of 1977, the OIRT represented organizations in twenty-three countries primarily located in Eastern Europe, Asia, and the Middle East.[59] The Intervision network has been of FFF concern for almost two decades.

Complementary EBU Agreement

FFF requests for an OIRT agreement regarding Intervision relays date back to July 1960. At that time, the OIRT declined to negotiate an agreement, noting that there was a relatively small number of FFF affiliates in Intervision countries and that the principle of supplementary payments to performers for the foreign use of their programs had not been incorporated in the national contracts of any OIRT affiliates. The OIRT was not opposed to general discussions in principle (FFF representatives did meet with the OIRT on several occasions), but the early discussions did not result in any firm agreements.[60]

In the absence of an OIRT agreement, both the FFF and the EBU were in an awkward position because relays *between* the Eurovision and Intervision networks were technologically feasible but of questionable legality. The EBU could freely relay artistic programs originating within the OIRT countries (subject only to national restrictions or quotas) but could not permit Eurovision broadcasts to be carried by Intervision.[61] In an attempt to eliminate this lack of reciprocity, the FFF and the EBU negotiated a "Complementary Agreement to Eurovision Agreement," which permitted EBU relays to OIRT countries to commence on July 1, 1965.[62] Participants in the relayed programs received an additional supplement amounting to 10 percent for each relaying OIRT organization. The maximum amount of the Intervision supplements was set at 50 percent of the performers' base fees. The Complementary Agreement was revised and incorporated into the Supplementary Agreement, which was in effect from January 1, 1968, to December 31, 1970. By the time of the Revised Eurovision Agreement (effective January 1, 1971, to December 31, 1973), individual supplements had been set for OIRT countries at an aggregate of 70 percent, a figure which was increased to 75 percent in the Eurovision Agreement that went into effect on January 1, 1974, and 81 percent by July 1980.

Although FFF/EBU agreements concerning Intervision served to protect (or at least to remunerate) performers employed in EBU productions which were relayed to OIRT countries, they did not protect artists who participated in OIRT programs that were relayed to other companies within the OIRT or the EBU. During 1967, however, the FFF decided not to extend the EBU agreement concerning the OIRT beyond December 31, 1967, unless the OIRT proposed a draft agreement which would regulate cultural broadcasts *within* the Intervision network. The OIRT met this demand, ultimately resulting in an "Intervision Agreement," which was signed on May 22, 1969.[63]

The Agreement and Its Effect

The FFF/OIRT agreement, like the EBU agreements, applies only to free-lance performers involved in international multilateral relays (i.e., "direct and deferred relays transmitted by at least two television organisations") and recommends that OIRT companies pay them supplements calculated as a percentage of the initial fees paid by the originating organization. During a "transitional period," the specific amounts of the supplements were to be fixed at the national level. It was noted, however, that "the parties should endeavor to unify the system which would subsequently take effect for all television organizations of OIRT participating in Intervision."[64]

It appears that the Intervision Agreement has not been widely implemented. It was reported in 1973, for example, that "since the individual unions concerned have not claimed that it be applied the agreement has not come into operation."[65] The agreement's lack of application largely results from the fact that most Intervision countries are communist states. Since the FFF/OIRT agreement is extremely general, a certain amount of union independence is required to set specific terms at the national level. In most communist countries, such independence is, of course, conspicuously absent. It is conceivable that FFF cooperation with the OIRT will increase if the latter becomes more actively engaged in satellite transmissions, but the desire for such cooperation has not yet been expressed by either party.

Summary

The agreements described above portray multinational entertainment union activity to be advanced beyond that in other industries. In certain respects, the International Federations of Performers have attained a degree of international union solidarity which is completely unprecedented. The most vivid example, perhaps, is the FFF boycott on Eurovision broadcasts, which led the EBU to recommend the payment of supplements to certain participating performers in 1957.

The agreements also demonstrate, however, that solidarity still has not reached the point where unions in more than one country are willing or able to demand identical terms and conditions of employment. None of the agreements attempt to establish basic absolute compensation levels for performers; they provide only for payments or supplements expressed as a percentage of a performer's initial fee or as a percentage of a record producer's distributive broadcasting revenue, both of which vary between individual countries. Moreover, since the agreements are not binding in character, the supplements are applied in each country to a varying degree, depending on the strength (or inclination) of the national unions involved. There may be some merit in the contention that the performers' contracts described herein are not really multinational agreements but rather multinational principles whose application depends upon the conventional exercise of industrial relations power on the national level.

In some ways, it is surprising that international union cooperation has emerged in the entertainment industry at all, for the industry is marked by a large number of different unions, a high degree of individual bargaining, a predominance of free-lance, short-term employment, and few objective standards by which employees can be evaluated.[66] Employee interest in multinational collective bargaining is not strong. As the FIA noted in 1979, decisions on an international level are increasingly made by people "remote from the day-to-day struggle of the performing artist."[67] One would expect the unusual nature of the industry's labor market to exaggerate, rather than dissipate, the national differences which normally make multinational collective activity impossible.

Ideological differences would also appear as a barrier to collective action in the entertainment field. The FIM, FIA, and FISTAV all attempt to be ideologically neutral. Their emphasis on strictly professional activity, however, does not change the fact that unions in communist countries are essentially organs of the state, and employees in those unions are usually incapable of engaging in industrial action to improve their own working conditions, much less those of workers abroad. The divisive role that national ideological differences can play in the entertainment industry's multinational union activity has been evident in the continuing struggle of the ISETU for national trade union support, the belated affiliation of many American unions with the FFF,[68] and the FFF's inability to implement fully its agreement with Eastern Europe's OIRT.

In spite of the obstacles, a number of factors in the entertainment industry favor multinational collective activity. The demand for entertainment, which has been traditionally cosmopolitan, is increasingly becoming more so thanks to faster and more inexpensive means of communication and travel. Films today are shot on location in every part of the world, and internationally renowned actors, recording artists, and symphony orchestras have long been a fact of life in the industry.

Another pervasive aspect of the industry which encourages multinational bargaining is the effect of technological change on employment and working conditions.[69] Automation in the entertainment industry (television and radio broadcasting, record production, and cable television, for example), while creating new types of employment, undisputedly reduces the demand for local musicians and actors. The introduction of even more advanced developments (direct television and radio reception from intercontinental satellites, for example) threatens further to extend this type of displacement on the international level. The impact of technological change on local, national, and international employment in the entertainment industry is highly visible and seems to ignore national ideological differences and geographic boundaries. This was the force behind the founding of the FIM and the FIA, and it remains their predominate ongoing concern.

Finally, in attempting to ascertain why multinational unionism has prospered in entertainment, one cannot avoid viewing the FFF agreements in their narrow European context. It has been noted that European Community officials avidly promote multinational industrial relations, viewing them as a "proper culmination of European integration."[70] Relations between the FFF and the EBU may have resulted not only from the entertainment industry's unique economic characteristics but also from the unique political structures of the European Community (EC). The FFF agreements with IFPI, the EBU, and the OIRT are only part of the overall protection that the FIM and FIA have sought to secure for performers on a broader level through work with the EC Commission and the Council of Europe. The fact that most European broadcasting facilities are government-owned may also increase their susceptibility to union pressure.

There are numerous indications that the limitations inherent in the FFF agreements and the national barriers to absolute union cooperation in the entertainment field will be slow to fall. The continuing viability of the EBU agreements to a large degree depends upon the use of professional performers in Eurovision broadcasts which, as noted above, has been steadily declining. The ability of the EBU and other employer groups to negotiate binding agreements instead of recommendations may be legally prevented by EC legislation.[71] Rigid reciprocity agreements among many national unions provide for only a one-to-one (or other fixed ratio) exchange of foreign and domestic performers. A principle of the FIM/IFPI London Principles provides that remuneration due to individual performers which cannot be distributed should nevertheless "remain in the country in which it has arisen."[72] The protection of narrow national interests is also demonstrated by the practice of the American Actors' Equity Association of charging resident members of the union substantially lower dues than alien (nonresident) members.[73] Finally, one of the stated reasons for FFF concern about direct satellite broadcasting is a desire to maintain the national distinctions which accompany "the use of TV as a medium of . . . cultural self-expression."[74]

These qualifications do not diminish the significance of the agreements described above, for they conclusively demonstrate a continuing commitment by at least the FFF, the EBU, and the IFPI to serious cooperation on an international level. As noted in the introduction, this type of commitment is unique to the entertainment industry and has not surfaced in any other field. The history of the

agreements indicates, however, that the multinational activity did
not evolve on its own but required great skill on the part of FFF officials in balancing their organizations' long-range international goals
with the national interests of affiliates, an unusually broad perception of interests by the national unions involved, and a belief on the
part of the IFPI, EBU, and OIRT that multinational cooperation
would, in the long run, also benefit their organizations.

The degree to which multinational collective bargaining will continue in the entertainment industry, and the extent to which it will
be duplicated in others, is not clear at the present time. Although every industry exhibits some characteristics that encourage multinational activity and usually many characteristics that discourage it,
the prevalence or absence of collective bargaining above the national
level is clearly dependent upon additional economic, political, and social factors that are not easily viewed in isolation. The experience of
the entertainment industry shows that multinational collective bargaining *can* occur, albeit in one industry under somewhat limited circumstances. Whether or when it will occur in more conventional industries is a question that remains to be answered.

NOTES

1.   See, for example, Charles Levinson, *International Trade Unionism*, Ruskin House
     Series in Trade Union Studies (London: George Allen & Unwin Ltd., 1972); J. A.
     Litvak and B. J. Maule, "Unions and International Corporations," *Industrial Rela-
     tions*, Vol. 9 (February 1972), pp. 62-71; Lloyd Ulman, "Multinational Unionism—
     Incentives, Barriers and Alternatives," *Industrial Relations*, Vol. 14 (February
     1975), pp. 1-31.

2.   For the Industrial Research Unit's findings and conclusions, see Herbert R. North-
     rup and Richard L. Rowan, *Multinational Collective Bargaining Attempts: The
     Record, the Cases, and the Prospects*, Multinational Industrial Relations Series,
     No. 6 (Philadelphia: Industrial Research Unit, The Wharton School, University
     of Pennsylvania, 1979).

3.   A reasonably thorough search of English literature prior to this study's commence-
     ment revealed isolated references to the FIM or FIA in only three sources: Richard
     N. Goldstein and Barry G. Cole, "Crossing National Boundaries: Labor-
     Management Problems;" Allen E. Koenig (ed.), *Broadcasting and Bargaining:
     Labor Relations in Radio and Television* (Madison: The University of Wisconsin
     Press, 1970), pp. 123-52; *The Yearbook of International Organizations, 1978-79*,
     17th ed. (Brussels: Union of International Associations, 1978); and a few issues of
     the *European Broadcasting Union (EBU) Review*.

4.   Edward Thompson, "International Protection of Performers' Rights—Some Cur-
     rent Problems," *International Labour Review*, Vol. 107, No. 4 (April 1973), p. 303.

5. FIM, *Report on the Activity of the Executive Committee to the 10th Ordinary Congress, Geneva, 5-9 May 1980*, Zurich, January 1980, pp. 4-5; *Addendum to the Report on the Activity of the Executive Committee to the 10th Ordinary Congress, Geneva, 5-9 May 1980*, Zurich, 11 April 1980, pp. 1-2.

6. The FFF originally incorporated all three performers' federations—the FIM, the FIA, and the FIAV.

7. FIA, *Report on Activities Since 10th Congress, 11th FIA Congress, Budapest, September 25-29, 1979*, London, June 30, 1979, Annexe 2: Unions affiliated to FIA, pp. 1-2; *Preliminary Documents for 10th Congress, Vienna, September 13-17, 1976*, "Fees Paid by Affiliated Organizations," pp. 1-3; Letter to the author from Gerald Croasdell, General Secretary, International Federation of Actors, September 10, 1980.

8. FISTAV, "FISTAV is a non-aligned, international federation of cinema, television, radio and film processing trade unions" (Informational Circular, 1978); Letter to the author from René Jannelle, General Secretary of FISTAV, November 16, 1979; *Bulletin*, No. 9 (July 1978), pp. 13-15.

9. At one point in the early 1970s, it looked as though some kind of ISETU-FFF cooperation might emerge. The chances for such cooperation vanished, however, when the ISETU initiated what the federations perceived as an attempt to have their consultative status with the Council of Europe withdrawn. FIM, *Report on the Activity of the Executive Committee to the 9th Ordinary Congress, Stockholm, August 30–September 3, 1976*, Zurich, March 1976, p. 32; *Minutes of the 9th Ordinary Congress, August 30–September 3, 1976*, Zurich, August 23, 1977, pp. 33-34; FIA, *Report and Resolutions of the 10th Congress, Vienna, September 13-17*, London, 1976, p. 6.

10. As of October 31, 1973 the ISETU's membership reportedly consisted of 56 unions representing 486,612 workers in 31 countries. By March 1977, however, all the North American and English organizations had withdrawn from the secretariat, in addition to three of the four Australian unions. The elimination of these unions alone would have reduced the total ISETU affiliated membership by 371,650. The fact that only four organizations had paid their proper dues for 1975 and 1976 (as of December 1976) indicates that many more unions had also effectively (even if unofficially) withdrawn from the organization. In spite of these developments, the ISETU still claimed a membership of 350,000 as of December 31, 1978, *ICFTU Reports on Activities and Financial Reports 1975-78*, Twelfth World Congress, Madrid, November 19-23, 1979, Brussels, 1979, p. 270; ISETU, *Preliminary Documents for 12th Executive Board Meeting*, Brussels, February 8-9, 1974; documents in author's possession.

11. ICFTU, *International Trade Union News*, November 1, 1979, p. 5. The ISETU's 1980 congress was actually financed by both the ICFTU and the Friedrich-Ebert Stiftung. ISETU, *Report on Activities by the Acting President Josef Schweinzer to the 5th ISETU Congress, Brussels, May 20-21*, Vienna, 1980, p. 4.

12. *Yearbook of International Organizations, 1978-79*, 17th ed. (Brussels: Union of International Associations, 1978), reference no. 2028 (unpaginated).

13. FIM/IFPI-Agreement on the Participation in Broadcasting Revenues, March 11, 1954, clause 1.

14. *Ibid.*, clause 3.

15. *Ibid.*, clause 8.

16. The Rome Convention (formally entitled "International Convention for the Pro-

tection of Performers, Producers of Phonograms and Broadcasting Organizations) was adopted on October 26, 1961 by a diplomatic conference jointly convened by the ILO, UNESCO, and the International Union for the Protection of Literary and Artistic Works (Berne Union) and lays down regulations for the protection of performers' rights. Article 12 of the Convention mandates that musicians be remunerated for the direct broadcast of phonograms published for commercial purposes. For an introduction to the Rome Convention, the Berne Union (now part of the World Intellectual Property Organization) and other intergovernmental copyright organizations, see Edward Thompson, "International Protection of Performers' Rights'—Some Current Problems," *International Labour Review*, Vol. 107, No. 4 (April 1973), pp. 303-14.

17. "IFPI/FIM Principles," FIM Circular Letter No. 5/19, May 16, 1963, p. 1.

18. International Federation of Musicians, *Report on the Activity of the Executive Committee on the 2nd Ordinary Business Period, Spring 1953–Spring 1956*, Zurich, 1956, p. 15. (Hereafter cited as *FIM 2nd Ordinary Business Period.*)

19. International Federation of Musicians, *Minutes of the 3rd Ordinary Congress, London, May 7-12, 1956*, Zurich, 1956, pp. 8-9.

20. International Federation of Musicians, *Report on the Activity of the Executive Committee to the 5th Ordinary Congress, Geneva, September 17-21, 1962*, Zurich, 1962, p. 17.

21. The five FIM/IFPI Principles specifically condemn or discourage (1) clandestine recordings, (2) the use of commercial records in film soundtracks, (3) the use of commercial recordings in stage productions, (4) the use of film soundtracks or recordings made by broadcasting organizations in commercial records, and (5) the use of commercial records in connection with nonmusical live productions.

22. International Federation of Musicians, *Report on the Activity of the Executive Committee to the 9th Ordinary Congress, Stockholm, August 30-September 3, 1976*, Zurich, 1976, p. 15. (Hereafter cited as *FIM 9th Ordinary Congress.*)

23. Protocol to the Agreement between the IFPI and the FIM on the Participation in Broadcasting Revenues of March 11, 1954, November 9, 1976, clauses 1-7.

24. By a separate agreement the FIM and the FIA have decided that the musicians in each country shall be entitled to 29⅙ percent of the IFPI's broadcasting revenue, leaving the actors with 4⅙ percent. It was pointed out, however, that "this ratio of distribution is not strictly binding; if on an amicable basis the organizations of musicians and actors can agree on different shares, they are free to do so." Cooperation FIM-IFPI-Protocol to the Agreement FIM-IFPI of March 11, 1954." FIM Circular Letter No. 9/8, January 24, 1977, p. 2.

25. "The Rome Convention," article 12, in *Copyright Laws and Treaties of the World*, CLTW Supplement 1962, Item B-1, pp. 1-7.

26. "FIM/IFPI London Principles," February 14, 1969, clauses 1-3; "London Principle No. 4," December 20, 1978.

27. FIM, *Report on the Activity of the Executive Committee to the 10th Ordinary Congress, Geneva, 5-9 May 1980*, Zurich, January 1980, p. 27.

28. Letter to author from General Secretary, International Federation of Musicians, November 10, 1980.

29. *Yearbook of International Organizations*, reference no. A0598; and *The Europa Year Book, 1971* (London: Europa Publications, Ltd., 1978), Vol. 1, pp. 168-69.

30. International Federations of Performers, [*Report of the*]*International Conference*

on *Television, Paris, 20-21 April 1954*, Zurich 1954, "Resolution 1: International Television Relays," p. 11.

31. *FIM 2nd Ordinary Business Period*, p. 18.

32. International Federations of Performers, *Report on a Conference held between the EBU and the FFF, Paris, 22-23 March 1956*, p. 5.

33. *FIM 4th Ordinary Congress*, p. 20.

34. International Federation of Musicians, *Report on the Activity of the Executive Committee to the 6th Ordinary Congress, Stresa, 3-7 May 1966*, Zurich, 1966, p. 11.

35. "Eurovision Agreement," FFF Circular Letter No. F/30, April 28, 1970, p. 1.

36. International Federation of Musicians, *Report on the Activity of the Executive Committee to the 8th Ordinary Congress, London, 7-11 May 1973*, Zurich, 1973, pp. 16-18. The supplements for Western Europe which are set out in the 1971 revised agreement actually total 188 percent. An additional 1 percent is added, however, for each of four "developing countries situated in the European Broadcasting Area and not included in the . . . list."

37. "Performing Artists Agreement with the International Federations of Performers, International Television Relays," Supplement No. 5, 1 January 1954, clauses 1 and 2.

38. Clause 12 of the 1974 Eurovision Agreement defines base fee as the "initial fees actually paid to performers for the creation (rehearsal and performance) of the programme as first broadcast by the originating organisation to its own audience."

39. FIM, *Report on the Activity of the Executive Committee to the 10th Ordinary Congress, Geneva, 5-9 May 1980*, Zurich, January 1980, p. 31.

40. FIM, *Addendum to the Report on Activity*, p. 7; Letter to the author from M. Cazé, Director, Legal Affairs Department, European Broadcasting Union, August 21, 1980.

41. "Authentic Interpretation of the Agreement between the European Broadcasting Union and the International Federations of Performers respecting international television relays," Supplement No. 5, January 8, 1974, clause 5. See also *EBU Review*, Vol. XXV, January 1974, p. 60.

42. Even the present Eurovision Agreement provides that its recommendations "shall not impugn the principles and practices obtaining in the field of sound broadcasting at the national or international level and can constitute no precedent in this respect . . . The Federations undertake not to revoke the present recommendations in order to put in issue the principles and practices affecting sound broadcasting or to make modifications of the said principles and practices a condition of a new agreement to supersede the present Agreement" (clause 3).

43. Use of sound recordings, outside their country of origin/Basic Agreement and 'Rules' UER/FFF, FFF Circular Letter No. F/11, February 1966, p. 1.

44. Performing Artists' Basic Agreement on certain exchanges of programmes in sound broadcasting, December 31, 1962, clause 1.

45. Article 6 of the "Basic Agreement" defines a "deferred international relay" as "an international relay which replaces a direct (live) relay when such a relay cannot be arranged for technical, programme schedule or other imperative reasons, and which fulfills the following conditions: (i) that the relaying organization has re-

quested or accepted the relay before the original broadcast takes place; (ii) that the transmission is made by the relaying organization not later than 15 clear days after the date of receipt of the said recording. Only the first transmission by the relaying organization, in the circumstances specified in (i) and (ii) above, shall be deemed to be a deferred relay."

46. "Basic Agreement," clauses 3 and 4. In a preliminary version of the "Basic Agreement," the following orchestras were specifically mentioned (after the FIM was assured that they were satisfactorily protected by national agreements): Filharmonish Sleskap (Norway), Musikselskabet 'Harmonien' (Norway), Orchestre de la Suisse Romande (Switzerland), and Orchestre de Chambre de Lausanne (Switzerland).

47. *Ibid.*, clauses 5 and 7.

48. *Minutes of the Joint Committee of the EBU and the International Performers' Federations, Zurich, January 28-29, 1965*, pp. 15-20.

49. *International Federation of Actors, Summary of Activities since the 7th Congress, Prague, October 2-8, 1967*, Stockholm, 1970, p. 7.

50. Letter from M. Cazé, Director, Legal Affairs Department, European Broadcasting Union, September 12, 1979.

51. FIA, *Report on Activities since 10th Congress, 11th FIA Congress, Budapest, 25-29 September 1979*, London, June 30, 1979, pp 5-6; FIM, *Report on the Activity of the Executive Committee to the 10th Ordinary Congress, Geneva, 5-9 May 1980*, Zurich, January 1980, pp. 31-33.

52. Letter to the author from M. Cazé, Director, Legal Affairs Department, European Broadcasting Union, August 21, 1980.

53. *Ibid.* (emphasis in original).

54. FIM, *Report on the Activity of the Executive Committee to the 8th Ordinary Congress, London, 7-11 May 1973*, Zurich, December 1972, p. 18.

55. The FFF federations vigorously opposed the Satellite Convention (which was fully endorsed by the EBU) on the grounds that it provided protection to broadcasting organizations without extending corresponding protection to performers. The FIA and FIM also feared that the Satellite Convention would diminish wider acceptance of the Rome Convention.

56. Letter to the author from Gerald Croasdell, General Secretary, International Federation of Actors, September 10, 1980.

57. International Federation of Musicians, *The major decisions of the 10th ordinary FIM congress, Geneva, May 5-9, 1980*, Zurich, June 27, 1980.

58. Burton Paulu, *Radio and Television Broadcasting in Eastern Europe* (Minneapolis: The University of Minnesota Press, 1974), p. 59. EBU and OIRT members constituted, at one time, a single organization, the International Broadcasting Union (UIR), which was founded in 1925 and succeeded, in 1946, by the International Broadcasting Organization (OIR). In 1949 the Western members of the OIR withdrew from the organization because of Cold War tensions and formed the EBU. By 1960 the two organizations had been separate for about ten years (the OIR became the OIRT in 1959), and each had its own broadcasting network: the EBU's Eurovision system primarily operated within Western Europe and North Africa, while the OIRT's Intervision system was functional in Eastern Europe. The two systems could provide for the exchange of programs between Eurovision

countries alone, between Intervision countries alone, or between Eurovision and Intervision countries.

59. *Yearbook of International Organizations*, reference no. A2391.

60. International Federation of Actors, *Report of Activity on the Period since the 5th Congress, Paris, 6-10 June 1961*, Paris, 1964, p. 12.

61. "Additional Agreement Eurovision," FFF Circular Letter No. FFF 10, July 24, 1965, p. 2.

62. The specific countries listed in article 1 of the Agreement are Bulgaria, Czechoslovakia, Eastern Germany, Hungary, Poland, Rumania, and the U.S.S.R. (European Broadcasting Zone).

63. *FIA 7th Congress*, p. 7.

64. FFF/OIRT Agreement of Recommendations respecting International Television Relays (Intervision Agreement), 1969, section V, clause 5.

65. International Federation of Actors, *Summary of Activities since the 8th Congress, Amsterdam, 21-25 September 1970*, Stockholm, 1973, p. 11.

66. Michael H. Moskow, *Labor Relations in the Performing Arts: An Introductory Survey* (New York: Associated Councils of the Arts, 1969), pp. 172-85.

67. FIA, *Report on Activities since the 10th Congress, Vienna, 13-17 September 1976*, London, June 30, 1979, p. 1.

68. No American union participated as a formal delegate in an FFF meeting until 1970, after the Screen Actors Guild (SAG) and Actors' Equity joined the FIA and attended its 8th Congress, Amsterdam, September 21-25, 1970. The American Federation of Television and Radio Artists (AFTRA) became an affiliate by the time of the FIA's 10th Congress, Vienna, September 13-17, 1976. Although the American Federation of Musicians (AFM) has had a cooperative relationship with the FIM since the mid-1950s (a formal cooperative agreement was signed in 1958), it never became an FIM member. The SAG, AFTRA, and the AFM were all once members of the ISETU but withdrew during the Secretariat's post-1974 period of inactivity. American Actors' Equity's application for ISETU membership in 1970 was rejected on the grounds that dual affiliations (to both the ISETU and the FIA) were unpalatable. Although the SAG and a few other ISETU members were also affiliated to FFF organizations at the time, the ISETU executive board did not want the situation "to go further than it had already." *ISETU, Report of Proceedings of the Third International Congress*, Vienna 19-22 May 1971, pp. 34-46, 39-42.

69. See Thompson, "International Protection of Performers' Rights," p. 303.

70. Northrup and Rowan, *Multinational Collective Bargaining Attempts*, p. 547.

71. Letter to the author from M. Cazé, Director, Legal Affairs Department, European Broadcasting Union, September 12, 1979.

72. "FIM/IFPI London Principles," clause 3.

73. This practice was recently found to be in violation of the National Labor Relations (Taft-Hartley) Act. *Actors' Equity Association*, 247 N.L.R.B. No. 172, 103 L.R.R.M. 1494, 1980.

74. "Activities of the FFF in 1977," FFF Circular Letter No. F/68, March 28, 1978, p. 4.

PART IV

NEW UNION-MANAGEMENT TACTICS

A. Private Sector

Plant Operation During Strikes

Charles R. Perry[†]

Collective bargaining is, in the final analysis, a process of economic power accommodation. The foundation of this process is the right of unions to strike and the right of companies to take a strike in the event of an honest impasse over mandatory subjects for good faith bargaining. One potentially significant power asset available to companies in collective bargaining is their right to continue to do business by operating production facilities during a strike using non-striking personnel. In theory, this option could play an important role in determining the basic balance of bargaining power in union-management relations in this country. In practice, however, it has not done so, because the right to operate has been little used and less discussed, at least in polite company, as a mangement option to augment the economic power inherent in its right to take a strike. This situation, however, seems to be changing judging by a growing number of widely publicized instances of plant operation in such firms as The Washington Post and Newport News Shipyard and such industries as the West Coast paper and San Francisco hotel industries, where operation during a strike seemed unthinkable. Thus, the time has come to bring plant operation out of the closet where it has been for the last twenty years since the prestigious Independent Study Group on the Public Interest in National Labor Policy last addressed the issue in polite company.

Plant operation is not an easy subject for dispassionate discussion and analysis. Any new power asset, whether plant operation, coalition bargaining, or mutual aid, that threatens to change significantly the balance of power already established in bargaining relationships is far more likely to be the subject of a holy war rather than of heavenly understanding. At the risk of becoming a hostage in just such a holy war, I propose to discuss and analyze the legal, philosophical, technological, and institutional considerations surrounding exercise of management's right to operate, based on the results of a study of

---

† Charles R. Perry is Associate Professor of Management and Industrial Relations at The Wharton School, University of Pennsylvania.

the experience of firms that have exercised the right. This study was conducted under the auspices of the Industrial Research Unit in 1980 and is scheduled for publication late in 1981.

The Right to Operate

The basic right of an employer to continue to do business in the face of a strike by operating production facilities has been clearly recognized by the courts and endorsed by the Independent Study Group, which stated that "as a matter of law, we stand without compromise for the employer's right to operate his plant and the right of individuals to enter that plant despite a strike."[1] The right of an employer to utilize temporary or permanent replacements for workers engaged in an economic strike in order to continue operation is also clearly recognized under law. That right extends to the use of temporary, but not permanent, replacements for workers subject to an offensive lockout.

The right to operate and to utilize replacement workers is not absolute. It is qualified by an extensive set of federal, state, and, in some cases, local regulations governing various aspects of bargaining and employment relationships. A detailed account of all such regulations is virtually impossible given varying state and local laws. It is, however, possible to identify a limited number of basic types of legal constraints that may impede the successful exercise of the right to operate. With no pretense of technical legal expertise, I suggest that the following are potential legal problem areas.

Federal Regulations

The basic obligation of an employer to bargain in good faith up to and beyond the point of an honest impasse is no different for an employer who operates during a strike than for one who does not. Most of the firms studied, however, indicated that they felt compelled to be particularly scrupulous in meeting this obligation in order to protect themselves from what they felt was a higher than average probability that charges would be filed by the union and pursued by the National Labor Relations Board (NLRB) because of plant operation. Two other areas in which firms felt it was advisable to be extremely careful were: (1) imposition of discipline for picket line activity; and (2) inducement of workers or replacement workers to cross the picket line.

A second area of federal regulation of concern to employers who operate during strikes is compliance with the Fair Labor Standards

Act (FLSA). Companies who operate using managerial, professional, technical, supervisory, and clerical personnel as temporary replacements must determine who among those personnel is exempt and nonexempt under the FLSA and how their status may be changed by assignment to production jobs on a full-time or part-time basis for varying periods of time. The fact that most plants that operate do so using extended shifts and workweeks can create some complex legal problems and expensive overtime pay obligations that few employers wish to violate, if only to maintain morale among replacement workers.

A third area of concern to employers who operate during strikes is the Occupational Safety and Health Administration (OSHA) and, to a lesser extent, the Equal Employment Opportunity Commission (EEOC). Compliance with the requirements of those agencies regarding working conditions and work force composition may be difficult to maintain when operating with replacement personnel. Thus far, none of the firms studied has encountered serious legal challenges to continued operation during a strike from either OSHA or the EEOC, but there is apprehension that those two agencies could cause problems in the future should they choose, as OSHA is alleged to have done at Newport News by becoming actively involved on a partisan basis in a strike situation. For the most part, however, OSHA and the EEOC seem to constitute more of a bother than a barrier in plant operation for the foreseeable future, particularly in light of the outcome of OSHA's efforts at Newport News.

State Regulations

There are three areas in which firms that have operated during strikes have encountered real or potential problems under state law in some states—unemployment compensation, licensing requirements, and antistrikebreaking laws. None of these problems has represented an insurmountable barrier to operation, but all have necessitated some accommodation in method of operation at some locations.

The eligibility for unemployment compensation of workers who are unemployed due to a labor dispute in the form of either a strike or a lockout is both a complex and an emotional issue in its own right— one which need not be discussed here. The issue is further complicated by plant operation in those states that have adopted a "stoppage of work" approach to eligibility for unemployment compensation. In these states, eligibility for benefits is based on a two-step analysis beginning with a determination of whether a labor dispute exists and proceeding to a determination of whether a labor dispute has resulted in a stoppage of work at the employer's place of business. If a labor dispute results in a stoppage of work, employees are not eligible for benefits; if it does not, employees are eligible for benefits. Courts in different states have arrived at different conclusions regarding what constitutes a stoppage of work, but as a general rule, a decrease in total output of less than 20 percent in a plant operation situation may not be considered a stoppage of work for purposes of determining benefit eligibility.

State licensing laws may profoundly affect the ability of a company to operate successfully during a strike. The operation of most production facilities requires certain technical skills. Nearly all states license individuals who practice such trades as electrician, boiler operator, or, closer to home, dealers in casinos. Thus, the ability to recruit an adequate supply of fully-qualified and licensed replacement personnel for such skilled jobs is crucial to successful operation during a strike without legal liability for violation of state law.

Both the federal government and certain states restrict the hiring of replacements for striking workers. The intent of both federal and state laws in this area is to prevent the use of professional strikebreakers. The relevant laws are not onerous, and most state laws may be meaningless by virtue of federal preemption of the field. Nonetheless, such laws, federal and state alike, continue to be a source of concern to employers who operate during strikes. None of the employers studied, however, yet had encountered any significant problem under those statutes.

The Decision to Operate

There are two basic constraints on management in utilizing its right to operate during strikes. The first is the "fear of confrontation" arising out of the potential union and public relations problems that can result from plant operation during strikes. The second is the "fear of failure" arising out of the practical problems anticipated in staffing and operating a struck production facility. In combination, these institutional and technological constraints have deterred most, but not all, managements from exercising their legal right to operate during a strike. There is, however, a growing minority of managements that have overcome the fear of confrontation and failure. The obvious question is why and how.

The Commitment to Operation

Plant operation may be either an offensive or a defensive weapon for management in its relationship with a union. Historically, plant operation has tended to be viewed primarily as an offensive weapon, most likely to be used in the context of what has been termed a "conflict" relationship in which management "strongly opposes the very existence of the union" and "does more or less everything it can to prevent or eliminate unionism."[2] More recently, plant operation has been admitted to the slightly more polite company of a "power bargaining" relationship in which management "concludes that the union is there to stay, and ceases open attempts to destroy it" but "will try to keep the union weak and defensive." The invitation of plant operation to join the truly polite company of "accommodation bargaining" relationships as an acceptable management alternative to "simply closing down production when a strike is called" remains to be sent.

It is difficult to discern the blend of offensive (philosophical) and defensive (pragmatic) considerations that leads firms to pursue their option to operate during strikes. It is possible, however, to gain some insight into the question of motivation by investigating the circumstances that surround the emergence and evolution of corporate commitments to plant operation as a bargaining tactic. On the basis of such an investigation, I would offer three general observations.

Firstly, the decision to risk confrontation through plant operation generally has some pragmatic foundation. Changes in corporate policy and practice with respect to plant operation have tended to come at discrete intervals over the past twenty years—around 1960, 1970, and 1980. Each of these changes came at a time of adjustment to change in basic economic and competitive conditions which served to increase management's potential strike costs in terms of losses of both sales and customers. At a more micro level, a number of the firms studied cited a particularly painful strike situation, either immediately past or imminently prospective, as a major factor in their initial decision to attempt plant operation.

Secondly, the decision to risk confrontation through plant operation rarely is motivated by purely economic considerations—institutional factors also play or come to play a major role. Two of the periods of expanded use of the plant operation option—1960 and 1980—coincided with growing general management resistance to unionism and the third—1970—came at a time of growing union pressure on management. Again, at a more micro level, several of the firms studied openly admitted that their commitment to plant operation was part of a more basic change in labor relations philosophy and posture designed to shift relations from accommodation to power bargaining in an effort to regain or maintain the offensive in dealing with unions.

In some cases, that change came about as a result of changes in top management and, in others, as a result of changes in union tactics—most notably, coalition bargaining.

Thirdly, plant operation, despite its offensive roots and potential, generally is not perceived or practiced as a weapon to be used to eliminate unionism. The breadth and depth of the commitment of most firms to plant operation as an offensive as well as a defensive weapon tends to grow over time, but seems to stop well short of using operation to break, rather than take, a strike. Specifically, most firms perceive the offensive limits of the plant operation to be a question of relative power, not absolute survival, and therefore avoid such measures as hiring permanent replacements or encouraging back-to-work movements that "challenge the union's status as exclusive bargaining agent . . . and thereby transform the strike from an incident in a long term bargaining relationship to a war for survival."[3]

The Logistics of Operation

There are three basic problems confronting management in implementing a decision to operate during a strike. The first, obviously, is the recruitment of an adequate supply of qualified replacement personnel to man production operations. The second is the establishment and maintenance of ingress and egress to the plant not only for replacement personnel, but for the transport of materials and the product. The third is the protection of the security of the replacement personnel and the production facility.

These problems are rarely solved easily and are never solved well without extensive planning and detailed preparation, which is now a routine part of preparations for negotiations in firms committed to plant operation as a possible response to strike action. Such operating plans and preparations vary from company to company and plant to plant. There is, however, a fairly consistent pattern among such plans in their approach to manning, access, and security which supports the following generalizations.

The basic source of replacement labor for plant operation is nonunion personnel regularly employed within the company, including managerial, professional, technical, supervisory, and, in some cases, clerical employees. Most firms have found this pool of potential replacement personnel adequate to meet their needs, although most have had to reach beyond the struck facility to meet their needs for skilled labor, particularly in the maintenance area and in jobs requiring licenses. A few have had to do the same for unskilled labor in some of their more labor-intensive operations. Where firms have found it necessary by virtue of the scale or duration of operation to augment their own personnel by hiring from the outside, they typically have done so on a temporary basis. The hiring of permanent replacements generally is not perceived as an option to be used except in unusual circumstances.

The problem of establishing and maintaining ingress and egress is a real one and may be sufficiently troublesome to deter operation in some locations. Mass picketing, with its attendant harassment, intimidation, and, possibly, violence is not uncommon in plant operation situations. Most firms choose not to confront such activity directly by forcing the picket line. Instead, they elect to operate the plant under siege until such time as they can secure the assistance of the courts and law enforcement agencies in limiting and controlling picket activity—a choice that necessitates stockpiling of raw materials and providing for the housing and feeding in the plant of company personnel. The disruption of deliveries and shipments by truck, rail, or water may not end with effective control over mass picketing, but generally has been overcome by reliance on carrier supervisory personnel, utilization of nonunion carriers, and, in a few cases, specially trained company personnel.

The problems of harassment, intimidation, and violence are not confined to the picket line, where they can be most easily observed, documented, and, with outside assistance, controlled by management. Such activity can extend both inward and outward from the picket line and be directed at either the plant or personnel. The possibility of attempts to interrupt operation by acts of violence directed at company facilities and/or personnel on or off the plant site is a real concern of any management that chooses to operate during a strike and succeeds in doing so. Such acts are not uncommon in plant operation situations, but they rarely, if ever, reach epidemic proportions. Most vulnerable are off-site facilities, such as utility connections and pipelines, and the homes of local company personnel which are not under the security control of management. For the most part, firms have been able to rely on local police for control of violence and harassment, but in a few cases they have felt it necessary to augment such protection by extended security measures off-site as well as on-site.

The Results of Operation

Plant operation during strikes clearly is not an easy or inexpensive option to pursue, which raises the obvious question of whether it is indeed a worthwhile option. Judging by the enthusiasm of most companies which are committed to plant operation, the answer to that question is most definitely yes. That answer raises a second question regarding both the nature and the magnitude of the benefits of plant operation. Unfortunately, those benefits are difficult, if not impossible, to measure, but they are not beyond the realm of informed speculation. On that basis, I would offer the following observations.

In the short run, plant operation serves primarily to cut losses, not to make a profit either in the marketplace or at the bargaining table, which, in effect, makes it more a defensive than an offensive tactic. Plant operation should serve to reduce the sales and revenue losses associated with a strike and limit the concessions made by management to avoid or curtail those losses. The magnitude of those benefits, not surprisingly, tends to be roughly proportional to the level of normal production attempted and achieved during strike operation . . . a level which varied among the companies studied from simply finishing work in progress to operation at close to normal capacity. Even firms at the upper end of this range, however, were reluctant to claim that their "savings" outweighed their "costs" on a short-term basis.

In the long run, plant operation during strikes appears to offer more substantial benefits in terms of both customer and union relations. Plant operation generally is felt to have beneficial long-term effects on customer retention and confidence. Similarly, plant operation also is felt to have a positive effect on union militancy, at least in the short term. In addition, firms reported that successful operation of a plant had a noticeable effect on the militancy of unions at other plants and even on the militancy of the union at the plant beyond the next one or two sets of contract negotiations. That phenomenon reflects basic union and worker skepticism regarding management's ability to operate—skepticism which seems to persist for a considerable period of time even in the face of successful operation during a strike and to reappear at varying intervals depending on degree of operating success.

Perhaps the most significant result of plant operation has been its impact on management attitudes. Success in operating plants during strikes has led many companies to be more aggressive in testing the institutional limits of their willingness to operate and the technological limits of their ability to operate. The result in most cases has been a clear lessening of both the fear of confrontation and the fear of failure with respect to specific situations and to general policies. Thus, there has been a tendency for nonoperation rather than operation to become the selective option among firms that have substantial experience in operating plants during strikes, to the point that operation is an accepted fact of life in some collective bargaining relationships.

Conclusions

The right to operate during a strike provides management with a potentially powerful weapon with which to give new meaning, and some would argue life, to its right to take a strike. Despite that fact, it is a right that has not been widely exercised by management, which has regarded plant operation as neither a popular nor an easy option to pursue. Thus, plant operation is not an integral element in our system of collective bargaining.

The fact that plant operation has not been an easy or a popular option does not mean that it has no role to play in the future of collective bargaining. Operation of struck facilities using salaried personnel has become an integral part of collective bargaining in at least two high-technology industries—telephone and oil refining—and has begun to work its way into collective bargaining in other industries such as chemicals, paper, and printing. The long-term trend toward less labor-intensive operations in most industries coupled with the growing ratio of salaried (white-collar) to hourly (blue-collar) workers in most companies suggests that plant operation may be, or may become, less difficult than has been perceived by management. That clearly has been the case for most firms that have exercised their right to operate.

Growing technological feasibility and/or management confidence in the ability to operate suggest that willingness, rather than ability, to operate will become even more important as a basic constraint on the exercise of the right to operate during strikes. Undoubtedly, the institutional costs of plant operation—short-run violence and long-run bitterness—continue to constitute a serious constraint on use of the option to operate. The desire for labor peace which underlies that constraint, however, now appears to be weakening in the management community at the same time that the costs of nonoperation during strikes seem to be increasing as a consequence of growing foreign and domestic nonunion competition.

The potential for expanded use of plant operation during strikes as a device to enhance management ability to take a strike has not gone unnoticed by the labor movement. Plant operation threatens to undermine the basic weapon used by unions in the process of economic power accommodation called collective bargaining—and it is unlikely that unions will accept this prospect passively. Thus, it is logical to expect unions to respond to any clear expansion in the use of plant operation by management with efforts to inhibit successful use of the option. The nature of such efforts remains to be seen, but several possibilities may be worth noting. One possibility is government intervention, either directly through legislation or indirectly through existing regulations. A second possibility is self-help measures such as sabotage, boycotts, and the organization of supervisory personnel.

There are few more perilous adventures than attempting to predict the future in labor relations, particularly when those in the field cannot agree as to whether the 1980s will be a decade of accommodation or of confrontation. Nonetheless, it appears that legally, economically, technologically, and, yes, philosophically, conditions in the early 1980s are favorable for expanded use of plant operation during strikes as a management power asset. What the result of these conditions will be remains to be seen and rests in your hands and the hands of the other practitioners of the arcane art of collective bargaining.

NOTES

1. Committee for Economic Development, *The Public Interest in National Labor Policy* (New York: Committee for Economic Development, 1961), p. 88.

2. E. Edward Herman and Alfred Kuhn, *Collective Bargaining and Labor Relations* (New Jersey: Prentice-Hall, Inc., 1981), p. 79.

3. Committee for Economic Development, *Public Interest*, p. 88.

8331
8310
U.S.

Labor's New Offensive: Neutrality Agreements

Andrew M. Kramer[†]

Introduction

From 1960 to 1978 union membership as a percentage of the total labor force has declined from 23.6 to 19.7 percent. In each and every year since 1969, during periods of both economic growth and recession, the percentage of union membership has declined. In the more heavily unionized manufacturing industries from 1968 to 1978, unions recorded a decrease in actual membership of approximately 1.1 million members, or approximately 12 percent.[1] Both employment and union membership in the auto and tire industries have continued to decline at a dramatic pace.

Although always a goal of organized labor, increasing union membership is even more critical today because of what has been described by Solomon Barkin, former research director for the Amalgamated Clothing and Textile Workers' Union (ACTWU), as a "crisis [resulting from] the cessation of the trade union movement's expansion into new areas and its decline in numerical strength."[2] In order to enhance its organizing efforts, labor has begun to employ new techniques. One of the most effective organizing tools being utilized by unions today is the neutrality agreement. Neutrality agreements are agreements whereby an employer, ordinarily one that already has a number of unionized plants, agrees to remain "neutral" in any organizing campaign conducted by the union with which it has such an agreement. Although the contractual language varies from agreement to agreement, a typical neutrality agreement is similar to the agreement entered into by the Goodrich Tire and Rubber Company and the United Rubber, Cork, Linoleum and Plastic Workers (URW). The relevant portion of that agreement reads as follows:

> In situations where the URW seeks to organize production and maintenance employees in a plant in which a major product is tires and which is not presently represented by a union, Goodrich management or its

---

† Andrew M. Kramer is a Partner of Seyfarth, Shaw, Fairweather & Geraldson and Managing Partner of its Washington office. For a more detailed analysis of the issues raised by neutrality agreements, *see* A. Kramer, L. Miller, and L. Bierman, *Neutrality Agreements: The New Frontier in Labor Relations—Fair Play or Foul* (to be published in the Boston College Law Review's Annual Labor Law issue, Fall 1981). The author wants to thank both Lee Miller and Leonard Bierman, associates in Seyfarth, Shaw, Fairweather & Geraldson (Washington office), for their contribution to the text.

agents will neither discourage nor encourage the Union efforts to
organize these employees, but will observe a posture of strict neutrality
in these matters.[3]

Neutrality agreements are of relatively recent origin. The first
union to have any major success in concluding such an agreement
was the United Automobile, Aerospace and Agricultural Implement
Workers (UAW), which succeeded in having "neutrality" adopted by
General Motors in 1976. This was followed in 1979 by the adoption of
"neutrality" by Goodrich, Firestone, and Uniroyal in the tire industry. During the most recent negotiations between the UAW and
General Motors, the UAW succeeded in extending the "neutrality"
concept. While retaining "neutrality," the UAW was able to negotiate transfer rights, which further facilitate the organization of new
plants, particularly in the South and Southwest. Employees were
given the right to transfer with full seniority to any new General
Motors plant that makes products similar to those produced at any
existing UAW plants.[4] In the past, such rights have applied only
when the opening of new plants resulted in layoffs at existing UAW
plants.

Neutrality agreements, however, are just one part of labor's
strategy to reverse the trend of declining union membership. The loss
of union membership has been linked to the movement of industry to
the South and Southwest and to labor's inability to wage successful
organizing campaigns there. Thus, the second prong of organized
labor's attempt to reverse these trends can be found in recent plant
closure legislation introduced both in Congress and in several northern states. While neutrality agreements make it easier to organize
plants in the South and Southwest, plant closure legislation is intended to stem the tide of industry relocation.

When viewed from a management perspective, it is difficult to see
any legitimate purpose served by neutrality agreements. Such agreements offer no benefit to employers or employees and are an attempt
by unions to gain an organizing foothold in the South and Southwest.
They enable unions to restrict the free flow of information needed
by employees in order to make an informed decision about unionization, and they are a device used by unions to circumvent the statutory protection of free speech set forth by Congress in section 8(c) of
the National Labor Relations Act.

Even a company with a positive relationship with its existing
unions ought to consider carefully the consequences of entering into a
neutrality agreement. Refusal to enter into a neutrality agreement
does not mean that an employer must oppose a particular union-

organizing effort. In the absence of such an agreement an employer can decide at the appropriate time what position is in its best interest and in the best interest of its employees. A company should not foreclose its option to speak out before an organizing campaign even is begun.

Employee interests are harmed when the only voice heard in an organizing campaign is that of the union. Indeed, the statutory principle of employee free choice is strengthened by having both sides set forth the respective issues so that a meaningful decision can be reached. Moreover, employers operating under a neutrality agreement will experience difficulties in organizing campaigns that otherwise they would not encounter. Public employers who ordinarily have taken no position with respect to organizing efforts have generally seen their employees vote for a union. While I believe that a campaign can be conducted by an employer under a neutrality agreement, such agreements place obvious limitations on the employer.

Because of the organizing advantages afforded by neutrality agreements, we can expect more unions to seek such agreements in the future. Because such demands might be made, it is important to look at the legal questions posed by such agreements. These include the duty to bargain about neutrality agreements, the scope of the restrictions imposed, and the application of such agreements when two rival unions are involved in an organizing campaign.

Compatibility of Neutrality Agreements with the Basic Policies of the National Labor Relations Act

The National Labor Relations Act was intended to protect "the exercise by workers of full freedom of association, self-organization and designation of representatives of their own choosing."[5] The act also gives workers the right to refrain from any and all such union activity.[6] Unlike the representation system in many other countries, the National Labor Relations Act provides that the employee representative selected by the majority of employees in an appropriate unit shall be the "exclusive representative of all the employees in such unit."[7] The act prevents employers and unions from coercing or restraining employees in the exercise of their right to select a majority representative or to remain unrepresented. In enforcing these sections of the act, the National Labor Relations Board (NLRB) has emphasized the importance of maintaining "laboratory conditions"[8] to allow employees to make a "free choice"—one that is "uncoerced," "reasoned," and "thoughtful."[9] Far from contributing to free choice, neutrality agreements undermine the "laboratory conditions" sought by the Board. Particularly if they are broadly drawn or construed, neutrality agreements prevent effective employer input into the election process. Such agreements cut off the flow of relevant information from the company to the employees. Employees hear only what the union wants to tell them. They are effectively cut off from the only source of information that can counterbalance union-organizing propaganda.

Neutrality agreements are analogous to contractual agreements that mandate that employees at any new stores in a retail chain automatically must become union members. In striking down such a provision, the U.S. Court of Appeals for the Ninth Circuit recently stated:

> All parties proceeded on the assumption that employees of any new store should simply be accreted to the respective multi-store units in accordance with the existing contracts. This, of course, denies employees of a new store their freedom of choice, for an election is never held. New store employees are simply subsumed into the larger unit without anyone ascertaining whether they desire union representation, and if so, whether they desire to join the larger unit. The new stores' clauses were relied on to justify this practice.
>
> The courts have frowned on this contractual usurpation of § 7 rights . . . Since contract rights cannot exist independent of the union's right to represent the unit, the new stores clause cannot bind the new employees despite the employer's acquiescence.[10]

While in the case of neutrality agreements elections are held, restriction of the free flow of information needed by the employees to make an informed decision often may, as a practical matter, make the election little more than a formality.

Neutrality agreements are subject to the same criticisms that led to the prohibitions against organizational picketing found in section 8(b)(7) of the National Labor Relations Act.[11] In describing organizational picketing, Senator McClellan, the sponsor of the 1959 Amendments to the National Labor Relations Act, stated:

> Unionizing and collective bargaining are premised on the free choice of individuals who work together to join a union of their choice, and to bargain collectively; it is not based upon compulsion to join a union.
>
> "Compulsion" is an ugly word. Decent unionism does not require it; decent unionism does not need it. Honest unionism does not need to apply that kind of tactics.
>
> If unionism is good, if it is sound, if it is right, if it is just, we can trust in the good faith and the quality and integrity of American workers voluntarily to accept it, to desire it honestly, and to be enthusiastic

to secure the benefits which flow from worthy unionism. The workers will seek to unionize. But they ought not to be compelled and hijacked to join unions whether they want to or not, when they are not given a free choice. Compulsion and hijacking are nothing in the world but top-down organization; and top-down organization has no place in American law or American institutions.[12]

Neutrality agreements share with organizational picketing many of these same characteristics. They are an attempt by organized labor to "coerce" or "buy" management silence in organizing campaigns at its unorganized plants through its bargaining strength at a company's unionized plants. Like organizational picketing, neutrality agreements are a form of top-down organizing. Unions seek to accomplish indirectly through such agreements what they are prohibited from doing directly through organizational picketing.

Such agreements clearly are a form of cooperation between labor and management that works to the detriment of employees' freedom of choice. The Supreme Court has recently inveighed against such limitations on the free flow of information in another context, stating that the first amendment presumes that "information is not in itself harmful, that people will perceive their own best interests if only they are well enough informed, and that the best means to that end is to open the channels of communication rather than to close them."[13]

In the long run, elections conducted pursuant to a neutrality agreement may result in workers feeling that they have been misled by the company's silence. The whole notion of free choice is undermined by such agreements. Moreover, the National Labor Relations Act's policy of reducing "industrial strife" and providing stability in labor relations is threatened by the use of neutrality agreements. From a policy standpoint, the value to the union of organizing a unit under such circumstances is also dubious. The union will have to expend both time and money in organizing the unit. Ultimately, however, an unstable relationship may result in plants organized without access to all the relevant information.

Duty to Bargain about Neutrality

An employer's initial concern when a union proposes a neutrality agreement is whether he has a legal obligation to bargain over such an agreement. As a practical matter, what the employer is ordinarily concerned about is whether the union can strike if he refuses to agree to "neutrality." Neither the Board nor the courts have yet had occasion to decide whether an employer must bargain about "neutrality." An analysis of the relevant statutory provisions and analogous cases, however, would suggest that he need not.

The National Labor Relations Act imposes on an employer the duty to "bargain collectively. . . [over] rates of pay, wages, hours of employment, or other conditions of employment."[14] Although the obligation to bargain "does not compel either party to agree to a proposal or require the making of a concession,"[15] if an employer is not required to bargain about a particular subject he need not even dignify the subject as a matter meriting serious discussion.

The subjects upon which an employer and a union may reach a legally binding agreement[16] are divided into two categories: mandatory subjects and permissive subjects. The parties are required to bargain in good faith about all mandatory subjects of bargaining. With respect to permissive subjects, neither side is obligated to bargain. In addition, strikes and lockouts may not be employed to support a proposal concerning a permissive subject of bargaining.[17]

The National Labor Relations Act does not specifically enumerate the items that are mandatory subjects of collective bargaining. As the Supreme Court made clear in *Allied Chemical and Alkali Workers v. Pittsburgh Plate Glass Co.*,[18] however, sections 8(d) and 9(a) of the act fix definitively the outer limits of the class. As stated by the Supreme Court:

> Together, these provisions establish the obligation of the employer to bargain collectively "with respect to wages, hours and other terms and conditions of employment" with "the representatives of his employees" designated or selected by the majority "in a unit appropriate for such purposes." *This obligation extends only to the "terms and conditions of employment" of the employer's "employees" in the "unit appropriate for such purposes" that the union represents.*[19]

In *Pittsburgh Plate Glass*, the Court determined that benefits for retirees did not satisfy the prerequisites of a mandatory subject of bargaining because retirees are not "employees" within the meaning of section 2(3) of the act. Moreover, irrespective of their status as employees, they were not and could not be members of the bargaining unit represented by the union. Accordingly, retiree benefits could only be a mandatory subject on the basis of their impact on active bargaining unit employees. The Court then established the test for whether such items could be considered mandatory subjects of bargaining based on their impact on members of the bargaining units. "[I]n each case the question is not whether the third-party concern is antagonistic to or compatible with the interests of bargaining-unit employees, but whether it *vitally affects* the 'terms and conditions' of their employment."[20] Applying this test, it concluded that the retiree benefits were not a mandatory subject of bargaining because "the benefits that active workers may reap by including retired employees under the same health insurance contract are speculative and insubstantial at best."[21]

Applying the Supreme Court's analysis in *Pittsburgh Plate Glass* to neutrality agreements would yield the same result. The essential principle of *Pittsburgh Plate Glass* is that the obligation to bargain extends only to terms and conditions of employment of bargaining unit employees. A neutrality agreement binds the employer not to oppose the union's organizational efforts in other bargaining units. In pressing for a neutrality agreement, the union is not advancing the working conditions of bargaining unit employees, but is using its status as their bargaining representative as leverage for its own organizational objectives completely outside the bargaining unit. The union's non-unit organizational efforts at best only tangentially affect the conditions of employment of bargaining unit employees.

Borg-Warner is also instructive on this issue. In *Borg-Warner*, the employer insisted on the inclusion in the agreement of a "ballot" clause calling for the employer's last bargaining offer in all future negotiations to be put to a vote of unit employees before a strike could be called. The Court held that the ballot clause was not a mandatory subject of bargaining. The decision rested in part on the fact that the clause dealt only with the relation between the employees and their unions, rather than employer-employee relations. It was also based on the Court's judgment that the clause undermined the independence of the union as the employee's representative by enabling the employer to bargain directly with the employees. Thus, the Court held that, although such a clause was not illegal, it could not be the subject of mandatory bargaining.

Similarly, the United States Court of Appeals for the Tenth Circuit has held that an "application of the contract" clause is not a mandatory subject of bargaining.[23] An "application of the contract" clause requires that an employer apply the terms of a collective bargaining agreement to any new operations acquired during the life of that agreement once the contracting union is recognized as the bargaining representative of a majority of the employees at the new facility. In a hearing before the Board, an administrative law judge (ALJ) found that such a clause did not relate to the terms and conditions of current employees and was therefore not a mandatory subject of bargaining. Moreover, he stated that " 'the principal purpose for the . . . clause is [as] an organizing device,' and was therefore not a mandatory subject of bargaining." The Board disagreed and held that such a clause did constitute a mandatory subject. The Tenth Circuit reversed the Board, however, adopting the ALJ's reasoning.

If an "application of the contract" clause does not properly constitute a mandatory subject of bargaining because it is primarily an organizing device, clearly a neutrality agreement would suffer from the same shortcoming. Moreover, a neutrality agreement, like a "ballot" clause, relates primarily to the relationship between the union and the employees. It has virtually no direct impact on the terms and conditions of employment in the bargaining unit covered by the agreement. Therefore, it would seem that neutrality agreements should, at most, properly be classified as permissive subjects of bargaining. Thus, employers would be free to refuse even to bargain with unions about "neutrality" proposals.

Impact of Neutrality Agreements on Management

The obvious purpose of a neutrality agreement is to prevent an employer from taking an active part in union organizational drives and elections. As such, neutrality agreements restrict an employer's right to express an opinion about a particular union or about unionism in general. The extent of the restriction will depend on the drafting of the specific neutrality agreement.

Unions generally maintain that "neutrality" requires management to refrain from making any statements concerning a union's organizing campaign. According to the president of one of the major unions to conclude a neutrality agreement, "neutrality" creates a zone of corporate silence. The typical neutrality agreement, however, should not be read so broadly.

Although a neutrality agreement would constitute a waiver by a company of its right of free speech, such a waiver probably does not extend so far as to prohibit management entirely from making statements regarding a union-organizing campaign. A strong argument can be made that a company retains its right to issue "neutral" remarks about unionization and the differences between union and nonunion plants, especially the effects these differences have on employees.

In this regard, it must be remembered that the union has the burden of establishing a waiver of a statutory or constitutional right.[24] Even if statutory or constitutional rights were not involved, the burden of proving a breach of contract would fall upon the union. "If a written contract is ambiguous, or open to different constructions, then it must be construed most strongly against the party who prepared it."[25] Since a neutrality agreement will ordinarily be prepared by the union or included at its insistence, a court or the Board should read any ambiguities in the agreement in the light most favorable to the employer.

In determining the scope of the restrictions imposed by neutrality agreements, some guidance can be garnered from the Railway Labor Act.[26] Unlike the National Labor Relations Act, which guarantees the employer freedom of speech, the Railway Labor Act provides that "representatives...shall be designated by the respective parties without *interference, influence,* or coercion by either party over the designation of representatives by the other; and neither party shall in any way *interfere with, influence,* or coerce the other in its choice of representatives."[27] In interpreting this proscription, the United States Supreme Court has stated:

> The intent of Congress is clear with respect to the sort of conduct that is prohibited. "Interference" with freedom of action and "coercion" refer to well-understood concepts of the law. The meaning of the word "influence" in this clause may be gathered from the context . . . The use of the word is not to be taken as interdicting the normal relations and innocent communications which are a part of all friendly intercourse, albeit between employer and employee. "Influence" in this context plainly means pressure, the use of the authority or power of either party to induce action by the other in derogation of what the statute calls "self-organization." The phrase covers the abuse of relation or opportunity so as to corrupt or override the will, and it is no more difficult to appraise conduct of this sort in connection with the selection of representatives for the purposes of this act than in relation to well-known applications of the law with respect to fraud, duress and undue influence.[28]

In more recent cases, the courts have interpreted the prohibitions against "influencing" elections of employee representatives even less restrictively.[29] The exact parameters of acceptable company conduct under a neutrality agreement cannot be determined with certainty. In light of the lack of any benefit to employers and their employees resulting from neutrality agreements, it is best to avoid entering into such agreements in the first place. If such agreements are entered into, however, one thing that is certain is that management cannot state that it opposes the union's organizing effort. As discussed above, it would seem that the company retains the right to give employees factual information concerning the company and the union. So long as the information given to employees is couched in a straightforward, unbiased, and frank manner, without the interjection of the employer's opinions, it would appear to come within the parameters of being "neutral."[30] Providing such information would constitute neither employer discouragement nor encouragement of the union efforts to organize its employees.

Often the right to provide factual information is set forth specifically in the neutrality agreement. For instance, the UAW agreement with Dana Corporation provides:

> Our Corporate position regarding union representation is as follows:
>
> We believe that our employees should exercise free choice and decide for themselves by voting on whether or not they wish to be represented by the UAW or any other labor organization.
>
> We have no objection to the UAW becoming the bargaining representative of our people as a result of such an election.
>
> Where the UAW becomes involved in organizing our employees, we intend to continue our commitment of maintaining a neutral position on this matter. The Company and/or its representatives will communicate with our employees, not in an anti-UAW manner, but in a positive pro-Dana manner.
>
> If a majority of our employees indicate a desire to be represented by the UAW, we will cooperate with all parties involved to expedite an NLRB election.
>
> In addition, we reserve the right to speak out in any manner appropriate when undue provocation is evident in an organizing campaign.[31]

Nevertheless, even when an employer such as Dana has negotiated as part of a neutrality agreement explicit provisions allowing it to speak out in order to set the record straight, such explicit provisions may still not be sufficient. For example, in the first arbitration case involving a neutrality agreement, which involved Dana and the UAW, an arbitrator found that Dana had violated its agreement by speaking out against the union in response to union misrepresentations regarding the rate of pay of other unionized employees, Dana hourly employees, and Dana executives.[32]

The arbitrator held that numerous union misrepresentations did not represent "undue provocation" by the union of the kind which permitted the company to speak out against the union. The arbitrator also, in an extraordinary move, awarded $10,000 in damages to the union because of the company's contractual breach, even though the union did not seek such monetary relief.

The Dana arbitration case makes it clear that the only way that an employer can be certain to protect its rights of free speech is by refusing to agree to a neutrality provision in the first place. Even when a neutrality clause expressly reserves the employer's right to speak out under certain conditions, that right may construe narrowly in subsequent arbitrations.

The Dana arbitration case was preceded by a court case in which the UAW successfully obtained a temporary restraining order prohibiting Dana, or persons acting on its behalf, "from making anti-union or anti-UAW oral or written statements or other communications to its employees at its Gastonia facility or otherwise departing from a position of neutrality with regard to [an] upcoming National Labor Relations Board election at that facility."[33] Then, based on a speech by the company president to employees of the Gastonia facility that followed, Dana was found in contempt. Judge Young ordered that Dana purge itself of contempt by:

> 1. [S]ending a written communication, in form satisfactory to the plaintiff, to all employees of . . . [the] Corporation repudiating both the written and oral statements of . . . [the Company President], promising to abide by the contents of its neutrality agreement, and indicating its neutrality in any forthcoming National Labor Relations Board election;
>
> 2. [P]rovid[ing] access to each plant of . . . [the] Corporation in which . . . [the Company President] addressed assembled workers, for a representative of the plaintiff to address each shift of workers, assembled, for the length of time that . . . [the President] addressed such shift, and . . . [the President] shall be and remain present throughout the giving of each such address;
>
> 3. [C]lear[ing] all the specially colored bulletin boards throughout the . . . Corporation plants of any and all anti-union materials, refrain[ing] from posting such material on any bulletin boards in the future, reserv[ing] no less than half the space upon said bulletin boards for the use of plaintiff to affix communications, and giv[ing] a representative of the plaintiff daily access to each such bulletin board for posting and for reviewing posted materials until a National Labor Relations Board election shall be held . . . .[34]

The decision in this case, which represented a clear instance of judicial prior restraint of speech, is currently being appealed.[35]

The *Dana* case, in particular, suggests that neutrality agreements are likely to involve employers in costly court litigation over any statements they make which could be construed as unfavorable toward unions. Neutrality agreements in this way provide unions with another weapon with which to enhance their organizing efforts. Throughout a campaign, a union can hold out the threat of litigation to inhibit an employer from communicating with his employees. If an employer does speak out and the union does not like the substance of management's comments, it can go to court in an attempt to gag the employer. At the very least, the act of litigating itself may assist the union by creating additional propaganda suggesting that the company cannot be trusted to keep its word.

As previously discussed, neutrality agreements facilitate union organizing by eliminating the primary source of informed opposition to the union's efforts—the employer. Moreover, some agreements extend beyond neutrality and provide an even greater organizing advantage to a union. Thus, the UAW's extension of its 1976 neutrality agreement with General Motors to guarantee employees the right to transfer with full seniority to new plants opened by the company greatly aids the union's ability to organize these new plants. The UAW's comments on this new agreement are revealing.

> Few challenges to labor are as critical as the organizing of new plants or runaway shops, especially those dotting the traditionally anti-labor areas of the Sunbelt and South.
>
> For GM workers, that challenge has focused on the fact that the corporation has opened or plans to open several new plants, many of which are in areas where workers have had limited contact with unions in the past and business and right-wing resistance to unions remains high . . . .
>
> [This agreement is a] major breakthrough . . . [which] is expected to build a more positive climate, especially in the South, for the UAW and for other unions.[36]

These developments in the use of neutrality agreements to enhance union ability to organize in the South and Southwest come at the same time that organized labor is seeking to maintain its membership in the North through legislation restricting a company's ability to close or relocate its plants. For example, at the time of the present Congress, H.R. 1037, a bill introduced on January 22, 1981, by Congressman Gaydos, would severely restrict the ability of businesses to relocate operations and shift capital as they see fit. A number of similar bills, including H.R. 5040, S. 1609, and S. 2400, were introduced in the previous Congress. The general scheme contemplated by these bills is to impose lengthy notice provisions and penalties in order to inhibit businesses from relocating their operations.

Under H.R. 1037, which is currently being considered by Congress, for instance, businesses generally must give at least two years prior written notice before closing an establishment or transferring operations. After such notice is given, the Department of Labor then investigates the "merits" of the business' decision. If the Department of Labor determines that the closing or transfer of operations is not "justified" or is otherwise improper, the business will then become ineligible under the Internal Revenue Code for: (1) investment credits, (2) accelerated depreciation, (3) foreign tax credits, (4) deferral of tax on income earned outside the United States, and (5) ordinary and necessary business expense deductions for expenses related to the transfer of operations. Such businesses will also not be entitled to derive benefits from the industrial development bond provisions of the Internal Revenue Code.[37] The entire act will be supervised by a new bureaucracy known as the National Employment Relocation Administration. Such proposed plant closure legislation represents an attempt by government to inhibit plant movement from the North to the South and Southwest, thereby protecting union membership.

Coupled with organized labor's efforts to enact plant closure legislation, unions are increasingly seeking to raise that issue at the bargaining table as well. The Oil Chemical and Atomic Workers (OCAW), for instance, intends to make plant closures a major issue in its 1982 negotiations.[38] From labor's perspective, however, legislation like H.R. 1037 is preferable, since enactment of legislation like H.R. 1037 would impose, by statutory mandate, restrictions on the transfer of capital of a kind which could not realistically be achieved through collective bargaining.

Legality of Neutrality Agreements under Section 8(a)(2) of the National Labor Relations Act

Section 8(a)(2) of the National Labor Relations Act provides, in part, that it is an unfair labor practice for an employer "to dominate or interfere with the formation or administration of any labor organization or contribute financial or other support to it."[39] The question thus arises whether an agreement between an employer and a union providing that the employer will be "neutral" with respect to future organizational efforts by that union presents the kind of employer support that poses a violation of section 8(a)(2).

In a sense, an employer remaining officially "neutral" when a union attempts to organize additional employees represents an expression of a point of view by the employer. The employer is simply saying that he has no real opinion one way or the other as to whether the employees should vote to have the union represent them or not. The law clearly allows employers the right to express that sort of opinion.[40] Indeed, the National Labor Relations Act explicitly protects that right.[41]

Thus, there is nothing wrong with an employer expressing its views on the representation of his employees by a particular union. An employer's simple statement that it feels it is in the best interest of its employees to be represented by a union does not constitute the kind of support for that union that violates section 8(a)(2) of the act. Furthermore, the right of employer free speech extends even to the situation where more than one union is competing to represent the bargaining unit. An employer's noncoercive declaration of a preference for one union over another does not constitute a violation of section 8(a)(2).[42]

Consequently, if neutrality agreements are read, from the point of view of the employer, as merely being an expression of its views toward unionization, such agreements seem to pose no real problems in terms of section 8(a)(2) of the act. The problem, however, is that it is unrealistic to view such agreements as having no more force than a mere public statement by the employer setting forth his views with respect to unionization. Neutrality agreements are binding contracts to assist, albeit through their silence, a union.

Neutrality agreements go beyond merely voluntarily refraining from taking a position against a particular union. Under a neutrality agreement, an employer contractually agrees, for the period of that contract, not to oppose the organizational efforts of the union with which the agreement was reached. The very fact of having reached such an agreement enhances the union's stature in the eyes of the employees. It goes beyond mere neutrality and borders on active assistance.

Overall, neutrality agreements clearly seem to violate the spirit, if not the precise language, of section 8(a)(2), which was enacted by Congress to guarantee employees "complete and unfettered freedom of choice."[43] The kind of "support" and "assistance" employers, by way of neutrality agreements, give unions tends to hamper employee free choice and should, as matter of policy, be found to violate section 8(a)(2) of the National Labor Relations Act.[44]

Whether or not neutrality agreements will, in fact, be found by the NLRB to violate section 8(a)(2) of the National Labor Relations Act is questionable. The NLRB has exhibited a distinct predilection toward upholding contractual commitments between unions and employers, even when such agreements tend to directly impinge on the rights of individual employees.

For example, the Board, under its *Briggs Indiana*[45] doctrine has upheld agreements under which the union agrees, for the term of the contract, not to represent certain groups of employees. The Board, in upholding such agreements, has flatly rejected assertions that such agreements work most unfairly to disenfranchise certain groups of employees.[46]

Similarly, the Board has upheld agreements which allow a union's majority status for purposes of recognition to be determined by methods other than a secret ballot election.[47] Such agreements are upheld despite the recognized questionable validity of those methods, and despite their seemingly obvious disadvantages in terms of encouraging uncoerced employee free choice.

Ultimately the protection of individual employee rights and the policies favoring "free" elections which underlie the National Labor Relations Act and which are threatened by neutrality agreements probably lies with the courts. The Supreme Court, particularly in the recent case of *Connell Construction Co. v. Plumbers Local 100*,[48] has shown a marked willingness to protect individual employee rights, even if it is necessary to read deeply into the National Labor Relations Act's underlying policy considerations to do so.

In *Connell*, despite seemingly clear language in section 8(e) of the National Labor Relations Act permitting such arrangements, the Court struck down an agreement between a construction industry employer and a union whereby the employer agreed to use only unionized subcontractors. The Court, in reaching its decision, displayed a willingness to look behind the specific statutory language to the policy considerations underlying the act. Focusing in part on how such agreements thwart the desires of individual employees, the Court held that such "top-down" organizing violated the National Labor Relations Act.[49]

Thus, while it seems rather unlikely that the National Labor Relations Board will strike down neutrality agreements, the courts may be sympathetic to the erosion of individual employee rights which such agreements produce. The courts may view neutrality agreements as representing much more than simply an employer's expression of opinion regarding unionization. Thus, they may find that neutrality agreements are inherently destructive of the right to free elections guaranteed by the National Labor Relations Act and that such agreements constitute improper aid to the unions with which they are concluded.

Conclusion

Even a brief examination of the trends in organizational activity in the 1980s makes clear that unions intend to use their "friends" in the business community and the legislatures to maintain and increase their membership. As union membership continues to decline, through the loss of jobs in the heavily organized industries in the North and through labor's continued inability to successfully organize in the South and Southwest, we can expect increased pressure on business and on Congress to come to the aid of organized labor. The International Union of Electrical Workers (IUE) has already vowed to make neutrality a key issue in its upcoming negotiations with General Electric and Westinghouse.

To date, however, the developments discussed above remain in an embryonic stage. Only a few unions have had any notable success in concluding neutrality agreements. Plant-closure legislation has yet to be enacted by Congress and has only been enacted in a limited form in two states.

Employers should resist entering into neutrality agreements. They should insist on allowing their employees the freedom to make an informed choice based on all the relevant information. In addition, industry should oppose the proposed plant-closure legislation. It must expose this legislation for what it really is—an attempt to restrict the flow of capital to its most productive uses. Industry must act instead of react. It must stand up to such unwarranted legislative interference with business that, in the long run, will reduce productivity and employment. It must stand up for the rights of its employees to determine, based on all the relevant data, whether they wish to be represented by a particular union. For if the business community will not, there is no one else who will.

NOTES

1. United States Department of Labor, Bureau of Labor Statistics, News Release (September 3, 1979).

2. Barkin, THE DECLINE OF THE LABOR MOVEMENT quoted in *Congressional Quarterly* (July 28, 1979), p. 1507.

3. [1979] 132 DAILY LAB. REP. (BNA) D-3.

4. The text of that letter agreement provides:
    During the current negotiations there have been discussions between the parties regarding the transfer of operations and employees affected by the opening of new plants.
    This will confirm our verbal commitment that during the term of the 1979 National Agreement any new plants opened by the Corporation in the United States to produce products similar to those now being produced at plants in which the Union is currently the bargaining representative of the production and maintenance employees will involve a 'transfer of major operations' (as histor-

ically applied by the parties) from an existing UAW-represented plant to the new plant so as to bring into play the provisions of Paragraph (96).

It is understood that the foregoing will not apply to those plants currently covered by the Preferential Consideration Procedure, nor will it apply to the current Chevrolet-Moraine, Ohio plant sites or to any new plant producing products which are similar to those produced in another existing plant where the production and maintenance employees are represented by some union other than the UAW. [1976] 237 DAILY LAB. REP. (BNA) A-13-14.

5. National Labor Relations Act, § 1, 29 U.S.C. § 151(1976).

6. *Id.*, § 7, 29 U.S.C. § 157.

7. *Id.*, § 9(a), 29 U.S.C. § 159(a).

8. As the Board stated in *General Shoe Corp.*, 77 N.L.R.B. 124, 126 (1948):
   In election proceedings, it is the Board's function to provide a laboratory in which an experiment may be conducted, under conditions as nearly ideal as possible, to determine the uninhibited desires of the employees. It is our duty to establish those conditions; it is also our duty to determine whether they have been fulfilled.

9. Sewell Mfg. Co., 138 N.L.R.B. 66, 70 (1962), where the Board stated:
   Our function, as we see it, is to conduct elections in which the employees have the opportunity to cast their ballots for or against a labor organization in an atmosphere conducive to the sober and informed exercise of the franchise, free not only from interference, restraint, or coercion violative of the Act, but also from other elements which prevent or impede a reasoned choice.

10. NLRB v. Retail Clerks Local 588, 587 F.2d 984, 986 (9th Cir. 1978) (citations omitted).

11. 29 U.S.C. § 158(b)(7).

12. LEGISLATIVE HISTORY OF THE LABOR-MANAGEMENT REPORTING AND DISCLOSURE ACT, 1959, at 1175 (1959)(statements of Sen. McClellan).

13. Virginia State Bd. of Pharmacy v. Virginia Citizens Consumer Council, Inc., 425 U.S. 748, 770 (1976).

14. National Labor Relations Act, §§ 8(a)(5) and 9(a), 29 U.S.C. §§ 158(a)(5) and 159(a)(1976).

15. *See generally* H.K. Porter v. NLRB, 397 U.S. 99 (1970).

16. Indeed, as developed *infra*, such neutrality agreements may represent a violation of section 8(a)(2) of the act and thus be an "illegal" subject of bargaining. For a general discussion of the "illegal" bargaining category, *see* R. GORMAN, *Unionization and Collective Bargaining*, in BASIC TEXT ON LABOR LAW, 528-31 (1976).

17. NLRB v. Wooster Div. of Borg-Warner Corp., 356 U.S. 342 (1958).

18. 404 U.S. 157 (1971).

19. *Id.* at 164 (emphasis added).

20. *Id.* at 179 (emphasis added).

21. *Id.* at 180.

22. *Supra* note 17.

23. Lone Star Steel Co. v. NLRB, 104 L.R.R.M. 3134 (10th Cir. 1980).

24. *See, e.g.,* Gary Hobart Water Corp., 210 N.L.R.B. 742 (1974), *aff'd*, 511 F.2d 284 (7th Cir.), *cert. denied*, 423 U.S. 925 (1975), where the Board stated: "While statutory rights may be waived, . . . the Board and the courts have repeatedly emphasized that such waivers will not be readily inferred, and there must be a clear and unmistakable showing that waiver occurred." 210 N.L.R.B. at 744.

25. Miravalle Supply Co. v. El Campo Rice Milling Co., 181 F.2d 679, 683 (8th Cir.), *cert. denied*, 340 U.S. 822 (1950).

26. 45 U.S.C. § 151 *et seq.* (1926).

27. *Id.* § 152 (emphasis added).

28. Texas & N.O.R. Co. v. Brotherhood of Railway & Steamship Clerks, 281 U.S. 548, 568 (1930) (citations omitted). *See also* Virginian Railway Co. v. System Federation No. 40, 300 U.S. 515 (1937).

29. Adams v. Federal Express Corp., 470 F. Supp. 1356 (W.D. Tenn. 1979); Brotherhood of Railway & Steamship Clerks v. Philadelphia, Bethlehem & New England Railroad Co., 428 F. Supp. 1308 (E.D. Pa. 1977); Teamsters v. Braniff Airways, Inc., 70 L.R.R.M. 3333 (D. D.C. 1969). *Contra,* Brotherhood of Railroad Trainmen v. Richmond, Fredericksburg and Potomac Railroad Co., 69 L.R.R.M. 2884 (E.D. Va. 1968).

30. *Webster's Third New International Dictionary* (1971 ed.) defines "neutral" as "not engaged on either side; not siding with or assisting either; lending no active assistance to either or any belligerent."

31. Letter of Neutrality Agreement between Dana Corporation and the UAW (December 7, 1979).

32. Decision of arbitrator in application of neutrality letter involving Wix Corporation and UAW, *printed in* [1981] 41 DAILY LAB. REP. (BNA) E-1.

33. UAW v. Dana Corporation, 104 L.R.R.M. 2687 (1980), *appeal docketed*, No. 80-3548 (6th Cir. 1981).

34. *Id.*

35. *Id.*

36. [1979] 183 DAILY LAB. REP. (BNA).

37. H.R. 1037, 97th Cong., 1st Sess., § 2701 (1981).

38. *See* [1981] 95 DAILY LAB. REP. (BNA) A-3.

39. 29 U.S.C. § 158(a)(2)(1976).

40. *See* NLRB v. Virginia Electric Power Co., 314 U.S. 469 (1941).

41. National Labor Relations Act, § 8(c), 29 U.S.C. § 158(c)(1976).

42. Rold Gold of California, Inc., 123 N.L.R.B. 285 (1959). *See also* Alley Construction Co., 210 N.L.R.B. 999, 1004 (1974); Stewart-Warner Corp., 102 N.L.R.B. 1153 (1953).

43. NLRB v. Link-Belt Co., 311 U.S. 584, 588 (1941).

44. The United States Supreme Court had made clear that an employer need not intend to unlawfully aid a union for a § 8(a)(2) violation to be found. As long as the result of the employer's actions is to unlawfully aid the union and hamper

employee free choice, a § 8(a)(2) unfair labor practice action will exist. ILGWU v. NLRB (Bernhard-Altman Texas Corp.), 366 U.S. 731, 739 (1961).

Furthermore, employees' subjective reactions to employer support of a union need not be proved for a § 8(a)(2) action to lie. What is of primary consequence is the tendency of the employer's assistance to the union to coerce employees in the exercise of their rights. NLRB v. Vernitron Electrical Components, Inc., 548 F.2d 24, 26 (1st Cir. 1977).

45. *See* Briggs Indiana Corp., 63 N.L.R.B. 1270 (1945).

46. *See* Allis-Chalmers Manufacturing Co., 179 N.L.R.B. 1 (1969).

47. *See* Snow & Sons, 134 N.L.R.B. 709 (1961), *enf'd*, 308 F.2d 687 (9th Cir. 1962).

48. 421 U.S. 616 (1975).

49. *Id.* at 632, n.11.

223-83

Labor Violence: The Inadequate Response of the Federal Anti-Extortion Statutes©

8331

8 U. S,

[1980]

Thomas R. Haggard[†]

I. Introduction

Of all kinds of human conduct, physical violence against person or property is undoubtedly the one which receives almost universal condemnation among civilized peoples. Even the fiercest of the classical liberals and modern libertarians, who view government's function very narrowly, recognize both the propriety and the necessity of state sanctions against aggression. Indeed, this may even be viewed as the *only* truly essential function of government, the nonperformance of which divests a corporated body of any legitimate claims to be our political sovereign. The state's control of violence is, in short, a very important matter.

Labor violence, however, has long been a major problem in this country. Perhaps the earliest reported instance of labor violence occurred in 1799 in connection with a strike among the cordwainers of Philadelphia. It involved numerous acts of misconduct, including the throwing of a tack-studded potato through a shop window, barely missing the head of the proprietor who had hired a "scab"[1]—a quaint but lethal way of making a point! The fifty-year period between 1880 and 1930 was especially marked by acts of violence committed in connection with the many strikes and lockouts of that era, which often took on the dimensions of "small wars."[2] In one two-year period, 1902-04, approximately 200 people were reported killed and over 2,000 injured in acts of labor violence.[3]

Although the days of company "armies" and the Molly McGuires[4] are thankfully gone, acts of violence continue to occur in labor disputes in this country. No hard data exist concerning the current scope

---

† Thomas R. Haggard is Professor of Law at the University of South Carolina School of Law. Research for this article was financed by a grant from the Foundation for the Advancement of the Public Trust to the Wharton School, University of Pennsylvania. The views expressed herein are, however, entirely those of the author.

© Copyright reserved, 1980, by Thomas R. Haggard. Reprint permission may be obtained from the Nebraska Law Review. Reprinted from the *Nebraska Law Review*, Vol. 59, No. 4, 1980. Copyright 1980 by the University of Nebraska

and origin of this violence. It would appear, however, that when management opposition to unionization does go beyond the bounds permitted by law, it consists mainly of economic reprisals against union sympathizers,[5] although physical violence by management officials does occur occasionally.[6]

Violence appears to be a more extensive problem for labor. In some instances, it undoubtedly represents the "semiofficial" policy of a labor union, a deliberate and all too effective tool for bargaining or organizing. In other instances, the official dereliction consists merely of a more-or-less passive indifference to the use of violence by rank-and-file members, including the failure by union leaders to take steps to prevent and correct these "unauthorized" acts. Also, there are still other instances of individual worker violence committed in open defiance of official and genuine union prohibitions against it. This conduct is of as much concern to responsible labor leaders as it is to the victims themselves.

At first glance it would appear that the law has responded fully and adequately to the problem of labor union violence. Such conduct is actionable under both the criminal[7] and the civil laws of every state,[8] and stiff penalties and high damage awards are certainly possible. In addition, the federal Labor Management Relations Act regards such violence as an unfair labor practice.[10] Although the use of injunctions is prohibited in the context of most labor disputes, the statutes seem to recognize an exception with respect to violence.[11] Futhermore, there are numerous other statutes, both state[12] and federal,[13] which either specifically or generally include labor violence within their ambit, or which have the potential of doing so.[14]

Despite the plethora of state and federal laws which potentially touch on the matter, the problem of labor union violence seems to persist. Even with due recognition that the law can never be expected to eradicate completely man's tendency toward aggression or to always provide a full measure of justice to its victims, the uneasy feeling remains that the law does not address the problem of labor union violence with the vigor that it should. The attitude seems to be that "boys will be boys"; that a certain amount of "animal exuberance"[15] is to be expected in the emotionally supercharged atmosphere of a labor dispute; and that, while this is to be regretted, the law should not overreact.[16]

This attitude can be seen in all three branches of government. Prosecution under the criminal statutes, especially at the state and local level, is reportedly lax in certain jurisdictions, perhaps because of the political sensitivity of the issue. Moreover, where vigorous attempts have been made to enforce these statutes against labor union violence, the administrative agencies and courts have often either construed the statutes so narrowly as to make them virtually worthless, or have judicially excluded labor violence from their coverage altogether. In addition, legislatures, especially Congress, have seemed either unable or unwilling to write statutes prohibiting labor violence with that degree of specificity that is apparently necessary in order to insure judicial and administrative enforcement.

In many respects, the federal anti-extortion statutes are an ideal microcosm of the problems that exist generally with respect to the law's response to labor violence. In particular, the history of these statutes and the cases construing them are an excellent example of the kind of legislative point and judicial counterpoint that has left the law in a virtual stalemate. Currently, as a part of the overall revision of the federal criminal code, the anti-extortion sections are being revised and their scope and applicability to labor union violence are again being hotly debated.[17] One cannot, however, fully appreciate the probable effect of the proposed changes except by reference to what has transpired before. The purpose of this article, thus, is to re-plow some ground that is concededly old in the hope that this may shed some useful light on the current controversy.

II. The Anti-Racketeering Act of 1934

A. *The Legislative History*

The original federal anti-extortion statute, known as the Anti-Racketeering Act,[18] was one of several bills that came out of the extensive investigations of "racketeering" conducted in 1933 by the Copeland Committee, a special subcommittee of the Senate Committee on Interstate Commerce.

As introduced in the Senate,[19] this bill did not specifically include or exclude the activities of labor unions. The Senate Report stated, however, that "[t]he provisions of the proposed statute are limited so as not to include the usual activities of capitalistic combinations, bona fide labor unions, and ordinary business practices which are not accompanied by manifestations of racketeering."[20] The report also stated that at the time "the nearest approach to prosecution of racketeers as such has been under the Sherman Antitrust Act."[21] It noted, however, the limitations of that act, as construed by the courts, in addressing this particular kind of abusive behavior. It is problematic, of course, whether framers of the Senate bill had in mind any of the cases in which the Supreme Court had found the Sherman Act to be inapplicable to various forms of strike violence.[22]

In any event, it is clear that S. 2248 was intended to go beyond the limitations of the Sherman Act in dealing with the problems of "racketeering" and violence in interstate commerce. It did this by separately prohibiting four things, as they would affect interstate commerce: (1) acts of violence, intimidation, or injury to person or property, or threats thereof; (2) extortion of money or other valuable consideration; (3) coercion of persons to join associations or make payments thereto; and (4) coercion of persons in the exercise of their rights to do or not to do as they choose.

This version of the bill passed the Senate with little or no debate. Moreover, it appears that the bill had been sent to the House before organized labor awoke to the possible implications insofar as labor activities were concerned. Senator Robinson, in belatedly requesting a reconsideration, stated: "Representatives of the American Federation of Labor informed me this afternoon that both bills [S. 2248 and a bill dealing with extortion by phone] might be very discriminatory against labor in this country, and that they wanted to be heard respecting them."[23]

It is not altogether clear why the American Federation of Labor (AFL) thought the bill was "discriminatory" or unfair to them. It seems unlikely that they believed that labor unions are simply entitled to a *blanket* exemption from the normal prohibitions against physical violence and extortion. In all probability labor feared that the historically elusive term "coercion" might be construed broadly to encompass, in addition to overt violence, the traditional labor activities of strikes and picketing, especially when such activities were directed at compelling an employer to recognize the union, to pay union wages, and to stop hiring nonunion labor.[24] These objectives would certainly seem to be encompassed by the third and fourth provisions of the bill as summarized above. Moreover, strikes to obtain these objectives had been held to be beyond the reach of the Sherman Act, and organized labor knew that the bill was intended to expand that reach in some unspecified fashion. Thus, the fears of the AFL may not have been totally unwarranted.

The House was apparently receptive to whatever fears labor had concerning S. 2248. When the bill was reported out of committee,[25] it had been rewritten so as to prohibit: (1) the use of force, violence, or coercion to obtain or attempt to obtain money or other valuable consideration, "not including, however, the payment of wages by a bona-fide employer to a bona-fide employee";[26] (2) the wrongful use of force to obtain the property of another without his consent; (3) conduct in furtherance of a plan or purpose to otherwise violate the act; and (4) conspiracies to engage in conduct otherwise prohibited by the act. A final proviso to the act also stated "[t]hat no court of the United States shall construe or apply any of the provisions of this act in such manner as to impair, diminish, or in any manner affect the rights of bona-fide labor organizations in lawfully carrying out the legitimate objects thereof, as such rights are expressed in existing statutes of the United States."[27]

The House Report, quoting a letter from the attorney general, noted that

> The original bill was susceptible to the objection that it might include within its prohibition the legitimate and bona fide activities of employers and employees. As the purpose of the legislation is not to interfere with such legitimate activities but rather to set up severe penal-
> ities for racketeering by violence, extortion, or coercion, which affects interstate commerce, it seems advisable to definitely exclude such legitimate activities.[28]

Assured that the new bill had the complete approval of organized labor,[29] the House and the Senate passed the act without further debate.

Despite the effort of Congress to direct the focus of the act *toward* organized crime and *away from* organized labor, some of the first indictments under the act were brought against labor union officials. Thus, it soon became necessary for the courts to clarify the scope of the labor exemption. One such case ultimately wound its way to the Supreme Court.

B. *The Case Law*

In *United States v. Local 807, International Brotherhood of Teamsters,*[30] members of the union met trucks as they came into New York City and used threats and violence to obtain from the owners of these trucks the equivalent of a day's wage for driving and unloading the trucks within the city. In some instances the defendant unionists did in fact perform *some* work for which they nevertheless obtained *full* payment. In others, the owners paid the money but rejected the offers of the defendants to do the driving and unloading. There were also instances in which the defendants apparently either failed to offer to do the work or refused to do any work when asked.

The issue in *Local 807* boiled down to whether the unionists were using force to obtain "*wages* by a bona-fide employer to a bona-fide employee,"[31] thus bringing the events within the Act's exception in that regard. Although the *Local 807* case involved a now repealed portion of the act, what the courts said in this case is important in evaluating the significance of the congressional repudiation of this interpretation, and in determining meaning of the act as presently written.[32]

A number of competing interpretations were proffered in the opinions of both the court of appeals and the Supreme Court. The interpretation that was the most obvious and the most reasonable, however, was dismissed out of hand by the court of appeals. Speaking of the exception, the court noted that "[t]heoretically it might indeed apply only to situations in which an employee procured by threats the payment of wages due under a contract which the employer had made without coercion."[33] In other words, a bona fide or uncoerced employment relationship must exist before the exception is even applicable.

Presumably, the unstated predicate of this interpretation was that actual physical violence can never really be considered a legitimate and bona fide labor union activity, insofar as the final proviso to the act is concerned,[34] and that the specific exemption with respect to wages should, therefore, be narrowly construed. Limiting the exception to violence used by a real employee to obtain the wages that are legitimately due him recognizes the general prohibition against violence, and at the same time, gives some meaning to the express words of the statute. Moreover, it makes sense to read the statute as recognizing a distinction between the use of force to obtain something that one is not entitled to without the consent of the other party (a wage contract), and the use of force to obtain something that one is actually entitled to (wages due under a previously consented to contract); the former but not the latter falls within the general meaning of the term "extortion,"[35] which was apparently the central concern of Congress in passing the act.

Nevertheless, the court had two objections to that interpretation. First, the court felt that there was no real distinction between using coercion to obtain a contract for wages, and using coercion to obtain the wages owed under an otherwise noncoerced contract. The court, however, was simply wrong in that regard; but the court's willingness to indulge in patently fallacious reasoning to reach that desired result is probably more important than the logical fallacy itself.[36]

More importantly, the court of appeals felt that the suggested interpretation would make the exception too narrow. The court noted that the exception was clearly intended to cover "labor disputes," that "[p]ractically always the crux of a labor dispute is who shall get the job and what the terms shall be," and that "[t]o confine the exception to cases where the original contract was voluntary would therefore leave out the great mass of instances in which theissue would ever arise."[37] This, however, simply begs the quetion of whether, with respect to the use of actual physical violence in contrast to the use of economic power, Congress intended the exemption to be narrow or broad.

In any event, the court of appeals obviously had to give the term "bona fide" some other meaning to avoid this particular interpretation. Accordingly, the majority held that the requirement of "bona fide" was not met and thus, the exception did not apply where the money was paid on a "pretext of service never in fact rendered."[38] Conversely, the exception was said to apply whenever the "employee really did the work for which he was paid."[39] The majority immediately expanded the exception, however, to include payments made to a person who offered to do the work but whose offer was refused by the person being coerced to make the payments. It was on this specific point that the dissent parted company with the remainder of the court.[40] The court noted that while it might be difficult to call such payments "wages," it would nevertheless be nonsensical to assume that Congress wanted to grant immunity to one who used coercion to the point of actually getting the job, but, at the same time, penalize another who did *not* persist "in pressing his unwelcome services upon the employer."[41] The court noted that this would "excuse the more heinous offense, and penalize the more venial."[42]

The majority also felt that interpreting "bona fide" to include any coercively obtained payments as long as work was performed or tendered was justified by reference to the evil that Congress intended to suppress by this act. The court noted that what Congress had in mind was the "blackmail" that "organized gangs of bandits" had levied upon many small businessmen, especially in New York City.[43] Labor violence, *aimed at the legitimate objectives of obtaining jobs and higher wages,* was said to be an altogether different matter. The court noted:

> Congress might indeed have gone further than it did; it might have included payments extorted by threats for services rendered or offered; that too is a grave evil. But, grave as it is, it is of a different kind from that at which this act was aimed. The history of labor disputes is studded with violence which unhappily is not yet obsolete; but, although the *means* employed may be the same as those here condemned, the *end* is always different, it is to secure work on better terms.[44]

This notion that the "legitimacy" of the *ends* somehow takes otherwise violent *means* outside the prohibitions of the statute has proved to be persistently appealing insofar as the courts are concerned. Although Congress expressly repudiated the Supreme Court decision which affirmed and restated this idea,[45] the theory was subsequently to reappear. Remarkably, today it represents the prevailing interpretation of the amended statute.[46]

On appeal, the Supreme Court again couched the issue in *Local 807* in terms of finding a correct construction of the wage proviso, and suggested three alternative interpretations. The Court first considered the possibility that "[t] he exception applies only to a defendant who has enjoyed the status of a bona fide employee prior to the time at which he obtains or attempts to obtain the payment of money by the owner."[47] Presumably, this interpretation had been considered and rejected by the court below. The Supreme Court rejected it, in part for the same reason—such a reading would allegedly exclude practically all labor disputes from the exemption, a result which the Court found incompatible with the probable intent of Congress. In addition, the Court found this interpretation inconsistent with the literal wording of the statute. The statute "does not except 'a *bona-fide employee* who . . . obtains . . . wages from a bona fide employer.' Rather, it excepts '*any person* who . . . obtains . . . the payment of wages from a bona-fide employer to a bona fide employee.' "[48] This is simply a disingenuous distortion of the suggested interpretation. The distinction underlying the interpretation focuses not on *who* uses coercion but *for whom* it is used. Coercion would be within the exception only when the person for whom it is used has an otherwise uncoerced employment relationship under which wages are owed.

The second possible interpretation considered by the Court was that the exception "does not apply if the owner's intention in making the payment is to buy 'protection' and not to buy service, even though the defendant may intend to perform the service or may actually perform it."[49] This was apparently the interpretation argued for by the government. The Supreme Court, however, rejected it on the ground that the state of mind of the victim could not properly be decisive of the guilt of the defendant. The Court made it quite obvious that it viewed the exception as clearly contemplating the use of violence in labor disputes, as long as it was for a "legitimate" end.

> For example, the members of a labor union may decide that they are entitled to the jobs in their trade in a particular area. They may agree to attempt to obtain contracts to do the work at the union wage scale. They may obtain the contracts, do the work, and receive the money. Certainly Congress intended that these activities should be excepted from the prohibitions of this particular Act, even though the agreement may have contemplated the use of violence. But it is always an open question whether the employers' capitulation to the demands of the union is prompted by a desire to obtain services or to avoid further injury or both. To make a fine or prison sentence for the union and its members contingent upon a finding by the jury that one motive or the other dominated the employers' decision would be a distortion of the legislative purpose.[50]

Given later developments in Congress and before the courts, one cannot overemphasize the critical importance of this language. It *clearly* suggests that, in the Supreme Court's view, the first principle of the statute was that it was not intended to apply to violence aimed at attaining traditional labor goals. The victim's state of mind was rejected by the Court as a relevant consideration *only* because its use might operate in derogation of that principle. Since the instructions of the trial judge to the jury had suggested the controlling importance of the victim's intentions in paying the money, the Supreme Court necessarily found that the conviction had to be set aside, and it, therefore, affirmed the court of appeals.

Finally, the Court discussed a third possible interpretation over which the court of appeals was divided—namely, whether the trial judge erred in suggesting that payments for work not actually done could never be considered "wages," notwithstanding the defendants' willingness to do the work. In this regard, the Court noted that both the majority and the dissent below had agreed that the payment of money to one who refuses to do any work is clearly not within the exception, but that payments to one who actually does the work clearly is within the exception. The Court apparently concurred with that view and stated that "[t] he doubtful case arises where the defendants agree to tender their services in good faith to an employer and to work if he accepts their offer, but agree further . . . that he should pay an amount equivalent to the prevailing union wage even if he rejects their proffered services."[51] The Court resolved the doubt in favor of finding such payments to be "wages" for the purposes of the statute.

The Court said that in determining whether the exemption applied or not, "[t]he test must . . . be whether the particular activity was among or is akin to labor union activities with which Congress must be taken to have been familiar when this measure was enacted."[52] Referring to the so-called " 'stand-by' orchestra device, by which a union local requires that its members be substituted for visiting musicians, or, if the producer or conductor insists upon using his own musicians, that the members of the local be paid the sums which they would have earned had they performed,"[53] the Court concluded that the practice of accepting payments even when the services are refused was within the contemplation of Congress and, therefore, within the exception.

The Court's holding on this point provides even further evidence of its preoccupation with the notion that if the objective is a traditionally legitimate one from labor's perspective, then conduct aimed at obtaining it does not constitute "extortion," no matter how violent it is. This, in sum, seems to be the recurring theme of the *Local 807* decision.

Chief Justice Stone registered a strong dissent in the case. His dissent is important because many in Congress later referred to it expressly as evidencing the proper approach to the problem of labor extortion. Unfortunately, it is difficult to pinpoint exactly where in the analysis the Chief Justice parted company with his brethren. In his view the elements of an offense under the act were: the defendants used force to compel the payment of money; these payments were made to purchase immunity from violence and for no other reason; and this end was knowingly sought by the defendants. With respect to the specific facts of the *Local 807* case, Chief Justice Stone clearly believed that illegal extortion occurs when an employer is forced to make payments for work not done, even when it is the employer himself who has elected not to use the services of an otherwise willing worker. He noted that "[u]nless the language of the statute is to be disregarded, one who has rejected the proffered service and pays money only in order to purchase immunity from violence is not a bona fide employer and is not paying the extorted money as wages."[54]

Moreover, the Chief Justice believed that the performance of some work did not necessarily bring forced payments within the exception. He cited with approval an instruction by the trial judge which stated that "[i]f . . . what the operator was paying for was not labor performed but merely for protection from interference by the defendants with the operation of the operator's trucks, the fact that a defendant may have done some work on an operator's truck is not conclusive."[55] Furthermore, he noted that "[t]he character of what the drivers or owners did and intended to do—pay money to avoid a beating—was not altered by the willingness of the payee to accept as wages for services rendered what he in fact intentionally exacted from the driver or owner as the purchase price of immunity from assault, and what he intended so to exact whether the proffered services were accepted or not."[56]

On the other hand, the Chief Justice did concede that "the procuring of jobs by violence is not within the Act . . . ." and that this may include "the 'stand-by' job where no actual service is rendered."[57]

What one may synthesize from these various assertions is that, from Chief Justice Stone's perspective, the critical issue was what constituted the "essential purpose" of the transaction. If the "essential purpose" of the transaction is to exchange money in return for work done (or for someone being available to work, as in a "stand-by" situation), there is no violation of the statute even if violence is used to accomplish the transaction. On the other hand, if the "essential purpose" of the transaction is to exchange money in return for freedom from violence, a violation does exist even if work is done or offered to be performed. The Chief Justice, however, did not suggest specific, objective indicia that can be used in identifying such purposes. He conceded, rather, that this is ultimately to be determined by a jury by reference to the perceived intent of the two parties. Since the instructions of the trial judge were consistent with Justice Stone's interpretation of the law, he believed that the convictions should stand.

The *Local 807* case virtually emasculated the Anti-Racketeering Act of 1934 insofar as its effectiveness as a tool against labor violence was concerned. Whether the case was consistent with the original legislative intent is hard to tell, given the obscurity and brevity of the legislative history on the issue. The intent of the Congress sitting at the time the case was decided is, however, a different matter.

III. The Hobbs Act Amendments

A. Legislative History

Congressional reaction to the *Local 807* case was as swift as it was negative. Bills were introduced in the 77th,[58] 78th,[59] and ultimately the 79th Congress[60] to correct what Congress considered to be an outrageous decision. The legislative solution that ultimately prevailed, the so-called Hobbs Act,[61] was originally introduced in the 1943 session.[62] It passed the House that year,[63] but died in the Senate. It was reintroduced the following year and finally enacted into law.[64]

Fearful that *any* repetition of the exact language of the 1934 Anti-Racketeering Act would give the Supreme Court an excuse for adhering to the *Local 807* approach, Congress completely rewrote the law and took special pains to eliminate the specific language on which the decision was based. The new act provided that:

> Whoever in any way or degree obstructs, delays, or affects commerce or the movement of any article or commodity in commerce, by robbery or extortion or attempts or conspires so to do, or commits or threatens physical violence to any person or property in furtherance of a plan or purpose to do anything in violation of this section shall be fined not more than $10,000 or imprisoned not more than twenty years, or both.[65]

The terms "robbery," "extortion," and "commerce" were defined, and the final paragraph of the act, the exact wording of which produced much debate, provided that "[t]his section shall not be construed to repeal, modify or affect" the Clayton Act, the Norris-LaGuardia Act, the Railway Labor Act, or the National Labor Relations Act.[66] Notably absent was anything akin to the wage exception of the 1934 act. Indeed, an amendment again exempting "wages" from the coverage of the Hobbs Act was rejected on the specific grounds that this would simply open the door to another *Local 807* decision.[67]

The legislative history makes absolutely clear that Congress viewed the *Local 807* case as wrongly decided.[68] Thus, the Hobbs Act was *at least* written to require a contrary result on those identical facts, but how much beyond that Congress intended to go is a matter of speculation.

To determine what impact the Hobbs Act was intended to have upon various kinds of violent labor union activity, one can conveniently break the legislative history down into five categories: (1) congressional interpretations of the holding and the dissent in the *Local 807* case; (2) specific examples of the kinds of conduct the new act was intended to reach; (3) interpretations of the "no repeal" proviso and the suggested alternative; (4) the basis of labor's opposition and the congressional responses thereto; and (5) the assertions of no intended "discrimination" for or against labor.

1. Interpretations of the Local 807 *Case.* Generally speaking, Congress read the *Local 807* case very broadly. The sponsor of one of the first bills introduced on the matter said the case "in effect, placed the Congress in the position of condoning and authorizing the use of force and violence in enforcing demands so long as such force and violence are practiced by members of labor organizations and unions."[69] Similarly, it was said that the case holds "in effect that the use of force and violence was not incompatible to the lawful settlement of disputes between employers and employees."[70] In the debates on the Hobbs Act as introduced the first time, one congressman said: "I think the intent of the Congress in the 1934 statute was to protect the lawful activities of organized labor. The construction put on it by the Supreme Court would authorize unlawful acts—certainly never intended by this Congress."[71]

In these and other instances the concern of Congress seemed to focus on the fact that the *Local 807* case allowed labor unions to use physical violence to enforce their demands against employers. It was, apparently, of no particular moment that in the *Local 807* case the demands specifically involved payments for unwanted, if not unused, labor. Assuming that the Hobbs Act was intended as a negation of a broad reading of the *Local 807* case, it follows that Congress intended to prohibit the use of all violence in the enforcement of labor union demands regardless of the particular nature of the demands.

On the other hand, a somewhat narrower interpretation of the *Local 807* case is reflected in the comments of Congressman Hancock, a proponent of the Hobbs Act. "[T] he Supreme Court," he said, "held that . . . members of Teamsters Union 807 in New York City were exempt from the provisions of that law when attempting by the use of force or the threat of violence to obtain wages for a job *whether they rendered any services or not*."[72] This suggests that the objectionable aspect of the *Local 807* case that was being legislatively overruled pertained not to the permitted use of violence alone, but to its use to achieve that particular result. Consequently, an intent to negate that aspect of *Local 807* would not support an inference that Congress intended to prohibit *all* forcibly backed union demands.

Perhaps the clearest indication of what Congress intended by its repudiation of *Local 807* can be found in the fact that the dissenting opinion of Chief Justice Stone was repeatedly referred to in approving terms.[73] Indeed, at one point Congressman Whittington expressly stated that "[t] he real purpose of the bill is to remove any doubt about the interpretation of the act by the Chief Justice being correct."[74] Unfortunately, as has been seen, Mr. Justice Stone's opinion is somewhat obscure as to the act's prohibition against violence in the labor context.[75]

2. Specific Examples of Prohibited Conduct. The examples given of the kind of union conduct the new act was designed to reach are much more helpful than are interpretations of *Local 807* in assessing the legislative intent. The facts of the *Local 807* case were, of course, cited time and time again as being prototypical of the kind of abusive labor conduct Congress wanted to reach through the Hobbs Act,[76] but other examples were also given. Congressman Anderson spoke of where the Teamsters used force in connection with a demand that drivers entering San Francisco either become members of the union or use Teamster drivers while within the city.[77] He also spoke of the situation where, in support of an organizational drive among dairy employees, a Teamsters Union refused to haul the dairy farmers' milk into the city, resulting in considerable spoilage.[78] This was considered an act of "coercion" in the colloquial sense, and one which the proposed act was intended to reach.[79]

Congressman Baldwin of Maryland cited the example of a strike in Baltimore where sabotage and other acts of violence had been directed against the employer and his property:

> This bill would not have been presented to the House if organized labor had recognized law and order in striking and in establishing their rights, *as they have a right to do.* Everyone can remember the taxicab strike in the city of Baltimore, . . . where cabs were overthrown, bricks thrown through the windows endangering the lives of people, innocent victims.
>
> . . . .
>
> Mr. Chairman, labor has a right to strike, but when labor perpetrates that sort of thing, they are going far beyond the bounds of reason. Certainly, I do not take the position that labor has not the right to organize or to strike, but when they do so they should abide by the- . . . laws of decency. If they had done that, we would not have this legislation before the House today.[80]

Thus, it is relatively clear that these members of Congress intended the Hobbs Act to prohibit forms of labor violence other than the kind of "featherbedding" practices that were at issue in *Local 807.* It appears that the proposed act was also intended to prohibit the use of violence and coercion to obtain otherwise legitimate objectives such as the organization of employees, membership in the union, the acquisition of work for union members, or a favorable collective bargaining agreement.

3. Debate Over the "No Repeal" Proviso. As drafted by Congressman Hobbs, the bill simply said that the four leading labor laws then in existence were not to be considered repealed, modified, or affected by the new legislation. Congressman Celler, however, proposed and strenuously argued for an amendment which would have provided that "no acts, conduct, or activities which are lawful under [the four acts in question] . . . shall constitute a violation of this act."[81] Congressman Celler felt that as drafted the exception to the bill would *not* protect labor in the exercise of rights guaranteed by the other statutes; the "no repeal" language, he conceded, would continue to protect the exercise of those rights from prosecution *under the former statutes,* but not necessarily from prosecution *under the proposed Hobbs Act.*[82]

Congressman Celler's interpretation of the language was not a reasonable one. Language of this kind would normally be construed to mean that if any of the four labor statutes grant labor unions an affirmative right to engage in a particular kind of conduct, the Hobbs Act should not be construed as taking that right away. It was repeatedly pointed out, however, that none of the four acts gave unions the affirmative right to engage in any acts of force and violence prohibited by the Hobbs Act.[83]

On the other hand, Congressmen Celler's version of the exception would have seriously limited the scope of the act insofar as labor union activities were concerned. It is reasonably apparent from his explanations of the proposed amendment that he construed the term "lawful" to mean "not illegal."[84] Saying that certain conduct is "not illegal" under a specific statute, as per Celler's version, is vastly different from saying that the statute makes such conduct a matter of "right." The Clayton Act,[85] for example, did not give labor unions an affirmative "right" to use force in the settlement of strikes; but the use of such force had also been held to be "not illegal" under that statute.[86] Arguably, under the Celler amendment it would not be subject to prosecution under the Hobbs Act either.[87] Thus, some labor leaders privately conceded that the Celler amendment would have nullified the Hobbs Act altogether, at least insofar as labor activities were concerned.[88] If an act was not already illegal under one of the four statutes, the Hobbs Act simply would not cover it.

Congressman Hobbs opposed the Celler amendment on slightly different grounds. He feared that if certain things which are generally "lawful" under the labor statutes were declared to be beyond the purview of the Hobbs Act, it would be construed as also excluding the pursuit of these "lawful" ends by "unlawful" means.[89] He said,

> Mr. Chairman, almost any crime may be committed while the perpetrator is engaged in otherwise lawful acts, conduct or activities.
> . . . Because a man is engaged in the perfectly lawful conduct of striking, is he guiltless if he commits rape?
> Picketing is lawful. But does that mean that a picket cannot be punished for stealing?
> The right of collective bargaining is guaranteed by law. Does that give collective bargainers the right to murder?
>
> . . . .
>
> Honestly and peaceably seeking employment is not only lawful, but commendable. However, it is equally lawful for one from whom employment is sought to refuse it. Does any sane and reasonable man contend that the right honestly and peacefully to seek employment gives the seeker the right to force employment or to beat the refuser?
>
> . . . .
>
> I submit that for these reasons the Celler amendment is dangerous, especially in view of the decision in the Local 807 case, which held that no matter how much violence might accompany a request for employment it was all right and you are perfectly innocent under the antiracketeering law. The same thing is true here. No matter what may be said about the Celler amendment, it still does not require, as do the acts to which it points, that lawful acts, conduct or activities must be done in a lawful and peaceful way. Without that or something like that the amendment should be defeated.[90]

The relevance and importance of this language used by the author of the Hobbs Act cannot be emphasized too strongly. In slightly different terms, what Congressman Hobbs was saying was that the fact that the objective or *end* is legitimate under one of the general labor statutes does not mean that such objective can be pursued by violent *means*. Rightly or wrongly, Congressman Hobbs feared that the Celler amendment would have that effect insofar as prosecutions under the proposed anti-extortion statute were concerned. Necessarily, Congressman Hobbs also believed that the statute as he drafted it did *not* have that effect. The Celler amendment was defeated.[91]

4. Objections to the Hobbs Act and the Responses. It is significant to note that, on a substantive level, the opposition to the act was *not* grounded on the fact that it was to be a violation of federal criminal law for labor unions to use actual physical violence in furtherance of their organizational or collective bargaining objectives. The substantive objection, rather, was that the act might be construed in such a way as to *also* preclude unions from pursuing these legitimate goals by the traditional methods of peaceful strikes and picketing. Congressman Celler, for example, noted:

> There are courts which have held that whenever workers seek to bring about a wage increase or other adjustment of their working conditions by a strike, however peacefully conducted, they are attempting to "force" their employer to grant the wage increase or grant the requested adjustment of their working conditions.[92]

He also feared that even a mere demand for a wage increase might be construed as an implied promise to strike if it were not granted, thus making it an illegal "threat."[93] Congressman Celler, concerned that the Hobbs Act might be similarly construed, also noted that "there are courts which have held that picketing, *however peacefully conducted,* is by its very nature an attempt to force the employer into action which he is not willing to take."[94]

Similarly, Congressman LaFollette said of the terms of the act that: "I think they are broad enough to cover a discussion between employees as to whether or not they shall join a union. Those things are often accompanied by heated discussions which might be called coercion and they would affect the right of labor to organize."[95]

The proponents of the bill, however, consistently denied these charges. It is important to note that the basis of their denial was *not* that the ends being sought in these examples were legitimate ones, thus putting the means being used to achieve them beyond the purview of the act. Instead, they answered that *otherwise peaceful* strikes and picketing are not acts of force or violence; such acts are specifically protected by federal statute and could not, thus, be considered a violation of the Hobbs Act. This point was made repeatedly. Congressman Hancock, in responding specifically to the claims of Congressman Celler, said: "A moment ago the gentleman said the threat of a strike came within the definition of extortion. This bill merely prohibits the wrongful use of force or threats. That cannot apply to a threatened strike because strikes are lawful, they are not wrongful."[96] Similarly, in giving a negative response to the question of whether a threat to go on strike would constitute a violation under the proposed bill, Congressman Sumners said, "as I . . . understand this bill, there is not a thing in it to interfere in the slightest degree with any legitimate activity on the part of labor people or labor unions, unless somebody thinks it is legitimate for them to rob and extort."[97]

That robbery and extortion were intended to connote acts of physical violence is also evident in Congressman Gwynne's listing of what the government would have to prove in order to obtain a conviction under the state—namely, that the conduct affects interstate commerce, that there be an actual taking of property, *and* that this be done "by violence, by personal violence, or by actual threats of personal violence."[98] Likewise, Congressman Fellows noted that "the so-called Hobbs bill is designed to make assault and battery and highway robbery unpopular. Its purpose is to protect trade and commerce [which would certainly include the negotiation of collective labor agreements and most other labor-related activities] against interference by violence, threats, coercion, or intimidation."[99]

Congressmen Savage was concerned about the act's effect on a "strike for better working conditions."[100] A response by Congressman Barden distinguished a *peaceful* strike from the type of activity the act was designed to prohibit. Focusing on the means used to accomplish the ends sought, he said:

> Do not talk to me about the man on strike. If he were an honest gentleman, he would not commit such offenses as robbery or extortion while on strike or off strike.
>
> . . . The fact that a man is on strike certainly does not license him to be an outlaw. . . .
>
> Good honest men do not commit robbery. They do not commit burglary. They do not beat up innocent people. They do not extort money. Good honest men do not do those things.[101]

A few moments later Congressman Michener said that "this bill will not interfere with legitimate strikes"[102]—presumably referring to strikes which are both peaceful and directed toward an otherwise legal end.

Congressman LaFollette also shared the fears of labor that the proposed Hobbs Act might be construed too broadly. Nevertheless, he did agree that the use of force or violence, *even if it was to obtain wages*, should be clearly prohibited. Thus, he proposed an amendment to that effect and said:

> If we put a construction into this statute which states that a bona fide payment of wages from an employer to an employee *shall not include wages* or the transfer of a thing of value *which is obtained by violence* or the threat of use of violence, then we reach the situation we are attempting to reach.[103]

The amendment was rejected presumably because the *Local 807* case caused the majority to avoid the "bona fide wages" language altogether and, instead, couch the prohibitions of the statute in even broader language. It would, however, be incongruous indeed to *now* construe the act as not reaching as far as even its opponents were willing to go.[104]

On the other hand, the most commonly cited indication that the act was *not* designed to reach *mere* strike violence is contained in the following exchange:

Mr. MARCANTONIO. All right. In connection with a strike, if an incident occurs which involves—

Mr. HOBBS. The gentleman needs go no further. This bill does not cover strikes or any question relating to strikes.

Mr. MARCANTONIO. Will the gentleman put a provision in the bill stating so?

Mr. HOBBS. We do not have to, because a strike is perfectly lawful and has been so described by the Supreme Court and by the statutes we have passed. This bill takes off from the springboard that the act must be unlawful to come within the purview of this bill.

Mr. MARCANTONIO. That does not answer my point. My point is that an incident such as a simple assault which takes place in a strike could happen. Am I correct?

Mr. HOBBS. Certainly.

Mr. MARCANTONIO. That then could become an extortion under the gentleman's bill, and that striker as well as his union officials could be charged with violation of sections in this bill.

Mr. HOBBS. I disagree with that and deny it in toto.[105]

Congressman Gwynne also indicated that the act was not intended to cover "a clash between strikers and scabs during a strike."[106] Presumably, Congressman Hobbs also had this kind of picket line violence in mind. If so, the import of what Congressman Hobbs was saying becomes clear. Based on what he said elsewhere in the record,[107] it is inconceivable that he intended to exempt violence simply because it occurred in conjunction with an otherwise legal strike. Although some of the opponents of the bill felt that "minor altercations on the picket line"[108] should not be treated as felonies, there is no basis for assuming that Congressman Hobbs or any other supporter of the bill intended any distinction between "major" and "minor" acts of violence.[109] Rather, Congressman Hobbs's statement must be viewed in the context of the specific crimes the bill purported to prohibit—extortion and robbery. The purpose of most picket line violence is to prevent persons against whom it is directed from entering the employer's premises, not to obtain money from them. It is difficult to see how such violence could be conceptualized as either extortion or robbery. In short, Congressman Hobbs was simply recognizing that the act did not reach *all* violence, but only that which would fit within the legal definition of extortion or robbery.

5. *The Intent Not to Discriminate For or Against Labor.* The fifth category of legislative remarks shedding light on the intended scope of the Hobbs Act are those which indicated that the act should not discriminate on the basis of whether the violent actor was or was not associated with a labor union. Many congressmen objected to the *Local 807* case because it seemed to grant a special license to labor unions alone to use violence in the pursuit of their goals. For example, Congressman Hobbs said that the case "decided that no matter how much

violence a *union* man might use *in seeking employment*, he could not be punished under the 1934 Anti-Racketeering Act."[110] He added,

> I am saying that is the effect of the construction put upon robbery committed while engaged in *otherwise lawful* conduct by the Supreme Court decision. No matter how much force is used, robbery is a perfectly innocent pastime, as Chief Justice Stone said, *if the perpetrator be a labor-union member seeking employment.*[111]

Similarly, it was also said that the *Local 807* case "in effect, placed the Congress in the position of condoning and authorizing the use of force and violence *in enforcing demands* so long as such force and violence are practiced by *members of labor organizations and unions.*"[112] Such favored treatment was clearly not acceptable to Congress; it was the nature of the act and not the status of the actor that Congress thought was of controlling importance, and the Hobbs Act was designed to implement that policy. On this point, the following exchange is revealing:

> Mr. SUMNERS of Texas. There is nothing in this bill dealing with persons connected with organized labor as such. It is just an attempt on the part of the Committee on the Judiciary to bring in a bill that will prevent this type of robbery in interstate commerce.
>
> Mr. MICHENER. That is all there is to it. The only way labor is involved is that if these offenders belong to the union, and by robbery or exploitation collect a day's wage—a union wage—they are not exempted from the law solely because they are engaging in a *legitimate union activity.*[113]

In other words, "[a] ll are treated alike and no group is given special permission to violate the law."[114] Moreover, as these remarks demonstrate, the legitimacy of a group's goal or objective is irrelevant.

A fairly clear pattern emerges from this legislative history. Congress did not intend to interfere with otherwise peaceful strikes and picketing. Yet, Congress did intend to prohibit the use of force, violence, and threats as a means of obtaining wages or other things of value from an employer despite the fact that obtaining such benefits might be otherwise completely legitimate. In other words, as brokers of employee services, labor unions were to be limited in the use of force to the same extent as were other brokers or sellers of commodities; in either instance, the effectuation of the exchange through the use of force was to be prohibited as extortion.

B. The Case Law

Although even a cursory review of the legislative history clearly indicates that Congress intended the Hobbs Act to prohibit labor from using force or violence as a means of obtaining concessions from employers, the initial judicial reaction was still somewhat hesitant.

For example, in *United States v. Kemble*[115] the Third Circuit Court of Appeals was faced with facts not unlike those in *Local 807*. A union official had used actual and threatened violence to cause an employer to hire a union member to unload a truck whenever it made deliveries to an RCA plant. These services were not otherwise desired by this employer. The court had little difficulty in finding that, on these particular facts, a violation existed. The court, however, did hedge somewhat when it stated that:

> The conclusion seems inescapable that Congress intended that the language used in the 1946 statute be broad enough to include, in proper cases, the forced payment of wages. We say "in proper cases" advisedly. For it is not necessary that we here consider the great variety of circumstances in which coercion may be involved in the payment of wages. We need not consider the normal demand for wages as compensation for services desired by or valuable to the employer. It is enough for this case, and all we decide, *that payment of money for imposed, unwanted and superfluous services* such as the evidence shows Kemble attempted to enforce here by violent obstruction of commerce *is within the language and intendment of the statute.*[116]

Although the majority decision was cautious in construing the scope of the new act, it still went too far in the opinion of dissenting Judge McLaughlin. Notwithstanding the legislative history, he felt that the disagreement Congress had with the *Local 807* decision was a relatively narrow one. He maintained that the Supreme Court there had held that: (1) the use of force to become a genuine employee (one who actually works and is paid for it) was within the "wage" exception, and (2) the use of force to compel the payment of wages when the services of the would-be employee are refused was also within this exception. According to Judge McLaughlin, Congress' quarrel with the decision and its repudiation thereof pertained only to the second point, and that the defendant's conduct in this case fell within the still exempt first point. As such, it merely represented "a reputable union's genuine attempt to organize a trucking corporation,"[117] which was not the kind of conduct that the Hobbs Act was intended to prohibit. Generally, he felt that the use of violence by a labor union in pursuit of a legitimate goal, such as obtaining work for its members, is not a violation of the Hobbs Act; instead, it is a matter for state and local prohibition.

Judge McLaughlin's theory was rejected not only by the Third Circuit in *Kemble* but also, later, by the Supreme Court;[118] but not without first picking up some support elsewhere. In *United States v. Green*,[119] Federal District Judge Adair reversed a conviction on the grounds that the facts as alleged in the indictment did not state an offense under the Hobbs Act. The indictment, tracking fairly closely the language used in the *Kemble* case, charged that the defendant had used "actual and threatened force, violence and fear" to cause "wages to be paid for imposed, unwanted, superfluous, and fictitious services of laborers."[120] In concluding that this did not state an offense under the act, Judge Adair relied on the proviso to the Hobbs Act which states that it was not designed to "repeal, modify or affect the provisions of . . . the Wagner Act."[121]

Given the legislative history of this section,[122] of which Judge Adair purported to have made "a personal investigation as to the intent of Congress,"[123] it is startling indeed to see how the section was used to support the result he reached. Noting that in several cases the Supreme Court had held that "a demand by a Union representative for 'feather-bedding' is not an unfair labor practice"[124] under the Wagner Act, Judge Adair stated, "[i] t seems incongruous that Congress intended that a lawful act"[125] under one statute would be punishable as a felony under another.

This reasoning is remarkable in two respects. First, it proceeds as if the Cellar version of the proviso had been adopted rather than the committee or Hobbs version. As previously discussed, Congressman Celler wanted the language to read, "no acts . . . which are lawful" under the labor statutes shall be considered unlawful under the Hobbs Act, with "lawful" apparently being equivalent to "not illegal."[126] Although Congress expressly rejected that approach, that is exactly the interpretation Judge Adair gave the statute.

In addition, Judge Adair simply ignored the warning of Congressman Hobbs that the "lawfulness" of the ultimate objective could not serve as a justification for the use of force to achieve it.[127] Congress, however, did apparently heed this admonition in that it rejected the Celler version which Hobbs said was susceptible to such a construction.

Nevertheless, Judge Adair concluded that—since obtaining wages, albeit for unwanted services, was within the defendant's "rights and responsibilities as a Union representative"[128]—no violation of the Hobbs Act existed even though violence was used to achieve that end. Instead, a violation is made out only when the end itself is "unlawful," as where the union representative is obtaining money for his own benefit.[129] Thus, on the question of the "legitimacy" of the end serving as an exoneration of violent means, Judge Adair was in line with the dissent in *Kemble*.

The Supreme Court, however, disagreed strongly. With respect to the notion that the act applied *only* to a union official's attempt to obtain money for his own benefit, the Court simply noted that while the union officials in the *Local 807* case were not attempting to get the money for that purpose, the Congress clearly intended for the Hobbs

Act to proscribe what they were doing.[130] Furthermore, the Court
noted that "[t] he legislative history makes clear that the new Act was
meant to eliminate any grounds for future judicial conclusions that
Congress did not intend to cover the employer-employee
relationship"[131]—including, one would presume, the primary incidents of that relationship, namely the obtaining of work and the
payment of otherwise legitimate wages.

With respect to Judge Adair's reliance on the proviso to the Hobbs
Act which stated that it did not affect any of the several labor statutes
the Court simply noted that: "There is nothing in any of those Acts,
however, that indicates any protection for unions or their officials in
attempts to get personal property through threats of force or violence.
Those are not legitimate means for improving labor conditions."[132]
The Court footnoted five cases that presumably illustrated labor
conditions or objectives which the labor statutes did not affirmatively
permit a union to seek through "threats of force of violence," and
which, therefore, fell within the parameters of the Hobbs Act when
those means are used. Significantly, in four of these cases, as in *Green*
itself,[133] what the unions were trying to attain was not intrinsically
"unlawful" or "illegitimate": in *United Construction Workers v.
Laburnum Construction Co.*,[134] the object was to get employees to join
the union and to get the employer to recognize it as the employees'
representative; *Allen Bradley Local 1111 v. Wisconsin Employment
Relations Board*[135] involved employer accession to the union's contract demand and employee observance of the picket line; *NLRB v.
Fansteel Metallurgical Corp.*[136] dealt with employer recognition of
and negotiation with the union over wages, hours, and working
conditions; and in *Kemble*[137] the object was to get the employer to hire
certain union helpers. Only *United States v. Ryan*[138] involved an
objective that was itself illegal—namely, the payment of money by an
employer to the representative of his employees. Thus, it would seem
that in *Green*, the Supreme Court was concerned with the use of force
and violence to obtain payments, not with the "legitimacy" or "illegitimacy" of the payments themselves.

This, certainly, is how the lower courts viewed the matter on
remand.[139] Following the Supreme Court decision, the defendants
asked that the verdict be set aside on the grounds that it was not
supported by sufficient evidence and that the trial judge erred in
refusing to submit a particular instruction to the jury. The instruction in question would have been to the effect that if the jury finds
that the defendant has a "labor dispute" of a jurisdictional nature
with another union at the time of the alleged threats to compel the
payment of wages to its members for unwanted services, the matter
was beyond the scope of the Hobbs Act.[140]

The Court of Appeals for the Seventh Circuit rejected that argument, noting the Supreme Court's admonition that the four labor statutes referred to in the proviso (which do generally regulate "labor disputes") in no way sanction the use of force or violence. The court added:

> We agree with the decisions that this statute encompasses illegal conduct which may be an outgrowth of a labor dispute just as any other criminal conduct may result from activity originally lawful. The mere fact that conduct originates in exercise of a lawful function does not prevent the ramifications and extensions thereof from becoming unlawful.[141]

This *exactly* reflects the position that Congressman Hobbs took with respect to the act. In sum, the *Green* decision on remand correctly stands for the proposition that the use of violence or threats of violence by labor union officials to enforce their demands, regardless of legitimacy, constitutes extortion under the Hobbs Act.

Despite the Supreme Court's willingness to construe the Hobbs Act broadly and as intended, judicial hostility to the Hobbs Act continued to surface. It was conceded that the express congressional reversal of the *Local 807* case necessarily meant that Congress intended to include a demand for wages for work not done within the prohibition of the act. In addition, the *Green* case necessarily meant that, at the very least, a demand for wages for *unwanted* work was covered. As one court framed it, the final issue was whether the act covered "violence to property as a part of a plan to extort a thing of value in the form of a collective bargaining agreement covering wages, hours and working conditions of *wanted* employees."[142] The issue was ultimately answered in the negative. But the path to that result was strewn with unfortunate distortions of the legislative history and embarrassing contortions of ordinary logic and semantics.

The first major case to reach the result was *United States v. Caldes.*[143] Since the United States Supreme Court was to later speak approvingly of this decision,[144] a detailed analysis is in order. First, the court took a narrow view of the disagreement between Congress and the Supreme Court's result in the *Local 807* case. It said that Congress thought *Local 807* was wrong in recognizing the union member's willingness to work as an excuse for violence, since this could be construed as also permitting the use of force to "bring about the hiring of unwanted, unneeded employees."[145] This particular result was predicted solely on the Supreme Court's interpretation of section 2(a) (the "wage exception"), and the fact that "[t]he legislative history of the Hobbs Act shows that the deliberate purpose of Congress was to eliminate Section 2(a)."[146] Thus, the court in *Caldes* reasoned that the purpose of the Hobbs Act was *merely* to compel a contrary result in cases like *Local 807*, where the work is either unperformed or unwanted. The court concluded that:

> By eliminating Section 2(a) however, Congress did not intend to eliminate traditional labor or union activity, albeit militant, which has as its object legitimate ends. The exclusion was not meant to provide impunity to the terroristic and extortionate activities of union members, but to protect union activity directed toward legitimate labor goals even when militantly pursued.[147]

The court then noted that the *Green* case fell within this pattern, since the purpose of violence there was to obtain wages for "imposed, unwanted and superfluous or fictitious services."[148] The court also distinguished other lower court cases which had found that "extortion occurred when a union member tried to *foist* himself or another union member on an employer by threats of force and violence."[149]

What the court seemed to ignore was that Congress did not merely repeal the "wage exception" which was the technical basis of the *Local 807* case. Instead, Congress entirely rewrote the act for the express purpose of precluding decisions *like* that in *Local 807*.[150] This suggests a broad rather than a narrow congressional overruling of the decision. Given the repeated emphasis in the debates on the element of violence, it is more likely that it was this aspect of the *Local 807* facts that Congress found offensive—not just the objective to which the violence was directed.

Moreover, euphemisms and pejoratives are no excuse for sound analysis. Pouring paint on the employer's trucks and the clean laundry he was delivering, as in *Caldes*, is no more acceptable when it is called "militant," (in the court's language) than it is when it is called "the use of violence against property." At a more substantive level, the fact that something can be disapprovingly called "foisting" one's "unwanted and superfluous or fictitious services" on an employer does not necessarily preclude that conduct from also being called a "legitimate labor goal." Thus, the distinction articulated by the court is totally without substance.

A classic example of this is the *Green* case. The union there simply wanted the employer to hire union members to scout ahead of bulldozers and warn the drivers of approaching pitfalls; the employer felt that this was an unnecessary precaution. But whatever the diseconomies of the situation, this kind of job acquisition and work sharing among union members is a traditional, legitimate, and otherwise entirely legal objective and purpose of American labor unions.[151] Stated differently, it was as legitimate for the union in *Green* to want to induce the employer to hire an additional man to walk in front of the bulldozer as it was for the union in *Caldes* to want to induce the employer to enter into a collective bargaining agreement. In short, the court really did not succeed in distinguishing the violence in the case before it from the violence in *Green*—not, at least, by reference to the alleged "legitimacy" of the goal.

The court, however, attempted to justify its distinction on another basis. It noted that the language of the Hobbs Act was derived from the New York extortion statute, and under that statute strikes and picketing had been found not to constitute "extortion" *if* the purpose was to accomplish some legitimate labor objective such as organization; but such conduct was actionable when merely "used as a pressure device to exact the payment of money as a condition of its cessation."[152] The Hobbs Act had been similarly construed, the court noted, in a case where a labor leader had threatened to call a strike unless the employer paid him some "under the table" money.[153] From this the court apparently concluded that the illegitimacy of the objective is *always* a necessary element in a Hobbs Act violation. This reasoning, however, is fallacious.

The distinction adopted by the New York cases with respect to strikes can be understood only in a historical perspective.[154] At one time in the history of American labor law, under the so-called "conspiracy doctrine," strikes and picketing were sometimes said to be inherently coercive, because of the economic injury-in-fact that they caused the person to whom they were directed. Even before the matter was almost totally preempted by federal statutory law, however, some of the common law courts had moved considerably away from that position and had adopted a "means/ends" approach. This approach declared the concerted activities of labor to be actionable or coercive only if they involved either "unlawful means"— conduct which was itself criminal, tortious, or perhaps even in breach of contract—*or* "unlawful ends"—a term capable of being construed as including almost anything a judge might find to be offensive.

Although this approach is certainly no longer the primary device for measuring the legality of strikes (that function having been assumed by the various federal labor statutes), ghosts of the theory do sometimes emerge in analogous contexts where the issue is whether an *otherwise peaceful* strike or picketing falls within the purview of some general statute prohibiting "acts of force" or "coercion." In such a case, if a violation exists at all it must necessarily be because the objective itself is unlawful or illegitimate.

The New York case, relied on by the *Caldes* court,[155] held that the otherwise peaceful picketing (the "means") became a coercive exer-

cise of force only when the objective shifted from attempting to organize the employer (a legitimate "ends") to obtaining money from
him as a condition of stopping the strike (an illegitimate "ends"). If
this holding was merely a reflection of the historically pervasive
"means/ends" theory of coercion, however, it becomes readily apparent that one cannot deduce from it what the *Caldes* court deduced—
namely, that *no* strike can be considered coercive unless the ends are
illegitimate. To the contrary, under the "means/ends" approach a
violent strike is coercive regardless of its objective; and there is
nothing in the New York case to suggest otherwise. Thus, the *Caldes*
court's reliance on that authority was misplaced.

Finally, at the policy level, the *Caldes* court simply noted that labor
unions should be allowed great latitude in pursuing the interests of
their members and that "[t]he expansive interpretation of 'extortion'
used in the Hobbs Act as urged by the Government would make criminal the activities of many militant labor organizations."[156]
The court contended, for example, that a strike in violation of a
contractual no-strike clause would be a " 'wrongful' use of force"[157]
and thus, constitute criminal conduct under the government's view.
This is a somewhat puzzling assertion, since it would seem that a
strike in violation of a "no-strike" clause would also be a violation
under the court's approach. The objective of such conduct certainly
could not be denominated a "legitimate labor goal"; thus, by analogy
to the New York cases, a strike to obtain that objective could be considered "coercive" and, therefore, a violation of the Hobbs Act.

As a second example of the possible overbreadth of the government's approach, the court noted that "[s]pontaneous and sporadic
fighting on the picket lines could also be condemned as the use of
wrongful force and as extortion if [the Government's] view was
allowed to prevail."[158] The court then indicated that in the year following passage of the Hobbs Act, Congress passed the Taft-Hartley
Act, containing "specific provisions which condemned this action as
unfair labor practices."[159] Furthermore, the court noted that during
the debates on the Taft-Hartley Act, "no congressman expressed an
opinion that the Hobbs Act of the preceding year covered union violence while a strike was in progress."[160]

The court's reasoning here is both obscure and factually incorrect.
In the first place, the section of the Taft-Hartley Act to which the
court specifically referred primarily prohibits secondary boycotts or
union attempts to require a neutral employer to stop doing business
with the employer with whom the union has a dispute.[161] Although
violence can occur in connection with such boycotts, it is certainly not
a necessary element of the offense. Moreover, even if violence did

occur in a specific situation, the objective of a secondary boycott is to force the victim to stop doing business with someone else, not to force him to pay the union money or anything else of value, *as is required in order for the crime of extortion to exist.* In short, what the Taft-Hartley Act prohibited and what the government in the *Caldes* case claimed that the Hobbs Act prohibited were two entirely different things. Thus, even if there had been no mention of the Hobbs Act during the Taft-Hartley Act debates, this would have in no way shown that the government's interpretation of the Hobbs Act was overly broad.

As a matter of fact, however, the court was simply wrong in suggesting that during the Taft-Hartley Act debates no one referred to the prohibitions of the Hobbs Act insofar as strike violence is concerned. In addition to making secondary boycotts, organizational picketing, and jurisdictional disputes unfair labor practices, the Taft-Hartley Act gave federal courts jurisdiction over private damage suits brought by a person injured as a result of such conduct. Senator Aiken, however, wanted to add an amendment which would also allow for injunctive relief in certain situations. He was specifically concerned with the small farmer who could not deliver his produce because of a labor dispute at the market, and for whom a damage action would be impractical. Senator Pepper, in discussing the proposed amendment said: "I do not recall exactly the terms of it, but last year we passed the Hobbs bill, the so-called antiracketeering bill, which gave jurisdiction to the federal court to act with respect to interruptions of and interference with people delivering their goods, in the way I think the Senator from Vermont has in mind."[162] Senator Aiken, however, responded:

> It has developed that the Hobbs bill was not worth the paper upon which it was written, so far as affording any protection to the farmer was concerned, because the farmer is not *molested* in taking his crop to the market, but when he arrives there may find that the commission man has an agreement for a closed shop, and the farmer cannot unload his produce, and therefore is turned back.[163]

Discounting the hyperbole, Senator Aiken was saying that the Hobbs Act is inadequate to solve the problem totally because it only applies to situations where the farmer has been "molested." The restraints upon delivery that are caused by certain kinds of agreements, secondary boycotts, or jurisdictional strikes cause just as real an injury to the farmer, but are not covered by the Hobbs Act. The correlative of his statement, however, is that the Hobbs Act does, in fact, cover acts of "molestation," including those that occur in connection with union activities that were, at the time he made this statement, not otherwise illegal under the existing labor statutes. In short, it would seem that the 1947 Congress *was* aware that the Hobbs Act applied to acts of violence aimed at achieving ends which were not otherwise illegal. This would tend to support the government's position in the *Caldes* case rather than refute it.

In summarizing its overbreadth argument, the court noted that "it appears to us that acts of vandalism of the type committed by these appellants would be more properly and suitably prosecuted in the state courts and it is doubtful if Congress intended . . . to elevate this type of conduct to the level of the federal court."[164] The opponents of the Hobbs Act, of course, made exactly the same kind of assertion.[165] It was of no moment to the *Caldes* court, however, that the majority of Congress apparently felt otherwise.

As specious as the reasoning in the *Caldes* case was, the same result was eventually reached by the United States Supreme Court without any firmer basis insofar as legislative history or analysis is concerned. In *United States v. Enmons*,[166] the defendants were indicted for firing high-powered rifles at three utility company transformers, draining the oil from a company transformer, and blowing up a transformer substation owned by the company—all done for the purpose of obtaining higher wages and other employment benefits from the company for the striking employees. The indictment was, however, dismissed by the district court on the theory that the Hobbs Act did not prohibit the use of violence in obtaining "legitimate" union objectives.[167] On appeal, the Supreme Court affirmed, advancing four separate justifications for its conclusion.

First, the Court focused on the fact that the statute prohibited only the "wrongful" use of force to obtain property.[168] The Court noted that Congressman Hobbs intended the term "wrongful" to modify the entire section;[169] if it modified only the term "force" it would be redundant because any force to obtain property is wrongful. Therefore, the Court concluded that "wrongful" has meaning in the act only if it limits the statute's coverage to those instances where the obtaining of the property would itself be 'wrongful' because the alleged extortionist has no lawful claim to that property."[170] The Court then added: "Construed in this fashion, the Hobbs Act has properly been held to reach instances where union officials threatened force or violence against an employer in order to obtain personal payoffs, and where unions used the proscribed means to exact 'wage' payments from employers in return for 'imposed, unwanted, superfluous and fictitious services' of workers."[171]

There are a number of things critically wrong with the Court's reasoning. First, the dilemma posed by the Court— "either construe the Act this way or make it redundant"—is essentially false since there are other possible interpretations. For example, one court of appeals previously suggested that "wrongful" referred to conduct constituting a breach of the peace in contrast to merely tortious conduct.[172] This interpretation gives the term "wrongful" a meaning as a modifier of the term "force" that is certainly as reasonable as the interpretation suggested by the Supreme Court.

A more compelling explanation of the intended meaning of the term "wrongful" can, however, be found through a thoughtful reading of the legislative history. As previously indicated, many of the opponents of the Hobbs Act were fearful that the act would be construed to prohibit legitimate strikes and picketing.[173] Some of them even suggested that a strike is, by definition, the assertion of a form of force.[174] The Hobbs Act proponents answered, of course, that the right to strike was protected by various federal labor statutes; that the rights affirmatively guaranteed by those statutes were not taken away by the Hobbs Act; but that there was nothing in those statutes which gave unions the right to use violence in the course of the exercise of the right to strike.[175]

It is against this background that Congressman Hobbs's assertion that the term "wrongful" "qualifies the entire section" must be viewed.[176] Congressman Voorhis, who was not an enthusiastic supporter of the bill, wanted to make sure that a simple threat to go on strike for higher wages would not be construed as extortion under the act. He was advised that it would not. He then immediately asked the additional question, "Does the word 'wrongful' apply to entire section?"[177] Presumably he wanted to make doubly sure that a *peaceful* strike would also not be considered wrongful under the Hobbs Act. Congressman Hobbs, in response to the question, then said that term wrongful "qualifies the entire section."[178] Congressman Hobbs undoubtedly intended this statement to assuage Congressman Voorhis's fears that the act, notwithstanding the proviso, might be so broadly construed as to prohibit even peaceful strikes. In other words, Congressman Hobbs was saying that even if strikes are considered a form of coercion or force, they are not "*wrongful* force" unless accompanied by violence. This interpretation easily removes the redundancy which so concerned the Court.

Even if the Court correctly concluded that the operative effect of the term "wrongful" in the statute is to identify the objective toward which the force must be directed in order for it to constitute extortion, the Court's reasoning on this point is still subject to question. It is based on the strange assumption that a person has no "lawful claim" to wages which are paid for unwanted services, as in the *Green* case, but that he does have such a claim to wages higher than those the employer would voluntarily pay in the absence of force "in return for genuine services which the employer seeks,"[179] as in the *Enmons* case. The distinction is analytically vacuous, however. A person has a no more "lawful claim" to work at $5.00 an hour for an employer who wants to pay only $4.75 than does another person who wants to work for an employer who does not want this person's services at all. In either case, the would-be employee's "legal claim" to wages is dependent upon the employer's voluntary or noncoerced agreement to pay such wages. Nevertheless, on the basis of a nonexistent distinction, the Court would apply the statute in one case but not the other.

The Court's second justification is somewhat related to this latter point; the Court simply claimed that "[t] he legislative framework of the Hobbs Act dispels any ambiguity in the wording of the statute and makes it clear that the Act does not apply to the use of force to achieve *legitimate* labor ends."[180] To support this extraordinary proposition, the Court first relied on the fact that Congress undoubtedly wanted to overrule the *Local 807* case which had permitted union members to "use their protected status to exact payments from employers for imposed, unwanted, and superfluous services"[181]—presumably *not* a "legitimate" labor objective, although the Court does not explain why. Assuming that overruling that aspect of the *Local 807* case was the limited intent of Congress, the Court then inferred an intent *not* to prohibit violence in the pursuit of "legitimate" objectives. In support of this conclusion, the Court referred to several assertions made during the debates to the effect that the bill was not intended to interfere "with any legitimate activity on the part of labor people or labor unions."[182]

This chain of reasoning is weak at almost every link. For example, the Court did not provide an *objective* basis for distinguishing "legitimate" labor goals from "illegitimate" ones—a basis which could be used to differentiate the objectives being pursued by the union in *Green* from those being pursued by the labor union in *Enmons*.[183] In neither case were the objectives independently illegal, that is, illegal regardless of the means used to achieve them. Also, while it is undoubtedly true that Congress intended to reverse the *Local 807* case, an impartial reading of the legislative history suggests that Congress was *at least* as concerned with the means that were being used in that case as it was with the ultimate objective being pursued. Finally, the statements relied upon by the Court to the effect that the act would not affect "legitimate" labor activity must be construed in *pari materia* with the more specific assurances that this result would be accomplished by the proviso guaranteeing that the existing labor statutes would not be modified or repealed. This guarantee was, however, tempered by the repeated reminder that these statutes in no way gave labor unions the right to use force or violence.[184]

In short, from conclusion that the act was not intended to prohibit "legitimate" labor activities, one simply cannot infer that the legitimacy of the objective justifies whatever means are used to achieve it.

The inference not only does not flow from the legislative history; indeed, it is affirmatively contradicted by it. Congressman Hobbs' *single* objection to Congressman Celler's amendment was that it would allow conduct which was aimed at "lawful" ends to escape the prohibitions of the act even though the conduct itself was "unlawful."[185] By rejecting the Celler amendment, Congress necessarily also rejected the interpretation given to the act by the Supreme Court in *Enmons*: that the legitimacy of the ends sought removes whatever means are used to achieve them from the prohibitions of the statute. Furthermore, while the Court was correct in saying that the Celler amendment was rejected because it "would have operated to continue the effect of the *Local 807* case,"[186] the Court was grossly incorrect in asserting that it was done "solely"[187] for that reason, and that "undoing the restrictive impact of that case"[188] *merely* means that violence directed at otherwise "illegitimate" ends is now illegal under federal law. To the contrary, it would appear that the legislative overruling of *Local 807* had a much broader purpose.

The *only* specific language in the legislative history from which the Court could derive support for its interpretation was a single, obscure dialogue between Congressman Marcantonio and Hobbs.[189] As was previously discussed, however,[190] that exchange cannot be construed as a condonation by Hobbs of violence directed toward achieving a "legitimate" end. The Court's reliance on this exchange in support of its interpretation of the statute is unwarranted if not totally misplaced.

The third justification advanced by the Court scarcely deserves mention. The Court simply noted that "[i]n the nearly three decades that have passed since the enactment of the Hobbs Act, no reported case has upheld the theory that the Act proscribes the use of force to achieve legitimate collective-bargaining demands."[191] The Court, without explanation, here cited *Green* and *Kemble* as cases allegedly involving "illegitimate" labor demands, and cited *Caldes* as a case involving "legitimate" labor demands where the indictment was properly dismissed. These cases, however, are either unpersuasive or simply not supportive of the Court's theory.

Nevertheless, from all this the Court concluded that Congress did not intend to legislate the manner in which labor enforced its various demands, since "[i]t is unlikely that if Congress had indeed wrought such a major expansion of federal criminal jurisdiction in enacting the Hobbs Act, its action would have so passed unobserved."[192] To say the least, this is a rather novel theory of statutory interpretation and one certainly not adhered to in other contexts.[193]

Finally, in justifying its narrow interpretaion of the Hobbs Act, the Court trotted out its "parade of horribles." The government's theory, the Court said:

> [w]ould cover all overtly coercive conduct in the course of an economic strike, obstructing, delaying, or affecting commerce. The worker who threw a punch on a picket line, or the striker who deflated the tires on his employer's truck would be subject to a Hobbs Act prosecution and the possibility of 20 years' imprisonment and a $10,000 fine.[194]

In the first place, as has been suggested before, a reasonable interpretation of the Hobbs Act need *not* include within its ambit *all* violence connected with a strike; in many instances either the victim or the purpose is different than would be required in order to constitute "extortion."[195] Moreover, if it is unlikely that Congress intended to severely punish a person who slices tires in the course of a strike to obtain $.50 more per hour, it is certainly no more likely that Congress intended to impose such punishment when that particular conduct occurs in the course of a strike to obtain additional but unwanted work for union members; yet that result could be reached even under the Court's theory. There is, in short, simply no logical relationship between the Court's concern over excessive punishments and its theory that the act should therefore be limited to conduct having an "illegitimate" objective.

In addition, the Court apparently lost sight of the fact that the Hobbs Act, like many other statutes, merely establishes the *maximum* possible punishments. While it is true that the opponents of the Hobbs Act thought these sanctions might be potentially excessive if applied to the so-called "milder" forms of labor violence,[196] the majority in Congress either felt otherwise or knew that judges would exercise the discretion inherent in their function and mold the punishment to fit the crime.[197] In any event, the Court's concern that an overzealous tire slasher might be fined to the point of impoverishment and incarcerated for the better part of his life is neither a necessary nor even a proper basis for construing the statute the way the Court did.

In sum, none of the reasons advanced by the Court for its reading of the statute can withstand hard analysis. The Court's distortion of the legislative history is particularly disturbing, and it was primarily this that led Mr. Justice Douglas, dissenting, to state:

> At times, the legislative history of a measure is so clouded or obscure that we must perforce give some meaning to vague words. But where, as here, the consensus of the House is so clear, we should carry out its purpose no matter how distasteful or undesirable that policy may be to us.[198]

The purpose, which Mr. Justice Douglas found evident from a careful review of the legislative history, was simply that "[t]he regime of violence, *whatever its precise objective*, is a common device of extortion and is condemned by the Act."[199] With respect to the majority's position, he bluntly but correctly observed that "[t] he Court today achieves by interpretation what those who were opposed to the Hobbs Act were unable to get Congress to do."[200]

C. Current Ambiguities in the Law

Although the *Enmons* decision resolved the specific issue that was before the Court, the opinion at the same time created two glaring points of uncertainty. First, the Court's holding that the act does not apply to the enforcment of "legitimate" union demands leaves open the question of what exactly an "illegitimate" union demand might be. At the very least, if the sought-after payment would itself be illegal, whether obtained through force or otherwise, a demand for such payment would potentially be within the purview of the Hobbs Act even under the *Enmons* decision. This would appear to cover certain proscribed payments by an employer to any representative of his employees,[201] as well as employer payments into pension funds, check-off payments, and other such payments when not done according to the strict mandates of the law.[202] Arguably, the payment of wages in excess of either mandatory wage guidelines or the terms of a collective bargaining agreement containing a no-strike clause could be included as well. True "featherbedding" would almost certainly be considered a proscribed objective.[203] An employer's requirement that his employees pay union dues in the absence of a valid union security agreement or each individual's voluntary agreement to pay would also seem to qualify,[204] as would the illegal recognition of a union.[205]

More troublesome, however, are those objectives which are not intrinsically "unlawful" but which are, nevertheless, susceptible to being called "illegitimate." The existence of this category is a necessary, though perhaps unintended,[206] corollary of the fact that the Court in *Enmons* clearly reaffirmed the *Green* decision. In point of fact, the objective of the union in *Green* was not independently unlawful. Although the union may have been seeking wages for services which the employer felt he did not need, the union members were apparently willing to actually do the work, and thus *Green* was not a true case of "featherbedding" in the statutory sense.[207] What other kinds of "illegitimate" but unlawful objectives the Court might have in mind is subject only to speculation.[208]

As has been shown, one source of ambiguity stems from the Court's conclusion in *Enmons* that "illegitimacy" of the objective is a necessary element of a Hobbs Act offense. Another ambiguity which the decision creates is whether physical force or violence is also a necessary element. Under prior case law it clearly was not. One of the recurring issues in the cases involving demands for personal payoffs to union officials was whether such demands, when backed *merely* by threats of strikes, picketing, or other presumably peaceful "labor difficulties," could constitute extortion under the Hobbs Act, or whether either actual force or threatened force was required. The courts had consistently held that "[r]easonable fear of economic loss was enough to come within the statute."[209] The Court in *United States v. Varlack*[210] explained:

> [I]t is . . . clear that it was not the intention of the Congress to interfere with the exertion of peaceful economic pressures by a union through the medium of strikes to achieve *legitimate* labor objectives. But it does not follow . . . that only violence or threats of violence are covered by the Act and that the Act is not violated when union leaders or representatives obtain . . . personal enrichment by using their . . . influence to instill in the minds of the employers with whom they deal a fear of work stoppages or the prolongation of strikes.[211]

Thus, the case law seemed to stand for the symmetrical proposition that it was extortion if *either* the ends *or* the means were independently illegal.[212] By requiring an "illegitimate" objective in every case, *Enmons* necessarily destroyed this formulation, but it is not clear what the decision provides by way of substitution. There are two alternatives: actual legality of the means used is no longer a relevant factor at all, thus making the "illegitimacy" of the ends both a necessary and a sufficient condition of the violation; or *both* illegitimate ends *and* otherwise illegal means (violence or threats of violence) are now necessary for a violation of the act.

The Court's statement in a footnote to its discussion of the term "wrongful," in *Enmons* is relevant to this issue:

> The Government suggests a convoluted construction of "wrongful." It concedes that when the means used are not "wrongful," such as where fear of economic loss from a strike is employed, then the objective must be illegal. If, on the other hand, "wrongful" force and violence are used, even for a legal objective, the Government contends that the statute is satisfied.[213]

The government's theory was, of course, consistent with the either/or proposition suggested above. In this footnote the Court was clearly rejecting the proposition that the means alone can render a demand illegal. Whether they were also rejecting the proposition that the ends alone can render a demand illegal, is only problematical. That such was *not* the Court's intent can perhaps be deduced from the fact that the Court also said that "the Hobbs Act has properly been held to reach instances where union officials threatened force or violence against an employer in order to obtain personal payoffs."[214] The Court here cited three lower court cases which stand unequivocally for the proposition that fear of economic loss, brought about by otherwise peaceful and not illegal strikes or picketing, can rise to the level of extortion under the Hobbs Act, provided the end being sought is itself an illegitimate one.[215] Presumably, the Supreme Court was of the same view.

On the other hand, there *is* specific language in the legislative history to suggest that the typical "shake down," where a union official uses his power to call or prolong strikes as a form of threat to induce an employer to make personal payoffs, is not extortion in the statutory sense. Presumably, Congress intended to not involve itself through the Hobbs Act in otherwise peaceful strikes and picketing. In dialogue supporting this proposition, Congressman Sumner stated: "There have been complaints that in the case of strikes an attorney has gone in and asked an operator something like $15,000 or $20,000 as a shakedown to stop a strike. Is there anything in this bill about that?"[216] Congressman Jennings responded: "Not a thing. This does not have a thing in the world to do with strikes."[217]

Since *Enmons*, there have been a number of cases where the courts have indicated that union officials can be convicted for extorting money or other benefits through threats of "economic harm" to an employer.[218] Apparently, the implications of *Enmons* on this issue and the significance of that bit of legislative history have not been discussed. This, however, is a matter of some concern. Where the end is affirmatively illegal, as in the personal payoff situations, perhaps the threatened use of economic force can be called "extortion" without doing undue violence to the term. Where the "illegality" flows from the fact that the objective is inconsistent with a previously agreed to contract term, however, one begins to get a little uneasy. Is it proper to make it a "crime" to strike to achieve such an objective? Regardless of one's judgment on this question, it is quite another matter to label as "extortion" the threatened use of *otherwise* peaceful and legal economic force for the purpose of achieving an end which is itself *merely* "illegitimate," as in the *Green* case. Although it seems unlikely that anyone would ever be convicted of extortion for striking in order to require a railroad to hire a "fireman" for a diesel locomotive, such a result flows logically from the *Enmons* decision. This is because the Court in *Enmons* characterized the objective of the union in *Green* as being "illegitimate" even though it was not in fact affirmatively illegal, and suggested that the use of economic force with respect to such ends can be considered extortionate. On the other hand, if the Court did not intend that result, one is necessarily left with the conclusion that the theoretical underpinnings of *Enmons* are hopelessly ambiguous. In either event, some clarification by the Court is certainly in order.

IV. Pending Legislation

At the time of the *Enmons* decisions, revisions to the Hobbs Act were already in the process of formulation. In 1966, Congress created the National Commission on Reform of Federal Criminal Laws,[219] commonly called the "Brown Commission" after its chairman, Edmund G. Brown, former governor of California. The mandate of this commission was to study the existing body of federal criminal laws, including the Hobbs Act, and to make recommendations to Congress for revision and recodification. In 1971 the commission submitted its final report, consisting primarily of a proposed draft of a federal criminal code with brief comments for each section.[220] Under this code, extortion, a separate offense under the Hobbs Act, was simply treated as a form of theft. Section 1732 provided that: "A person is guilty of theft if he: . . . (b) knowingly obtains the property of another by deception or by threat with intent to deprive the owner thereof, or intentionally deprives another of his property by deception or by threat. . . ."[221] Section 1741 further provided that

> 'threat' means an expressed purpose, however communicated, to (i) cause bodily injury in the future to the person threatened or to any other person; or (ii) cause damage to property; or (iii) subject the person threatened or to any other person to physical confinement or restraint . . . or (x) bring about or continue a strike, boycott, or other similar collective action to obtain property or deprive another of his property which is not demanded or received for the benefit of the group which the actor purports to represent; or (xi) cause anyone to be dismissed from his employment, unless the property is demanded or obtained for lawful union purposes.[222]

Part (x) of the definition stated that a strike or boycott which is not for the purpose of obtaining benefits for the whole group, as in the typical "payoff" or "shakedown" situation, is to be considered illegal. Presumably this is true even though the strike or boycott is an otherwise peaceful one. It also seems clear from the structure of the definition that violence intended to coerce the settlement of a strike (*i.e.*, causing bodily injury, property damage, or physical restraint to obtain an otherwise legitimate group benefit) is also illegal. Finally, as the comments to this section of the draft make clear, part (xi) was clearly designed to exclude from the coverage of the section any threatened or actual enforcement of a union security agreement as long as the dues received under threat of discharge were used for lawful union purposes.[223] Thus, the Brown Committee draft would not have accomplished any major changes in the Hobbs Act as it had been construed before *Enmons*.

The Brown Committee report was submitted to Congress, where it was referred to the Senate and House Committees on the Judiciary and to the President, who created a Criminal Code Revision Unit within the Department of Justice for further study and revision. The Senate Committee's end product, after two years of hearings, was bill S. 1,[224] introduced by Senators McClellan, Hruska, and Ervin on January 4, 1973.[225] Although it was derived from the Brown Committee draft, S. 1 differed from that draft in many ways. With respect to the extortion provisions, S. 1 opted in favor of a return to the carefully hammered out language of the existing Hobbs Act. Section 2-9C3 provided that: "A person is guilty of extortion if he intentionally obtains services or property of another from another person, with the consent of the other person, where such consent is induced by wrongful use of actual or threatened force, violence or fear, or under color of official right."[226]

The section-by-section explanation of S. 1 simply stated that "[t]he language is taken from [section] 1951 to carry forward its judidial construction,"[227] presumably including, insofar as Supreme Court cases are concerned, the *Green* decision. It is significant to note that the *Enmons* decision, appearing on February 22, 1973, had not been handed down at the time this explanation was written.

In the meantime, the Criminal Code Revision Unit of the Justice Department had also been working on a draft ciminal code. S. 1400[228] was introduced by Senators Hruska and McClellan on March 27, 1973,[229] after *Enmons* had been rendered, and it was clearly drafted with the intent of repudiating the decision. Section 1722 (a) provided that: "A person is guilty of an offense if he knowingly obtains property of another by force, or by threatening or placing another person in fear that any person will be subjected to bodily injury or kidnapping or that any property will be damaged."[230] The explanation to this section of the bill said that it was "worded to overcome the adverse effects of a recent Supreme Court opinion construing the legislative intent as to one aspect of the existing statute in an unusually restrictive manner."[231] Presumably, the authors of S. 1400 believed that they accomplished this by the omission of the word "wrongful" in the definition of the crime, since the rationale of the *Enmons* decision hangs fairly heavily on the presence of that word in the Hobbs Act.

Hearings were subsequently held on all three versions of a proposed federal criminal code—the Brown Commission draft, S. 1, and S. 1400. On January 15, 1975, Senator McClellan, for himself and several other senators, introduced a new S. 1[232] which incorporated elements of all three of the proposals. Significantly, this S. 1 adopted the language of S. 1400 insofar as extortion was concerned, and the draft report clearly indicated that the subcommittee intended to overrule the *Enmons* decision.[233] Some doubt was expressed, however, as to whether the language used was capable of having that effect. A statement by the Associated Builders and Contractors suggested that in order to make the matter clear the following be added after the final word "damaged" in section 1722 (a): "Notwithstanding that the same acts or conduct may also be a violation of state or local law, and notwithstanding that such acts or conduct were used in the course of a legitimate labor dispute or in the pursuit of legitimate union or labor ends or objectives."[234] The second S. 1, with some amendments, was reported by the Subcommittee on Criminal Laws and Procedures to the full Committee on the Judiciary on October 21, 1975, where the bill was allowed to die.

The next step was taken on May 2, 1977, when Senators McClellan and Kennedy introduced S. 1437,[235] the Criminal Code Reform Act of 1977.[236] This bill allegedly represented a compromise on several controversial and important points, the lack of agreement on which had kept prior bills from moving through the legislative process. The extortion offense, however, was again simply defined, as obtaining property of another "(1) by threatening or placing another person in fear that any person will be subjected to bodily injury or kidnapping or that any property will be damaged; or (2) under color of official right."[237]

The Committee Report on S. 1437[238] contains an excellent summary of the then existing law with respect to extortion under the Hobbs Act and indicates approval of the judicial decisions holding that "fear" under the statute applies not only to fear of physical violence but also fear of economic harm to the victim's property or business. Moreover, the report is unequivocal in its repudiation of the *Enmons* "legitimate objectives" rationale. Noting that such an exception had not been recognized with respect to extortion by other persons, the committee felt that labor union officials were not entitled to such a privileged treatment.

The thrust of an extortion statute should be to punish violent extortionate means to obtain the property of another regardless of the legality of the ends sought, and this principle should apply in the collective bargaining context as well as elsewhere. Thus, an employer who blows up a union office or causes a union official to be assaulted in order to instill fear and thereby obtain property of the union ought to be guilty under the Act irrespective of whether the property could have been obtained lawfully through collective bargaining. And the same should be true in the reverse situation. Accordingly, the Committee has proposed in effect to overturn the *Enmons* result by treating the parties engaged in a labor dispute no differently from other persons in terms of the applicable prohibitions under this section, which is limited to extortionate means involving actual or threatened violence.[239]

The Committee Report, however, also responded to the concern expressed by the *Enmons* Court that minor acts of picket line violence might, but for a narrow reading of the statute, be elevated into a federal felony. The report noted that

in the Committee's view such acts do not fall within the purview of the Hobbs Act (nor should they be Federally punishable) since there is no intent thereby to obtain the employer's property through the use of force and the acts do not in fact cause the employer to part with his property; in short, such isolated acts of violence do not partake of the nature of extortion.[240]

To insure that the act would be construed in that fashion, the proposed extortion provision contained an additional section specifically recognizing that "[i]t is an affirmative defense to a prosecution under subsection (a)(1) that the threatened or feared injury or damage was minor and was incidental to peaceful picketing or other concerted activity in the course of a bona fide labor dispute."[241] Senator Kennedy, who introduced S. 1437 in the Senate, explained that "a defense is added to the extortion provision to make it clear that minor incidents occurring in the course of legitimate labor picketing are not punishable under the extortion statute."[242]

Immediately thereafter, however, Senator Kennedy introduced an amendment to the extortion provision which deleted the "affirmative defense" section altogether and substituted the following:

(b) PROOF.—In a prosecution under subsection (a)(1) in which the threat or fear is based upon conduct by an agent or member of a labor organization consisting of an act of bodily injury to a person or damage to property, the pendency at the time of such conduct, of a labor dispute, as defined in 29 U.S.C. 152(9), the outcome of which could result in the obtaining of employment benefits by the actor, does not constitute prima facie evidence that property was obtained 'by' such conduct.[243]

In Senator Kennedy's view, the amendment simply clarified existing law, which, as he understood it, required proof not only of acts of violence but also of the fact that the violence was done with the intent of extorting. Beyond saying that and restating what the amendment itself said directly,[244] he offered no explanation.

Senator Thurmond's remarks, on the other hand, were considerably more enlightening. In explaining his lack of objection to the amendment, he noted that:

> This amendment would add a "proof" subsection designed to prevent a trial judge from holding that, in a case described in the new subsection, mere proof that personal injury or property damage occurred during a labor dispute constitutes a sufficient showing of the causal relationship between the obtaining of property and the threat of fear based on that injury or damage to justify submission of that issue to the jury. It prevents such a holding directly, by providing that proof of the coincidence of the labor dispute and the injury or damage in such a case is not "prima facie evidence" of the causal relationship. It is true, of course, that such a causal relationship sometimes does exist where injury or damage occurs during a labor dispute. This proposed subsection, however, is based on the belief that where there is a cause and effect relationship, or the intent to obtain property by means of a threat or fear resulting from injury or damage, it should be possible to prove, in addition to that coincidence, some other circumstances adding to the strength of the inference of causation.
>
> The proposed subsection does not address the question of which particular additional circumstance or circumstances, when proven along with that coincidence, will suffice to justify the submission of the issue to the jury. One which clearly would be sufficient in many cases to avoid a directed verdict is the circumstance that the defendant was, or conspired with, a person negotiating on behalf of the union involved in the labor dispute. The same result might obtain, where the repetitive or systematic nature of property damage, or its exact timing, contributed to an inference, based also on the fact that a labor dispute was pending at the time the damage was done, that the damage was purposeful rather than mindlessly vindictive.[245]

The amendment was adopted[246] and S. 1437 passed the Senate on January 30, 1978;[247] however, the bill was allowed to die in the House.

Undaunted by this lack of prior success, Senator Kennedy, on behalf of himself and several other senators, reintroduced a proposed recodification of the federal criminal laws[248] in the Criminal Code Reform Act of 1979, S. 1722.[249] As introduced, the extortion provisions of this bill were identical to those as contained in S. 1437 as passed by the Senate.

Hearings were again held on this bill, and to at least some of the representatives of management the extortion provisions of the bill were apparently satisfactory. The published comments of the Associated Builders and Contractors, Inc. noted, for example, that the omission of the word "wrongful" in the act properly eliminated the "legitimate objectives" exception read into the Hobbs Act by the Court in *Enmons*.[250] Furthermore, the comment stated that, properly construed, the "proof" provision was acceptable as well. In their view, if the violence was something more than a minor and unrelated incident, and the employer could testify "that there was a direct connection between the violence and his decision to increase benefits,"[251] then the requirements of the section would be satisfied and a prima facie case of violation made out.

For the most part representatives of organized labor agreed with this interpretation of the proposed statute, and, for that reason, were vehemently opposed to it. They objected to the overruling of the *Enmons* decision by elimination of the term "wrongful" in the definition of extortion on many of the same policy grounds that were advanced by the Court in that case. Witnesses cited numerous reasons why *Enmons* should not be overruled: The danger of making minor picket line misconduct a federal criminal felony; the danger of overactive and politically ambitious prosecutors using this as an excuse to intrude unnecessarily into strike situations; the resulting unwarranted incursion of federal jurisdiction into an area traditionally left to the states; the disruption of the balance already struck by Congress in the labor-management relations area; the chilling effect upon the exercise by employees of other federally protected rights; and the existence of other remedies for labor violence.[252]

Moreover, the "proof" provision was regarded by labor as inadequate to guard against the evils that would result from making labor activity generally subject to the statute. Thomas X. Dunn, general counsel for the Building and Construction Trades Department, AFL-CIO, stated:

> It is clear that section 1722(b) is designed to create an additional burden of proof in prosecutions for misconduct which occurs in the course of a labor-management dispute. The Government would be required to establish a nexus between the alleged misconduct and the obtaining of otherwise legitimate employment benefits. As a practical matter, however, this burden of proof could be satisfied easily in almost every economic strike where misconduct occurs. It appears that all that the Government need do to satisfy its burden is present the employer involved in the strike who will testify that the alleged violence or threat of violence was a factor in his decision to agree to workers' demands for higher wages or other employment benefit.
>
> Thus, section 1722(b) would not be an effective means of discouraging the Government from applying the proposed extortion statute to any misconduct which occurs in the course of an economic strike.[253]

Robert M. Baptiste, Counsel for the International Brotherhood of Teamsters, expressed a similar sentiment:

While the amendment was proposed in "recognition that tempers often flare in labor disputes" and all strike-related misconduct should not be a Federal criminal offense, we submit that the proof provisions can so easily be satisfied that virtually all economic strikes where misconduct occurs could be subject to this new Federal extortion penalty.[254]

Lance Compa, Washington representative of the United Electrical, Radio and Machine Workers of America, was fearful of the undesirable consequences that could result if the interpretation advanced by Senator Thurmond[255] was taken as controlling. He stated:

Furthermore, Senator Thurmond offered a detailed interpretation of the Kennedy Amendment that constitutes dangerous legislative history. Senator Kennedy made no careful explanation of his amendment. Senator Thurmond said the proof requirement would not be necessary if the defendant "was or conspired with" a union negotiator or if the damage was "repetitive," "systematic" or "purposeful rather than mindlessly vindictive."

Applying this interpretation would, first of all, chill any contact between a union negotiating committee and the rank and file members. Instead of keeping a firm hand on the strike—which is essential if the committee is to be effective at the bargaining table—a committee will be forced into a "hear no evil, see no evil" position, sequestered from the membership in order to avoid possible prosecutions. Even so, a prosecutor out to nail an aggressive union leader could frighten or entice with promises of immunity a rank and file member to implicate the union official in some damage.

Second, the "purposeful rather than mindlessly vindictive" interpretation effectively removes any protection the Kennedy Amendment might have provided, since any damage in a strike, misguided as it may be, is connected to the purpose of winning the strike.[256]

As drafted, the extortion provisions of S. 1722 represented a compromise which could not be held together because of the strong opposition of organized labor. This, however, opened the door anew to the full range of possibilities, including reaffirming the *Enmons* approach in its entirety, on the one hand, or providing no special exemptions for labor, on the other, as well as several intermediate possibilities.

Eventually, a new compromise was hammered out. It was agreed that the basic definition of the offense of extortion would remain the same, but that the "proof" provision would be replaced with a "bar to prosecution" provision; the "grading" and "jurisdiction" provisions remained unchanged. In relevant part, the extortion section, as finally approved and reported out by the Senate Judiciary Committee, reads as follows:

§ 1722. EXTORTION.

(a) OFFENSE.—A person is guilty of an offense if he obtains property of another—

(1) by threatening or placing another person in fear that any person will be subjected to bodily injury or kidnapping or that any property will be damaged; or

(2) under color of official right.

(b) BAR TO PROSECUTION.—It is a bar to prosecution under this section that the offense occurred in connection with a labor dispute as defined in 29 U.S.C. 152(9) to achieve legitimate collective bargaining objectives, unless there is clear proof that the conduct which constitutes the threat or placing in fear required under subsection (a)(1) consists of a felony and the conduct was engaged in for the purpose of causing death or severe bodily injury in order to secure such objectives; and the Attorney General, Deputy Attorney General, or Assistant Attorney General for the Criminal Division certifies in writing that—

(A) the facts establish the existence of the additional elements of the offense required under this subsection;

(B) a federal prosecution should be commenced under this section; and

(C) the State is unable or unwilling to proceed with any equivalent prosecution relating to such conduct.[257]

The Committee Report summarized the compromise in these terms: "The Committee has concluded over the objection of a substantial minority that, except in the circumstances set forth in subsection (b) of section 1722, for the purposes of this bill the *Enmons* decision should not be modified."[258] The committee, in other words, was willing to accept the *Enmons* proposition that the "legitimacy" of a union's objective was sufficient to justify even the use of physical violence to achieve it, at least in the sense of rendering the violence not illegal under federal law. "On the other hand, the Committee believes that the thrust of an extortion statute should be to punish violent extortionate means to obtain the property of another regardless of the legality of the ends sought and has carried forward current law to that effect in situations not involving a labor dispute."[259]

That is what the proposed statute says, but what it means is another matter. For example, S. 1722 does nothing to clarify the two main ambiguities of the existing case law. By carrying forward the *Enmons* rationale of "legitimate" union objectives, the proposed statute also carries forward the ambiguities associated with that rationale.[260] Furthermore, the Committee Report on the bill does nothing to clarify the ambiguity. At one point the report notes that the committee intended to reaffirm the *Enmons* principle "to the effect that labor officials were not covered for their extortionate activities against employers in the course of a labor dispute, if the objective sought was *a permissible goal of collective bargaining.*"[261] Similarly, in discussing the meaning of the phrase "legitimate collective bargaining objectives," the Committee Report notes that this "encompasses activities to secure *non-corrupt* labor union objectives even if, as in *Enmons*, those activities would violate other laws and excludes such objectives as efforts to obtain personal payoffs or payments for superfluous services."[262]

The difficulty, as with the *Enmons* decision itself, is in fitting the *Green* facts into such a formulation. Although the objective sought in *Green* was certainly to obtain "payments for superfluous services," in the colloquial sense, as a legal matter the objective was both "non-corrupt" and "a permissible goal of collective bargaining"; yet a violation was found to exist in that case, undoubtedly because of the presence of violence. The committee, like the Court in *Enmons*, obviously did not intend to overrule *Green*. Since the presence of violence is no longer a sufficient condition for a violation, however, the reconciliation of results of *Green* with the wording of the proposed statute is somewhat less than obvious.

With respect to the second major ambiguity, the Committee Report does make it clear that the damage to property referred to in the definition of extortion includes only *physical* damage to property and does not include mere economic loss or injury. Those kinds of Hobbs Act injuries were, the Committee Report notes, intended to be covered by the proposed section on blackmail rather than the extortion section.[263] Section 1723 provides that "a person is guilty of an offense [of blackmail] if he obtains property of another by threatening or placing another person in fear that any person will . . . (4) improperly subject any person to economic loss or injury to his business or profession . . . ."[264] The Committee Report comments that

> [t]his carries forward . . . the present reach of the Hobbs Act, . . . as interpreted by judicial decisions. It is designed to make clear that this section does not reach legitimate activity, such as strikes, boycotts, or picketing activity undertaken in support of such objectives as increased wages or improved working conditions for employees.[265]

The significance of this language should be readily apparent. The word "improperly," as used in the proposed section on blackmail, is obviously intended to have the same connotation as the word "wrongful" contained in the Hobbs Act and construed by the Supreme Court. This means that the objective must be an "illegitimate" one. So construed, the blackmail section ties in nicely with the extortion section. If the objective being sought is other than a "legitimate" one, the extortion section is relevant if the "means" involve threats of physical damage to person or property, but if the "means" involve mere threats of economic injury, the blackmail section is relevant.

With respect to the latter, an unduly broad definition of "illegitimate" (*i.e.*, broad enough to encompass the objective sought by the union in *Green*) would create some difficult problems. It is *highly* unlikely that the committee intended to include within the offense of blackmail a union's peaceful picketing to cause an employer to add jobs which he considers unnecessary or superfluous. But, the ambiguities inherent in the central concept of the two sections —namely, the fuzzy notion of "legitimate" versus "illegitimate" ends—makes the statute, in theory at least, susceptible to that construction.

To summarize: If, under the extortion section, the union's objective is other than a "legitimate" one, whatever that means, it is not covered by the bar under subsection (b) and a prosecution can commence under the main provisions of the section.[266] On the other hand, even if the union is attempting to achieve "legitimate collective bargaining objectives,"[267] the use of force to that end can still be considered extortion if the requirements spelled out in the "unless" clause of subsection (b) are all met. With respect to these, the Committee Report, which presumably represents an authoritative interpretation of the language, deserves to be quoted in full, because it adds things which are certainly not apparent on the face of the language itself:

> The exception to the bar stated in subsection (b) is intended to spell out the exclusive circumstances which may give rise to a Federal extortion prosecution involving unlawful conduct that occurs during a labor dispute to achieve legitimate collective bargaining objectives. In essence this exception adds two elements to the crime. First, the government must prove that the defendant engaged in conduct against the person which, if there were Federal jurisdiction, would be a felony under the code. This element requires an act and not a mere statement or threat to act. Second, the government must prove that the defendant acted not merely "knowingly" as that term is used in the code but with the preestablished intent to (a) cause death or severe bodily injury, and (b) by so doing to force acceptance of the union's demands. "Severe bodily injury" means protracted disabling or disfiguring bodily injury that precludes the individual from gainfully working.
>
> The phrase "clear proof," which has its origin in Section 6 of the Norris-LaGuardia Act (29 U.S.C. Section 106), as used here imposes on the government the obligation to establish by direct evidence that the conduct against the person included in the exception was undertaken for the purpose specified therein. Without such proof, violence, no matter how serious, during a labor dispute is outside the Federal extortion law.

In order to reinforce traditional principles of federalism the bar is not overcome (and the Federal government may not initiate an investigation or prosecution of the illegal conduct) unless the Attorney General, Deputy Attorney General, or Assistant Attorney General for the Criminal Division certifies in writing that (a) the facts establish the existence of the additional elements of the offense required by the exception to the bar; (b) a Federal prosecution should be commenced under this section; and (c) for reasons other than insufficient evidence the State refuses to proceed with a prosecution relating to the conduct against the person specified in the exception to the bar. Such a certification must be based on evidence obtained by or available to the State prior to the Federal government's involvement in the matter; however, once the certification is made, this provision does not limit the Federal government's ability to secure and rely on additional evidence.[268]

Construed in this fashion, it would appear that section 1722 would result in federal prosecution of violence in connection with collective bargaining only in the rarest of situations. The "clear proof" standard has, for example, been a difficult one to meet in Norris-LaGuardia cases, and one could expect it to be a popular and successful ground of defense under the proposed extortion section as well. Similarly, the limits on federal *initiation* of investigations and prosecutions under the extortion section, as suggested by the Committee Report, would severely hamstring the enforcement of the statute. The exclusion of threats to cause property damage and the definition of "severe bodily injury" in terms of "protracted disabling or disfiguring bodily injury that precludes the individual from gainfully working"[269] further limits the circumstances under which the section could be applied to labor violence. Moreover, insufficiency of the evidence as a basis for non-prosecution by the state is not, according to the Committee Report, sufficient to permit federal involvement, an ironic limitation since the state's lack of sufficient evidence may well be attributable to its inability to effectively investigate a crime having interstate dimensions. Finally, the requirement of what amounts to an *affirmative* recommendation from someone at the *highest* levels of the Justice Department that a prosecution be commenced seems to create almost a presumption against prosecution, immediately makes the decision a politically sensitive one, and also suggests that the discretion involved there is somewhat broader than that which would exist otherwise. Nevertheless, the Criminal Code Reform Act of 1979, S. 1722, containing the extortion provision thus described, was reported out favorably by the Senate Judiciary Committee, and is currently pending before the full Senate.

Although most of the attention was initially focused on the Senate committee hearings, the House of Representatives was at this time also quietly proceeding on the matter of revising and recodifying the federal criminal laws. The Brown Commission draft itself was, for example, introduced in the House as H.R. 300,[270] but no hearings were ever held on it. As the reforms began to solidify in S. 1 and S. 1400, "liberal" representatives, alarmed at the direction the legislation was taking, introduced their own proposed code of federal criminal laws, H.R. 10850[271] in 1975 and H.R. 12504[272] in 1976. One commentator has called these "belated and hastily drafted alternatives"[273] to S. 1, and they do not really warrant any detailed analysis.

The first proposal to receive serious consideration by the House was H.R. 6869.[274] This was the so-called "companion bill" to S. 1437 which omitted the term "wrongful" (thus overruling *Enmons*) and provided an affirmative defense if the threatened injury was "minor and incidental to peaceful picketing."[275] Organized labor was not, however, happy with the wording of this defense. Lance Compa, Washington representative of the United Electrical, Radio and Machine Workers of America, stated that:

> H.R. 6869 provides a defense, not a bar to prosecution, that the threatened or feared injury or damage was "minor" and "incidental" to a "bona fide labor dispute." Each of these terms is dangerously unclear. How much damage is minor? What is incidental? Who determines whether there is a bona fide labor dispute? Suppose, for example, what an employer labels a "wildcat" strike is later found by the NLRB to be protected Unfair Labor Practice strike? Where would this leave a prosecution based on the "bona fide" requirement?[276]

The bill was never reported out of committee. That year, however, the Subcommittee on Criminal Justice did report H.R. 13959[277] to the House Committee on the Judiciary. This bill was designed merely to reorganize the federal criminal laws, but not, at that point in time, to change their substance. Thus, it carried forward the law as construed by the Court in *Enmons*.

The next proposed revision to the federal criminal laws appeared in the form of H.R. 6233.[278] As introduced, section 2522 of this bill provided, with respect to the extortion offense that:

> (a) Whoever knowingly threatens or places another person in fear that—
> (1) any person will be subjected to bodily injury or kidnapping; or
> (2) that any property will be damaged; and thereby obtains property of another, or attempts to do so, commits a class C felony.
> (b) It is not a defense to a prosecution for an offense under this section that the conduct constituting the offense was in furtherance of a legitimate objective or activity.[279]

Subsection (b) obviously makes express what the omission of the term "wrongfully" in subsection (a) leaves only implicit—namely, that the *Enmons* approach was to be repudiated in its entirety.

When H.R. 6233 was later reintroduced as H.R. 6915,[280] however, the extortion provision had been changed by the insertion of the term "wrongfully" before the term "obtains" in subsection (a), thus making subsection (a) directly contradictory to the language in subsection (b). Apparently, the legal and logical effect of that was to reaffirm the "legitimate objectives" defense of *Enmons*.[281] The resolution to that conundrum ultimately adopted by the House Judiciary Committee was simply to delete subparagraph (b), thus apparently leaving the law exactly as it is under *Enmons*.

In this form, H.R. 6915 has been reported out of committee and is currently pending before the House of Representatives. Whether this bill, the Senate version, some compromise worked out by a Senate-House Conference Committee, or no bill at all is to be passed is, of course, purely a matter of conjecture.

V. Conclusion

The response of the federal extortion laws to the problem of labor union violence does not reflect favorably on the state of American jurisprudence in three broad respects. First, as a matter of judicial process, serious questions can be raised about the way the courts have handled the extortion statutes. The *Local 807* case was poorly reasoned, and both the majority opinion and the dissent leave the scope of the statute somewhat obscure. The "legitimate objectives" rationale of the *Enmons* decision is not only inconsistent with the prior *Green* decision, thus creating a yet unresolved ambiguity in the statute, but also ignores the overwhelming evidence of a contrary legislative intent. The reasoning in the opinion is weak in other respects as well, and one must share Mr. Justice Douglas's suspicion that the Court's own predelictions about labor policy played a more instrumental role in the decision than the traditional tenets of statutory construction, thus creating, as he also recognized, serious separation-of-powers problems.[282] Specifically, it would appear that the Court used the *judicial process* to achieve a *political result* that probably could not have been achieved by the *legislative process* and which, as indicated by the current status of pending legislation, probably cannot now be reversed by the *legislative process*.[283]

In addition, as a matter of legislative process, the manner in which

Congress has responded to the problem leaves much to be desired. Although a relatively clear legislative intent can, on some critical points at least, be distilled from the Hobbs Act debates, they do make for agonizing reading for they are often rambling, obscure, filled with many irrelevancies, and in general reflect the lack of a clear understanding of finer nuances of the matter under discussion. Furthermore, the statutory draftsmanship is frequently flawed. The use of the word "wrongful" in the Hobbs Act without a clear indication of what was intended and the ambiguous words and phrases of much of the pending legislation serve only as an invitation to judicial license.

Finally, at a substantive level, the *Enmons* creation of a doctrinal exception applicable *only* to the agents of organized labor, and the currently pending legislation, which, in whole or in part, perpetuates that policy of favored treatment, raise serious and far reaching questions about the quality and the equality of federal criminal justice in this country. Congressman Hobbs said of the Hobbs Act that "[t]his bill is grounded on the bedrock principle that crime is crime, no matter who commits it; and that robbery is robbery and extortion extortion, whether or not the perpetrator has a union card."[284] The view today, however, is that this is not necessarily so. Instead, the prevailing view seems to be that criminality under federal law is as much a matter of the actor's *status* as it is of his conduct, and that the status of a labor union official is an especially privileged one in our society.

Admittedly, state law remedies may still be available for labor violence falling within the *Enmons* exception. Furthermore, even an intelligently drafted and impartially construed federal extortion statute may not be the cure-all for labor violence, since much of it does not have extortionate objectives, proof problems will always be somewhat more difficult with respect to this particular form of violent crime, and limited federal resources may sometimes call for selective enforcement, thus still leaving the bulk of the responsibility for combating this evil to other sources of law. But, given the *almost* universal agreement that labor violence, even when aimed at otherwise legitimate ends, is to be deplored, there are no sound reasons why such violence should not be covered by a federal extortion statute of general application. The deterrent effect alone would be of immense value in promoting a central policy of labor law—namely, the encouragement of collective bargaining, reasoned persuasion, and the *peaceful* use of economic power. To that end the *Enmons* decision should be overruled, either by the Court itself after a more reflective review of the legislative history, or by Congress.

NOTES

1. Nelles, *The First American Labor Case*, 41 YALE L.J. 165, 176 (1931).

2. *See generally* J. BRECHER, STRIKE! (1972); S. LENS, THE LABOR WARS (1973); Taft & Ross, *American Labor Violence: Its Causes, Character, and Outcome,* in THE HISTORY OF VIOLENCE IN AMERICA 281-395 (1969).

3. National Commission on the Causes and Prevention of Violence, Violence in America 288-89 (1969).

4. The Molly McGuires, the name of a group whose *formal* existence is a matter of some historical dispute, is generally used to refer to the Irish miners who engaged in widespread acts of violence, sabotage and murder in the eastern Pennsylvania coal fields during the bitter strikes of the 1870's. *See generally* S. LENS, *supra* note 2, at 11-35.

5. This kind of conduct, of course, constitutes an unfair labor practice. Labor Management Relations Act §§ 8(a)(1), (a)(3), 29 U.S.C. §§ 158 (a)(1), (a)(3) (1976).

6. The section 8(a)(1) prohibition against employer interference, restraint, or coercion of employees in the exercise of their statutory rights is certainly broad enough to also encompass acts of physical violence or intimidation. *See, e.g.,* Jacques Syl Knitwear, Inc., 247 N.L.R.B. No. 191 (1980). In 1979, however, only nine violations of this kind were found by the National Labor Relations Board.

7. Such things as assault and battery, riot, burnings, and trespass against land and chattels, all of which can easily occur within the context of a labor dispute, are routinely prohibited by the criminal codes of the various states. *See, e.g.,* S.C. CODE §§ 16-3-620,-5-70 to -140, -11-120 (1976).

8. *See* Comment, *Tort Liability of Labor Unions for Picket Line Assaults,* 10 U. MICH. J.L. REF. 517 (1977).

9. *See, e.g.,* Pipeliners Local 798 v. Ellerd, 503 F.2d 1193 (10th Cir. 1974); C.E. Thurston & Sons, Inc. v. Barber, 78 L.R.R.M. 2719 (M.D.N.C. 1971).

10. Labor Management Relations Act § 8(b)(1)(A), 29 U.S.C. § 158(b)(1)(A) (1976); Local 30, United Slate, Tile & Composition Roofers, 227 N.L.R.B. 1444 (1977); Union de Operadores y Conteros de la Industria del Cemento de Ponce, 231 N.L.R.B. 171 (1977); Teamsters Local 695, 204 N.L.R.B. 866 (1973).

11. Norris-LaGuardia Act §§ 3(e), 3(i), 29 U.S.C. §§ 104(e), (i) (1976).

12. *See, e.g.,* S.C. CODE § 41-7-70 (1976).

13. The Hobbs Act, 18 U.S.C. § 1951 (1976), which is the subject of this article, represents the primary attempt of Congress to deal with the *specific* problem of labor violence. The Labor Management Relations Act has a broader scope and direction.

14. *See, e.g.,* 18 U.S.C. § 241 (1976), prohibiting conspiracies to injure persons in the exercise of their federal rights. In United States v. DeLaurentis, 491 F.2d 208 (2d Cir. 1974), the court held, however, that this statute did not apply to violence by union officials against employees who were attempting to exercise their federal statutory right of refusing to participate in certain union activities. The court conceded that a violation *literally* existed, but went on to ask: "Can Congress have intended the consequences of such improper, but nevertheless not uncommon acts, to be up to ten years in prison, or a $10,000 fine, or both? The thought does more than give one pause; it brings one to a halt, and to a further, more careful look at the Government's position." *Id.* at 211.

15. Under the so-called "Thayer Doctrine," an employee who has been fired for engaging in conduct so designated is, despite the otherwise unprotected nature of the conduct, entitled to reinstatement if the employer has engaged in unfair labor practices which are *theoretically* assumed to have provoked such exuberance. The Board only draws the line where "the misconduct is so flagrant or egregious as to require subordination of the employee's protected rights [*sic*] in order to vindicate the broader interests of society as a whole." W.C. McQuaide, Inc., 220 N.L.R.B. 593, 594 (1975), *modified in other respects,* 522 F.2d 519 (3d Cir. 1977).

16. *See* United States v. DeLaurentis, 491 F.2d 208 (2d Cir. 1974).

17. *See generally* § IV of text *infra.*

18. Ch. 569, 48 Stat. 979 (1934) (current version at 18 U.S.C. § 1951 (1976)).

19. S. 2248, 73d Cong., 2d Sess. (1934), 78 CONG. REC. 457 (1934).

20. S. REP. NO. 532, 73d Cong., 2d Sess. 2 (1934).

21. *Id.* at 1.

22. *See, e.g.,* United Leather Workers v. Herkert & Meisel Trunk Co., 265 U.S. 457 (1924); United Mine Workers v. Coronado Coal Co., 259 U.S. 344 (1922).

23. 78 CONG. REC. 5859 (1934).

24. Under certain forms of the "conspiracy doctrine," labor activities could be considered actionable or, in legal contemplation, "coercive" if either the ends or the means were impermissible. Thus, non-violent strikes to obtain a closed shop could be enjoined in some cases. *E.g.,* Plant v. Woods, 176 Mass. 492 (1900); *see* T. HAGGARD, COMPULSORY UNIONISM, THE NLRB, AND THE COURTS 21-24 (1977). Organized labor, which had vigorously and more-or-less successfully opposed the "conspiracy doctrine" in other contexts, may have feared its resurrection in the form of this federal criminal law.

25. 78 CONG. REC. 11402-03 (1934).

26. *Id.* at 11403.

27. *Id.*

28. H.R. REP. NO. 1833, 73d Cong., 2d Sess. 2 (1934).

29. 78 CONG. REC. 11482 (1934) (remarks of Sen. Copeland).

30. 118 F.2d 684 (2d Cir. 1941), *aff'd,* 315 U.S. 521 (1942).

31. Ch. 569, 48 Stat. 979 (1934) (current version at 18 U.S.C. § 1951 (1976)).

32. For discussion of the congressional repudiation of *Local 807* and the current version of the act, see § III-A of text *infra.*

33. 118 F.2d at 686.

34. *See* note 27 & accompanying text *supra* .

35. The common definition of criminal extortion is as follows: "Extortion is a crime when . . . any person extorts that which is not due, or more than is due, or before the time when it is due." BLACK'S LAW DICTIONARY 525 (5th ed. 1979).

36. In order to demonstrate that there was no distinction between the two, the court noted that "if any employer is coerced into making a contract, the coercion ordinarily persists until the wages fall due, so that it is proper to speak of them as being 'obtained' by the original threats, or violence . . . . " 118 F.2d at 686. While

that assertion may well be true, the converse cannot be inferred, namely that if the wages due are obtained through coercion, this necessarily means that the original contract was obtained in like fashion. Nevertheless, this is what would have to be inferred in order to be consistent with the court's notion that the statute recognized no distinction between these two uses of force.

37.   118 F.2d at 686.

38.   *Id.*

39.   *Id.*

40.   *Id.* at 690 (Hand, J., dissenting).

41.   118 F.2d at 687.

42.   *Id.*

43.   *Id.* at 688.

44.   *Id.* (emphasis added).

45.   *See* § III-A of text *infra.*

46.   *See* notes 152-53 & accompanying text *infra.*

47.   315 U.S. at 527-28.

48.   *Id.* at 531.

49.   *Id.* at 528.

50.   *Id.* at 532-33.

51.   *Id.* at 534.

52.   *Id.* at 535.

53.   *Id.*

54.   *Id.* at 540 (Stone, C.J., dissenting).

55.   *Id.* at 542.

56.   *Id.* at 540.

57.   *Id.* at 541.

58.   S. 2347, 77th Cong., 2d Sess. (1942); H.R. 6872, 77th Cong., 2d Sess. (1942); H.R. 7067, 77th Cong., 2d Sess. (1942).

59.   H.R. 653, 78th Cong., 1st Sess., 89 CONG. REC. 3218 (1943).

60.   H.R. 32, 79th Cong., 1st Sess. (1945), becoming Hobbs Act §§ 1-6, 18 U.S.C. § 1951 (1976).

61.   18 U.S.C. § 1951 (1976).

62.   *See* note 59 *supra.*

63.   The debates in the House on H.R. 653 were fairly extensive and are as much a legitimate source of legislative history from which probable legislative intent may be deduced as are the debates on the identical bill in the following session. United States v. Enmons, 410 U.S. 396, 404 n.14 (1973).

64. After passing the House in independent form, 91 CONG. REC. 11922 (1945), the substance of the Hobbs Act was also incorporated into the Case Bill, H.R. 4908, 79th Cong., 2d Sess. (1945), which passed Congress but which was vetoed by President Truman, 92 CONG. REC. 674 (1946). Immediately after the veto, the Senate took up and passed the Hobbs Act as previously approved in independent form by the House, 92 CONG. REC. 7308 (1946), thus making it law in spite of the veto. *See generally* Comment, *Labor Law—A New Federal Antiracketeering Law*, 35 GEO. L.J. 362 (1947); Comment, *The Hobbs Act—An Amendment to the Federal Anti-Racketeering Act*, 25 N.C.L. REV. 58 (1946).

65. 18 U.S.C. § 1951 (1976).

66. *Id.*

67. 91 CONG. REC. 11913-19 (1945). Speaking of the *Local 807* case, Congressman Sumners also said: "It was the purpose of the Judiciary Committee to prevent the rendition of that sort of decision by any court in the future, so the language upon which that holding was based was eliminated." *Id.* at 11909.

68. Congressman Hancock called the *Local 807* case "a gross misinterpretation of the law and a distortion of the intent of Congress." 91 CONG. REC. 11900 (1945). *See also* 88 CONG. REC. 2071, 5334-35 (1942); 89 CONG. REC. 3193, 3201, 3202, 3206-07, 3220 (1943).

69. 88 CONG. REC. 2071 (1942) (remarks of Sen. Holman).

70. *Id.* at 5334-34.

71. 89 CONG. REC. 3202 (1943) (remarks of Rep. Gwynne).

72. 91 CONG. REC. 11900 (1945) (emphasis added).

73. *See, e.g.,* 88 CONG. REC. 2071 (1942); 89 CONG. REC. 3206, 3210, 3217 (1943).

74. 89 CONG. REC. 3221 (1943).

75. *See* text accompanying notes 54-57 *supra.*

76. *See* note 68 *supra.*

77. 91 CONG. REC. 11904 (1945).

78. *Id.*

79. *Id.*

80. *Id.* at 11918 (1945) (emphasis added).

81. 89 CONG. REC. 3220 (1943).

82. *Id.*

83. *Id.* at 3193, 3202.

84. *See id.* at 3220.

85. 15 U.S.C. §§ 12-27 (1974).

86. *See., e.g.,* Apex Hosiery Co. v. Leader, 310 U.S. 469 (1940) (Court held that labor union activity that was illegal under local law could be legal under the Sherman Antitrust Act).

87. *See* 89 CONG. REC. 3202 (1943) (remarks of Congressman Gwynne).

88. *Id.* at 3203, 3224 (remarks of Rep. Baldwin).

89. *Id.* at 3194-95, 3220-21 (remarks of Rep. Hobbs).

90. *Id.* at 3220-21.

91. *Id.* at 3225.

92. 91 CONG. REC. 11901 (1945).

93. *Id.*

94. *Id.* (emphasis added).

95. *Id.* at 11920.

96. *Id.* at 11902.

97. *Id.* at 11908.

98. *Id.* at 11903.

99. *Id.* at 11907.

100. *Id.* at 11841 (remarks of Rep. Savage).

101. *Id.* (remarks of Rep. Barden).

102. *Id.* at 11843 (remarks of Rep. Michener).

103. *Id.* at 11846 (remarks of Rep. LaFollette) (emphasis added).

104. Nevertheless, such a result was, in effect, reached by the Supreme Court in United States v. Enmons, 410 U.S. 396 (1973), where the Court held that the use of violence to obtain a more favorable collective bargaining agreement (covering, among other things, the payment of wages) was not within the prohibitions of the Hobbs Act. *See* text accompanying notes 166-200 *infra*.

105. 89 CONG. REC. 3213 (1943).

106. *Id.* at 3202 (remarks of Rep. Gwynne).

107. *See* notes 89-90 & accompanying text *supra*.

108. 91 CONG. REC. 11901 (1945) (remarks of Rep. Celler).

109. United States v. Enmons, 410 U.S. 396, 410 n.20 (1973).

110. 89 CONG. REC. 3195 (1943) (emphasis added).

111. *Id.* (emphasis added).

112. 88 CONG. REC. 2071 (1942) (remarks of Sen. Holman) (emphasis added).

113. 91 CONG. REC. 11843-44 (1945) (emphasis added).

114. *Id.* at 11844 (remarks of Rep. Michener).

115. 198 F.2d 889 (3d Cir.), *cert. denied,* 344 U.S. 893 (1952).

116. 198 F.2d at 891-92 (emphasis added).

117. *Id.* at 895 (McLaughlin, J., dissenting).

118. *See* notes 130-38 & accompanying text *infra*.

119. 135 F. Supp. 162 (S.D. Ill. 1955), *rev'd,* 350 U.S. 415 (1956).

120. 135 F. Supp. at 162.

121. 18 U.S.C. § 1951 (1976).

122. *See* § III-A-3 of text *supra.*

123. 135 F. Supp. at 162-63.

124. *Id.* at 163. Judge Adair was undoubtedly correct in concluding that the union's objective in this case was "not illegitimate." This conclusion, as well as its significance insofar as the current law is concerned, will be discussed subsequently. *See* note 151 & accompanying text *supra.*

125. 135 F. Supp. at 163.

126. *See* note 84 & accompanying text *supra.*

127. *See* notes 89-90 & accompanying text *supra.*

128. 135 F. Supp. at 163.

129. *Id.* Most of the cases under the Hobbs Act have involved attempts by labor union officials to extort money for their own personal use. *See, e.g.,* United States v. Daley, 564 F.2d 645 (2d Cir. 1977), *cert. denied,* 435 U.S. 933 (1978); Anderson v. United States, 262 F.2d 764 (8th Cir. 1959); United States v. Varlack, 225 F.2d 665 (2d Cir. 1955); United States v. Compagna, 146 F.2d 524 (2d Cir. 1944), *cert. denied,* 324 U.S. 867 (1945). In some instances the money was not obtained through the threatened use of physical violence, but through the threatened use of "economic force," *i.e.,* otherwise nonactionable strikes, picketing, and the like. How these cases fit into the conceptual scheme will be discussed at § III-C of text *infra.*

130. United States v. Green, 350 U.S. 415, 419-20 (1956).

131. *Id.* at 419 (footnote omitted).

132. *Id.* at 420 (footnote omitted).

133. *See* note 124 & accompanying text *supra.*

134. 347 U.S. 656 (1954).

135. 315 U.S. 740 (1942).

136. 306 U.S. 240 (1939).

137. 198 F.2d 889 (3rd Cir.), *cert. denied,* 344 U.S. 893 (1952).

138. 350 U.S. 299 (1956).

139. *See* United States v. Green, 143 F. Supp. 442 (S.D. Ill. 1956), *aff'd,* 246 F.2d 155 (7th Cir.), *cert. denied,* 355 U.S. 871 (1957).

140. 246 F.2d at 160.

141. *Id.*

142. United States v. Caldes, 457 F.2d 74, 75 (9th Cir. 1972).

143. 457 F.2d 74 (9th Cir. 1972). *See generally* Willis, *Labor Violence—The Judiciary's Refusal to Apply the Hobbs Act,* 28 S.C.L. REV. 143 (1976).

278 *Private Sector*

144. *See* United States v. Enmons, 410 U.S. 396, 409 (1973).

145. 457 F.2d at 77.

146. *Id.* at 76.

147. *Id.*

148. *Id.* at 77.

149. *Id.* (emphasis added).

150. *See* notes 69-71 & accompanying text *supra*.

151. Although the Labor Management Relations Act § 8(b)(6), 29 U.S.C. § 158(b)(6) (1976) contains a so-called "anti-featherbedding" provision, it would not prohibit the kind of conduct that was involved in *Green*. In American Newspaper Publishers Assoc. v. NLRB, 345 U.S. 100 (1953), the Court noted that the LMRA "limits its condemnation to instances where a labor organization or its agents exact pay from an employer in return for services not performed or not to be performed." *Id.* at 110. This conclusion is bolstered by Senator Taft's observation that although the Senate did not approve of featherbedding in the broader sense, it "felt that it was impractical to give a board or a court the power to say that so many men are all right, and so many men are too many." 93 CONG. REC. 6441 (1947). Moreover, a demand for the kind of work that was involved in *Green* would not only be a legitimate subject of bargaining, but also a mandatory one. As the Court in *American Newspaper Publishers* put it, the Act "leaves to collective bargaining the determination of what, if any, work, including bona fide 'made work,' shall be included as compensable services." 345 U.S. at 111.

152. 457 F.2d at 78.

153. United States v. Kramer, 355 F.2d 891 (7th Cir. 1966).

154. *See generally* T. HAGGARD, COMPULSORY UNIONISM, THE NLRB, AND THE COURTS 11-24 (1977), which contains, from a slightly different perspective, a comprehensive overview of the evolution of the "criminal conspiracy" doctrine.

155. People v. Dioguardi, 8 N.Y.2d 260, 168 N.E.2d 683, 203 N.Y.S.2d 870 (1960).

156. 457 F.2d at 78.

157. *Id.*

158. *Id.*

159. *Id.*

160. *Id.*

161. *See* Labor Management Relations Act § 8(b)(4)(A), 29 U.S.C. § 158(b)(4)(A)(1976).

162. 93 CONG. REC. 4860 (1947).

163. *Id.* (emphasis added).

164. 457 F.2d at 79.

165. *See, e.g.,* 89 CONG. REC. 3201, 3225 (1943); 91 CONG. REC. 11901 (1945).

166. 410 U.S. 396 (1973).

167. United States v. Enmons, 335 F. Supp. 641 (E.D. La. 1971), *aff'd*, 410 U.S. 396 (1973).

168. Specifically, the Act defines extortion as "the obtaining of property from another, with his consent, induced by *wrongful* use of actual or threatened force, violence or fear . . . ." 18 U.S.C. § 1951(b)(2) (1976) (emphasis added).

169. 410 U.S. at 399 n.2.

170. *Id.* at 400.

171. *Id.* (footnotes omitted).

172. Bianchi v. United States, 219 F.2d 182 (8th Cir.), *cert. denied*, 349 U.S. 915 (1955).

173. *See, e.g.,* 89 CONG. REC. 3194, 3218 (1943); 91 CONG. REC. 11901 (1945).

174. Congressman LaFollette, for example, said that "[o]f course, there is an element of coercion in strikes. It is the only right labor has." 91 CONG. REC. 11920 (1945).

175. *See* 89 CONG. REC. 3193, 3202 (1943); 91 CONG. REC. 11904-05 (1945).

176. This assertion, and other matters summarized in the text, occurred in the course of remarks among Congressmen Voorhis, Sumners, and Hobbs, recorded at 91 CONG. REC. 11908 (1945).

177. *Id.*

178. *Id.*

179. 410 U.S. at 400.

180. *Id.* at 401 (emphasis added).

181. *Id.* at 403.

182. *Id.* at 404 (quoting 91 CONG. REC. 11908 (1945) (remarks of Rep. Sumners)).

183. In *Enmons*, the objective of the violence was simply to obtain a more favorable collective bargaining agreement, an obviously legitimate goal in itself, while in *Green* the objective was to obtain job opportunities for union members, a similarly legitimate and entirely traditional goal of the labor movement. *Cf.* United States v. Green, 246 F.2d 155, 160 (7th Cir. 1957) ("There is no doubt that unions have the right to settle disputes [such as the one involved in that case] peacefully by means of negotiation . . . ."); *see also* note 151 *supra*.

184. *See* notes 173-78 & accompanying text *supra*.

185. *See* notes 89-90 & accompaning text *supra*.

186. 410 U.S. at 408.

187. *Id.*

188. *Id.*

189. *See* text accompanying note 105 *supra*.

190. *See* text accompanying notes 105-09 *supra*.

191. 410 U.S. at 408.

192. *Id.* at 410.

193. For example, it apparently "passed unobserved" for roughly a hundred years that in the Civil Rights Act of 1866 Congress intended to prohibit purely private as well as public discrimination. However, this did not prevent the Court from so

holding in the first case where the issue was squarely presented. Jones v. Alfred H. Mayer Co., 392 U.S. 409 (1968).

194. 410 U.S. at 410 (footnotes omitted).

195. *See* text following note 109 *supra.*

196. *See, e.g.,* 89 CONG. REC. 3201 (1943), where Congressman Celler voiced the concern that the bill may permit simple assaults to be converted into felonies.

197. *See* Livers v. United States, 185 F.2d 807, 809 (6th Cir. 1950) ("In the enactment of our national laws against crime, the Congress has vested United States District Judges with wide discretion in assessing punishment within the limits of the various federal statutes.").

198. 410 U.S. at 418 (Douglas, J., dissenting) (footnotes omitted).

199. *Id.* (emphasis added).

200. *Id.* at 413.

201. *See* United States v. Quinn, 514 F.2d 1250 (5th Cir. 1975), *cert. denied,* 424 U.S. 955 (1976). Under the circumstances of that case, the payment of the money was itself thought by the court to be an independent violation of the Taft-Hartley Act, 29 U.S.C. § 186(a) (1976), which generally prohibits payments by an employer to the representative of his employees, thus making it an "illegitimate" objective under the *Enmons* approach.

202. *See, e.g.,* 29 U.S.C. § 186(c)(4) & (5) (1976) (pertaining to payments made under check-off authorizations and employer contribution into pension funds).

203. *See* 29 U.S.C. § 158(b)(6) (1976); United States v. Arambasich, 597 F.2d 609 (7th Cir. 1979); United States v. Callahan, 551 F.2d 733 (6th Cir. 1977).

204. *See* 29 U.S.C. § 158(a)(3) (1976).

205. *See* United States v. Jacobs, 543 F.2d 18 (7th Cir. 1976), *cert. denied,* 431 U.S. 929 (1977).

206. The Court may have simply misread the *Green* decision, for there is some suggestion in the opinion that the Court viewed the facts in *Green* as substantially similar to those in the *Local 807* case. *See* 410 U.S. at 408. This, however, is not accurate in that, in at least some instances, the union members in *Local 807* did not even offer to do any work, thus making it a case of true "featherbedding," and, under *current* law at least, an illegitimate union objective. *See* note 151 *supra.* There was no suggestion of that in *Green.*

207. *See* note 151 *supra; see also,* United States v. McCullough, 427 F. Supp. 246 (E.D. Pa. 1977).

208. In United States v. Warledo, 557 F.2d 721 (10th Cir. 1977), a non-labor case, members of a certain Indian tribe were indicted for attempting to obtain money from a railroad to redress past wrongs aginst the tribe. Payment by the railroad would not, of course, have been illegal, and they alleged that their belief in the validity of their claim was sufficient to bring them within the *Enmons* exception. The Court of Appeals disagreed. "To say that the pursuit of a payment from the railroad for *alleged* past wrongs is not wrongful taxes the statutory language to a highly unreasonable degree." *Id.* at 730.

209. United States v. Stirone, 262 F.2d 571, 575-76 (3d Cir. 1958).

210. 225 F.2d 665 (2d Cir. 1955).

211. *Id.* at 669.

212. Comment, *Featherbedding and the Federal AntiRacketeering Act,* 26 U. CHI. L. REV. 150, 159 (1958).

213. 410 U.S. at 400 n.3.

214. *Id.* at 400 (footnote omitted).

215. United States v. Iozzi, 420 F.2d 512 (4th Cir. 1970); United States v. Kramer, 355 F.2d 891 (7th Cir.), *cert. granted and case remanded for resentencing,* 384 U.S. 100 (1966); Bianchi v. United States, 219 F.2d 182 (8th Cir.), *cert. denied,* 349 U.S. 915 (1955).

216. 91 CONG. REC. 11912 (1945).

217. *Id.*

218. *See, e.g.,* United States v. Arambasich, 597 F.2d 609 (7th Cir. 1979); United States v. Nell, 570 F.2d 1251 (5th Cir. 1978); United States v. Daley, 564 F.2d 645 (2d Cir. 1977), *cert. denied,* 435 U.S. 933 (1978).

219. Act of Nov. 8, 1966, Pub. L. No. 89-801, 80 Stat. 1516, *as amended,* Act of July 8, 1969, Pub. L. No. 91-39, 83 Stat. 44.

220. *Reform of the Federal Criminal Laws: Hearings Before the Subcommittee on Criminal Laws and Procedures of the Senate Committee on the Judiciary, Part I,* 92d Cong., 1st Sess. 129 (1971) [hereinafter cited as *Hearings, Part I*].

221. *Id.* at 359.

222. *Id.* at 373-74.

223. *Id.* at 374.

224. S. 1, 93d Cong., 1st Sess. (1973); *Reform of the Federal Criminal Laws: Hearings on S. 1, S. 716, S. 1400, S. 1401 Before the Subcommittee on Criminal Laws and Procedures of the Senate Committee on the Judiciary, Part V,* 93d Cong., 1st Sess. 4211-748 (1973) [hereinafter cited as *Hearings, Part V*].

225. 119 CONG. REC. 92 (1973).

226. *Hearings, Part V, supra* note 224, at 4346.

227. *Id.* at 4786.

228. S. 1400, 93d Cong., 1st Sess. (1973), *Hearings, Part V, supra* note 224, at 4862-5197.

229. 119 CONG. REC. 9634 (1973).

230. *Hearings, Part V, supra* note 224, at 5966.

231. *Id.* at 4847.

232. S. 1, 94th Cong., 1st Sess. (1975).

233. SENATE COMMITTEE ON THE JUDICIARY, 94TH CONG., 2D SESS., DRAFT REPORT TO ACCOMPANY S. 1 644-59 (Comm. Print 1975).

234. *Reform of the Federal Criminal Laws. Hearings on S. 1 Before the Subcommittee*

on *Criminal Laws and Procedures of the Senate Committee on the Judiciary, Part XII*, 94th Cong., 1st Sess. 215 (1975).

235. 123 CONG. REC. S6831 (daily ed. May 2, 1977).

236. S. 1437, 95th Cong., 1st Sess. (1977), *Reform of the Federal Criminal Laws: Hearings on S. 1437 Before the Subcommittee on Criminal Laws and Procedures of the Senate Committee on the Judiciary, Part XIII*, 95th Cong., 1st Sess. 9485-792 (1977) [hereinafter cited as *Hearings, Part XIII*].

237. *Id.* at 9602.

238. S. REP. NO. 605, 95th Cong., 1st Sess. (1977).

239. *Id.* at 624-25.

240. *Id.* at 624.

241. *Hearings, Part XIII, surpa* note 236, at 9602-03.

242. 124 CONG. REC. S12 (daily ed. Jan. 19, 1978).

243. *Id.* at S17.

244. *Id.* at S17-18.

245. *Id.* at S17.

246. *Id.* at S18.

247. *Id.* at S860.

248. 125 CONG. REC. S12204 (daily ed. Sept. 7, 1979).

249. S. 1722, 96th Cong., 1st Sess. (1979), *Reform of the Federal Criminal Laws: Hearings on S. 1722, S. 1723 Before the Senate Committee on the Judiciary, Part XIV*, 96th Cong., 1st Sess. 11090-484 (1979)[hereinafter cited as *Hearings, Part XIV*].

250. *Hearings, Part XIV, supra* note 249, at 10707.

251. *Id.*

252. *Id.* at 10045-48, 10691-92.

253. *Id.* at 10693.

254. *Id.* at 10049.

255. *See* note 245 & accompanying text *supra*.

256. *Hearings, Part XIV, supra* note 249, at 10764.

257. S. 1722, 96th Cong., 2d Sess. (1980)(as reported with amendments).

258. S. REP. NO. 553, 96th Cong., 2d Sess. 645 (1980).

259. *Id.*

260. *See* § III-C of text *supra*.

261. S. REP. NO. 533, 96th Cong., 2d Sess. 649 (1980) (emphasis added).

262. *Id.* at 651 (emphasis added).

263. *Id.* at 648 n.58.

264. S. 1722, 96th Cong., 2d Sess. (1980) (as reported with amendments).

265. S. REP. NO. 553, 96th Cong., 2d Sess. 657 (1980) (footnote omitted).

266. *See* text accompanying note 257 *supra.*

267. S. 1722, 96th Cong., 2d Sess. (1980).

268. S. REP. NO. 553, 96th Cong., 2d Sess. 651-52 (1980).

269. *Id.* at 651.

270. H.R. 300, 92d Cong., 2d Sess. (1972).

271. H.R. 10850, 94th Cong., 1st Sess. (1975).

272. H.R. 12504, 94th Cong., 2d Sess. (1976).

273. Schwartz, *Reform of the Federal Criminal Laws: Issues, Tactics, and Prospects,* 41 LAW & CONTEMP. PROB. 12 (1977).

274. H.R. 6869, 95th Cong., 2d Sess. (1978).

275. *Id.*

276. *Hearings, Part XIV, supra* note 249, at 10763.

277. H.R. 13959, 95th Cong., 2d Sess. (1978).

278. H.R. 6233, 96th Cong., 1st Sess. (1979). A "working draft" of this bill was also introduced in the Senate as S. 1723, 96th Cong., 1st Sess. (1979), but with subsection (b) omitted.

279. *Id.*

280. H.R. 6915, 96th Cong., 2d Sess. (1980).

281. One logical, but somewhat unlikely explanation, of this draft was that it made "legitimate objectives" a defense in all cases *except* those involving labor extortion, thus turning on its head the uniquely favored treatment afforded labor unions by the *Enmons* decision.

282. Mr. Justice Douglas noted that "[w]hile we said in . . . [case citation omitted] that it is 'retrospective expansion of meaning which properly deserves the stigma of judicial legislation,' the same is true of retrospective contraction of meaning." 410 U.S. at 419 (Douglas, J., dissenting).

283. The *Enmons* decision is, of course, only one example of this rather curious phenomenon. For an insightful analysis of the underlying constitutional (separation of powers) problems posed by this particular use, or abuse, of the judicial process, see Walker, *The Exorbitant Cost of Redistributing Injustice: A Critical View of* United Steelworkers of America v. Weber *and the Misguided Policy of Numerical Employment,* 21 B.C.L. REV. 1 (1980).

284. 89 CONG. REC. 3217 (1943).

285-305

83/0
8/20

,0S

[1981]

Union Organization Among Engineers: A Current Assessment

Geoffrey W. Latta[†]

The decline since 1958 in the percentage of the American labor force that is unionized can be attributed partially to the difficulty unions have had attracting white-collar employees in the private sector. In their efforts to counteract stagnating membership levels, particularly in the early 1970s, a number of unions began seeking to organize engineers and scientists. The results have been very disappointing so far, from the unions' standpoint. Few groups have been successfully unionized and some that voted for union representation later decertified their unions.

This article outlines the history of the attempts to organize engineers and scientists in the private sector in the 1970s, analyzes the reasons why attempts to unionize this key group have not met with significant success, and discusses how the situation could change in the future. The research for this study was conducted through interviews with company and union officials and with representatives of professional societies and other relevant groups. A total of forty-two persons from twenty-six organizations were interviewed between June 1978 and May 1979. The companies and unions selected were known to have been involved in organizing campaigns. In most cases, cooperation was given freely, but representatives of two unions and one company refused to be interviewed.

The History

The first serious attempt to organize engineers was made by the American Association of Engineers (AAE), which was founded in 1915.[1] In the following decades, unions affiliated with the American Federation of Labor (AFL) and the Congress of Industrial Organizations (CIO) competed for the allegiance of engineers in independent unions, which were affiliated with neither the AFL nor the CIO and

† At the time this research was conducted, Geoffrey W. Latta was a research specialist at the Industrial Research Unit at the Wharton School at the University of Pennsylvania. He is now affiliated with a consulting firm. He would like to thank Herbert R. Northrup and Janice R. Bellace for their comments on this paper and the Pew Memorial Trust for their research grant. Reprinted by permission from the *Industrial and Labor Relations Review*, Vol. 35, No. 1 (October 1981).

each of which drew membership from only a single company. Neither type of organization achieved major success, although the years between 1943 and 1948 were the most fruitful period of organizing. The modest growth of engineering unionization in that period reflected the wider trends that encouraged union membership in the years following the passage of the Wagner Act. By 1948, independent organizations of engineers had established a firm foothold in such companies as Westinghouse, RCA, Lockheed, and Boeing.

The major AFL and CIO unions regarded the single-company independents as pale imitations of real trade unions, although some of the independents were sometimes quite aggressive in the sphere of collective bargaining. The independent at Westinghouse, for example, conducted a three-week strike against the company in Pittsburgh in 1945.[2] The skepticism of affiliated unions toward the independents reflected the fact that the latter were sometimes established as a defensive reaction by engineers against organizing campaigns launched by AFL or CIO unions. At other times the formation of an independent was encouraged by the professional societies that represent engineers and scientists.[3]

In 1952, a number of the independents united to form a federal organization called the Engineers and Scientists (ESA), which by 1955 had fifteen affiliates representing about 50,000 employees.[4] In the late 1950s, however, ESA experienced pressures from three different directions, the first coming from several major independents affiliated with AFL-CIO unions. The Engineers Association of Arma and the Engineers Association of Sperry both joined the International Union of Electrical Workers (IUE), for example, and the Federation of Honeywell Engineers affiliated with the United Automobile Workers (UAW). These moves created internal conflict within the ESA, as a number of the affiliates objected to any affiliation with AFL-CIO unions. At the same time a battle raged between independents that sought to restrict their membership to technicians. The third pressure arose from the decertification in 1960 of ESA's largest affiliate, the Council of Western Electric Professional Employees. As a result of these problems, by 1961 ESA had only five member associations with about 9,700 actual members,[5] and so it was dissolved in March 1961.

Between 1961 and 1968 union-organizing efforts among engineers were limited; the Sperry engineers decertified the IUE in 1962, and the Western Electric independent lost an election in 1963.[6] In 1968-69, however, the IUE won back its Sperry unit and was selected as bargaining agent by a unit of 700 engineers at Western Electric in Kearny, New Jersey. These victories seemed to usher in an era of

TABLE 1

Representation Elections in Private Sector Units of Over 100 Engineers, December 1968 to December 1980.

Date		Company	Location	Union	Vote		Percentage	
					For Union	*Against Union*	*For Union*	*Against Union*
December	1968	Western Electric	Kearny, N.J.	*IUE*	373	294	55.9	44.1
July	1969	Sperry Gyroscope	Long Island, N.Y.	*IUE*	827	492	62.7	37.3
May	1971	North American Rockwell	Cape Kennedy, Fla.	*MEBA*	98	124	44.1	55.9
August	1971	Amoco Chemicals	Napierville, Ill.	*MEBA*	44	131	25.1	74.9
October	1971	Western Electric	Kearny, N.J.	*IUE*	349	356	49.5	50.5
				(decertification)				
June	1972	Lockheed	Sunnyvale, Calif.	*MEBA*	1,618	2,690	37.6	62.4
June	1972	Boeing Vertol	Philadelphia, Pa.	*SPEEA*	354	436	44.8	55.2
June	1972	North American Rockwell	Cape Kennedy, Fla.	*MEBA*	93	100	48.2	51.8
November	1973	General Electric (Knolls)	Schenectady, N.Y.	*KASE*	423	629	40.2	59.8
November	1974	General Dynamics (Convair)	San Diego, Calif.	*NEPA*	607	468	56.5	43.5
July	1975	Leeds and Northrup	Norty Wales, Pa.	*PESA*	138	117	54.1	45.9
				(decertification)				
August	1976	General Dynamics (Convair)	San Diego, Calif.	*NEPA*	334	462	42.0	58.0
				(decertification)				
February	1977	Rohr Industries	Chula Vista, Calif.	*NEPA*	160	277	36.6	63.4
August	1977	North American Rockwell	Los Angeles, Calif.	*NEPA*	2,366	3,192	42.6	57.4
August	1977	North American Rockwell	Tulsa, Okla.	*NEPA*	28	81	25.7	74.3
June	1978	North American Rockwell	Los Angeles, Calif.	*NEPA*	2,161	2,690	44.5	55.5
				(rerun)				
June	1979	Boeing	Cape Kennedy, Fla.	*MEBA*	86	59	59.3	40.7
May	1980	Boeing Vertol	Philadelphia, Pa.	*SPPEA*	281	373	43.0	57.0

Source: National Labor Relations Board Data.

greater promise for engineering unionization. Data on the major private-sector elections among engineers in the period between December 1968 and December 1980 are presented in the table below. Although the period 1968-80 witnessed more elections per year than had the previous decade, unions only won four major certification elections, and in two of these units they lost decertification elections within three years of their initial victories.

One factor inhibiting organizational success has been the absence of a union that has been concerned primarily with organizing engineers. In theory one might think that the AFL-CIO affiliated International Federation of Professional and Technical Engineers (IFPTE), founded in 1918, would be the focal point of the attempt to unionize engineers, but this union, which has about 15,000 members, consists largely of technical employees. (The IFPTE has also concentrated its attention in the public sector, and therefore its largest recent success, which came in 1972 when it was chosen to represent a unit of 1,614 professional scientists and engineers at the Marshall Space Flight Center in Huntsville, Alabama, falls outside the scope of this study.[7]) In the five years between 1975 and 1979, the union participated in only fifteen National Labor Relations Board (NLRB) elections, mainly in technical units, and won representation rights for only 105 employees in five units.[8]

A number of other unions have been active in seeking to organize engineers, with the IUE, the UAW, and the Marine Engineers Benevolent Association (MEBA) taking the lead. The tactics adopted by different unions have varied. Both the International Association of Machinists (IAM) and the International Brotherhood of Electrical Workers (IBEW) undertook some campaigns among engineers, most of which did not reach elections. These two unions, as well as the IUE, relied on traditional organizational tactics, with an effort made to sign up individual employees. Both the MEBA and, later, the Teamsters were more inclined to attempt to secure the affiliation of existing independent organizations of engineers. In 1969-70, for example, the MEBA secured the affiliation of independents at Pacific Gas and Electric in San Francisco, at the Shell Development Company in Emeryville, California, and at Amoco's facility in Whiting, Indiana. At North American Rockwell, the MEBA took over the Aerospace Professional and Technical Association (APTA), which had fought an unsuccessful election in the Autonetics Division in 1969, but a campaign by MEBA-APTA in 1971 petered out. The MEBA seemed to have secured a major victory for its policy in 1971, however, when the executive board of the Southern California Professional Engineering Association (SCPEA) at McDonnell-Douglas recommended affiliation to the MEBA; a membership ballot, however, narrowly rejected this proposal.[9] After 1972, the MEBA's organizing initiative lost momentum, although the union later won an election at Bechtel Corporation in San Francisco (in a unit of fewer than 100 employees and therefore not shown in the table), and in 1979, its affiliate, the Florida Association of Professional Employees (FAPE), was selected as bargaining agent by 190 professional engineers at Boeing Services International in Cape Kennedy.

The Teamsters followed a similar strategy and in 1975 gained the affiliation of the SCPEA at McDonnell-Douglas. The company refused to recognize this affiliation, and a period of maneuvering ensued during which officials of Teamsters Local 911 were able to appear at the SCPEA negotiations as "consultants," only. While the Teamsters filed unfair labor practice charges against the company, the company announced that it would only accept the link with the Teamsters if the union would go through an NLRB election to change the certification.[10] The company was confident that the Teamsters lacked sufficient support among the engineers to contemplate this course of action. It appears to have been right, for in December 1978 the SCPEA disaffiliated from the Teamsters, reportedly with 84 percent of its members voting in favor of disaffiliation.[11]

The UAW chose a different strategy by creating a separate section for engineers in 1975, called the National Engineers and Professionals Association (NEPA). This body owed its origins to the affiliation to the UAW in 1972 of an organization of the same name that had been established at North American Rockwell, and that had been building up its membership in order to file for an election.[12] NEPA sought both to organize directly and to take over independents. Its greatest victory occurred in 1975 when it was selected as bargaining agent for a unit of 1,300 engineers at General Dynamics' Convair Division in San Diego.

In other attempts to organize directly, the NEPA fought several elections, such as that at Rohr Industries in Chula Vista, California in 1977 and at Rockwell in 1978. In its attempt to organize through taking over independents, it secured the affiliation of the Professional Engineers and Scientists Association (PESA) at the Leeds and Northrup Company in North Wales, Pennsylvania. It suffered a major blow, however, when it was decertified at General Dynamics in 1976. Thereafter, its continuing lack of success led to a reevaluation by the UAW, and in 1978 the NEPA informed the PESA, its only affiliate with bargaining rights, that the NEPA could no longer provide it with bargaining support. The PESA then reverted to independent status.[13]

Among engineering independents, the aim of establishing a national federation remained alive and the Association of Professional Engineering Personnel (ASPEP), the independent at RCA in New Jersey, took the lead in discussing federation with a body that had been set up for that purpose in California, the Council of Engineering and Scientific Organizations-West (CESO-W). As a result, in 1968 a national CESO was formed.[14] The CESO enjoyed a rather checkered history as several major independents disaffiliated from it for varying periods of time. By 1979, however, it seemed to have established a stable base, with eleven affiliated members.[15] In contrast to the situation in the ESA, the CESO affiliates adopted a less hostile attitude to mainstream trade unionism and admitted into membership both the NEPA in 1977 and the IFPTE in 1978.

In terms of organizing, the ASPEP was the only independent actively to seek new members in companies different from those in which it had traditionally organized. In 1972, it fought an election in a unit (too small for inclusion in the table) at Lockheed Electronics in Plainfield, New Jersey, but it was defeated; several other ASPEP organizing campaigns, including one at Allied Chemical in Morristown, New Jersey, proved abortive. The largest independent union of engineers, the Seattle Professional Engineering Employees' Association (SPEEA) at Boeing, adopted a different growth strategy, seeking to extend its membership within the company. In 1971, it won an election in Seattle for a technical unit, which marked its movement away from a purely professional membership. This evolution was further emphasized in May 1980 when the SPEEA fought an election in a professional and administrative unit in Seattle. The union lost by a vote of 2,333 to 1,440. At the same time, the SPEEA unsuccessfully fought an election in a unit of Boeing Vertol in Philadelphia, where it had lost a previous election in 1972.

In summary, except in the unusual circumstances of the 1940s, engineers have never been very susceptible to union organization. Between 1968 and 1980, however, it looked as though the situation might have altered and, in fact, that period saw more major elections per year in the private sector among engineers than had taken place in the previous decade. Despite the number of elections, however, union victories were scarce, and as the 1980s commence, the little momentum the unions had achieved is slowing markedly. The following section will try to explain why the number of elections increased in recent years and also why the unions were usually unsuccessful.

Unionization Campaigns

One means of assessing the attraction of unionism to some groups of engineers is to examine the issues raised during union-organizing campaigns. In many cases, these issues are not dissimilar to those one might have expected in any union campaign. Job security occupied a high place in a number of campaigns, for example, especially after 1968 in the aerospace industry. Elections were not concentrated in the period between 1968 and 1972, however, when employment fell sharply in aerospace, but in the years after 1972 when employment remained static. Organization was thus not an immediate response to layoffs, but a longer-term effort to prevent the recurrence of the conditions of the period from 1968 to 1972. Although it was not always apparent what unions could do to halt the layoffs, unions such as the NEPA at Rockwell and Rohr often cited past layoffs as reasons for organizing. In part this was an attempt to offset company appeals for loyalty by reminding engineers that the company was not always so solicitous of their interests.

The union criticism of employers on this issue usually centered on the method of selecting individual employees for layoff. Unions rarely pushed for seniority to be the sole factor in determining layoffs, but they would also not accept management's unfettered right to decide on a "skill and ability" basis. The potency of this issue had been illustrated by the ASPEP at RCA, which in 1967 conducted a 77-day strike largely on the question of selection for layoff. The SPEEA contract with Boeing has long included the provision of a "retention index," which determines selection for layoff. Length of service is an important component, although not the sole one, in this index.[16] Unions have dealt carefully on this issue in campaigns, both for fear of alienating shorter service engineers and because they realize some engineers do not regard strict seniority as compatible with a professional role.

The remuneration of engineers relative to other groups of employees was also a common campaign theme. At Electric Boat Company, an organizing campaign by the IUE followed the granting of wage increases to draftsmen and technicians, who were unionized, in excess of those given to engineers. Both union and company personnel agree that this was a major factor in the campaign.[17] Similarly, in the Convair Division of General Dynamics, merit increases for engineers in 1971 were less than the pay increases achieved by unionized employees in the company, and that disparity provided the initial impetus to a union-organizing drive that led eventually to the NEPA's victory in 1974. In many other cases, even absent specific instances, there seems to have been a feeling by engineers that they were being left behind by unionized groups.

Many of the company and union officials who were interviewed during the course of this study asserted that engineers embraced unionism partly as a response to a perceived decline in their status relative to other groups of employees. This situation seemed to arise most frequently where engineers worked in large units. Although status is always a somewhat nebulous concept, campaigns often drew on specific instances of managerial action, such as attempting to tighten up on engineers' coffee-breaks. The following comment of one manager is typical of many managers' views:

> Professional engineers feel a significant loss of status during the last decade. . . . [They] do not feel they are part of management and in fact they feel isolated from the mainstream of management decision making.[18]

While, as might be expected, union officials did not always agree with managers about the reasons for engineers' interest in unionization, the comments of the two groups on status concerns were often similar. As one union official put it:

> Professionalism is not fully utilized by management. . . . They don't bring them into the decision-making process so the engineers get frustrated at their non-involvement; they think management "doesn't give a damn," and if the employer won't adequately recognize their professionalism, professional engineers may go the collective bargaining route therefore, since they can't get recognition as individuals.[19]

In the campaign at Rohr Industries, the company claimed that a vote for the NEPA would endanger the engineers' role as part of the management team. The NEPA response was clear:

> The company suddenly "claims" us as a part of management . . . going so far as to infer we will lose our "management" standing if our union is certified. The question is, how can we *lose* something we *do not* have?[20]

The nature of engineers' work could also be an underlying campaign issue, especially at times when economic conditions reduce employment opportunities for engineers. As one manager expressed it, "Engineering work used to be glamorous, but then that fell apart. There was less R and D work and more routine maintenance."[21]

This problem was linked to the obsolescence of engineering skills, sometimes mentioned by managers. The notion was that sometimes older, longer service engineers tended to be in the forefront of union organization because they were no longer able to keep pace with rapid changes in technology and knowledge and so sought to find in union activity an interest their own careers had ceased to provide. In addition, it was claimed that skill obsolescence made engineers more fearful of layoffs, thus encouraging unionization. Also, the lack of potential for career progression may encourage unionization, independent of the argument about obsolescence: those engineers who both aspire to managerial jobs and have a realistic hope of attaining them are probably less receptive to unionization than those who neither seek nor expect such advancement.[22]

The argument for this managerial view may be treated with some skepticism. The evidence is highly subjective, not least because it is difficult in practice to define an "obsolescent" engineer. Also, other evidence from management itself contradicted this view. Many managers pointed out that often the major supporters of unionization campaigns were highly-skilled and well-respected engineers. In a number of cases these people were subsequently promoted to managerial positions. The organizational ability required to take a leading role in a union-organizing campaign would suggest that the more able engineers would be involved. The fact that the leading unionization campaigners were older is also not entirely surprising, because the more experienced group would probably be the ones who received the highest respect from their colleagues and would therefore be more likely to act as leaders of their peer group.

Union officials were usually not prepared to accept the validity of the argument about skill obsolescence. They typically would argue instead, "They are not obsolescent. Management doesn't give older engineers sufficient opportunity to maintain their skills."[23]

The importance of the lack of career progression received some support from union officials, although they pointed out that management frequently misled engineers about the potential scope for career advancement. Many union officials also agreed that the leading internal supporters of unionization were often the most skilled engineers.

The issues raised in engineers' election campaigns serve mainly to show that most engineers were similar to other employees in the reasons that attracted them to organize. The key issue is why the initial interest in unionization so rarely bore fruit for unions. This study suggests that the reasons for union failure fall into four categories: employer opposition, the attitudes and values of engineers, the lack of bargaining power of engineers, and union attitudes and organizing policies.

Employer Opposition

Those four categories are merely analytically distinct, of course; in practice they are closely intertwined. Nevertheless, the first two reasons appear to be the most important causes of the union defeats. This study suggests that although engineers' attitudes tend to make them wary of unions, they would probably have voted to unionize in many of the cases studied if employer opposition had not been present. In these campaigns, management often adopted a subtle approach, drawing heavily upon the engineers' own ambivalence about unions, contrary to the more normal, fairly direct antiunion propaganda that employers generally rely on.

All the union officials interviewed believed that strong employer opposition was the major cause of union defeats. One union official who had worked as an organizer for both a major public sector union and one that was primarily in the private sector, provided the following comparison:

> The reasons for wanting to organize are identical [in the private and public sectors]; the problems are identical. The big difference is employer attitude . . . . In the public sector employers are basically neutral.[24]

It might be argued, of course, that union officials seek to blame employer opposition for defeats, both as a way of avoiding the possibility that engineers merely do not want unions and as a means of deflecting attention from the unions' shortcomings. Thus the nature of employer campaigns requires some attention.

In all the elections studied, employers waged active campaigns against unions. One aspect of the employers' strategy was usually an effort to remedy some of the grievances that had led to union activity. In one company, for example, the immediate response to an organizing campaign was the introduction of a dental plan, previously limited to unionized employees, and the raising of meal and mileage allowances.

While one aspect of the company response was thus to woo engineers with concessions, company propaganda also involved an undercurrent of threat, stressing the negative results that could occur if engineers voted for unions. The use of the argument that a barrier would be created between management and engineers was very common. Companies frequently asserted that engineers would no longer be able to complain as individuals, but would have to follow a formalized procedure. The cost of union dues was usually raised, along with the loss of "professional status" from joining a union. One issue that surfaced in every company campaign was the argument that voting for a union would inevitably lead to engineers being forced into taking strike action. Union officials in general corroborated management's view that engineers were hesitant to be seen as potential strikers.

In addition to employer opposition during election campaigns, a tough policy usually followed either an election victory or a union takeover of an independent. A classic instance was the tough management bargaining that led the NEPA to lose support and be decertified at General Dynamics' Convair Division. Management tactics were geared to the belief that it is an essential weakness of engineers' unions that strike action is unpopular among their members and would probably be ineffective in any case. The company negotiators at Convair believed that if the NEPA called a strike, engineers would provide insufficient support to make the strike viable. The union began bargaining in June 1975 and a year later had still not obtained an agreement. Although the membership voted in February 1976 to authorize strike action and the NEPA officers thought management's final offer was unacceptable, they refrained from actually calling a strike, preferring to continue to negotiate rather than risk an ineffective strike. This suggests that willingness to strike is a less important constraint than the perceived inability to damage the employer significantly.

Without an agreement with Convair after a year of bargaining, however, the NEPA found itself faced with a decertification petition in June 1976. During the decertification campaign, the employee group opposed to the NEPA attacked the union for not achieving results and depicted the union's final position as a sellout. The basis for the latter charge was that the union's initial demand for a one-year agreement with a "substantial," though unspecified, wage increase had been pared down to a final offer to accept a three-year agreement providing increases of 5.5, 4, and 4 percent. Thus the union was blamed for the results of managerial intransigence and lost the decertification election held in August 1976. In November, Convair awarded their engineers merit and promotional increases averaging 13 percent.[25]

Not only was the issue of bargaining power relevant to the decertification vote, but it surfaced in later NEPA activity. At Rohr, an employee group opposed to the NEPA distributed a handbill in 1977 saying:

> In order to negotiate a contract which provides more than we are currently receiving requires some power at the bargaining table. The *only* power a union has is the threat of a strike. . . . The union did not accomplish anything at Convair because they did not have any *bargaining power*.[26]

Thus Convair's award of large pay increases to engineers after decertification carried a simple but effective message to engineers in
other companies.

These tough management tactics are only a variant on the common
theme of increased employer hostility to unions in recent years. Employers in these cases generally felt that engineers were more susceptible to management arguments than were blue-collar workers,
and the employers were sophisticated enough to avoid unfair labor
practice charges being filed against them. At Convair, for example,
there were fifty-seven negotiating sessions with the NEPA, during
which company negotiators were careful to make some concessions.
In election campaigns, a number of companies used management
consultants who specialize in union election campaigns. This practice
seemed to ensure that threats and promises were made in a manner
that almost entirely precluded challenges before the NLRB.

Engineers' Attitudes and Values

Although it is clear that engineers as a group are not highly receptive to unionization, the focus in this study has been on those situations in which engineers had overcome their distaste for unions sufficiently to make a campaign viable. The attitude of engineers toward
unionism can be illustrated partially by a study of the role of those
professional societies to which engineers belong.

Until the 1970s, the professional societies maintained a generally
hostile attitude toward unions. The recession of 1970 and the resulting layoffs of engineers provoked membership demands for greater
involvement in the employment field. The involvement manifested
itself mainly in attempts to draw up employment guidelines that
companies would then be encouraged to follow. The interest in guidelines is an example of the degree to which many engineers felt that
fair treatment from their employers was not dependent on unionization and that employers could be persuaded to act reasonably on a unilateral basis.

The use of employment guidelines was not new, but to avoid the
proliferation of possibly conflicting guidelines, the National Society
of Professional Engineers (NSPE) took the initiative in bringing
together twenty different societies, which agreed in 1973 on a set of
guidelines.[27] The guidelines proposed standards to govern employers' recruitment and professional development activities and
urged that an engineer's salary should be "in keeping with his professional contribution."[28] They also recommended a notice period for
layoffs of one month, plus one week per year of service.

Although the guidelines were mild and stressed loyalty to the employer, they aroused considerable opposition from aerospace employers on whom the layoff notice provisions could have had a definite effect. Whether as a result of employer opposition or not, the guidelines do not seem to have had a great deal of impact. Hoffman's 1976 survey of 172 companies showed that only 25 percent claimed to have received the guidelines and only about half of these to have reviewed them.[29] The lack of impact reflected both the generalized manner in which the guidelines were written and the absence of any mechanism for enforcement. The reliance on guidelines is a good example of a certain degree of naiveté in engineers' views about employee relations.

It has sometimes been suggested that the professional societies might develop into something resembling unions, paralleling the evolution of the National Educational Association. In practice, however, this seems a remote possibility, and Hoffman has cogently pointed out the barriers to such a transformation.[30] One major factor is that society dues are too low to finance a wide range of union services. In addition, most societies have a disparate membership that includes employees, employers, and self-employed. Even among the employees, there is a lack of common interest among those employed in government, teaching, and private industry.[31] The NSPE brings together engineers from different specialties and has regarded the study of employment conditions as part of its role. It has consistently opposed trade unionism among engineers. In 1972 a task force, established in response to membership pressure, concluded that:

> The National Society of Professional Engineers believes, on the basis of extended experience and study over a long period, that collective bargaining is not a desirable, effective or appropriate mechanism to achieve the objectives of professional employment practices.[32]

The NSPE argues that unionism and professionalism do not mix. Its Code of Ethics depicts participation in strikes by engineers as unethical.[33]

A study of the attitudes of engineers, as expressed through their professional organizations, illustrates some of the factors that inhibit the growth of union membership. Companies have regularly argued that unionism would undermine the engineers' professional status. Unions in response argue that doctors and lawyers believe in self-organization and that engineers should follow suit. Both sides agree that engineers seem very conscious of any challenge to their professionalism. Engineers appear less confident of their status than doctors or lawyers, a reflection both of public perception of their position and of the fact that most engineers are employees. The 1970 census data showed that only 3 percent of engineers were self-employed, compared to 59 percent of lawyers and 60 percent of physicians.[34] The absence of a strong central professional body on the lines of the American Medical Association or the American Bar Association is probably also a factor. One result of the engineers' status consciousness is that independents like the SPEEA at Boeing, which also organize technicians, have been careful to place the latter in separate bargaining units. Others have not wished to go even that far and have turned away potential recruits. In one case in 1960, the inclusion of non-professionals in a unit led engineers at Western Electric to surrender their NLRB certification and file for an election as an independent and purely professional unit. The independent lost this election.[35]

Several empirical research projects have illustrated that engineers may fear that unionism will undermine their professional status. A study of federal government engineers by Manley and McNichols is a case in point.[36] There is, however, an apparent lack of consensus among researchers on this point. Kleingartner's research in the late 1960s showed that three-quarters of the two hundred engineers interviewed saw no conflict between unionism and professionalism, and those whom he defined as the "highest" professionals were least likely to see such a conflict.[37] In this context, he defined the degree of professionalism in relation to the level of education, the professional's self-image, and his occupational commitment. Kleingartner concluded that the argument about professionalism was really an employers' argument about unionism and not one put forward by engineers.[38]

It is not impossible to reconcile these apparently divergent results. Kleingartner's study was carried out in two unionized aerospace companies. It seems likely that experience with unionization serves to reduce professionals' fears of potential conflict, and also that engineers, like other employees, have an interest in not defining their own situations as involving conflicting roles. This does not mean that fear of such conflict is not an important force in reducing the attraction of unionism to unorganized engineers. Many union officials felt that engineers were unrealistic in their belief in their status. Although they are often in the same objective situation as other employees in relation to their employer, the engineers' perception is that there is a difference.

Some managers have argued that engineers are often not seriously interested in union membership but are seeking, rather, to attract the attention of management. Even some union officials expressed a certain cynicism about the degree to which engineers really wished to accept the obligations of union membership. The evidence on this point is mixed. On the one hand, early concessions by employers often seemed to erode the unions' initial support. On the other hand, the degree to which employers resorted to tough tactics suggests a greater amount of tenacity among engineers than a mere desire to attract attention would entail.

Bargaining Power

The concept of relative bargaining power is an important one in looking at engineers and unionization. Slichter, Healy, and Livernash defined bargaining power as "the ability to induce the other side to make concessions that it would not otherwise make. It means more than the mere fact of obtaining concessions."[39] In this context, most groups of engineers cannot immediately paralyze the employer's operations and in an industry like aerospace, with long production lead-times, strike power may not be very great. As the protracted negotiations at Convair illustrated, union officials are conscious of this lack of bargaining power. Thus, even if an engineering union wins an election, it may have difficulty achieving significant gains in the ensuing negotiations.

It might seem that bargaining power is a relevant factor only after an election has been held. Most of the campaigns studied, however, also drew attention to the difficulty engineers would face in applying sanctions against their employers. It is here, particularly, that the ambivalence of engineers toward strike action would often need to be protracted to prove effective.

Bargaining power is also influenced by the engineers' individualistic orientation. Kuhn has pointed out that engineers, like some other white-collar employees, have opportunities for individual bargaining that are not available to most blue-collar employees.[40] Even when engineers are organized, for example, both sides attest to their relatively low use of the formal grievance procedure, which reflects both the engineers' ability to use other channels to solve problems and their unwillingness to be seen to be in a conflict with management.

Union Attitudes and Organizing Policies

One important issue for international unions in campaigns to organize engineers was the balance they should strike between appealing to engineers' professional interests and to their desire to be represented by an effective union. It seems clear that unions that projected a strong blue-collar image felt it was necessary to stress their ability to adapt to the special interests of professionals. On the other hand, a blue-collar image could sometimes be identified with effectiveness, even by the engineers themselves.

This issue arose most directly in relation to the links between the engineers' groups and the international unions. Most major unions apparently accepted the view that engineers wanted some distance between themselves and the blue-collar members. The establishment of the NEPA within the UAW was a specific instance of this attempt to provide separate representation. In its campaigns, the NEPA stressed its independence from the UAW hierarchy of locals by pointing out that it reported directly to international headquarters. The Teamsters similarly offered the SCPEA considerable autonomy as an inducement to affiliate.

Companies certainly seemed to believe that it benefitted them during campaigns to identify the NEPA as closely as possible with the UAW and to stress the extent to which membership dues would not be retained locally. Unions made no effort to play down the relationship and, however, frequently cited access to professional advice in bargaining and legal and research services, as well as to the additional resources available from a union should a strike occur. On balance, it does not seem that the issue particularly hurt the NEPA, not least because the UAW could not be attacked as undemocratic or corrupt. The company campaigns against the Teamsters and the MEBA played more heavily on a perception of "corruption." That this tactic had an effect need not be left to management to attest. After its disaffiliation from the Teamsters, the SCPEA issued a notice that pointed it out:

> SCPEA has a tremendous rebuilding task. Our membership is now below 30% from a high of 70% prior to affiliation with the Teamsters. SCPEA knows there are a number of eligible candidates who are hesitant about rejoining because of their feelings toward Teamsters.[41]

The moral is probably the relatively unspectacular one that unions cannot escape from their general image and that engineers may be more concerned about the problem of corruption than are blue-collar workers.

Conclusion

Not for the first time in the history of engineering unionization is it tempting to write an epitaph for an unsuccessful period of organizing. It is sobering to reflect that in the period since July 1969—when

1,300 Sperry engineers voted for the IUE— only about 2,500 private sector engineers have unionized, and the largest group of these, at General Dynamics, voted within two years to decertify the union. By any criterion, the unions cannot regard their efforts in organizing this occupation to be successful.

In part, the lack of union success in organizing engineers is another instance of the broader problem of union organizing at present in this country. The continuing decline in the unionized percentage of the labor force and the recent increase in union decertification are two obvious examples of this problem. It is clear that there are certain common elements that affect unions in organizing all types of workers. Private sector employers in the United States have generally shown a particular aversion to white-collar unionism and there are signs among some employers of an increasingly hostile attitude toward all unionism. This employer response is one that would not be socially or often legally acceptable in many Western European countries. The hostility to unions flourishes because a significant section of American society is imbued with values drawn from individualistic, free-market capitalism which are no longer widely espoused in Europe. The greater acceptance of the role of unions at all levels in Europe than in the United States means that in Europe, even employees who tend to identify with management have only limited objections to unionization.

Employer propaganda against unions finds a much more receptive audience in this country than in Europe. In the United States, white-collar workers in general, and engineers in particular, are likely to accept management criticisms of unions. Studies of occupational choice suggest that those who select engineering as a profession may be more individualistic and less willing to join any organization than those in most other occupational groups.[42] This view received support from several union officials, including one who was himself an engineer.[43] Even in the United Kingdom, where white-collar unionism is far more extensive than in the United States, engineers have been a more difficult group to organize than other white-collar employees in the private sector.[44]

For engineers willing to unionize, there arises the practical problem that they often lack significant bargaining power. This is particularly important in the United States, where unions are judged by their members and potential members on strongly practical criteria and where they lack the underpinning of ideological support on which European unions can draw. In the United States, members tend to see their unions more as external service organizations than as the embodiment of the collective will of a group of employees. The corollary of this attitude is that a union that fails to deliver tangible benefits may be rejected. Thus, with limited bargaining power, engineers' unions often are unable to resist aggressive management tactics and are seen as failures by their members.

In this context it is tempting, but unfair, to blame unions for being the authors of their own misfortunes. The argument that unions have become inflexible and conservative and unable or unwilling to respond to problems with innovative solutions is common. The evidence from this study, however, shows that a number of unions, especially the UAW, have adopted a flexible approach to organizing engineers. In addition, it is difficult for anyone familiar with the British trade union movement to believe that British unions have been any more flexible or innovative than American unions, yet in the United Kingdom the organization of white-collar employees in the private sector has expanded significantly during the 1970s.[45] The problem for American unions is basically not internal; it arises because they are operating in a political and social environment that is not supportive of their role and because they are subject to a high degree of management opposition.

If this argument is valid, the extent to which unions can improve their position is limited and gains in organizing engineers are unlikely. Naturally, major economic or political changes could alter this picture, but the higher levels of inflation of the 1970s have not resulted in significant increases in union membership. In the political sphere, the failure to enact the innocuous Labor Reform Bill in 1978 offers little hope of developments in the legislative arena that will aid union organizing.

This conclusion may seem unduly fatalistic. The key questions from several of the campaigns studied are why engineers, a majority of whom had signed authorization cards, voted against the union and why engineers who voted union later voted for decertification. In both cases, the simple answer is that management arguments often swayed sufficient engineers to vote against unions in the first place and that lack of bargaining success later provoked decertification. In the short term, it is difficult to foresee circumstances in which engineers suddenly develop greater bargaining power or become less receptive to management persuasion. In the long term these two issues are linked. Bargaining power is not a totally objective phenomenon; it depends in part on employee attitudes. Engineers have so far not generally been willing to face the protracted battles that might be required to prove their bargaining power. Only when American unions can persuade engineers to do so will the potential for engineering unionization be translated into reality.

NOTES

1. William C. Rothstein, "The American Association of Engineers," *Industrial and Labor Relations Review*, Vol. 22, No. 1 (October 1968), pp. 48-72.

2. "The AWSE Story," *AWSE Reporter*, Vol. 7, No. 9 (September 1948), pp. 5-6.

3. Herbert R. Northrup, *Unionization of Professional Engineers and Chemists* (New York: Industrial Relations Counselors, Inc., 1946), pp. 15-20.

4. Donald W. Jarrell, *A History of Collective Bargaining at the Camden-Area Plants of the Radio Corporation of America with Special Attention to Bargaining Power* (Ph.D. thesis, University of Pennsylvania, 1967), p. 87.

5. *Ibid.*, p. 90.

6. George Strauss, "Professional or Employee-Oriented: Dilemma for Engineering Unions," *Industrial and Labor Relations Review*, Vol. 17, No. 4 (July 1964), p. 521.

7. Bureau of National Affairs, *Daily Labor Report*, No. 244 (December 18, 1972), p. A-2.

8. Bureau of National Affairs, *Bulletin to Management*, No. 1587 (August 7, 1980), pp. 4-6.

9. Interview with union official, Los Angeles, July 24, 1978.

10. Interview with company official, Los Angeles, July 24, 1978.

11. Southern California Professional Engineering Association, *SCPEA: An Independent Union* (Los Angeles: SCPEA, January 1979).

12. Bureau of National Affairs, *White Collar Report*, No. 773 (January 7, 1972), p. A-6.

13. Interview with company official, North Wales, Pa., April 19, 1979.

14. Bureau of National Affairs, *White Collar Report,* No. 611 (December 21, 1968), p. A-9.

15. Bureau of National Affairs, *White Collar Report*, No. 1149 (May 11, 1979), p. A-2.

16. "Collective Bargaining Agreement Between the Boeing Company and the Seattle Professional Engineering Employees Association (Engineering Bargaining Unit), Article 8," (February 1, 1978).

17. Interview with union official, Washington, D.C., April 25, 1979. Interview with company official, St. Louis, Mo., June 22, 1978.

18. Interview with company official, San Diego, July 25, 1978.

19. Interview with union official, Washington, D.C., April 25, 1979.

20. National Engineers and Professionals Association—San Diego, California. Chapter No. 3001, Handbill (January 20, 1977). (Emphasis in original.)

21. Interview with company official, St. Louis, Mo., June 22, 1978.

22. Henry S. Farber and Daniel H. Saks, "Why Workers Want Unions: The Role of Relative Wages and Job Characteristics," *Journal of Political Economy*, Vol. 88, No. 2 (April 1980), pp. 364-65, supports this finding.

23. Interview with union official, Washington, D.C., March 15, 1979.

24. Interview with union official, Washington, D.C., April 25, 1979.

25. This account of events at Convair is based on interviews with a company official, St. Louis, Mo., June 22, 1978, and a union official, Washington, D.C., March 13, 1979.

26. Al Alter and 45 others, "Look at the Big Picture,"—Handbill (February 3, 1977). (Emphasis in original.)

27. Twenty Engineering Associations, *Guidelines to Professional Employment for Engineers and Scientists* (Washington, D.C., 1973).

28. *Ibid.*, p. 9.

29. Eileen B. Hoffman, *Unionization of Professional Societies* (New York: The Conference Board Inc., 1976), p. 33.

30. *Ibid.*, p. 48.

31. Interview with a society official, Washington, D.C., March 13, 1979.

32. National Society of Professional Engineers, *Collective Bargaining v. Collective Action*, Report of Task Force on Collective Bargaining (Washington, D.C.: NSPE, 1973).

33. *Ibid.*, p. 34.

34. Data cited in Hoffman, *Unionization of Professional Societies*, p. 2.

35. Strauss, "Professional or Employee-Oriented: Dilemma for Engineering Unions," p. 526.

36. T. Roger Manly and Charles W. McNichols, "Attitudes of Federal Scientists and Engineers Towards Unions," *Monthly Labor Report*, Vol. 98, No. 4 (April 1975), pp. 57-60.

37. Archie Kleingartner, "Professionalism and Engineering Unionism," *Industrial Relations*, Vol. 8, No. 3 (May 1969), p. 229.

38. *Ibid.*, p. 235.

39   Sumner H. Slichter, James J. Healy, and E. Robert Livernash, *The Impact of Collective Bargaining on Management* (Washington, D.C.: The Brookings Institution, 1960), p. 918.

40. James W. Kuhn, "Success and Failure in Organizing Professional Engineers," in Industrial Relations Research Association, *Proceedings of the 16th Annual Meeting* (Boston: IRRA, December 1963), pp. 194-208.

41. Southern California Professional Engineering Association, *SCPEA: An Independent Union*.

42. Ann Roe, "Early Determination of Vocational Choice," *Journal of Counseling Psychology*, Vol. 34 (1963), p. 357.

43. Interview with union official, Washington, D.C., March 15, 1979.

44. The author here draws on his experience in 1975-77 as an organizer for the major union of professional engineers in the United Kingdom, the TUC-affiliated Engineers' and Managers' Association (EMA). See also, Council of Engineering Institutions, *Professional Engineers and Trade Unions* (London: CEI, 1975). For the most thorough recent estimate of white-collar union density in the U.K., see Robert Price and George Sayers Bain, "Union Growth Revisited: 1948-1974 in Perspective," *British Journal of Industrial Relations*, Vol. 114, No. 3 (November 1976), p. 347. These authors estimated that 39.4 percent of white-collar workers belonged to unions in the U.K. in 1974.

45. Price and Bain, "Union Growth Revisited," pp. 339-55; Trades Union Congress, *Annual Report 1977* (London: TUC, 1978), pp. 610-22.

Union Decertification under the NLRA

Janice R. Bellace†

The labor law of the United States is premised on the belief that employees have a right to bargain collectively through representatives of their own choosing[1] and that an employer must recognize this right when a majority of his employees designates a union as its bargaining agent.[2] That employees should also have the right to refrain from bargaining collectively if they so desire can be viewed as a logical corollary of this premise. In 1947, Congress, accepting this line of reasoning, amended the Wagner Act[3] to provide a means whereby employees may decertify their union as bargaining agent.[4]

In the years immediately following the enactment of the Taft-Hartley Act,[5] rival unionism between affiliates of the American Federation of Labor (AFL) and the Congress of Industrial Organizations (CIO) led frequently to the raiding of each other's locals, thus focusing attention on the decertification procedures of the National Labor Relations Act.[6] Since the merger of the AFL with the CIO in 1955, the incidence of raiding has declined greatly[7] and, with it, the interest in decertification. The recent sharp increase in the number of decertification petitions filed with the National Labor Relations Board (NLRB)[8] has generated renewed interest in the subject of union decertification. In order to discuss the balance between employees' free choice and industrial stability that the rules and regulations governing decertification have achieved, this article first outlines the development of these rules through decisions of the NLRB and the courts.

Types of Decertification

The label "decertification" is correctly used to describe two very different situations. In the first, an incumbent union loses its status as exclusive bargaining agent and is not replaced by another union. In the second, the employees' allegiance is transferred from one union to another, either immediately or within the year. Unfortunately, the

† Janice R. Bellace is Assistant Professor of Legal Studies and Senior Faculty Research Associate—Industrial Research Unit, The Wharton School, University of Pennsylvania. The research for this article was supported in part by unrestricted grants to the Industrial Research Unit from the Pew Memorial Trust.

literature on the subject of decertification frequently fails to acknowledge this crucial distinction. This failure may be attributed in part to the record-keeping method of the NLRB, which does not indicate whether a rival union was involved in a decertification effort, thereby making research on this point difficult.

For the most part, the process of decertification falls within the first category described above. Decertification petitions are usually filed by employees pursuant to section 9(c)(1)(A)(ii)[9] of the act and, if successful, usually lead to a "no union" situation. In some instances where there is an incumbent union, an employer will file a petition for an election under section 9(c)(1)(B)[10] of the act on the grounds that it has a good faith doubt about the union's continuing majority status. Although uncommon, it is possible for an initial certification election to result in the loss of bargaining rights for an incumbent union that had previously been voluntarily recognized by the employer.

Rival unionism undoubtedly does account for some proportion of decertification activity, although it is extremely difficult to glean any information on this from the statistics. A rival union acting on behalf of the unit employees may directly file a decertification petition. With the requisite showing of interest, a rival union can secure a position on the ballot. In some instances, rival unions more or less explicitly instigate an employee decertification petition but do not make any attempt to appear on the ballot, preferring to wait out the twelve-month period prescribed by section 9(c)(3)[11] before seeking a representation election. This strategy is usually followed by AFL-CIO unions not wishing to violate openly the federation's no-raiding pact.[12] In order to clarify which union it should recognize for the purposes of collective bargaining, an employer may also file an election petition if two or more unions are competing to represent its employees.

Finally, it is possible for a union to lose its bargaining rights without any party approaching the National Labor Relations Board to file a petition or unfair labor practice charges. This occurs when an incumbent union voluntarily relinquishes its role as bargaining agent upon realizing that it no longer commands majority support within the unit. Without pertinent data, it is not possible to speculate on the frequency of such occurrences, but labor practitioners mention that it is not unknown.[13]

The NLRB's Decertification Caseload

In examining the NLRB's statistics on decertification cases since the passage of the Taft-Hartley Act in 1947,[14] the most striking figure that emerges is the nearly threefold increase in the number of employee decertification petitions since 1967. In addition, the period since 1975 has marked a sharp decline in the fortunes of unions. Unions now win less than 30 percent of decertification elections; a record low was reached in 1977 when unions won only 22.8 percent of decertification elections.

The number of "RD" cases, the Board's designation for employee decertification petitions, hovered in the 330-490 range during the decade 1948-1958. During the next decade, there was a slow, slight movement upward. Since 1967, however, the decertification caseload has nearly tripled, from 624 petitions in 1967 to 1,793 petitions in 1979. The number of decertification elections conducted has followed a similar pattern; likewise, the number of eligible voters has almost tripled since 1967.

The average size of units in which decertification elections are held, however, has been declining gradually since 1962. The decline may explain to some extent why the union success rate has also declined, since it is generally believed that unions are more likely to win a decertification election in larger bargaining units.[15] In 1979, for instance, unions won elections in units averaging ninety employees and lost in units averaging thirty-eight employees.[16] Although the number of decertification elections had been increasing, the success rate of unions showed no consistent fall prior to 1975. In that year, unions won under 30 percent of decertification elections, and this lower success rate (in the mid-20 percent range) now seems to be the pattern.

The data also reveal that fewer decertification cases are now being withdrawn or dismissed. Prior to 1953, only about 30 percent of decertification cases reached an election. This figure hovered in the 35 to 40 percent range until 1974. Here, too, a major change has occurred since 1975. Significantly fewer cases are being withdrawn or dismissed, with a record high of 47.9 percent of cases reaching an election in 1977.

The Statutory Framework

When the Wagner Act[17] was enacted in 1935, section 9 set out the procedure enabling employees in an appropriate bargaining unit to select a union as their exclusive bargaining representative.[18] The Wagner Act, however, contained no provision whereby employees dissatisfied with their union could rescind their choice. Nor did the act provide a means whereby an employer could initiate the NLRA's election process. In 1947, as part of the revision of national labor poli-

cy embodied in the Taft-Hartley Act,[19] section 9(c)(1)(A) was inserted
to provide that an election petition could be filed:

> by an employee or group of employees or any individual or labor organ-
> ization acting in their behalf alleging that a substantial number of em-
> ployees . . . (ii) assert that the individual or labor organization, which
> has been certified or is being currently recognized by their employer as
> the bargaining representative, is no longer a representative as defined
> in subsection [9](a).[20]

Section 9(c)(1)(B) of the Taft-Hartley Act gives an employer the right
to file a representation election petition "alleging that one or more
individuals or labor organizations have presented to him a claim to
be recognized as the representative defined in subsection [9](a)."[21]

In debating the amendments to section 9 of the Wagner Act,[22] Congress focused its attention in large measure on the desirability of
curbing industrial conflict arising from the rampant rival unionism
of the era. In the Senate, proponents of the amendment bill repeatedly referred to the plight of the employer who, having recognized and
bargained with a union, found itself helpless when a union from the
rival federation picketed its plant and neither union would file for an
election.[23] In response to this predicament, opponents of the bill unsuccessfully supported an amendment that would have given employers the right to request certification but would have left decertification solely within the discretion of the NLRB.[24]

When the proposed statutory decertification process was addressed, its proponents emphasized that it was necessary to ensure
employee freedom of choice, an argument to which labor's backers
had difficulty responding directly. Not until near the end of the Senate debate did one senator point out what impact section 9(c) could
have in conjunction with section 9 as it then read. Senator Pepper
presented the hypothetical situation of a bargaining unit in which no
election had occurred during the previous year and where workers
who were engaged in an economic strike had been replaced.[25] He
noted that, since only the replacements would vote, it was nearly certain that the union would be decertified.[26] He concluded that, if an
employer wanted to break a union, it had the power to do so. Curious-
ly, most other opponents of the bill predicted rather unlikely effects
for section 9(c). For example, it was feared that employers would repeatedly file for a decertification election at the expiration of every
collective agreement or that unions would be tempted to make unreasonable bargaining demands as a means of retaining their members' allegiance in the face of an employer decertification attempt.[27]

Raising a Valid Question of Representation

In order to secure a decertification election, a petitioner must satisfy the Board that a number of requirements have been met, some of which are dictated by the act and others of which have resulted from the Board's policy and procedures. Essentially, the petitioner must demonstrate that a "question of representation"[28] exists at the time the election is directed. To make such a determination, the regional director checks that:

1. the petitioner can establish the requisite showing of interest;
2. the petition emanates from an appropriate source;
3. the petition relates to a unit that is appropriate for collective bargaining;
4. there is currently a union that claims bargaining rights;
5. the petition is "timely"; and
6. there are no pending unfair labor practice charges which serve to "block" the petition.

If the petition meets these conditions, the regional director will direct an election; otherwise, the petition will be dismissed. The regional director's decision can be appealed to the five-member Board in Washington.[29] This paper examines the requirements that must be satisfied to secure a decertification election and then considers the likelihood of an election's being held, given the Board's policy on presumption of majority.[30]

The Showing of Interest

In decertification cases, the party filing for an election must show within forty-eight hours of filing the petition that 30 percent of the employees in the appropriate bargaining unit desire an election. The Board has consistently held that determining the adequacy of the showing of interest is an administrative matter within the Board's discretion that is not subject to subsequent challenge. The Board supports its position by noting that any election held will effectively protect the interests of the parties.[31]

Employee decertification petitions are checked to determine if 30 percent of the unit employees have signed the petition. Representation election petitions filed by rival unions may be validated in the same way, or the rival union may present signed authorization cards.

Before 1966, employer petitions were allowed solely on the grounds that the employer had shown that it was faced with a claim for recognition. When an employer petitioned for a decertification election, the employer merely had to show that the union was currently recognized, either voluntarily or as a result of certification, for the unit concerned, that the union had expressed its intention of remaining the bargaining agent, and that the employer had rejected or otherwise questioned the union's continued majority status. Believing that the legislative history of the Taft-Hartley Act did not support any qualification of the employer's right under section 9(c)(1)(B) to question the majority status of an incumbent union, the Board did not question the good faith of the employer's doubt of the union's majority status.

In 1966, in *United States Gypsum Co.*,[32] the Board modified its policy on employer petitions after concluding that not only did the statute not prohibit the Board from exercising its discretion to dismiss employer petitions where there was no good faith doubt, but that its exercise of such discretion actually accorded with the legislative intent. In *United States Gypsum*, the Board announced that it would require employers not only to show that the union claimed recognition and that this had been questioned, but also to "demonstrate by objective considerations that it has some reasonable grounds for believing that the union has lost its majority status."[33] Supporting this change in policy, the Board stated that the requirement of objective evidence would enhance bargaining stability. Unless there was some basis in reality for the employer's doubt of its majority status, a union would no longer have to fight an election campaign at a time when it should be preparing for negotiations on a new collective agreement.[34]

The Appropriate Source

Under section 9(c)(1)(A)(ii) of the act, decertification petitions may be filed by employees or by agents acting on behalf of the employees. Thus, the Board has found petitions filed by lawyers and labor relations consultants acceptable.[35] A union's objection to the filing of a petition by a lawyer or consultant who has previously done work for the employer will be dismissed unless it is determined that the petitioner has, in reality, been acting as an agent for the employer in the decertification campaign.[36]

The Board has taken the view that an employer cannot instigate or encourage decertification, since such activity would be incompatible with the performance of his continuing statutory obligation to recognize and bargain with the union as the representative of his employees. It should be noted that this restraint on the employer's freedom of speech ceases to operate once it is decided that there exists a valid question of representation regarding the unit.

Consonant with this view, the Board will not entertain any decertification petition filed by managerial or supervisory personnel, since it does not regard such a petition as raising a valid question of representation.[37] As with cases dealing with inclusion or exclusion of alleged supervisors in the bargaining unit, this policy has required the Board to make a number of judgments about the nature of a supervisor's work. The Board's starting point is section 2(11) of the act, which states:

> The term "supervisor" means any individual having authority, in the interest of the employer, to hire, transfer, suspend, lay off, recall, promote, discharge, assign, reward, or discipline other employees, or responsible to direct them, or to adjust their grievances, or effectively to recommend such action, if in connection with the foregoing the exercise of such authority is not of a merely routine or clerical nature, but requires the use of independent judgment.[38]

The extent of similarity between the alleged supervisor's duties and the work of other unit members is a major factor in the determination.[39] In view of the very great diversity of work situations, coupled with the changing duties a person may assume in a small, informal company, it is not surprising that the members of the Board often disagree on a person's status.[40]

Even if the person who filed the petition is found not to be a supervisor, the petition may still be dismissed if the Board belives it has been tainted by the employees' perception that the person was a supervisor or that the person was acting at the behest of the employer. For instance, in *Columbia Building Materials, Inc.*,[41] the son of a plant supervisor prepared and circulated the decertification petition. The son's work tasks, while varied, were clearly superior to those of the other unit employees in the job hierarchy. In addition, the son was the only unit employee not on the timeclock. The Board found that the circulation of the petition was attributable to the employer, even assuming that the son was not a supervisor, since a number of employees reasonably believed that the son was in charge when his father was absent from the plant premises.[42]

Similarly, in *Maywood Plant of Grede Plastics*,[43] the person who circulated the decertification petition was one of only two bilingual employees in a unit where many employees, but none of the supervisors, spoke Spanish. Her bilingualism and the fact that she had substantially more seniority than any other employee combined to place her in a powerful intermediary position between management and the other unit employees. Although she was clearly at a level below the other members of the supervisory staff, the Board found that she was a supervisor within the meaning of the act since she assigned and checked work and effectively had the power to hire and to impose minor discipline. In finding her decertification petition tainted, the Board relied not only on her supervisory status but also on her conduct. As the administrative law judge stated:

> She was the dominant figure, leading employees to believe that she was reflecting management's desires in soliciting their signatures, promising better things if the Union were ousted, and threatening loss of jobs if it were not. Even if higher supervision and management had been totally unaware of Martinez' activities and representations, the effect on employees would have been the same as if it had encouraged and approved her conduct.[44]

Supervisory status becomes an issue in a decertification case when it is asserted that the alleged supervisor was instrumental in preparing the decertification petition and in soliciting support for the decertification. If the alleged supervisor takes a direct role in the preparation of the petition itself, the petition will usually be dismissed on the grounds that it emanated from an improper source. If the incumbent union suspects supervisory participation in the decertification campaign, it may file a charge under section 8(a)(1).[45] If the regional director issues a complaint, the decertification petition will nearly always be dismissed under the Board's blocking charge policy.

Prior to 1958, Board policy dictated that, before finding that a decertification petition raised a valid question of representation, the regional director should consider whether the petition had been instigated by the employer. In *Georgia Kraft Co.*,[46] the Board altered this policy by stating that allegations of supervisory participation in the decertification effort should not, in the future, be entertained in the representation proceedings and should be investigated only administratively by the Board.[47] The Board has clearly distinguished the principle of excluding the issue of supervisory participation from hearings on the petition from its continuing refusal to accept decertification petitions filed by supervisors.[48]

Not all interference by a supervisor during a decertification campaign is unlawful. The Board has long distinguished between employer instigation of a decertification petition and assistance rendered after the employees have decided to act. Since employees dissatisfied with their union but uninformed of their statutory options will often enter into a discussion with their supervisor regarding what can be done about the union, the line between employer instigation and assistance can be extremely fine. In general, the Board seeks to determine who initiated the conversation and whether the employee's questions to the supervisor indicated that decertification was already in the employee's mind.[49] Although a supervisor may outline the decertification procedure in response to an employee's question, the more active a role the supervisor takes in assisting the employee-generated decertification, the more likely it is that the employer will be found to have violated section 8(a)(1).

If a supervisor merely adds "individual and isolated encouragement to an independently originated decertification drive,"[50] his conduct may violate section 8(a)(1) but not taint the decertification petition. In *GAF Corp.*,[51] a supervisor suggested to an employee dissatisfied with the union that an in-plant committee be formed to oust the union, a suggestion that was never acted upon. One month later, the same employee initiated a conversation critical of the union with the same supervisor. At this time, the supervisor suggested that the employee telephone the regional office of the NLRB to obtain information concerning the filing of a decertification petition. The Board found the in-plant committee suggestion unlawful but held that it was not sufficiently closely connected with the petition conversation so as to render the later conversation violative of section 8(a)(1).[52] Hence, the employer was found not to have instigated or unlawfully assisted the decertification campaign.

When it is clear that a supervisor has discussed decertification with unit employees, thus violating section 8(a)(1), and an employee decertification petition is later filed, the question becomes whether the supervisor's comments amount to employer inducement of the decertification petition. Since first-line supervisors are in constant, close, and informal contact with unit employees, their seemingly insignificant comments may be interpreted as having great import and influence. Not surprisingly, as *National Cash Register Co.*[53] illustrates, the Board and the courts do not always agree on whether a supervisor's comments have had a coercive impact.

In *National Cash Register*, the union won elections in the winter of 1970 in Duluth, Detroit, and New York City to represent a unit of technical services representatives. In May 1970, the union signed a one-year contract, backdated to January 1. In July, the union filed a charge under section 8(a)(1) alleging that a supervisor in New York City had outlined the procedure for decertification and had stated that certain pay increases would be retroactive if decertification occurred. The supervisor's comments were made to some unit employees during routine performance appraisal interviews. It was alleged that in all three cities, supervisors were noting during performance appraisal interviews that the employees would normally have been entitled to wage increases under the company's merit plan but that this was not permitted under the union contract. With the contract due to expire at the end of 1970, decertification petitions were timely filed in late October.[54]

In November, the regional director decided against issuing a complaint on the union's charge. The union appealed, and the regional director's decision was reversed. The decertification petitions were then dismissed under the Board's blocking charge rule,[55] and the case proceeded to a hearing on the unfair labor practice complaint. In June 1972, the administrative law judge recommended finding that the General Counsel had failed to prove by a preponderance of the evidence that the employer had induced the filing of the employee decertification petitions in all three cities. In February 1973, the Board unanimously rejected this recommendation.

Emphasizing that the supervisors' conversations with employees during performance appraisals constituted a pattern of direct dealing with employees over terms and conditions of employment in derogation of the union's status as bargaining agent, the Board concluded that the company's "conduct, although widely scattered geographically . . . was pursuant to a carefully orchestrated plan to sow dissatisfaction among the employees with union representation for the purpose of inciting the filing of decertification petitions."[56] The Board pointed out that the General Counsel had conceded that there was no direct evidence of company involvement in the filing of the decertification petitions but had argued that it could be reasonably inferred that there was such involvement. Agreeing that such an inference could be reasonably drawn, the Board noted that the filing of the petition "resulted in large measure if not entirely," from the company's unlawful conduct.[57]

On appeal, the Eighth Circuit agreed that the supervisors' comments regarding the employees' entitlements under the merit plan violated section 8(a)(1), but the court did so "reluctantly" since there was much disputed testimony and the Board's finding of coercive impact was "highly speculative."[58] The Eighth Circuit, however, refused to accept the Board's finding that the decertification petition was the intended effect and direct product of the employer's misconduct, and held that the Board's inferences were impermissible.[59] Impressed by the fact that the employee filing the petition in New York City had not been present during any conversation in which a supervisor made unlawful comments, the court took the administrative law judge's position that there was no substantial evidence linking the employer to the filing of the petition.[60]

The Appropriate Unit

The question of what constitutes an appropriate bargaining unit arises in all representation election cases. After the passage of the Taft-Hartley Act, the Board decided to apply the same general principles it had developed in certification cases to decertification cases. Ordinarily, the unit appropriate for decertification is "the unit previously certified or the one recognized in the existing contract unit."[61] The main unit issues that the Board has had to resolve relate to the attempts of employees to secure decertification elections in distinct sections of multiplant or multiemployer bargaining structures.

In the years immediately following the passage of the Taft-Hartley Act, the Board permitted severance by specific subgroups within certified units. Craft and professional employees were the main beneficiaries of this policy.[62] In 1955, however, the Board reversed its stance and held that decertification elections should no longer be used to achieve severance.[63]

In general, the Board has refused to direct decertification elections for subgroups where there has been a demonstrable history of multiunit or multiemployer bargaining.[64] The mere fact that the unit in question had previously been certified separately does not per se justify separate decertification where those employees have participated in a joint negotiating structure. The Board's view on this point with regard to multiemployer bargaining is open to serious criticism. Where a number of employers bargain as a group with one union and the employees of one employer no longer want that union as their bargaining agent, the employees' objective of ridding themselves of the union could be achieved easily if their employer would take appropriate action to withdraw from the multiemployer bargaining group. The Board's view, however, allows the employer to lock the employees into a situation not to their liking. Hence, it would seem that this view denies the employees the right to select representatives of their own choosing as guaranteed by the act.

Each case is examined on its own merits. For instance, the technicality that the employers sign separate collective agreements will not outweigh a factual analysis that points to multiemployer bargaining.[65] In cases involving multiemployer bargaining, the Board has viewed a significant history of multiemployer bargaining as an important factor arguing for a finding that a multiemployer unit exists. But it is not the controlling factor. Rather, the Board seeks to determine "whether the parties have demonstrated an unequivocal intention to be bound by group action."[66] Not unexpectedly, unit determinations under this test are less predictable than under a history-of-bargaining test.

Similar problems arise when decertification for a subgroup of employees subject to a multiplant agreement is sought. The Board's position on subunit decertification has not been entirely consistent. For instance, in 1961, the Board held that, despite a history of wider bargaining, elections would be appropriate in separately certified subunits.[67] Where joint bargaining had only existed for a short while and there was evidence that the employees had accepted its introduction only under pressure from the union, decertification petitions would be accepted by the Board.[68] After *Duke Power Co.*,[69] some observers believed that the Board was once again taking a more favorable view toward subunit decertification. In *Duke Power*, the short length of time in which multiplant bargaining had been applied to the subunits was considered by the Board, which directed decertification elections in three units that had all been certified less than five years and had been added to a system-wide bargaining unit.[70] Yet, in *Westinghouse Electric Corp.*,[71] the Board found that a unit which had been certified only fourteen months had been effectively merged into a nationwide bargaining agreement that permitted local agreements to supplement the national master agreement. In *Westinghouse*, the Board declared that the local union had failed to retain "a sufficiently separate, independent bargaining position from the other locals . . . in matters of collective bargaining."[72]

The current status of the Board's policy is difficult to evaluate. It can be said with some certainty that the Board will refuse to accept decertification petitions from units that are included in a multiplant bargaining arrangement that has a long and stable history. But where the history of multiplant bargaining is shorter and where supplemental local agreements are of considerable importance, the Board's determination cannot be predicted with any certainty.

Timeliness

A decertification petition does not raise a question of representation unless it is timely, both in relation to the one-year election bar under the act and to the contract bar created by the Board. Under section 9(c)(3) of the act, no election can be held in a unit within twelve months of a valid representation election. The twelve-month period runs from the date the election was held. If a union wins a representation election, however, the twelve-month period runs from the date of the certification, absent unusual circumstances. The Board established this one-year certification bar on the basis that the union is entitled to a full twelve months as bargaining agent and that its status as bargaining agent is not definite until certification. In a case where the employer voluntarily recognized a union and concluded a one-year contract with it prior to a certification election, the Board held that the certification identifies the bargaining agent "with certainty and finality" for one year.[73] In *Brooks v. NLRB*,[74] the United States Supreme Court accepted the Board's view that the one-year period should run from the date of certification rather than from the date of election as within the allowable area of the Board's discretion in carrying out the purposes of the act.[75] A much more frequently encountered barrier to the filing of a decertification petition is an existing collective bargaining agreement, which may bar the petition under long-standing Board policy.

Contract Bar

In attempting to effectuate the sometimes conflicting statutory objectives of fostering stability in labor relations while according employees freedom to select representatives of their own choosing, the Board has resorted to a policy whereby the employees' ability to vote in a Board election is postponed for a certain period of time because a valid collective agreement is in effect. This doctrine, called contract bar, is premised on the belief that

> [c]ontracts established the foundation upon which stable labor relations usually are built. As they tend to eliminate strife which leads to interruptions of commerce, they are conducive to industrial peace and stability. Therefore, when such a contract has been executed by an employer and a labor organization . . . the postponement of the right to select a representative is warranted for a reasonable period of time.[76]

The Board's contract bar doctrine dates from 1939, when it was applied to postpone a representation election.[77] After the passage of the Taft-Hartley Act, the doctrine was extended to decertification cases.[78] The precise application of the doctrine has been modified several times, with a thorough reconsideration of the rules in a series of cases in 1958.[79] The establishment of the contract bar doctrine and various rules implementing it has usually been deemed to be within the discretion of the Board as an exercise of its administrative expertise.[80]

The contract bar rules are complex and embrace several issues. The major issues include (1) the duration of the contract, (2) the adequacy of the agreement, (3) changed circumstances during the life of the contract, (4) the status of the contracting union, and (5) the existence of unlawful contract provisions.

Duration of the Contract

The contract bar doctrine restrains the employees' right to select
their representatives at certain times, a restraint that is not mentioned in the statute. Because of this, the Board has several times
considered whether the length of the contract bar was proving an unwarranted restraint of the employees' section 7 rights. In *Pacific
Coast Association of Pulp & Paper Manufacturers*,[81] the Board recognized that not only must employees be afforded an opportunity to
select their representatives at reasonable intervals, but such intervals should occur at easily predictable times.[82] As a result, the Board
announced in *Pacific Coast* that a contract would serve as a bar to the
filing of a petition for the life of the contract or two years,[83] whichever
came first. The Board further reasoned that, since the main justification for the contract bar doctrine was the promotion of industrial
peace, no contract should operate as a bar unless it represented a
commitment to stability in industrial relations. Hence, contracts
having no fixed duration, such as contracts lacking termination or
duration provisions or contracts terminable at will, do not serve as a
bar to the filing of a petition.[84]

The Board construes its rules strictly, and, at times, with unnecessary inflexibility. For instance, in *Cind-R-Lite Co.*,[85] a three-year
contract expired on April 1, 1978. On April 4, the employer submitted
a final proposal to the union that included no termination date but
did call for three annual wage increases to take effect on April 1,
1978, 1979, and 1980. The union accepted the offer on April 5. The
following day, a decertification petition was filed. The regional director dismissed the petition as untimely on the basis of the contract bar
doctrine. The Board, however, adhered strictly to its rule that the
contract must contain an expiration date that is apparent from the
face of the contract.[86] Since, on its face, the contract's final annual
wage increase could be construed to continue indefinitely, the Board
held that the contract contained no express expiration date and,
therefore, it was no bar to a decertification election.[87]

The precision of these rules is of great help to those employees seeking to file a decertification petition, since the NLRB will consider a
petition timely only if it is filed not more than ninety nor less than
sixty days before the expiration of the contract for a contract not exceeding three years in length, or at any time after three years for a
longer contract.[88] The filing period has been longer in the past[89] and
it can be argued that it is too short at present, but the length of the
filing period is an issue only when its reasonableness is questioned.

Thirty days is a reasonable filing period if employees have adequate advance notice of the period so that they can mount a campaign and collect sufficient signatures on a decertification petition in due time. Since many employees are likely to have only a thirty-day period once every three years in which to file for decertification, it is of utmost importance that the filing period should be easily calculated in advance, and the Board's present rules ensure that this can be done.

A more serious objection to the present rules concerning the filing period relates more to its placement than its duration. The Board has set sixty days prior to the expiration of a contract not exceeding three years in length as the termination of the filing period, since unions are required by section 8(d)(1)[90] of the act to serve notice in writing to the employer at least sixty days before the expiration of the contract of their intent to modify the contract.[91] If the union's status as bargaining agent is in doubt, this should be known before the employer sits down to bargain with that union. Under the Board's present rules, however, it is not unusual for a union to mail notice of its intent to modify the contract at about the same time a decertification petition is being filed.[92] The employer may well receive the union's letter with its request that a date for negotiations be set before he receives notice from the regional director that employees have filed for decertification. The employer may be aware of the decertification campaign and may be uncertain whether to begin bargaining or to delay responding to the union's request. Likewise, the union may have concentrated its energies on the imminent negotiations only to discover suddenly that bargaining will be delayed pending the outcome of the decertification effort. Clearly, it would foster stable labor relations if the possibility of such uncertainty were removed from the onset of negotiations. Such a goal could be achieved merely by moving back the filing period fifteen days, which would enable the regional office of the NLRB to process the petition prior to the commencement of the bargaining period.

Adequacy of the Agreement

In keeping with its view that postponing the employees' right to select their representative is warranted by the stability a collective agreement promotes, the Board held in *Appalachian Shale Products Co.*[93] that a contract would not serve as a bar to a decertification election unless it contained "substantial terms and conditions of employment deemed sufficient to stabilize the bargaining relationship."[94] The Board, therefore, seeks to determine whether the agreement being put forward as a contract barring decertification contains terms sufficiently important and definite so as to minimize the likelihood of industrial conflict during the life of the contract.

The contract must be in writing[95] and signed by the parties.[96] This does not, however, require that a formal document be signed for the contract to serve as a bar.[97] In *Valley Doctors Hospital, Inc.*,[98] the employer mailed a complete contract proposal to the union with a cover letter that clearly indicated that a contract would result if the union accepted the offer without modification. The employees voted to accept the contract on May 7, at which time the union telephoned the employer with this information. The following day, a decertification petition was filed. On May 14, the union mailed the employer a copy of the contract signed by the union officers and dated May 7. The Board held that the exchange of a written proposal and a written acceptance satisfied the contract bar rule of *Appalachian Shale*. A similar case, *Diversified Services, Inc.*,[99] highlighted the common practice of attorneys acting for the parties at the bargaining table. There, the union's attorney sent a telegram to the employer's attorney, stating that the union accepted the employer's last offer and requesting that the attorney forward a contract for signature. The employer's attorney then sent two unexecuted copies of a contract based on the parties' written agreements during bargaining and on the employer's position on unresolved issues. The contract was accompanied by a cover letter signed by the employer's attorney, requesting that the two copies be signed and returned. The union promptly did so. Shortly thereafter, a decertification petition was filed. The regional director found that the contract did not serve as a bar on the grounds that the attorney's signature on the cover letter did not constitute the employer's signature on the contract and that the employer had not given the attorney power to bind the employer without approval of the employer's executive board. The Board disagreed. Emphasizing that the attorney conducted all the negotiations for the employer and that throughout the negotiations he had represented to the union that he had the authority to bind the employer on matters arising at the bargaining table, the Board found that the attorney's signature on the cover letter and the union's signature on the contract were sufficient to satisfy the rule in *Appalachian Shale*.[100]

Once the contract's expiration date has passed, the parties are often committed to reaching an agreement as quickly as possible so that a strike may be averted or terminated. As a result, the employer's last offer may be communicated to the union's membership before it is fully set down in writing. Members dissatisfied with the union's performance at the bargaining table may, at this point, seek to file a decertification petition if it seems likely that the membership will accept the employer's offer. Whether or not a decertification petition will be accepted in such situations depends on whether the petition is filed before the agreement is set down in writing to some extent. *Liberty House*[101] illustrates the uncertainty of the application of *Appalachian Shale* in such circumstances.

In *Liberty House*, the employer operated two department stores in different shopping centers. The union represented salesclerks at both stores in one unit and office employees at both stores in another unit. In June 1975, the contracts expired. In November, a new contract covering the salesclerks was concluded. On December 4, the employer wrote to the union concerning the office employees' contract. Referring to a telephone conversation in the interim about a new wage scale, the employer stated that he would make other appropriate changes to bring the office employees' agreement into line with the salesclerks' agreement. On December 9, an early morning meeting was called at which time the employees present voted to accept the employer's offer. The union president signed the employer's letter and immediately after the meeting contacted the stores to inform them that the contract had been accepted. Within the hour, a decertification petition was filed. Following *Appalachian Shale*, the regional director found that the petition was not barred by the agreement since there existed neither a formal document executed by both parties nor an exchange of a signed written proposal and acceptance.

The Board, however, disagreed. The Board held that the employer's proposal, which included a wage scale and incorporated by reference to the salesclerks' contract other terms and conditions of employment, contained "substantial terms and conditions of employment."[102] By signing this proposal, the union formed a contract that would serve to bar the petition.

The Board's contract bar rules in this area are thus open to varying interpretation. For the sake of certainty, it would seem preferable to adhere closely to the rule that the contract, either in a formal document or set out in a proposal, must be in writing and that this written statement of the agreement must contain substantial terms and conditions of employment. If such a rule were consistently applied, unions would be on notice that the contract should be reduced to writing as soon as its terms are known. To be lenient in this regard places the Board in a position of allowing certain agreements to operate as a bar when important contractual terms can only be filled in on the basis of oral understandings; yet oral contracts do not serve as a bar. In addition, the tenor of such a policy does not comport with the Board's general rule in contract bar cases that extrinsic evidence should not be introduced in order to clarify the meaning of ambiguous contract terms.

In certain circumstances, the terms of the contract must be examined to determine whether the contract serves as a bar. For instance, to serve as a bar, a contract does not have to be ratified by the membership except when the contract itself specifies that it will take effect only upon ratification.[103] Thus, if a union's bylaws require ratification and a decertification petition is filed before the membership ratifies the union's acceptance of the contract, the contract will serve as a bar. Similarly, a requirement that an international union approve the contract will not prevent the contract from serving as a bar if a decertification petition is filed prior to the international's expressing its approval unless the contract by its own terms makes the international union's approval a condition precedent to the contract's validity.[104] In most instances, union members will be aware of ratification or international approval requirements. Hence, they will normally presume that the contract is not valid until such requirements are met. The Board's view, however, results in these reasonably based expectations being upset with very little justification. Surely, it would not be difficult for the Board to examine a copy of the local union's or international union's bylaws to determine whether a ratification or approval requirement exists.

Changed Circumstances

In certain situations, a contract may cease to serve as a bar to a decertification election because of changed circumstances between the date of signing the contract and the date of petition. In 1958, in *General Extrusion Co.*,[105] the Board laid down a series of rules relating to situations in which the contract bar rule might not operate because of changed circumstances.

In *General Extrusion*, the Board modified prior cases by adopting the rule that a contract would not serve as a bar if the contract had been executed:

> (1) before any employees had been hired or (2) prior to a substantial increase in personnel. When the question of a substantial increase in personnel is in issue, a contract will bar an election only if at least 30 percent of the complement employed at the time of the hearing had been employed at the time the contract was executed, *and* 50 percent of the job classifications in existence at the time of the hearing were in existence at the time the contract was executed.[106]

In *General Extrusion*, the Board also modified its view on mergers and relocations. It decided that there would be no bar if changes had occurred in the nature of the operation involving a merger of two or more operations into an entirely new operation with major personnel changes or if there was a resumption of operations after an indefinite period of closure with new employees. Mere relocation of a plant with substantially the same employees, management, and type of work would not prevent the contract from serving as a bar.[107] Although there have been some minor modifications to the *General Extrusion* principles,[108] their flexibility, yet reasonably predictable certainty, has not created a need for any substantial revision.

Schism and Defunctness

A contract can stabilize the bargaining relationship only if the signatory union is able and willing to enforce it. Situations have arisen in which the union is either so fragmented or so weak that it is unable to perform its duties as bargaining agent. As a result, the Board has been required to assess whether a contract should serve as a bar when the union's status as bargaining agent is in doubt.

The Board has taken the view that, when a union becomes defunct, its contract does not bar a decertification election. In *Hershey Chocolate Corp.*,[109] a schism case, the Board stated that a bargaining agent is defunct "if it is unable or unwilling to represent the employees."[110] The Board further stressed that "mere temporary inability to function does not constitute defunctness; nor is the loss of all members in the unit the equivalent of defunctness if the representative otherwise continues in existence and is willing and able to represent. the employees."[111] Under the *Hershey Chocolate* doctrine, the status of the signatory union is examined only if the issue of defunctness is raised. It is irrelevant that a nonsignatory parent body indicates its willingness to administer the local union's contract.[112]

The Board has given the defunctness exception to the contract bar doctrine a narrow application. In *Road Materials, Inc.*,[113] where the union had not processed any grievances or visited the plant for several years and where the employer had implemented unilateral pay increases, the Board still refused to hold that the union was defunct.[114] In overruling the regional director's determination in this case, the Board regarded the union's willingness to represent the employees as the crucial issue. Since the employees had not approached the union for grievance handling or the holding of meetings, the Board found no evidence of any unwillingness on the part of the union to represent the employees.[115] It seems that for defunctness to be found to exist, the union either must have disappeared by virtue of losing all its members or it must have abandoned its status as bargaining agent, since a union that is able to sign a collective agreement periodically will probably be held to have demonstrated its willingness to represent the employees.[116] The defunctness doctrine, then, can have the unintended effect of locking unit employees into a situation where the union, for some reason, does not actively represent its members during the life of the contract. Although this arrangement may satisfy the union and the employer, the Board should adopt a position that does not unjustifiably penalize employees.

The Board has recognized that there are times when a schism within a union so disrupts bargaining relationships that an exception should be made to the contract bar doctrine. In the 1950s, when revelations of corruption and communist infiltration within certain unions led to a rash of schism cases, the Board reconsidered the application of the contract bar doctrine to schism situations in the leading case of *Hershey Chocolate*.[117] That case concerned a split within the Bakery and Confectionery Workers International Union (BCWIU)[118] caused by the members' reaction to its expulsion from the AFL-CIO for uncorrected corrupt practices. The AFL-CIO subsequently chartered a rival union, the American Bakery and Confectionery Workers International Union (ABCWIU),[119] with the same jurisdiction as the BCWIU. When BCWIU locals attempted to disaffiliate and affiliate with the new ABCWIU, the BCWIU informed employers that they should not recognize the ABCWIU locals for the purposes of collective bargaining. Faced with claims by two unions for recognition, the employer filed for an election. The question presented was whether the existing contract between the employer and the BCWIU local barred the election. Observing that it had generally found a schism to exist when a local union's disaffiliation occurred "in the context of a basic intraunion conflict," the Board held that such "a basic intraunion conflict is a necessary prerequisite to a finding that a schism exists warranting an election."[120] The Board then defined "basic intraunion conflict" to be "any conflict over policy at the highest level of an international union . . . which results in a disruption of existing intraunion relationships."[121] Since the split within the BCWIU was at all levels and was disrupting intraunion relationships, the contract bar doctrine was held not to apply.[122]

The Board does not lightly classify dissident movements within a union as a "schism." For instance, in *B & B Beer Distributing Co.*,[123] a Teamsters local sought to affiliate with another international union when the International Brotherhood of Teamsters was expelled from the AFL-CIO for corruption. When the rival union, which traditionally had overlapping jurisdiction with the Teamsters in beer distributing, petitioned for an election, the petition was dismissed. On appeal, the Board agreed with the regional director that the narrow exception carved out of the contract bar doctrine in *Hershey Chocolate* should not be applied on these facts. The Board distinguished *Hershey Chocolate* by pointing out that there was no open split within the Teamsters union; that the AFL-CIO had not assigned the Teamsters' existing jurisdiction to any other union so that two unions, with some claim of right, could assert bargaining rights; and that no group was intensively campaigning to win the allegiance of Teamsters locals. Finding that the facts did not amount to a basic intraunion policy conflict and that there was no evidence that the Teamsters' expulsion threatened the stability of its bargaining relationships, the Board held that the existing contract was a bar to an election.[124]

A local union that wants to disaffiliate from its parent union and affiliate with another international union without waiting until the current collective bargaining agreement expires may find its path blocked, as *Allied Chemical Corp.*[125] demonstrates. There, a weak international union, District 50, was a prime candidate for merger with one of two large international unions. Two District 50 national officers were actively seeking to have the national executive board support their respectively favored unions. A District 50 local preferred a third international union and voted to affiliate with it. This international union, the Oil, Chemical and Atomic Workers (OCAW),[126] then filed to have certification of the bargaining representative amended to reflect the local's change in affiliation. On the basis of the contract bar doctrine, the regional director dismissed the case. District 50 subsequently placed the local in trusteeship. On appeal to the Board, the OCAW argued that, under *Hershey Chocolate*, a schism existed; therefore, the contract was no bar to an election. Reviewing the principles enunciated in *Hershey Chocolate*, the Board emphasized that a schism exists only where a basic intraunion policy conflict disrupts existing intraunion relationships.[127] The Board pointed out that the local's disaffiliation was not related to any policy conflict, observing that there was no split within District 50 as there had been in *Hershey Chocolate*. Critical to the Board's determination was its characterization of the dissension within the union: the rivals were trying to gain control of District 50; they were not fragmenting it.[128] The *Allied Chemical* case exemplifies the limited nature of the schism exception as set out in *Hershey Chocolate*. As the Board stated in *Hershey Chocolate*, an election should not be directed in a unit with a current contract unless the existing contract no longer serves to promote industrial stability.[129] A contract may fail to further industrial stability where there is such confusion that bargaining relationships are unstable. This would seem to be the case only where the employer is confronted with two groups, each of which can, with some show of legitimacy, claim to be the certified bargaining agent or its heir.[130] Accordingly, routine disaffiliation by a local dissatisfied with its parent body would rarely, if ever, qualify as a "true schismatic situation" under the Board's view.[131]

If the identity of the contracting local can still be pinpointed at the time a decertification petition is filed, the Board will find an election barred by the existing contract. It can be argued, however, that the Board's narrow schism exception unjustifiably restrains employee freedom of choice in situations where it is unlikely that industrial stability will be disrupted. In *Allied Chemical*, for instance, where both the membership and the leadership of the contracting local supported the transfer of affiliation from District 50 to the OCAW, there was no indication that the change of affiliation would have any impact on the existing collective bargaining relationship between the local and the employer. Since the relationship between the employer and the union was stable, the underlying rationale for the contract bar doctrine was absent. Nevertheless, the doctrine was applied, thereby compelling the employees to accept affiliation with an international union not of their choosing.[132]

Unlawful Contract Provisions

Since 1935, the Board has taken the view that contracts contravening the basic policies of the National Labor Relations Act do not bar an election. After the Taft-Hartley Act was enacted, application of this principle was extended to union security clauses. Thus, if a clause was not executed in conformity with the requirements of section 8(a)(3),[133] the contract was not a bar. The mere existence of such a clause was sufficient to eliminate the bar, even if the clause had not been put into effect.[134]

In 1958, during its thorough reconsideration of the contract bar doctrine, the Board decided *Keystone Coat, Apron & Towel Supply Co.*,[135] which represented a codification of prior cases on unlawful contract clauses. Under *Keystone,* any contract containing a union security clause that did not, on its face, conform with the requirements of the act or that had been found unlawful in an unfair labor practice proceeding would not bar an election. Any union security clause with ambiguous language would not constitute a bar. To assist the parties in drafting a clause that would meet the Board's standards, a "model clause" was set out. Supporting its stance, the Board argued forcibly that it could not be regarded as burdensome to observe the law in express terms. Three years later, in *NLRB v. News Syndicate Co.*,[136] the Supreme Court faulted the Board's approach, holding that a collective bargaining agreement could not be deemed unlawful merely because it did not affirmatively disclaim all illegal objectives.[137] The Board accordingly modified its policy in this respect in *Paragon Products Corp.*[138]

In *Paragon Products*, the Board stated that only those contracts containing a "clearly unlawful" union security clause or a clause that had been declared unlawful in an unfair labor practice proceeding would not bar an election.[139] A clearly unlawful clause was defined as "one which by its express terms clearly and unequivocally goes beyond the limited form of union-security permitted by Section 8(a)3 and is therefore incapable of a lawful interpretation."[140] Hence, ambiguous clauses, unless determined to be unlawful in an unfair labor practice proceeding, would not bar an election since extrinsic evidence of actual practice would not be considered in a representation proceeding.[141]

The Board's self-imposed rule against considering extrinsic evidence can have a harsh impact. In *Jet-Pak Corp.*,[142] the union security provision was lawful on its face, but the contract that was executed on September 16, 1976, was made effective retroactive to July 1, 1976. As a result, some new employees might have been denied their thirty-day grace period in which to join the union. The regional director considered extrinsic evidence, which took the form of stipulations by both parties to certain facts, since he believed that such uncontroverted evidence did not present "dangers normally present in a non-adversary representation hearing."[143] Having considered this evidence, the regional director found that an election was barred. The Board, however, adhered strictly to its rule and stated, "[W]e are permitted only to examine the terms of the contract as they appear within the four corners of the instrument itself."[144]

The application of the Board's rule against extrinsic evidence in cases such as *Jet-Pak Corp.* seems unduly inflexible since "boilerplate" contract clauses are often drafted in advance of contract expiration to take effect at 12:01 A.M. on the day following the date of expiration of the old contract. In so doing, the drafters anticipate that, even if a new contract is not actually settled by that date, it will often be made retroactive to it. That the union security clause as stated could then be construed to be unlawful is a fact that may well escape many local union officials.[145]

The Board's rigid adherence to this rule also produces cases in which minor technicalities have a major impact. In one case, for example, the contract was concluded on May 20, 1968, but the formal document was not signed until June 10, 1968.[146] The formal contract document stated that the contract had been made and entered into on May 20 and was effective from May 20. When a decertification petition was filed, the regional director found it was not barred by the contract because the union security clause was unlawful in possibly denying some employees the full thirty-day grace period. In so finding, the regional director stated that the different effective and signing dates transformed the contract into one that was retroactively effective. The Board disagreed, stating that, by its very terms, the contract took effect on the very day it was entered into.[147] As a result, the union security clause was unlawful, and the contract was a bar to an election. There is no reason to believe, however, that the nonunion employees in this case received any more notice of the contents of a contract that had not yet been reduced to writing than the employees in *Jet-Pak*. The Board's position is that the rights of these employees could be vindicated in an unfair labor practice proceeding, a position that is equally applicable to the employees in *Jet-Pak*.

The scope of the unlawful contract exception to the contract bar doctrine extends beyond union security clauses. Contracts that on their faces contained provisions clearly unlawful with regard to such issues as dues checkoff, seniority,[148] preferential hiring,[149] and racial discrimination[150] have been held not to bar an election. Somewhat inconsistently, an unlawful hot cargo clause did not influence the employees' choice of a bargaining representative.[151] Such reasoning would seem to be equally valid on the question of a seniority clause. If a union breaches its duty under a contract that is lawful on its face, that contract will serve to bar a decertification election.[152]

Presumption of Majority

If an employer suspects that a union no longer has the support of a majority of the employees in the bargaining unit, he may wish to cease recognizing the union for the purposes of collective bargaining. Whether he can do this without violating his section 8(a)(5) duty to bargain in good faith depends on whether he has a good faith doubt of the union's continued majority status and whether, at that particular time, the presumption of continued majority status is rebuttable. Since an employer will often doubt the union's majority status once he learns that there is a campaign to decertify the union, the issue of presumption of majority frequently arises in a decertification context.

Irrebuttable Presumption of Majority

There are certain protected periods of bargaining when the presumption of the union's continuing majority cannot be challenged, for instance, during the certification year and for a reasonable period following voluntary recognition, the issuance of a bargaining order and the settlement of 8(a)(5) charges. At those times, decertification petitions will be dismissed as untimely even if the signatures on the petition indicate that a clear majority of the employees in the unit wants to oust the union.[153]

During Certification Year

In *Brooks v. NLRB*,[154] the Supreme Court held that, absent unusual circumstances,[155] an employer has a duty to bargain with the union certified as the bargaining agent for his employees for one year from the date of certification.[156] In *Brooks*, where the union lost a majority of its members shortly after the election through no fault of the employer, the Supreme Court affirmed the longstanding Board position that the union should still have one year in which to carry out its mandate.[157] While noting that this rule promoted "a sense of responsibility in the electorate and needed coherence in administration,"[158] the Court was not unaware of other, more pragmatic considerations underscoring such a policy. The Court stated:

> It is scarcely conducive to bargaining in good faith for an employer to know that, if he dillydallies or subtly undermines, union strength may erode and thereby relieve him of his statutory duties at any time, while if he works conscientiously toward agreement, the rank and file may, at the last moment, repudiate their agent.[159]

Consonant with the Court's reasoning in *Brooks* is the Board's rule, promulgated in *Mar-Jac Poultry Co.*,[160] that the certification year will be extended if the employer's unfair labor practices have frustrated the union's ability to carry out its duties as bargaining agent during the original certification year. In *Mar-Jac*, the company shut down six months after bargaining had commenced. Two years later, the same stockholders resumed business under a different name. The union requested that the company resume bargaining. When the company refused, stating that the union no longer had majority support,[161] the union filed a charge under section 8(a)(5). When an employee decertification petition was filed, it was dismissed by the Board on the grounds that the union had not received the benefit of bargaining for a substantial part of the certification year, a period, as the Board noted, "when Unions are generally at their greatest strength."[162]

In remedying the unfair labor practices in *Mar-Jac*, the Board ordered the employer to bargain for a full year, thus taking no account of the six months during which bargaining had occurred in the original certification year. In *Brooks*, the employer had been ordered to continue recognizing the union for the remainder of the certification year. Although the Board did not do so, *Mar-Jac* can be distinguished from *Brooks* on the grounds that the employer in *Mar-Jac* had displayed an intransigent attitude toward the union, which, in large part, contributed to its loss of majority, whereas in *Brooks*, the employees repudiated the union on their own.

Whether employees who no longer support the union and who perhaps have never supported the union should be locked into an extended period of union representation without the opportunity of expressing their choice raises difficult questions, both legal and practical in nature. Practically, the efficacy of such a remedy is questionable. In such situations, the employees' confidence in the union's ability to win concessions may have been severely undermined, if not destroyed, by the employer's tactics.[163] At most, the union will have one year in which to regain the allegiance of the employees. Aware that the only way the union is likely to accomplish this is by concluding a collective agreement that represents a substantial improvement in terms and conditions of employment, the employer will doubtless be in no haste to sign such an agreement. At the end of the year, the employees may very well decertify the union. If the end result is the same,[164] the justification for applying the *Mar-Jac* rule, which postpones the employees' section 7 rights, must lie elsewhere.

The Fifth Circuit responded to this point in a case where it enforced a Board order that extended the certificatn year. The court asserted:

> It would be particularly anomalous, and disruptive of industrial peace, to allow the employer's wrongful refusal to bargain in good faith to dissipate the union's strength, and then to require a new election which "would not be likely to demonstrate the employees' true, undistorted desires,". . . since employee disaffection with the union in such cases is in all likelihood prompted by the employer-induced failure to achieve desired results at the bargaining table.[165]

The Fifth Circuit's observation was made in a case where the employer displayed a particularly belligerent and obstructionist attitude toward bargaining with the union and had committed numerous unfair labor practices.[166] This fact is of utmost importance since the Board's remedial power "is merely incidental to the primary purpose of Congress to stop and to prevent unfair labor practices."[167] If there has been no unfair labor practice, a Board order requiring bargaining for an extended certification year would seem to be a punitive, rather than remedial, measure.[168]

The limitations on the Board's remedial powers were raised by the Seventh Circuit in *NLRB v. Gebhardt-Vogel Tanning Co.*[169] In that case, the union was certified on July 9, 1963. During the certification year, the employer delayed in disclosing wage information to the union during bargaining. The union filed a charge under section 8(a)(5) in October alleging that the employer had delayed five months in handing over the information. In November, the employer furnished the wage information, and the union withdrew the unfair labor practice charge. On July 28, 1964, a decertification petition was filed. The regional director, dismissing the petition on the basis of the rule in *Mar-Jac*, stated that the union did not have the benefit of the full certification year since the employer had unlawfully delayed in disclosing the wage information. The Seventh Circuit refused to enforce the Board's order extending the certification year since, on the facts presented, there was no finding that the employer had committed an unfair labor practice.[170] Although the Seventh Circuit was technically correct, its decision had the effect of penalizing a union which had declined to use the procedures of the NLRB to engage in unnecessary litigation. Such a decision can only lead other unions to refuse to withdraw charges for fear that it may redound to their disadvantage.

Although the *Mar-Jac* rule remains a vital remedy in the Board's enforcement scheme for 8 (a)(5) violations,[171] the Board will, in its discretion, refuse to extend the certification year in circumstances where the rule arguably applies. In one case,[172] the union was certified to represent a unit of dental laboratory technicians in March 1973. Shortly thereafter, the employer contracted out the lab work, and all the technicians were dismissed. The union immediately filed unfair labor practice charges. Several months later, the employer reopened the lab, and by mid-1974 the number of employees in the unit had attained its earlier level. In 1974, the Board found that the closing of the lab was economically motivated but that the employer had violated section 8(a)(5) by not bargaining about the impact of the closing.[173] In January 1976, the Ninth Circuit enforced the Board's order and the issue of back pay was referred to the NLRB's regional office. At this point, the parties voluntarily agreed to negotiate a contract covering the lab technicians, none of whom had been employed in March 1973. Bargaining ceased after six sessions when the parties learned that a decertification petition had been filed. The union appealed the regional director's direction of an election,[174] claiming that since it had bargained for a total of only three months under its certification, the certification year should be extended and the decertification election barred. Considering the applicability of the *Mar-Jac* rule, the Board held that the extension of the certification year was not warranted in these "rather unusual circumstances."[175] In reaching this conclusion, the Board found persuasive the fact that the closing of the lab was economically motivated and that the hiatus in bargaining was not attributable to an employer unfair labor practice.

Following Voluntary Recognition

For a reasonable period of time following an employer's voluntary recognition of a union, the employer cannot lawfully refuse to bargain with that union even when it is clear that the union has lost its majority; the union's presumption of majority is irrebuttable. The genesis of this rule can be traced to the 1944 United States Supreme Court decision in *Franks Brothers Co. v. NLRB.*[176] In *Franks*, an employer refused to bargain with the union on the basis of its having authorization cards from a majority of the employees. When the union filed for an election, the employer engaged in a course of antiunion conduct, and the union filed unfair labor practice charges, which blocked the holding of the election.[177] More than a year later, it was held that the employer had violated sections 8(a)(1) and 8(a)(5) of the act. Rather than direct an election, the Board ordered the employer to bargain with the union even though the turnover in the work force indicated that the union had lost its majority status.[178] The Supreme Court enforced the Board's order, stating that, if the bargaining order remedy were unavailable and elections had to be held when shifts in the work force during the pendency of unfair labor practice charges had occurred, then recalcitrant employers might be tempted to commit unfair labor practices in order to postpone indefinitely their bargaining obligation.[179] In responding to the employer's arguments, the Court pointed out that the bargaining order was not designed to establish a permanent bargaining relationship but that "a bargaining relationship once rightfully established must be permitted to exist and function for a reasonable period in which it can be given a fair chance to succeed."[180] The Board regards this statement as support for its rule that an employer can be ordered to continue bargaining with a union that has lost its majority support even when the employer in no way caused the loss of support.[181]

The Board took this position in *Keller Plastics Eastern, Inc.,*[182] where the employer had voluntarily recognized the union and commenced bargaining. Within three weeks of recognition, raiding by a rival union had caused the bargaining agent to lose its majority. Citing the statement quoted above from *Franks Brothers*, the Board held that the employer was required to continue recognizing the union for a reasonable period of time. In *Keller*, the Board found it unnecessary to decide what constituted "a reasonable period of time" since clearly it is more than three weeks.[183]

The *Keller* doctrine becomes operative as soon as an employer recognizes a union. In one case,[184] a majority of the employees signed a petition to oust the union only three days after the employer and voluntarily recognized it on the basis of a card check. The decertification petition was dismissed on the grounds that it was untimely since the union had not yet had a reasonable period of time in which to carry out its mandate as bargaining agent.[185] Similarly, the employer's refusal to engage in bargaining once the decertification petition was filed was held unlawful since the presumption of the union's majority at that point was irrebuttable.[186] In responding to the employer's argument that it was unfair to bind the employees for a lengthy period on the basis of such an informal and uncertain method of selection, the Seventh Circuit noted that there was no reason to distinguish between the two modes of bargaining agent selection authorized by section 9 of the act in deciding that the bargaining relationship, once rightfully established, should have an opportunity to function.[187] The court observed that the employer or employees should have challenged the lawfulness of the voluntary recognition if they doubted its validity.[188]

If the union at the time of the employer's voluntary recognition did not have a majority, the bargaining relationship will not be given a reasonable period in which to function since it was not rightfully established. The Board has held that it is irrelevant under *Keller Plastics* that the employer's recognition was "purely voluntary"; recognition must be based on a demonstrated showing of majority.[189]

The Board has long held that an employer who agrees to bargain with a union, in return for the union's withdrawing an unfair labor practice charge, is obligated to honor that agreement "for a reasonable time after its execution without questioning the representative status of the Union."[190] The Fourth Circuit, affirming the Board's order in *Poole Foundry & Machine Co. v. NLRB*,[191] stated, "If a settlement agreement is to have real force, it would seem that a reasonable time must be afforded in which a status fixed by the agreement is to operate."[192] Hence, an employer who has agreed to bargain with the union as part of a settlement agreement cannot refuse to do so on the grounds that a majority of its employees have signed a decertification petition.[193] In such circumstances, the petition will be dismissed as untimely.

Subsequent to a Bargaining Order

Following similar reasoning, the Board has held that once bargaining commences in compliance with an NLRB bargaining order, the bargaining relationship must have a reasonable period of time in which to function regardless of the union's actual majority status. In *NLRB v. Kaiser Agricultural Chemicals*,[194] the employer asserted that the employee decertification petition meant that the employees no longer wanted the union as their bargaining agent. In upholding the Board's dismissal of the decertification petition as untimely, the Fifth Circuit suggested that it was an equally plausible assumption that the unfair labor practices continued to affect employee sentiment, making a fair election impossible.[195]

Rebuttable Presumption of Majority

Once a union has established its majority status on the basis of either a certification election or a lawful voluntary recognition by the employer, there is a presumption that the union continues to enjoy majority status.[196] This presumption is irrebuttable at certain times, as discussed above.[197] At other times, the presumption of majority is rebuttable.

To rebut the presumption of majority status, an employer must show that the union, in fact, no longer enjoys majority status or that it has a good faith doubt about the union's continuing majority status.[198] To constitute a "good faith doubt," the employer's doubt must be based on objective considerations, and it must be raised in a context free of unfair labor practices.[199]

If the collective bargaining agreement is due to expire shortly and the employer suspects that the union no longer commands majority support in the unit, the employer may contemplate refusing to bargain with the union on a new contract. Such a course of action, however, presents a dilemma. If an employee decertification petition is timely filed subsequent to the employer's refusal to bargain,[200] it will most likely be dismissed under the Board's blocking charge rule, assuming that the union has filed an 8(a)(5) charge in response to the employer's refusal to bargain.[201] If the employer does refuse to bargain and it is later determined that his suspicions did not amount to a "good faith doubt;" he will be found to have violated section 8(a)(5). A bargaining order will be issued, and he will not be permitted to question the union's majority status for a reasonable period of time. As a result, in deciding whether or not to bargain with the union, it is of utmost importance to the employer that he be able to estimate with reasonable certainty whether his suspicions constitute a "good faith doubt" in the Board's view.

Good Faith Doubt of Majority Status

It can be said with reasonable certainty that the employer's doubt must arise in an atmosphere free of unfair labor practices if there is to be any likelihood that it will be classified "good faith."[202] A finding that the employer's conduct violated section 8(a)(1) or 8(a)(5) will undermine his claim of good faith. Even if the employer's conduct does not amount to an unfair labor practice, if it is claimed that the conduct was "aimed at causing disaffection from the union,"[203] the Board may well conclude that the atmosphere has become tainted so that any doubt of the employer cannot be classified as a good faith one.

Much more difficult to predict are the factors on which an employer may reasonably rely in concluding that the union has lost its majority. While certitude is not required, the Board has tended to look with disfavor on anything less than a very high degree of probability. The Board has admitted that there is no simple formula for determining when a good faith doubt exists.[204] As such, the Board examines the totality of the circumstances in which the doubt arises.

The Board takes the view that the employer's doubt must be based on "objective considerations" of the union's loss of majority.[205] Reliable information that more than 50 percent of the unit employees support decertification usually suffices to raise a good faith doubt. The employer must, however, possess more or less precise information; statements that "many" employees do not want to be in the union are too vague.[206] An estimate that more than 50 percent of the employees probably no longer support the union, based on a commonsense appraisal of the situation, will usually be insufficient to raise a good faith doubt. For instance, in *Massey-Ferguson, Inc.*,[207] the employer based its doubt on the fact that the union had won a narrow victory shortly before, that there had been high turnover in the unit, and that supervisors had reported that many employees were dissatisfied with the union. The Board held that the employer did not possess a good faith doubt.[208] Stating that the narrow election victory was insignificant, the Board observed that high turnover was a factor to consider but in itself was not sufficient to establish good faith doubt since new employees are presumed to support the union in the same ratio as those they have replaced.[209]

The weight that can be placed on supervisors' reports of employee sentiments is unclear. In *Massey-Ferguson*, the Board stated that the evidence of employee dissatisfaction must come from the employees themselves, not from supervisors on their behalf.[210] Some weight, however, seems to be given to supervisors' observations when they are buttressed by employee comments. For instance, in *Stresskin Products Co.*,[211] a good faith doubt was based primarily on "numerous and substantially identical reports from presumably trustworthy supervisors and employees."[212] Comments evincing dissatisfaction with the union made by employees directly to supervisors are persuasive evidence of the union's loss of support, but supervisory personnel must be extremely careful in their contacts with employees regarding the union. Since supervisors cannot interrogate employees about their feelings about the union without violating section 8(a)(1), the employer must depend on employees' volunteering their opinions to supervisory personnel. Likewise, attempts by supervisors to steer the conversation toward the subject of the union's popularity, unless done neutrally, might be construed as attempts to cause disaffection with the union.

The Board carefully scrutinizes the objective considerations put forward by the employer to determine whether they indicate that the employees no longer want the union to be their bargaining agent. As a result, the fact that less than 50 percent of the employees in the unit belong to the union, in itself, is not determinative since it can be argued that there are employees who want the benefits of union representation without the obligations of union membership.[213] Similarly, the fact that some employees abandoned a strike and crossed the union's picket line cannot necessarily be interpreted as a sign that they no longer wish the union to represent them since their return to work might have been wholly for personal reasons unrelated to the union's stance.[214]

In some cases, the employer lists several reasons why he doubted the union's majority status. Taken individually, each factor may be insufficient to support a finding of good faith doubt, but if taken together, the reasons may well provide the basis for such a finding. Although the Board has not been altogether consistent in its approach, it has displayed a marked tendency toward a weighing of each factor on its own.

Six cases in which the employer questioned the majority status of the hotel and bartenders union in the same city illustrate this tendency.[215] In all six cases, the employer belonged to the Reno Employers' Council, which had a collective bargaining relationship with the union dating from 1959. Realizing in early 1974 that the union's membership was so low as to jeopardize the negotiation of a new contract later in the year,[216] local union officers sought to enlist the aid of the international union. In June 1974, the international sent out organizers in a campaign to increase the local's membership. In mid-summer, local newspapers ran articles on this union activity and quoted an international trustee as stating that only about 20 percent of eligible employees in the area were members of the union.[217] In this same period, the employers noted union activity within the casino-hotels, and supervisors received complaints from employees who did not want to join the union. In late summer, each employer timely withdrew from the multiemployer association and subsequently refused to bargain with the union, asserting doubt about the union's majority status. Except for this refusal to bargain, there was no allegation that any employer had engaged in unfair labor practices.

In its defense to the 8(a)(5) charge, one employer made the following arguments: (1) the union had never demonstrated a majority since it had been voluntarily recognized; (2) the size of the unit had tripled since the union was recognized; (3) turnover in the unit since the last contract was 500 percent; (4) the statements of the international trustee indicated that the membership of the local union was very low, and the union was engaged in an organizing drive; (5) many employees had indicated to their supervisors that they were dissatisfied with the union and were not interested in joining it; (6) the union had filed only one grievance in a twelve-year period during which there had been 10,000 employees at the hotel; and (7) there was no union security or dues checkoff provision in the contract.[218] The Board considered each argument on its own and found only two arguments relevant to the issue of majority status: the employees' complaints and high turnover. Since only 29 out of 202 employees had complained to their supervisors and since new employees are presumed to support the union in the same ratio as the employees they replace, the Board found that the employer could not have possessed a good faith doubt about the union's majority status in the particular unit. Coming to the same conclusion in all six cases, the Board demonstrated that what an employer believes to be true after a careful review of the situation may fall short of what the Board demands as the basis for a good faith doubt.

Effect of a Decertification Petition

In many cases, the employer's doubts of the union's majority status are heightened when a decertification petition is filed. The question, therefore, often arises whether an employer can refuse to bargain with the union because a decertification petition has been filed with the NLRB.

The mere filing of a decertification petition, which requires only that 30 percent of the employees desire an election, does not raise a real question of representation.[219] Therefore, if an employer ceases to recognize the union as the representative of his employees subsequent to the filing of a decertification petition, he will violate section 8(a)(5) of the act, unless it is determined that he possessed a "good faith doubt" of the union's majority status at the time he ceased recognizing the union.[220] It should be noted that if an absolute majority of the unit employees sign the decertification petition, the real question of representation is usually raised, and the employer may refuse to bargain with the union.[221]

In *Telautograph Corp.*,[222] the Board considered the predicament of an employer who sought to postpone bargaining on a new contract until after the decertification election was held. In *Telautograph*, the employer and the union had agreed to meet on September 14, 1970, to commence bargaining on a new contract. On September 3, an employee decertification petition was filed. On October 23, the regional director found that the petition was timely filed. The bargaining session did not take place as scheduled. Shortly after the hearing on the petition, the union contacted the employer regarding meeting to begin bargaining. Awaiting the regional director's decision, the employer did not respond. After the regional director found that the petition was timely filed and directed an election, the employer replied that it would not enter into bargaining on a new contract at that time because the question of representation remained to be settled. The union then filed an 8(a)(5) charge, at which point the regional director applied the Board's blocking charge rule and indefinitely postponed the holding of the decertification election pending the outcome of the unfair labor practice charge.

The employer in *Telautograph* did not possess a "good faith doubt" about the union's majority status under the criteria discussed above.[223] Ordinarily, it would have been found to have violated section 8(a)(5), but the administrative law judge refused to recommend the finding of a violation in the "special circumstances" of that case,[224] namely that the employer refused to bargain only after the regional director had determined that a question of representation existed. The administrative law judge emphasized that a "critical factor" in his recommendation was that the employer's refusal to bargain had occurred in a context totally devoid of any antiunion animus.[225] In adopting the administrative law judge's findings and recommendations, the Board stressed that the decertification petition must raise a "real question of representation" in order for it to justify an employer's refusal to bargain on a new contract.[226] The Board further clarified its stance by stating that the union could continue to administer the contract and could still process grievances.

Telautograph provides guidance for an employer confronted with a union demand that bargaining on a new contract take place even though a decertification petition has been filed. The employer should not refuse to bargain until the regional director finds that a question of representation exists and directs an election. Providing that the employer has engaged in no antiunion conduct, his refusal to bargain on a new contract while continuing to recognize the union should not block the prompt holding of the decertification election, assuming that the regional director does not mechanically apply the blocking charge rule.

The Blocking Charge Rule

In an exercise of its discretion under the act, the Board has long taken the position that it will generally not conduct an election in a unit during the pendency of unwaived unfair labor practice charges relating to that unit.[227] Since the unfair labor practice charge "blocks" the holding of the election, this policy has been labelled the "blocking charge" rule.

The blocking charge rule is based on the premise that it would contravene the purposes of the act to proceed with an election arguably tainted by an employer's unfair labor practices.[228] As one court succinctly noted, "it would surely controvert the spirit of the Act to allow the employer to profit by his own wrongdoing."[229] The evident rational underpinning to this rule has led numerous courts to cite it with approval.[230] The Board's application of the rule, however, has not always met with the uncritical approval of the courts.

In a series of cases arising in the Fifth Circuit, the courts have had occasion to scrutinize the Board's procedures for delaying the holding of a decertification election upon the filing of unfair labor practice charges. In each case, the threshold question was whether the federal district court had jurisdiction, since the challenged ruling was an interim order in a representation case. Generally, decisions of the NLRB in representation cases are not reviewable by the district courts,[231] and under section 10(f),[232] only final orders of the Board are subject to review by the circuit courts. The United States Supreme Court decision in *Leedom v. Kyne*[233] was seen as providing the basis for jurisdiction in the blocking charge cases. In *Leedom v. Kyne*, the Court held that the federal district courts are empowered to grant injunctive relief in representation cases where the Board has acted contrary to a specific provision in the act and where the employees' rights under the statute will otherwise be denied because there is no statutory mechanism by which they can enforce their rights.

In *Templeton v. Dixie Color Printing Co.*,[234] employees brought suit complaining that their decertification petition filed in 1968 had been held in abeyance for three years because of an unfair labor practice charge filed in 1964.[235] Stating that the only issue in the case was the arbitrary use of the blocking charge procedure, the Fifth Circuit commented, "The short of the matter is that the Board has refused to take any notice of the petition."[236] The court limited the applicability of its holding by stating that it was not considering how the blocking charge rule should be applied against employers or when it would be within the Board's discretion to refuse to process a decertification petition.[237] The thrust of the *Templeton* court's decision is that by delaying, the Board had failed to act in accordance with a specific provision of the act[238] and, as a result, employees were being denied their statutory right to determine whether they wanted to be represented for the purposes of collective bargaining. The court, therefore, ordered the Board to consider the decertification petition without delay.[239] Although the court in *Templeton* did not order that the decertification election be held, it made quite clear in dicta that the underlying rationale for the blocking charge rule was inapposite in that case and that the election should be held promptly.[240]

The ramifications of *Templeton* were explored the following year in *Surratt v. NLRB*,[241] a case also arising in the Northern District of Alabama. In *Surratt*, an employee decertification petition was filed in December 1970, fourteen months after the union had been certified. After the petition was filed, the union filed charges under section 8(a)(5), alleging that the employer had not been bargaining in good faith since June 1970. Approximately six weeks later, the regional director dismissed the decertification petition on the basis of the blocking charge rule. After the Board affirmed the dismissal, employees filed suit in federal district court. When the case came before the Fifth Circuit, the Board has not yet rendered its decision on the 8(a)(5) complaint, but it was known that the administrative law judge had recommended that the charges be dismissed. The court in *Surratt* stated:

> The Board should not be allowed to apply its "blocking charge practice" as a *per se* rule without exercising its discretion to make a careful determination in each individual case whether the violation alleged is such that consideration of the election petition ought to be delayed or dismissed.[242]

The court clarified its position when responding to the Board's argument that *Surratt* should be distinguished from *Templeton* on the grounds that the delay in *Templeton* was much longer. The court noted that this was a difference of degree, not principle, and that the Board should make a careful determination before deciding to delay the decertification election.[243]

The limited utility that *Templeton* has for employees seeking to compel the Board to conduct a decertification election became apparent in *Bishop v. NLRB*.[244] In *Bishop*, the union filed unfair labor practice charges against the employer. Winn-Dixie Stores,[245] in late 1969. The case was still slowly making its way up to the Board when an employee decertification petition was filed in April 1972. The regional director determined that the unfair labor practice charges had merit and then applied the blocking charge rule and dismissed the petition. The employees then filed suit in federal district court seeking an order compelling the National Labor Relations Board to process their petition.[246] The Fifth Circuit responded by noting that the district court should have dismissed the case for lack of jurisdiction over the subject matter since the "carefully circumscribed jurisdiction" carved out in *Leedom v. Kyne, Templeton,* and *Surratt* did not reach the instant case.[247] The court noted that jurisdiction would exist only where the Board had failed to act in accordance with a specific provision of the act. Here, the Board had acted in accordance with section 9(c)(1). It had investigated the petition when it was filed, and it had made a determination to dismiss the petition after careful consideration of the merits of the individual case. The court emphasized that the Board had not followed a mechanistic approach as it had in *Templeton* and *Surratt* in applying the blocking charge rule as if it were a per se rule.[248]

Subscribing to the view that the employees' desire to rid themselves of the union might well be the result of the employer's unfair labor practices, the court in *Bishop* commented that if the employees still wanted to oust the union after it had had an opportunity to operate free from the employer's unlawful conduct, then they could file another decertification petition.[249] As *Hamil v. Youngblood*[250] illustrates, however, the employees may be stymied the second time around.

In *Hamil*, the Board found in 1972 that the employer had violated section 8(a)(5). The following year, the Tenth Circuit enforced the Board's order and bargaining commenced. In late autumn of 1973, the union charged that the employer was still bargaining in bad faith[251] and asked that the Tenth Circuit hold the employer in contempt. A decertification petition filed in 1975 was dismissed. In February 1976, the union and the employer signed a collective agreement.[252] On September 8, 1976, a Special Master for the Tenth Circuit recommended that the employer be held in contempt of the court's 1973 order. Two weeks later, the employees filed their second decertification petition. It was dismissed two days later by the regional director on the basis of the blocking charge rule. In his letter, the regional director cited the contempt charge still pending in the Tenth Circuit, a charge that related to conduct during negotiations for a contract that was by then approaching expiration.

Asserting that it is the responsibility of the court to determine whether the Board has rationally exercised its discretion in applying the blocking charge rule, the district court in *Hamil* found that it could not make such a determination because the regional director had not made an investigation or subjective determination on the merits of the individual case and that he had not articulated his reasons for dismissing the petition. Accordingly, the court held that, before the regional director applies the blocking charge rule, an investigation should be made to determine whether the alleged unlawful conduct of the employer was of such a nature as to make a free election unlikely.[253] Further, the regional director should set out the factors on which he based his decision, thereby providing the basis for proper judicial review.

The court in *Hamil* would not go so far as to detail the nature of the required investigation. The court did note that such an investigation would be tailored to the requirements of each case, which would reflect whether the Board was already familiar with events relating to the unit.

The *Hamil* court's formulation strikes a balance between permitting unfettered Board discretion and hampering the Board unnecessarily in the application of the blocking-charge rule. As the court indicated, the Board will, in some cases, possess sufficient knowledge of the unfair labor practices affecting the unit employees, and these facts, if not stale, will obviate the need to undertake a time-consuming and costly formal investigation.

The court in *Hamil* was sensitive to the rationale behind the blocking-charge rule: that the employer's alleged unlawful conduct could prevent a reasoned choice by the employees. Unless it is determined that the employer's conduct is likely to restrain the employees in exercising their free choice, there is no reason to dismiss a decertification petition, thereby thwarting the employees' statutory rights.[254] The *Hamil* decision also eliminates one unintended side effect of the blocking charge rule: that unions, anticipating a mechanistic application of the rule, might be encouraged to file unfair labor practice charges to forestall a decertification election.[255]

Conclusion

With management attorneys and labor relations consultants explaining the mechanics of the decertification process at seminars for company executives,[256] it is not surprising that the unions' success rate in decertification elections have been declining. What is more difficult to pinpoint are the reasons why the number of petitions filed has increased so sharply in the past five years and how much of this increase can be attributed to the activities of labor relations consultants. One spokesman for the labor movement has charged that companies encourage "spontaneous" decertification drives as part of a "deliberate, calculated campaign" to destroy unions.[257] Regardless of the accuracy of this allegation, it is clear that an increasing number of employers have become more sophisticated in the ways in which they communicate to their employees their viewpoint that the employees do not need the union.[258]

The decertification scenario envisioned by opponents of the Taft-Hartley Act does occur, but only infrequently. In briefly discussing "the power of an employer to break a labor union if he chooses to do so," Senator Pepper in 1947 argued that an employer who had taken a very hard bargaining stance and thereby provoked a strike could permanently replace economic strikers and then petition for a decertification election in which the striking employees would not be entitled to vote.[259] Now that striking employees retain their right to vote in an NLRB election for one year,[260] an employer must be in a position to operate during a very long strike in order to achieve decertification in this fashion.[261] Hence, few decertifications are of this type, although the ones that are tend to excite very strong emotions.[262]

Labor relations practitioners commonly believe that, in the majority of cases, the employees' main reason for filing a decertification petition is their perception that the union has been ineffective at the bargaining table.[263] The employees' disenchantment with the union is especially likely to occur during the life of the first contract when their expectations of improvements in wages and conditions are not met.

It may be that employers are now more attuned to the possibility of decertification when confronting a vulnerable union as contract expiration draws near.[264] As one court noted, "there comes a point when hard bargaining ends and obstructionist intransigence begins."[265]

Admittedly, this dividing line is not always easy to detect,[266] but if an employer takes a vigorous hard bargaining stance yet is able to remain within the arena of lawful good faith bargaining, there is the distinct possibility that it may undermine the employees' confidence in the union's ability sufficiently so that the employees are moved to decertify the union. One example of this occurred in *Firestone Synthetic Rubber & Latex Co.*[267]

In *Firestone*, the union was certified in 1965. Not until August 1966 was a contract concluded, and this contract was for one year only with provision for a wage reopener after three months. In November 1966, the union reopened negotiations on wages. Unable to reach agreement on this issue, the union struck in mid-January 1967. On April 28, 1967, the employer wrote to each employee to communicate its last offer. Within a week, the union indicated that it would accept this offer but conditioned its acceptance on certain terms relating to the resumption of work, terms that the company found unacceptable.[268] May went by with no settlement. On June 2, 1967, an employee decertification petition was timely filed. On June 7, the union gave notice, as required by statute, of its desire to begin bargaining on a new contract because the current one was due to expire on August 5. At this point, the company refused to bargain, claiming that it had a good faith doubt about the union's majority status.[269] On July 27, 1967, the employer unilaterally implemented its last wage offer[270] and cancelled the striking employees' medical and life insurance.[271] The union then filed unfair labor practice charges. The Board held that at no point did the employer violate the act; hence, the strike at all times was an economic strike.[272] In addition, the employer was found to have a good faith doubt of the union's majority status; therefore, its refusal to bargain on a new contract was lawful.[273]

In *Firestone*, it is not surprising that the employees were disenchanted with the union. In the eighteen months following certification, they had worked under a union contract for less than six months, had been out on strike over four months, and had seen their union achieve little more than could have been expected with no union on the scene.

Similarly destructive of the union's support is an inability to conclude a first contract, particularly where the employer's conduct is deemed to be lawful.[274] Even when unlawful employer conduct occurs, the impact on the employees may be just as likely to inspire decertification. When hard bargaining slips over the line into bad faith bargaining, the remedy for the section 8(a)(5) violation will normally be an order to cease and desist from such conduct and to undertake bargaining in good faith. As noted above, a decertification election will not be held for a reasonable period following the commencement of good faith bargaining, but it has never been suggested that this period should exceed one year; and yet, as one court has noted, "some practices may be of such pernicious nature that their effect upon employees is clearly apparent and longlasting."[275] Thus, if this second round of bargaining should be drawn out, the employees may become demoralized. From their perspective, they have waited during one fruitless period of (bad faith) bargaining; then nothing happened for a substantial period of time (while the case worked its way up through the Board and the courts); and now, renewed bargaining still has not yielded a contract. The reaction of employees in one such case, as expressed in their decertification petition, was predictable: "It is our feeling that [the union] has accomplished nothing in our favor, therefor [sic] we would like a new election."[276]

Unlike Western European unions, which draw on a well of class-based ideological support, American unions have always appealed to workers on the basis of the material results that unions can achieve. Yet, as the *Firestone* case indicates, American employers are increasingly willing to take a firm stance[277] to demonstrate to their employees their conviction that unionization does not necessarily bring better terms and conditions of employment. In some instances, no doubt, the employer's hard bargaining stance is largely the product of the employer's refusal to accept collective bargaining and the concomitant resolve to thwart the bargaining process.[278] In such cases, whether the employer *actually* bargains in good faith and whether the employer will be found to have bargained in good faith by the Board are issues that have little impact on the dynamics of industrial relations. When the unit employees come to the conclusion that the union's achievements fall short of the anticipated standard, decertification becomes a distinct possibility.

NOTES

1. Section 7 of the National Labor Relations Act provides:
   Employees shall have the right to self-organization, to form, join, or assist labor organizations, to bargain collectively through representatives of their own choosing, and to engage in other concerned activities for the purpose of collective bargaining or other mutual aid or protection, and shall also have the right to refrain from any or all of such activities except to the extent that such right may be affected by an agreement requiring membership in a labor organization as a condition of employment as authorized in section 158(a)(3) of this title.
   29 U.S.C. § 157 (1976). [The National Labor Relations Act is hereinafter referred to as the NLRA or the Wagner Act.]

2. The principle that the will of the majority controls is set out in § 9(a) of the National Labor Relations Act, 29 U.S.C. § 159(a)(1976).

3. Ch. 372, 49 Stat. 449 (1935)(current version at 29 U.S.C. §§ 151-169 (1976)). The Wagner Act was amended by the Taft-Hartley Act, ch. 120, 61 Stat. 136 (1947)(current version at 29 U.S.C. §§ 141-197 (1976)). Section 9(c) was amended to provide for decertification as well as for certification of bargaining agents.

4. Such a statutory provision is one which may well be unique. In Western Europe, for instance, no country provides a statutory mechanism whereby employees can oust their union. Few countries, however, have statutory procedures akin to union certification.

5. Ch. 120, 61 Stat. 136 (1947)(current version at 29 U.S.C. §§ 141-197 (1976)).

6. Ch. 372, 49 Stat. 449 (1935), *as amended by* Labor Management Relations (Taft-Hartley) Act, ch. 120, 61 Stat. 136 (1947), *as amended by* Labor-Management Reporting and Disclosure (Landrum-Griffin) Act of 1959, Pub. L. No. 86-257, 73 Stat. 519, *as amended by* Act of July 26, 1974, Pub. L. No. 93-360, 88 Stat. 395 [hereinafter referred to as the act].

7. *See* note 13 *infra* and accompanying text. The decline is attributable in great part to the no-raiding pact among AFL-CIO affiliates. Non-AFL-CIO affiliates, such as the UAW and the Mineworkers, tend to avoid raiding other unions' members. Some Teamsters' locals continue to engage in raiding as part of their general organizing effort.

8. Hereinafter referred to as the NLRB or the Board.

9. 29 U.S.C. § 159(c)(1)(A)(ii)(1976). *See* text accompanying note 20 *infra*.

10. *Id.* § 159(c)(1)(B)(1976). *See* text accompanying note 21 *infra*.

11. Section 9(c)(3) of the Act provides:
   No election shall be directed in any bargaining unit or any subdivision within which in the preceding twelve-month period, a valid election shall have been held. Employees engaged in an economic strike who are not entitled to reinstatement shall be eligible to vote under such regulations as the Board shall find are consistent with the purposes and provisions of this subchapter in any election conducted within twelve months after the commencement of the strike. In any election where none of the choices on the ballot receives a majority, a runoff shall be conducted, the ballot providing for a selection between the two choices receiving the largest and second largest number of valid votes cast in the election.
   29 U.S.C. § 159(c)(3)(1976).

12. In December 1953, officers of the American Federation of Labor and the Congress of Industrial Organizations signed a "no-raiding" agreement which pledged their respective affiliates to refrain from organizing another union's members. The protection against raiding has been seen as the chief benefit of affiliation to the AFL-CIO. *See* A. SLOANE & F. WHITNEY, LABOR RELATIONS 144-46 (3d ed. 1977).

13. *See, e.g.*, R. Prosten, Special Analysis of 1970 NLRB Election Victories (June 23, 1976) (internal AFL-CIO memorandum from Research Director to the Executive Board of the federation's Industrial Union Department).

14. These figures were obtained from the NLRB Annual Reports for the years 1948 through 1979. 13-14 NLRB ANN. REP. (1948-1979).

15. Between 1951-1962, the average size of units was fairly stable, not falling below 65. The average has declined since 1962, with the average unit size in 1979 being 51 employees. Charles J. McDonald, Assistant to the Director, Organizing and Field Services Dep't, AFL-CIO, estimates that unions win 40% of all decertification elections in units having more than 100 employees, but only 20% of those elections involving units of less than 100 employees. *See* Cook, *Divorce Union Style*, INDUSTRY WEEK, June 25, 1979, at 38 [hereinafter referred to as Cook].

16. 44 NLRB ANN. REP. 18 (1979).

17. *See* note 3 *supra.*

18. 29 U.S.C. § 159(1976).

19. *See* note 4 *supra.*

20. 29 U.S.C. § 159(c)(1)(A)(1976).

21. *Id .*§ 159(c)(1)(B).

22. For the Senate debates, *see* II NLRB, LEGISLATIVE HISTORY OF THE LABOR MANAGEMENT RELATIONS ACT, 1947(1948)[hereinafter referred to as LEGISLATIVE HISTORY II].

23. *See, e.g., id.* at 965, 983, 990, 1066, 1077, 1496, 1523.

24. *Id.* at 1452-53.

25. *Id.* at 1606 (statement of Senator Pepper).

26. Between 1935-1947, the right of replaced economic strikers to vote was in dispute. Section 9(c)(3) of the Taft-Hartley Act denied economic strikers the right to vote in representation elections. In 1959, § 9(c)(3) was amended so that economic strikers who are not eligible for reinstatement are entitled to vote in an NLRB election for 12 months following the commencement of the strike. *See* note 11 *supra.*

27. LEGISLATIVE HISTORY II, *supra* note 22, at 1042 (statement of Senator Murray).

28. Section 9(c) of the Act provides that the Board shall direct an election upon finding that a question of representation exists. 29 U.S.C. § 159(c)(1976).

29. In 1959, § 3(b) of the Act was amended, enabling the five-member NLRB to delegate to its Regional Directors its powers under § 9 to process and decide representation cases. The Board delegated this authority in 1961. The five-member Board may, at its discretion, accept representation cases for review. If the Board refuses to review, the Regional Director's decision becomes final.

30. For a thorough discussion of the NLRB's policies, *see* R. Williams, P. Janus & K. Huhn, NLRB REGULATION OF ELECTION CONDUCT (1974). For an article dealing specifically with conduct during decertification campaigns, *see* Krupman & Rasin, *Decertification: Removing the Shroud,* 30 LAB. L.J. 231 (1979). *See also* Krislov, *Decertification Elections Increase but Remain No Major Burden to Unions,* MONTHLY LAB. REV., Nov. 1979, at 30; Anderson, Busman & O'Reilly, *What Factors Influence the Outcome of Decertification Elections,* MONTHLY LAB. REV., Nov. 1979, at 32.

31. 15 NLRB ANN. REP. 33 (1950).

32. 157 N.L.R.B. 652 (1966).

33. *Id.* at 656.

34. The question of what constitutes a good faith doubt of majority status often arises in the wider context of a charge under § 8(a)(5), 29 U.S.C. § 158(a) (5)(1976). Section 8(a)(5)makes it an unfair labor practice for an employer to refuse to bargain collectively with the representative of his employees. For a discussion of good faith doubt of majority status, *see* text accompanying notes 202-18 *infra.*

35. Alexander Mfg. Co., 120 N.L.R.B. 1056 (1958).

36. *See, e.g.,* Armco Drainage & Metal Prods., Inc., 116 N.L.R.B. 1260 (1956).

37. *See* Clyde J. Merris, 77 N.L.R.B. 1375 (1948).

38. 29 U.S.C. § 152(11)(1976).

39. *See, e.g.,* Doak Aircraft Co., 107 N.L.R.B. 924 (1954).

40. A typical case is Custom Bronze & Aluminum Corp., 197 N.L.R.B. 397 (1972), where Chairman Miller dissented from his colleagues' finding that the petition-er was a supervisor on the grounds that he was really only a leadman. *Id.* at 398-99.

41. 239 N.L.R.B. 1342 (1979).

42. *Id.* at 1346-47.

43. 235 N.L.R.B. 363 (1978), *modified,* 628 F.2d 1 (D.C. Cir. 1980)(per curiam).

44. *Id.* at 376.

45. Section 8(a)(1) of the Act provides:
It shall be an unfair labor practice for an employer . . . to interfere with, re-strain, or coerce employees in the exercise of the rights guaranteed in Section 157 of this title.
29 U.S.C. § 158(a)(1)(1976).

46. 120 N.L.R.B. 806 (1958).

47. *Id.* at 808. Such evidence is now presented by the parties to the Regional Director.

48. Modern Hard Chrome Serv. Co., 124 N.L.R.B. 1235 (1959).

49. *Compare* Bond Stores, Inc., 116 N.L.R.B. 1929 (1956) *with* Southeast Ohio Egg Producers, 116 N.L.R.B. 1076 (1956).

50. Maywood Plant of Grede Plastics, 235 N.L.R.B. 363, 376 (1978), *modified,* 628 F.2d 1 (D.C. Cir. 1980)(per curiam).

51. 195 N.L.R.B. 169 (1972).

52. *Id.* at 169.

53. 201 N.L.R.B. 1034 (1973), *enforcement denied in material part,* 494 F.2d 189 (8th Cir. 1974).

54. Petitions were filed in New York City and Detroit in late October. The Duluth unit did not file a petition until early 1971.

55. *See* text accompanying notes 227-55 *infra.*

56. 201 N.L.R.B. at 1034.

57. *Id.*

58. National Cash Register Co. v. NLRB, 494 F.2d 189, 192-93 (8th Cir. 1971).

59. *Id.* at 193.

60. *Id.*

61. W. T. Grant Co., 179 N.L.R.B. 670 (1969).

62. *See, e.g.,* Kelsey Hayes Wheel Co., 85 N.L.R.B. 666 (1949); Gabriel Steel Co., 80 N.L.R.B. 1361 (1948).

63. Campbell Soup Co., 111 N.L.R.B. 234 (1955).

64. *See* General Motors Corp., 120 N.L.R.B. 1215 (1958) and cases cited therein.

65. *See, e.g.,* Wm. T. Kirley Lumber Co., 189 N.L.R.B. 130 (1971).

66. Taylor Motors, Inc., 241 N.L.R.B. 711 (1979).

67. Goodyear Tire & Rubber Co., 130 N.L.R.B. 889 (1961); Mission Appliance Corp., 129 N.L.R.B. 1417 (1961).

68. Jos. Schlitz Brewing Co., 206 N.L.R.B. 928 (1973).

69. 191 N.L.R.B. 308 (1971).

70. *Id.* at 311. Member Brown sharply criticized the Board's decision as a departure from previous practice. *Id.* at 312-13. *See* Owens-Illinois Glass Co., 108 N.L.R.B. 947, 950 (1954), where the Board specifically held that inclusion in a multiplant unit for a period of one year was sufficient to merge the certified unit into the larger bargaining unit.

71. 227 N.L.R.B. 1932 (1977). At issue here was the IUE's coordinated bargaining approach toward Westinghouse through the IUE-Westinghouse Conference Board. *See also* General Elec. Co., 180 N.L.R.B. 1094 (1970), which dealt with the attempted decertification of a unit included in the IUE-GE Conference Board.

72. 227 N.L.R.B. at 1933.

73. Kimberly-Clark Corp., 61 N.L.R.B. 90, 92 (1945).

74. 348 U.S. 96 (1954).

75. *Id.* at 104.

76. Paragon Prods. Corp., 134 N.L.R.B. 662, 663 (1961).

77. National Sugar Ref. Co., 10 N.L.R.B. 1410 (1939).

78. Snow & Neally Co., 76 N.L.R.B. 390 (1948).

79. Keystone Coat, Apron & Towel Supply Co., 121 N.L.R.B. 880 (1958); Hershey Chocolate Corp., 121 N.L.R.B. 901 (1958); Pacific Coast Ass'n of Pulp & Paper Mfrs., 121 N.L.R.B. 990 (1958); Deluxe Metal Furniture Co., 121 N.L.R.B. 995 (1958); Appalachian Shale Prods. Co., 121 N.L.R.B. 1160 (1958); General Extrusion Co., 121 N.L.R.B. 1165 (1958).

80. *See, e.g.*, Local 1545, United Bhd. of Carpenters v. Vincent, 286 F.2d 127 (2d Cir. 1960); NLRB v. Efco Mfg., Inc., 203 F.2d 458 (1st Cir. 1953)(per curiam).

81. 121 N.L.R.B. 990 (1958).

82. In *Pacific Coast*, the Board abandoned its "substantial part of the industry" test which required it to determine in which industry the employer belonged and what was the normal length of contracts in that industry. In many cases, the answer to one or both questions was far from predictable. *Id.* at 992.

83. In General Cable Corp., 139 N.L.R.B. 1123 (1962), the Board adopted its current three-year rule. *Id.* at 1125.

84. 121 N.L.R.B. at 993-94.

85. 239 N.L.R.B. 1255 (1979).

86. *Id.* at 1256.

87. *Id.*

88. Leonard Wholesale Meats Co., 136 N.L.R.B. 1000 (1962).

89. Deluxe Metal Furniture Co., 121 N.L.R.B. 995 (1958), set the filing period at not more than 150 nor less than 60 days before the expiration of the contract.

90. Section 8(d)(1) provides:
    [W]here there is in effect a collective-bargaining contract covering employees in an industry affecting commerce, the duty to bargain collectively shall also mean that no party to such contract shall terminate or modify such contract, unless the party desiring such termination or modification—
    (1) serves a written notice upon the other party to the contract of the proposed termination or modification sixty days prior to the expiration date thereof, or in the event such contract contains no expiration date, sixty days prior to the time it is proposed to make such termination or modification . . . .
    29 U.S.C. § 158(d)(1)(1976).

91. The filing period is 120-90 days prior to contract expiration for health care employees since 90 days notice of intent to modify is required in health care units by § 8(d)(4)(A). 29 U.S.C. § 158(d)(4)(A)(1976).

92. *See, e.g.*, Telautograph Corp., 199 N.L.R.B. 892, 893 (1972).

93. 121 N.L.R.B. 1160 (1958).

94. *Id.* at 1163. The term specifically mentioned by the Board in *Appalachian Shale* was wages.

95. *Id.* at 1161.

96. *Id.* at 1162.

97. *Id.*

98. 222 N.L.R.B. 907 (1976).

99. 225 N.L.R.B. 1092 (1976).

100. *Id.* at 1092.

101. 225 N.L.R.B. 869 (1976).

102. *Id.* at 869.

103. 121 N.L.R.B. at 1162. The ratification requirement must be in writing. *Id.*

104. *See, e.g.,* Lane Constr. Corp., 222 N.L.R.B. 1224 (1976); Western Roto Engravers, Inc., 168 N.L.R.B. 986 (1967); Standard Oil Co., 119 N.L.R.B. 598 (1957).

105. 121 N.L.R.B. 1165 (1958).

106. *Id.* at 1167 (emphasis in original).

107. *Id.* at 1167-68.

108. In 1970, the Board reconsidered the impact of *General Extrusion* in successor employer cases. *See* Wm. J. Burns Int'l Detective Agency, Inc., 182 N.L.R.B. 348 (1970), *modified*, 441 F.2d 911 (2d Cir. 1971); Kota Div. of Dura Corp., 182 N.L.R.B. 360 (1970); Travelodge Corp., 182 N.L.R.B. 370 (1970); Hackney Iron & Steel Co., 182 N.L.R.B. 357 (1970).

109. 121 N.L.R.B. 901 (1958).

110. *Id.* at 911.

111. *Id.*

112. *Id.* at 911-12.

113. 193 N.L.R.B. 990 (1971).

114. *Id.* at 991.

115. *Id.*

116. *See, e.g.,* Sahara-Tahoe Corp., 229 N.L.R.B. 1094, 1109 (1977), *aff'd*, 581 F.2d 767 (9th Cir. 1978); Sierra Dev. Co., 231 N.L.R.B. 22, 24 (1977), *aff'd*, 604 F.2d 606 (9th Cir. 1979), where the union had maintained an extremely low profile, filing virtually no grievances over a 10-year period in a unit of over 10,000 employees and rarely, if ever, visiting the casinos to enforce the contract. A series of three-year contracts were signed despite this inactivity. The union may have been quiescent but the Board dismissed the suggestion that it was defunct.

117. 121 N.L.R.B. 901 (1958).

118. Herinafter referred to as the BCWIU.

119. Hereinafter referred to as the ABCWIU.

120. 121 N.L.R.B. at 906-07.

121. *Id.* at 907.

122. *Id.* at 908-09.

123. 124 N.L.R.B. 1420 (1959).

124. *Id.* at 1422-23.

125. 196 N.L.R.B. 483 (1972).

126. Hereinafter referred to as the OCAW.

127. 196 N.L.R.B. at 484.

128. *Id.*

129. 121 N.L.R.B. at 906.

130. 196 N.L.R.B. at 484.

131. *See, e.g.*, Kimco Auto Prods., Inc., 183 N.L.R.B. 993, 995 (1970). *See also* Hershey Chocolate Corp., 121 N.L.R.B. 901, 909, 911 (1958).

132. District 50 subsequently merged with the United Steelworkers of America.

133. 29 U.S.C. § 158(a)(3)(1976). Section 8(a)(3) was amended in 1947 by the Taft-Hartley Act so that employers and unions could execute a union shop agreement requiring union membership as a condition of continued employment on or after 30 days following the employee's employment. *See* G. Bloom & H. Northrup, ECONOMICS OF LABOR RELATIONS 222-24 (9th ed. 1981) for a description of the most common union security arrangements.

134. Eagle Lock Co., 88 N.L.R.B. 970 (1950).

135. 121 N.L.R.B. 880 (1958).

136. 365 U.S. 695 (1961).

137. *Id.* at 699-700.

138. 134 N.L.R.B. 662 (1961).

139. *Id.* at 666.

140. *Id.*

141. *Id.* at 667.

142. 231 N.L.R.B. 552 (1977).

143. *Id.* at 553.

144. *Id.* The Board's final consideration was whether the clause in the contract was lawful on its face. The Board found the clause lawful since it gave employees a statutory 30-day grace period to become union members. Accordingly, it found that an election was barred. *Id.*

145. *See, e.g.*, Standard Molding Corp., 137 N.L.R.B. 1515 (1962), and cases cited therein.

146. National Seal Div. of Federal-Mogul Corp., 176 N.L.R.B. 619 (1969).

147. *Id.* at 619.

148. Pine Transp., Inc., 197 N.L.R.B. 256 (1972).

149. Peabody Coal Co., 197 N.L.R.B. 1231 (1972).

150. Pioneer Bus Co., 140 N.L.R.B. 54 (1962).

151. Food Haulers, Inc., 136 N.L.R.B. 394 (1962).

152. *See, e.g.,* Loree Footwear Corp., 197 N.L.R.B. 360, 360 (1972), where it was asserted that the contract was no bar to an election because the union had breached its duty of fair representation. Because the contract was lawful on its face and because of the Board's policy of not permitting extrinsic evidence to be introduced at the hearing on a decertification petition, the Board held that the contract did serve as a bar to an election.

153. *See* NLRB v. Big Three Indus., Inc., 497 F.2d 43, 52 (5th Cir. 1974).

154. 348 U.S. 96 (1954).

155. The Court cited defunctness and schism as examples of unusual circumstances. *Id.* at 98.

156. *Id.* at 104.

157. The Board had taken the position as early as 1939 that a union should have a reasonable period in which to carry out its mandate. *See* Whittier Mills Co., 15 N.L.R.B. 457, 463 (1939), *enforced,* 111 F.2d 474 (5th Cir. 1940)(seven months). For the formalization of the one-year rule, *see* Thompson Prods., Inc., 47 N.L.R.B. 619, 621 (1943).

158. 348 U.S. at 99.

159. *Id.* at 100.

160. 136 N.L.R.B. 785 (1962).

161. The company's statement was probably factually accurate since the composition of the work force had changed substantially.

162. 136 N.L.R.B. at 787.

163. Particularly destructive of the union's support may be the substantial length of time which can elapse between the filing of the unfair labor practice charge and the handing down of a decision by a federal court of appeals enforcing the Board's order. *See, e.g.,* Bishop v. NLRB, 502 F.2d 1024 (5th Cir. 1974), where five years had passed without the unfair labor practice charge being resolved.

164. There is no empirical data on the efficacy of Board orders extending the certification year. Labor relations practitioners on both sides pinpoint as the most common factor motivating decertification the members' perception that the union is ineffective at the bargaining table. Cook, *supra* note 15, at 38.

165. NLRB v. Big Three Indus., Inc., 497 F.2d 43, 51-52 (5th Cir. 1974)(citations omitted).

166. *Id.* at 45. For example, the employer had threatened to shut down the plant, had dismissed a union activist, had told employees they would get nothing more and had taunted employees to go on strike. *Id.*

167. UAW v. Russell, 356 U.S. 634, 643 (1958).

168. Although the punitive/remedial terminology is less than clear conceptually, a punitive order is one where there is a "patent attempt to achieve ends other than those which can fairly be said to effectuate the policies of the Act." Virginia Elec. & Power Co. v. NLRB, 319 U.S. 533, 540 (1943).

169. 389 F.2d 71 (7th Cir. 1968).

170. *Id.* at 75. There had never been a hearing on the unfair labor practice charge and no evidence relating to it was offered at the hearing on the decertification petition.

171. *See* Downey, *The Mar-Jac Rule Governing the Certification Year*, 29 LAB. L.J. 608 (1978).

172. Jack L. Williams, D.D.S., 231 N.L.R.B. 845 (1977).

173. Jack L. Williams, D.D.S. (Empire Dental Co.), 211 N.L.R.B. 860 (1974).

174. The Regional Director considered whether the principles of Keller Plastics Eastern, Inc., 157 N.L.R.B. 583 (1966) were applicable. *See* text accompanying notes 182-83 *infra*.

175. 231 N.L.R.B. at 847.

176. 321 U.S. 702 (1944).

177. *See* text accompanying notes 227-55 *infra*.

178. The union had gained a card majority in June 1941. The Board's decision was handed down in October 1942. The high turnover stemmed mainly from the mobilization following America's entry into World War II. Franks Bros. Co., 44 N.L.R.B. 898 (1942).

179. 321 U.S. at 705.

180. *Id.*

181. *See* Keller Plastics Eastern, Inc., 157 N.L.R.B. 583, 586 (1966).

182. 157 N.L.R.B. 583 (1966).

183. *Id.* at 587.

184. NLRB v. Montgomery Ward & Co., 399 F.2d 409 (7th Cir. 1968).

185. The court did note that, unlike the situation in *Franks*, there were no employer unfair labor practices in *Montgomery Ward* which contributed to the union's loss of majority. The court, however, found persuasive the Supreme Court's reasoning in Brooks v. NLRB, 348 U.S. 96 (1954), supporting an enforced year of bargaining. 399 F.2d at 411-12.

186. *Id.* at 412-13.

187. *Id.* at 412.

188. *Id.* It can be seriously argued that it is unrealistic to expect employees, on their own, to challenge the employer's voluntary recognition of a union.

189. In Jack L. Williams, D.D.S., 231 N.L.R.B. 845 (1977), after the dental laboratory reopened, the employer voluntarily recognized the union for the purpose of representing the unit employees, most of whom were new, without any showing of majority. The Board upheld the Regional Director's refusal to apply *Keller Plastics. Id.* at 846.

190. Poole Foundry & Machine Co., 95 N.L.R.B. 34, 36 (1951).

191. 192 F.2d 740 (4th Cir. 1951), *cert. denied*, 342 U.S. 954 (1952).

192. *Id.* at 743.

193. *See, e.g.,* Foster & Foster, Inc., 240 N.L.R.B. 955 (1979).

194. 473 F.2d 374 (5th Cir. 1973).

195. *Id.* at 385.

196. Terrell Machine Co. v. NLRB, 427 F.2d 1088, 1090 (4th Cir.), *cert. denied,* 398 U.S.929 (1970).

197. *See* text accompanying notes 153-93 *supra.*

198. Sierra Dev. Co., 231 N.L.R.B. 22, 23 (1977); Terrell Machine Co., 173 N.L.R.B. 1480, 1481 (1969), *enforced,* 427 F.2d 1088 (4th Cir.), *cert. denied,* 398 U.S. 929 (1970).

199. Firestone Synthetic Rubber & Latex Co., 173 N.L.R.B. 1179, 1180 (1968); Celanese Corp. of America, 95 N.L.R.B. 664, 673 (1951).

200. *See* notes 81-92 *supra* and accompanying text. Since a union seeking to modify the contract is statutorily required to give the employer 60 days advance notice of this fact, a union often sends a letter to the employer in the period 90-60 days before contract expiration. This same period of time is the open period for the filing of decertification petitions. As such, an employer who is aware that a decertification campaign is afoot may receive the union's letter before he is certain that a decertification petition will be filed or before the NLRB's regional office notifies him that a petition has been filed. *See* Telautograph Corp., 199 N.L.R.B. 892 (1972).

201. For a discussion of the circumstances where the filing of a charge under § 8(a)(5) will not block a decertification election, *see* notes 222-26 *infra* and accompanying text. For a more typical case, *see* Stresskin Prods. Co., 197 N.L.R.B. 1175 (1972).

202. Celanese Corp. of America, 95 N.L.R.B. 664, 673 (1951).

203. *Id.* at 673.

204. *Id.*

205. Firestone Synthetic Rubber & Latex Co., 173 N.L.R.B. 1179, 1180 (1968). The Board's determinations in this area are accorded great deference. *See* NLRB v. Gulfmont Hotel Co., 362 F.2d 588 (5th Cir. 1966).

206. Sierra Dev. Co., 231 N.L.R.B. 22, 24 (1977). *But see* Stresskin Prods. Co., 197 N.L.R.B. 1175 (1972).

207. 184 N.L.R.B. 640 (1970).

208. In *Massey-Ferguson,* the employer had unilaterally implemented a wage increase after reaching impasse which was better than its last offer to the union, thereby violating § 8(a)(5). Thus, the employer's doubt did not arise in a context free of unfair labor practices. The Board did not consider separately the issue of whether the doubt was based on objective considerations. *Id.* at 641.

209. *Id.* This presumption was applied in a case where there was 100% turnover in the unit and the size of the unit had doubled. King Radio Corp., 208 N.L.R.B. 578, 581-83 (1974), *enforced,* 510 F.2d 1154 (10th Cir. 1975). *See also* Strange & Lindsey Beverages, Inc., 219 N.L.R.B. 1200, 1201 (1975).

210. 184 N.L.R.B. at 641.

211. 197 N.L.R.B. 1175 (1972).

212. *Id.* at 1180. About 400 employees were in the unit. Nowhere was it contended that a majority of those employees spoke individually with a supervisor.

213. *See, e.g.,* Sierra Dev. Co., 231 N.L.R.B. 22, 24 (1977).

214. Celanese Corp. of America, 95 N.L.R.B. 664, 674 (1951).

215. Sierra Dev. Co., 231 N.L.R.B. 22 (1977), *aff'd,* 604 F.2d 606 (9th Cir. 1979); Sahara-Tahoe Corp., 229 N.L.R.B. 1094 (1977), *aff'd,* 581 F.2d 767 (9th Cir. 1978); Carda Motels, Inc., 228 N.L.R.B. 926 (1977); Barney's Club, Inc., 227 N.L.R.B. 414 (1976), *modified,* 623 F.2d 571 (9th Cir. 1980); Nevada Lodge, 227 N.L.R.B. 368 (1976), *aff'd,* 584 F.2d 293 (9th Cir. 1978); Tahoe Nugget, Inc., 227 N.L.R.B. 357 (1976), *aff'd,* 584 F.2d 293 (9th Cir. 1978).

216. Tahoe Nugget, Inc., 227 N.L.R.B. 357, 360 (1976), *aff'd,* 584 F.2d 293 (9th Cir. 1978). The local union had approximately 900-1000 members out of a possible 10,000 at that time. Sahara-Tahoe Corp., 229 N.L.R.B. 1094, 1109 (1977), *aff'd,* 581 F.2d 767 (9th Cir. 1978).

217. The local union had been placed in trusteeship by the international union. The trustee stated that the local's membership had increased from 900 to 1800 since the campaign began and estimated a 20% unionized rate. 229 N.L.R.B. at 1109.

218. Sierra Dev. Co., 231 N.L.R.B. 22, 23-24 (1977), *aff'd,* 604 F.2d 606 (9th Cir. 1979).

219. Massey-Ferguson, Inc. 184 N.L.R.B. 640 (1970).

220. *See, e.g.,* Firestone Synthetic Rubber & Latex Co. 173 N.L.R.B. 1179 (1968), where the employer refused to bargain after a decertification petition was filed but before the Regional Director determined that a question of representation existed. The employer was able to establish that it possessed a good faith doubt as to the union's majority status. *Id.* at 1180.

221. This assumes that no employer unfair labor practices have contributed to the undermining of the union's status. If this is the case, such a decertification petition clearly indicates that the union has lost its majority status and an employer relying on such a petition would be basing his refusal to bargain on objective considerations.

222. 199 N.L.R.B. 892 (1972).

223. The employer and the union had a longstanding collective bargaining relationship covering a unit of 11 employees. The employer did not assert that it had possessed any doubts prior to the filing of the petition. *Id.* at 893.

224. *Id.*

225. *Id.* at 894.

226. *Id.* at 892.

227. The blocking charge rule was first applied in United States Coal & Coke Co., 3 N.L.R.B. 398 (1937).

228. *See* text accompanying note 165 *supra. See also* Newport News Shipbldg. & Dry Dock Co. v. NLRB, 631 F.2d 263 (4th Cir. 1980).

229. Bishop v. NLRB, 502 F.2d 1024, 1029 (5th Cir. 1974).

230. *See id.* and cases cited therein.

231. R. GORMAN, BASIC TEXT ON LABOR LAW 59-65 (1976).

232. Section 10(f) provides in pertinent part:
Any person aggrieved by a final order of the Board granting or denying in whole or in part the relief sought may obtain a review of such order in any United States court of appeals in the circuit wherein the unfair labor practice in question was alleged to have been engaged in or wherein such person resides or transacts business, or in the United States Court of Appeals for the District of Columbia, by filing in such a court a written petition praying that the order of the Board be modified or set aside.
29 U.S.C. § 160(f)(1976).

233. 358 U.S. 184 (1958).

234. 444 F.2d 1064 (5th Cir. 1971).

235. The union filed charges in 1964. In early 1966, the Board found that the employer had violated §§ 8(a)(1) and 8(a)(5), and ordered reinstatement of the unfair labor practice strikers. Dixie Color Printing Corp., 156 N.L.R.B. 143 (1966). In 1966, the Board's order was enforced. Dixie Color Printing Corp. v. NLRB, 371 F.2d 347 (D.C. Cir. 1966). Bargaining ceased in October 1967 when impasse was reached. 444 F.2d at 1066. In January 1968, an employee decertification petition was filed. *Id.* Later in the year, both the Board and the union went back to the District of Columbia Circuit seeking a contempt citation. This was still pending in 1971. *Id.*

236. *Id.* at 1069.

237. *Id.* at 1070.

238. Section 9(c)(1) provides in pertinent part:
[W]henever a petition shall have been filed, . . . the Board *shall* investigate such petition.
29 U.S.C. § 159(c)(1)(1976)(emphasis added).

239. 444 F.2d at 1070.

240. For instance, the court observed that it was "unlikely that there are past unfair labor practices which have a present impact upon the fair and free choice of bargaining representatives by the employees." *Id.* The court's observations are problematical since in the seven years since the original unfair labor practice charge, no contract had ever been concluded and 17 strikers had not yet been reinstated. In addition, the contempt citation was still pending.

241. 463 F.2d 378 (5th Cir. 1972).

242. *Id.* at 381.

243. *Id.*

244. 502 F.2d 1024 (5th Cir. 1974).

245. The Fifth Circuit noted that the employer was "no stranger to this Court in unfair labor practice proceedings." *Id.* at 1025 n.1 (listing five such cases involving the employer).

246. *Id.* at 1026 n.2. The court commented that the matter seemed moot since the Board had "processed" the petition by virtue of affirming the Regional Director's determination that no real question of representation existed. The Fifth Circuit

rendered a decision in the case in order not to add its "mite to this intolerable delay." *Id.* at 1027 n.2.

247. *Id.* at 1027.

248. *Id.* at 1031.

249. *Id.* at 1029.

250. 96 L.R.R.M. 3016 (N.D. Okla. 1977).

251. The charge alleged that the employer refused the union access to the plant in 1973, and that there were some unilateral job classifications and merit increases during this period. *Id.* at 3021.

252. The contract was made retroactive to November 1975. *Id.* at 3022.

253. *Id.* at 3021-23.

254. *Id.* at 3021.

255. *Id.* at 3022. *See also* NLRB v. Minute Maid Corp., 283 F.2d 705, 710 (5th Cir. 1960).

256. Krupman & Rasin, *Decertification: Removing the Shroud*, 30 LAB. L.J. 231, 231 n.1 (1979). *See also Oversight Hearings Before the Subcomm. on Labor-Management Relations of the House Comm. on Education and Labor*, 96th Cong., 1st Sess. 45, 51, 315 (1979) [hereinafter cited as *Oversight Hearings*]. *See, e.g.*, statement of Robert A. Georgine, President, AFL-CIO Building & Construction Trades Dep't before the Subcommittee. *Id.* at 410-19.

257. Remarks of Thomas Donahue, Executive Assistant to AFL-CIO President George Meany, before the convention of the Louisiana AFL-CIO, Mar. 20, 1979. DAILY LAB. REP. (BNA), MAR. 20, 1979, AT E1-2.

258. *See, e.g.*, Raskin, *Big Labor Strives to Break Out of Its Rut*, FORTUNE, Aug. 27, 1979, at 32-40. *See also Oversight Hearings, supra* note 256, at 246, for a report of a labor consultant's specific recommendations on how companies can achieve and maintain nonunion status.

259. LEGISLATIVE HISTORY II, *supra* note 22, at 1606. At that time, the only statutory limitation on the immediate holding of the decertification election would have been if an election had been held in the same unit within the preceding year.

260. In 1959, § 9(c)(3) of the Taft-Hartley Act was amended so that economic strikers who are not eligible for reinstatement are nevertheless entitled to vote in an NLRB election for 12 months following the commencement of the strike.

261. Typically, the employer is able to hire persons who are willing and able to permanently replace the strikers. Now that an increasing number of plants can be operated, if not at full capacity at least near full capacity, by non-exempt, non-unit personnel, the employer may be given time at the beginning of a strike to consider hiring replacements.

262. *See, e.g., Coors Undercuts Its Last Big Union*, BUSINESS WEEK, July 24, 1978, at 47-48. *See also* Cook, *supra* note 15, at 38.

263. *Id.*

264. Whether an employer wishes to capitalize on this vulnerability is a strategic question. An employer who is aware of the union's weakness may not welcome decertification if another, more aggressive union is actively organizing in the

area. It cannot be denied, however, that some labor consultants view bargaining to impasse as a "prelude to union ouster." *See Oversight Hearings, supra* note 256, at 32 (statement of Alan Kistler, Director of the AFL-CIO's Dep't of Organization and Field Services). *See also Unions: Turning Them Out*, THE SOUTH MAGAZINE, Nov. 19, 1979, at 40, for the advice of a management labor lawyer.

265. NLRB v. Big Three Indus., Inc., 497 F.2d 43, 47 (5th Cir. 1974).

266. *See, e.g.*, Murphy, *Impasse and the Duty to Bargain in Good Faith*, 39 U. PITT. L. REV. 1, 11 (1977).

267. 173 N.L.R.B. 1179 (1968).

268. The union demanded that there be no reprisals and no layoffs. The company responded that it would not take back anyone who had engaged in violence. Management also noted that as a result of a nationwide strike against Firestone Tire Company, demand for their product was reduced; therefore, not everyone on strike would be recalled immediately. *Id.*

269. The company calculated that 202 employees in a unit of 365 no longer supported the union. (Of 120 employees who had spoken with supervisory personnel, only 30 had signed the decertification petition containing 112 signatures.) In addition, 70 strikers had returned to work. *Id.* at 1179-80.

270. The company took the position that on May 6th, impasse had been reached on the wage issue. The Board agreed. *Id.* at 1180.

271. This was done after notice to the employees. The employer had informed the strikers of such a possibility as early as February.) *Id.* at 1179.

272. *Id.* at 1180.

273. *Id.*

274. *See, e.g.*, Stresskin Prods. Co., 197 N.L.R.B. 1175 (1972), where the union was certified on September 29, 1969. When the employee decertification petition was filed in October 1970, the parties were still bargaining on the first contract. *Id.* at 1175-76.

275. Hamil v. Youngblood, 96 L.R.R.M. 3016, 3023 (N.D. Okla. 1977). The court in *Hamil* was referring to the validity of applying the blocking charge rule when the conduct complained of had occurred three years earlier. The unfair labor practice case had not yet been closed.

276. NLRB v. Big Three Indus., Inc., 497 F.2d 43, 52 (5th Cir. 1974). In this case, the employer challenged the NLRB's bargaining order and extension of the certification year as a means of remedying the § 8(a)(5) violation. *See* text accompanying note 164 *supra*.

277. Unions charge that some employers deliberately offer unacceptable terms during bargaining as part of a strategy to force the union to go out on strike. Having already planned to operate during the strike, the employer suffers minimally from the strike while inflicting serious damage on the union. *See* AFL-CIO NATIONAL ORGANIZING COORDINATING COMMITTEE, 21 REPORT ON UNION BUSTERS 3 (Oct. 1980).

278. *See, e.g., Taking Aim at "Union-Busters,"* BUSINESS WEEK, Nov. 12, 1979, at 98, 102 for a report on tactics advocated by some labor consultants.

PART IV

B. Public Sector

365-86

832²
V.S.

[1979]

Teacher Bargaining:
The Experience in Nine Systems[*]

Charles R. Perry[†]

The past decade has produced a staggering abundance of scholarly literature on the process and results of collective bargaining in the public sector. That literature is as diverse as it is abundant, encompassing "theoretical" works on the basic nature of bargaining relationships,[1] empirical studies of the character of bargaining outcomes,[2] and efforts to relate the two through analyses of determinants of bargaining outcomes.[3] Relatively little attention, however, has been given to the way in which bargaining relationships develop over time or to the institutional and economic forces that shape the evolution of those relationships.[4] This study endeavors to fill that gap through a longitudinal analysis of bargaining processes and results in nine public school systems of widely varying size and circumstance. All of these systems were engaged in hard bargaining with teacher unions by 1965, when they were the subject of an earlier study of bargaining in public schools,[5] and all have continued to engage in bargaining with teachers since then.

An intensive analysis of bargaining process and results can only be undertaken in a limited sample of relationships. The virtue of such a sample rests in the detailed information that can be obtained. The obvious weakness in this approach rests in the problem of generalizing any findings, particularly if there is substantial diversity in experience within the sample. At this point in the development of the literature on collective bargaining in the public sector and in public education, there is a need for institutional detail to test more global theories and generalizations. To meet this need, nine systems were chosen from among the larger set of twenty-four studied in 1965, which had then been selected on the basis of size of the system, character of the community, and evidence of teacher militancy at an early stage in the evolution of bargaining.

---

[*] Reprinted with permission from *Industrial and Labor Relations Review,* Vol. 33, No. 1 (October 1979). © 1979 by Cornell University.
[†] Charles R. Perry is Associate Professor of Management and Industrial Relations and Senior Faculty Research Associate in the Industrial Research Unit of The Wharton School, University of Pennsylvania. This study was conducted under a grant from the Pew Memorial Trust as part of its support of the Labor Relations and Public Policy Series of the Unit.

The sample of nine systems used in this study encompasses a diverse cross-section of school districts. Two of the systems are large urban districts, two are much smaller urban districts, two are suburban systems of varying size, and three are essentially rural systems, again, of varying size. The systems are also diverse with respect to their operating structure and fiscal condition. (These characteristics are summarized in Table 1.)

In each of the nine systems, school or union officials or both were interviewed at length and asked to describe the character and course of their bargaining relationships since the conclusion of their 1965 negotiations. In addition, interviewees were asked a series of specific questions regarding such matters as: (1) the relationship of bargaining to the budget cycle; (2) the role played by the press and the public in the bargaining process; (3) the issues that have been the most significant source of conflict in bargaining; (4) the incidence of full-scale impasses in negotiations (those resulting in a strike, strike threat, or recourse to some procedure other than mediation); and (5) the response of the public in general, and of public officials, in impasse situations. Finally, interviewees were asked to evaluate the impact of bargaining in three general areas: (1) teacher compensation; (2) teacher work loads; and (3) administrative procedure and educational policy.

The descriptive information gained through interviews was augmented by contractual and budgetary data for each of the systems. In all cases, interviewees were asked to provide copies of each contract covering the classroom bargaining unit beginning with the 1967-68 school year. In some situations, copies of all contracts could not be provided, but it was possible in all to secure at least copies of the 1967-68 and 1977-78 contracts, plus copies of the salary schedules for all the intervening years. In addition, copies of the system budget or audit report were obtained to provide data on expenditures, enrollment, and employment over the 1967-77 period.

Bargaining Relationships

It is difficult, if not dangerous, to draw conclusions from a study of only nine bargaining relationships in public education, but two conclusions appear to be justified by the experience of the systems studied. First, collective bargaining relationships in public education, as in the private sector, have become incredibly diverse in almost every respect. Second, collective bargaining relationships in public education, as in the private sector, have matured quite rapidly, judged by the acceptance of the legitimacy of bilateral decision making.

TABLE 1

Characteristics of the Systems Studied

System	Type	Population	Fiscal Control	Pupil/ Teacher Ratio in 1977	Expenditure/ Pupil 1977	Percentage Change from 1967-1977		
						Teachers	Pupils	Budget
1	Urban	2,000,000	Dependent	17.4	2400	-13	-10	+190
2	Urban	1,500,000	Independent	23.8	1460	-9	-14	+90
3	Suburban	200,000	Independent	21.2	1370	+22	+30	+180
4	Suburban	50,000	Dependent	19.8	1700	+5	-7	+108
5	Urban	80,000	Dependent	16.5	1400	+24	-5	+165
6	Urban	70,000	Independent	16.8	1890	0	-10	+138
7	Rural	50,000	Dependent	21.7	1540	+10	+20	+200
8	Rural	40,000	Dependent	18.0	1850	+20	+3	+250
9	Rural	25,000	Independent	20.3	1310	+48	+44	+270

Source: Data supplied by the school systems.

The most striking characteristic of this set of bargaining relationships was its diversity in terms of procedure and process. In most of the systems, management was represented in negotiations by the administration; in two of the systems, however, board members continued to play a leading, or at least active, role in negotiations. Most systems operated with relatively compressed timetables to conclude an agreement, but two scheduled regular weekly negotiation sessions throughout the school year as the basis for bargaining. Most used closed negotiation sessions, but some opened bargaining sessions formally or informally to the press; and one system conducted negotiations entirely through bargaining sessions open to both the press and the general public.

The tone of individual relationships varied almost as much as their procedures. In all of the relationships, however, "institutional" issues of principle and control had given way to more pragmatic questions of power and money as those relationships matured. Notably absent were serious vestiges of the basic institutional conflict over "lay vs. professional" control that had characterized these same relationships in the early 1960s. Also absent were the questions of personal and institutional integrity that had been associated with early impasses in many of these systems.

Basic questions of money and power have not been easily resolved in any of the nine systems. Many reported repeated recourse to mediation in their negotiations over the period. All acknowledged that they had been close to the point of a formal impasse in one or more of their negotiations between 1967 and 1977, but only five of the nine systems had actually reached that point. (See Table 2.) The overall conflict record of these nine systems suggests two interesting patterns: (1) overt conflict has been concentrated in larger, urban systems, and (2) overt conflict intensified in the early 1970s. The explanation for these cross-sectional and longitudinal conflict patterns must be sought in the basic constraints on the parties to these public sector bargaining relationships. Those constraints can be placed in three overlapping categories— political, economic, and institutional.

Political Constraints

The existence of political constraints on bargaining relationships is difficult to deny, but the character, strength, and mode of operation of such constraints are equally difficult to pinpoint. The clearest manifestation of such constraints would be the emergence of true "multilateral" bargaining in which community groups seek and receive full and independent participation rights in the bargaining process.[6] The existence and operation of such constraints can also be inferred from efforts by either or both protagonists to appeal directly to the public for its support on substantive conflict issues.

The experience in the nine systems over the past decade provides little concrete evidence of an emerging system of explicit political or public constraints on the bargaining process, particularly short of a strike. In most cases, both parties expressed the view that the community was not actively interested in what went on in negotiations either procedurally or substantively. Few of the protagonists reported any serious efforts to enlist the support of community groups in the negotiation context on a regular basis. As a result, collective bargaining in most systems was a remarkably private and apolitical process.

The most significant exceptions to this apolitical rule were the two large urban systems, in which bargaining did become highly politicized in the early 1970s. In both cases, there was evidence of conscious efforts by both sides to frame and publicize conflict issues in such a way as to enlist the support of specific interest groups, both in anticipation of and in reaction to an impasse and a strike. In both cases, management took the initiative in such action, an initiative that has since been repeated in one of the systems with the same result—a strike. The success of all three of these management initiatives is open to serious question.

TABLE 2

The Bargaining Record of the Nine Systems

System	First Impasse	1967	1968	1969	1970	1971	1972	1973	1974	1975	1976	1977
1	—	—	Strike Threat	—	Strike Threat	—	Strike	—	—	—	X	—
2	—	Strike	—	X	—	X	—	Strike	X	X	—	X
3	1965	X	—	—	Strike	Strike	—	Strike	—	X	X	—
4	1965	X	X	X	X	X	X	—	X	—	X	—
5	1965	X	X	Strike Threat	X	X	X	Strike	—	Strike	X	—
6	1965	X	Strike Threat	X	Strike	X	—	X	X	—	X	—
7	1965	X	X	X	X	X	X	X	X	Near Impasse	—	X
8	1964	X	X	X	X	Near Impasse	X	X	X	X	X	X
9	1965	X	X	X	X	X	X	X	—	X	—	Near Impasse

X = Agreement reached without recourse to a strike, strike threat, or some dispute-resolution procedure other than mediation.

— = No negotiation held that year (multiyear contract).

The only evidence of community pressure for multilateral bargaining appeared in these two urban systems and then only in the context of a strike. In both cases, more militant and radical community groups attempted to gain hearings in the bargaining process; in both cases, they failed. In one case, a "radical" group in the form of a "parents' union," which emerged as a result of a strike, sued to overturn the resulting contract and, in the subsequent set of negotiations, published a formal position paper on substantive issues. The suit was dismissed and the paper largely ignored by all concerned, including the press. Interestingly, in this same system, "responsible" community groups, such as the PTA or established civic groups with a special interest in education, had been invited to sit in on negotiations at one point, but had quickly lost interest in light of the time required. In the second system, a similar group attempted to gain a formal role in negotiations on two separate occasions, but was rebuffed by the union. The union did, however, agree to meet outside negotiations with the group in the first instance but not the second.

Outside the major urban systems, there was almost no management or union activity intended to involve the community in bargaining, except through a strike. A few of the systems did maintain active community-public relations programs, but in all cases those programs were directed toward building or sustaining favorable attitudes toward the system generally, not merely in the bargaining context. There were a few isolated cases of community relations efforts by teacher organizations, but those, too, were not designed or used to seek strategic advantage in bargaining. Even in strike situations, public relations efforts were remarkably limited. Only one Board of Education went so far as to hold a series of public board meetings at various schools across the community during one of its strikes.

Outside of the major urban systems the level of community interest in participation in or understanding of decisions reached through bargaining appeared to be surprisingly limited, even in the smaller rural communities. In one such system in which the press was welcome at all negotiation sessions, the only sessions that were attended regularly were those at which money issues were to be discussed, and even those sessions were not reported in any detail. Similar reports of the extent of press interest were made by interviewees in most of these systems. The system with totally open negotiations reported that public attendance and participation were extremely limited, to the point of making "off-the-record" meetings unnecessary. It was clear, however, that neither party encouraged public attendance and that both parties were capable of being deliberately "oblique" in any discussions of issues on which they perceived that the public was and should be kept "vague."

The absence of evidence of the emergence of growing community interest or participation in decision making through bargaining does not mean that political constraints do not exist or are not significant. It does suggest, however, that such constraints operate primarily through normal political channels. Thus, bargaining in public education, as in the private sector, is a bilateral process of decision making. The primary difference between the two sectors is the potential diffuseness of constituent expectations and control on the management side, which can create both opportunities and problems for unions in the bargaining process. Thus far, unions in most of these nine systems have not actively sought to exploit their opportunities, except at the point of impasse, nor have managements sought consciously to negate those opportunities. It may well be that both sides gain from the flexibility accorded them by an "uncommitted" community that leaves open the possibility of a non-zero-sum bargain for a management and union that share a common interest in the "educational system."

Fiscal Constraints

The budgetary resources available to a public school system in the short run constitute the most significant potential constraint on the decisions reached in collective bargaining, particularly since education is a highly labor-intensive industry. The existence of such fiscal constraint, in theory, is difficult to dispute. The practical clarity and stringency of such constraint, however, has been seriously debated. At the core of this debate is the question of whether available resources determine bargaining outcomes or whether bargaining outcomes determine available resources.

The budgetary cycle, itself, imposes a form of potential discipline on the bargaining process. That discipline played a prominent role in the early stages of bargaining in virtually all of the nine systems in two ways: (1) management often was reluctant to move on basic economic issues until it had a clear picture of what its revenues were likely to be and (2) management often was forced to hold the line once it had such a picture of its resources. The same is true today, but to a far less significant extent. The integration of bargaining and budgetary cycles has become far more a matter of convenience than principle with management, although a number of smaller systems have resisted multiyear contracts that involve a clear break in the bargain-budget link. Smaller systems generally maintained stronger budget-bargain links over the period—in terms of timing of settlements, one-year contracts, and avoidance of a cost-of-living allowance (COLA)—than did their larger counterparts in the sample.

Decisions in bargaining necessarily continue to be made with far less than perfect knowledge of the resources available to finance the costs of even a one-year agreement, due to uncertainty over such matters as state-aid formulas, appropriations from local fiscal authorities (in the case of dependent districts), and the outcome of millage (taxing-authority) referenda (in independent districts). Despite such uncertainty, it was clear that management generally approached negotiations with some concept of the total package it could afford to accept, based on estimates of probable revenues and expenditures in the coming year or years. The fact that such estimates could only be highly tentative at the outset of negotiations provided the basis for some flexibility. Problems tended to arise when this flexibility disappeared as budget deadlines approached and passed, making it increasingly clear that further compromise might require either deficit financing, either then or in the immediate future, or an internal reallocation of resources.

The original study revealed that many school managements were willing to accept one or both of these alternatives to resolve an impasse at the time of their first impasse in the mid-1960s, despite the economic or educational risks involved. For the most part, those risks turned out to be minimal at the early stage, given the ability of most

systems to pass on the costs of settlements to the community or to local or state government in the short run. Subsequent experience in
these nine systems suggests little change in this basic predisposition
of management until or unless an actual or imminent budget crisis
makes risk-avoidance imperative. Thus, much of the intensified
overt conflict in the nine systems in the early 1970s was the product of
short-run budget crises rather than emerging managerial concern
over the long-run fiscal stability of the system.

None of the nine systems faced particularly stringent fiscal constraints during the latter part of the 1960s. All experienced growing
enrollments and employment and were the beneficiaries of growing
real revenues. In this context, overt conflict was limited and relatively easily resolved in all the systems. Four of the nine did, however,
experience impasses in this period; but none of these impasses resulted in long or serious strikes. In all cases, the disputes were
perceived by the parties, and particularly by the unions involved, as
having been necessary to pave the way politically to "free-up" some
available resources for the school system or the salary bargain. In
all cases, the impasse appeared to have served this purpose very
effectively.

The three rural systems have continued to operate without serious
fiscal constraints since 1970 and have continued to be successful in
concluding agreements without overt conflict. The roots of this success rest in both the ability of school management to neutralize
community pressure for fiscal restraint and its willingness to share
the fruits of its efforts with teachers. Managements in these systems
have been able to offset pressure for fiscal restraint by building
strong political support for the public schools through extensive community relations and services programs, close cooperative relationships with the local fiscal authority, and, where necessary, active
bargaining with the community through real or threatened curtail-
ments in services—most notably athletics and extracurricular activities. Managements in these systems generally have not sought to
impose more stringent limits in negotiations than they themselves
are subject to in dealing with the community. In two of these systems,
however, management recently has attempted to impose such limits
in negotiations—in one case on the issue of resistance to the introduction of COLA and in one case on the issue of fringe benefit cost
containment. In both cases, the result was a near impasse and substantial managerial withdrawal from its initiative.

The six remaining systems did not fare as well after 1970 as the
three rural systems. Two of the three fiscally independent systems
experienced an absolute drop in local tax support as a result of fail-

ures of millage issues in the early 1970s and the third experienced a relative decline in the real rate of growth of such support as its tax base ceased to grow. The three fiscally dependent systems experienced similarly adverse circumstances in the form of budget cuts or limits imposed by local fiscal authorities. As a result, management in all six systems felt compelled to impose stringent limits in negotiations, which led to strikes in five of the six cases. These strikes were generally both prolonged and bitter, which is not surprising in that they marked a transition from what was described as the "easy affluence" of the 1960s to the "hard reality" of the 1970s. This transition was not easy and may not yet have been completed in all of the systems, for the following reason. The credibility or legitimacy of fiscal constraints is still open to question in the minds of teachers in at least three of the systems—those in which such constraints stem from seemingly arbitrary limits on the growth rate of local tax support imposed by the allocational decisions of either city or system management in the budgetary process. Thus far, teachers have been reasonably successful in challenging such "arbitrary" allocational decisions where they are internally imposed by managerial reluctance to reallocate resources or to seek additional resources, but not where they are externally imposed by a city government or similar outside agency.

Institutional Constraints

The basic strategies of the parties, and particularly teacher organizations, in these nine systems in dealing with impasses in negotiations have changed markedly. At the early stage, considerable emphasis and faith were placed on factfinding, a process that worked reasonably well in a number of cases. Over time, however, the emphasis on, faith in, and effectiveness of factfinding have waned rapidly and dramatically, and the parties have turned to the strike and related activities as the basis for impasse resolution.[7] This phenomenon was evident even in "non-impasse" systems (those four systems in which no full-scale open impasse occurred). In those systems, those unions confronting a possible impasse have considered such activities as picketing of schools and board offices in nonschool hours, distribution of literature, and one-day protest strikes or sickouts rather than factfinding or arbitration.

The growing emphasis on the strike model does not mean that impasse procedures have not proved helpful in isolated cases. Mediation was relied on heavily in a few systems. In two systems ad hoc interest arbitration was used to resolve issues of implementation that threatened to renew or prolong a strike. In a third system, the parties faced with the possibility of their second prolonged strike in two years were able to accept factfinding and to agree to abide by the recommendations of the factfinder before the fact.

The reaction of the local community to strikes generally took the form of demands that some solution be found so that schools could be opened. The sources of these demands were varied, including organized and unorganized groups of parents, ad hoc groups of civic or religious leaders, and the local press. The primary focus of such demands tended to be on management. There was little evidence, particularly in the eyes of management, that community reaction extended beyond the question of simply ending the strike to a concern about the substance of the issues in dispute.

Information from the five systems that experienced formal impasses over the period suggests a growing willingness on the part of school management to "stand the political heat" of a confrontation with teachers. In only one of these five districts did the Board of Education attempt to open schools during their first strike experience. Three of the five, however, threatened or actually attempted to open schools in subsequent impasse situations. Similarly, in the first strikes management in none of these five systems sought legal sanctions against the union, but in subsequent impasses, management in three of the systems sought and secured injunctions against strikes, which in two cases resulted in the jailing of union leaders.

The effectiveness of these managerial actions is open to serious question, particularly in large systems and urban areas. The two systems that did not attempt to open schools simply perceived no prospect of success in such a move; the three systems that did attempt to open schools fared little better. One system tried and failed, whereupon groups of parents responded by opening schools in their homes, but with little real effect on the strike situation. A second system tried twice to open schools one fall, finally succeeding by hiring substitute teachers and running double shifts. The third system was able to operate schools with administrative personnel and some nonstriking teachers, but not effectively enough to preclude one parent group from seeking a court order directing the system to provide "adequate education." Attempts to open schools generated considerable teacher bitterness and handed unions in the large cities a potent basis for appealing to the larger labor movement for support—the charge of "union busting." This action may ultimately have increased the price of a settlement in some systems.

The changing posture of school management in responding to strikes has been paralleled by changes in the response of other public officials to strikes. The potential for political credit constitutes a powerful incentive for intervention by elected officials at the local level, particularly in fiscally dependent districts, and at the state level, particularly in the case of large urban systems. Several instances of such intervention noted in the original study resulted in tripartite or multilevel bargaining, based on the ability of the intervening party to provide or promise added resources.[8] Over time, both the frequency and form of such intervention has changed. After 1970, there was a marked drop in the apparent propensity of local and especially state officials to intervene in disputes and, where such intervention occurred, it was increasingly confined to mediation in search of agreement within the limits of available resources rather than negotiations in search of added resources.

The changing fiscal environment and attitudes of management and other officials seem to have resulted in longer strikes and less generous settlements. For example, one fiscally dependent district experienced a one-week strike in the early years, which led to intervention by the mayor and a settlement involving a deficit for that year, which would become the mayor's problem in the following year. In a later three-week strike in the same system, the same mayor declined to intervene and a settlement was reached that did not involve additional resources. Similarly, the first strike in a fiscally independent district ended after four weeks when the district accepted a settlement that involved deficit financing, but the same district later took a twelve-week strike to avoid such a settlement. Finally, another system in which a strike threat and later a short strike had produced intervention and augmentation of resources in the 1967-70 period, finally took a twelve-week strike without either intervention or augmentation.

Bargaining Results

The accommodations made and agreements concluded in nine diverse bargaining relationships cannot provide a basis for definitely assessing the impact of bargaining in public education. The experience in those relationships, however, can provide valuable insight into the direction in which collective bargaining and collective action are moving public school systems, the extent to which such movement has been substantial, and the potential implications of that movement for the educational process.

The first problem that confronts any effort to assess bargaining outcomes in the public sector is that of defining the effective scope of bargaining. The original study found that the formal scope of teacher bargaining (all the terms and conditions of employment dealt with in contracts) was actually far broader than the effective scope of bargaining (the terms and conditions that teachers try to change).

Teacher contracts, that is, were found to contain many provisions that simply called for the continuation of "past practices" that had been established by the employer and that teacher unions made no effort to change. Subsequent research has added another dimension to this problem—recognition that effective bargaining can and does occur over issues not covered in the contract.[9]

The formal scope of bargaining in the nine systems covered in the present study became both broader and more uniform across districts than had been the case in the mid-1960s. The effective scope of bargaining within the contractually defined range also was broader and more uniform than had been the case earlier, although to some extent this effective bargaining range varied directly with size of school system. Finally, the "true" effective scope of bargaining in all districts was significantly expanded by formal and informal commitments to discuss or to confer or consult on various matters independent of the normal process of contract negotiation or administration. The scope of this "informal" bargaining varied greatly among the systems.

The original study identified three central thrusts of unions in the collective bargaining arena—compensation, work loads, and participation rights in "policy" decisions. Clearly, all three remain relevant today to the interests both of teachers and the public in the outcome of bargaining. It seems worthwhile, therefore, to ask the question, "As a consequence of bargaining, have teachers gained more pay for less work while achieving more control?"

Wage Bargains

It is difficult to measure the wage gains of teachers over time, much less to assess the contribution of collective bargaining to any such gains. Teachers usually receive, at one time or another, three kinds of wage increases: across-the-board increases, increments for service (up to some maximum), and differentials for added academic credit (at established credit-hour intervals). Unions can enhance teachers' wage gains by expanding the magnitude of those three types of increase, of course, and also by increasing the frequency or number of increments and differentials that produce added compensation. Consequently, the wage gains of individual teachers, groups of teachers, or teacher organizations will not be reflected accurately in average teacher salary in either growing or shrinking systems.

The original study concluded that collective bargaining did produce larger salary increase packages for teachers than would have been forthcoming in the absence of bargaining, with much of the gains of bargaining coming in the form of increased service increments or educational differentials.[10] The marginal impact of these gains on the earnings of individual teachers, the level of incremental resources required by the system, or the way in which such incremental resources were allocated was significant in several cases; the overall impact on average teacher salary, budget size, and budget structure, however, was not equally substantial.[11]

The experience of the nine systems over the 1967-77 period offers little evidence to contradict the conclusions of the earlier study. Collective bargaining in these systems has continued to add varying amounts to the total cost of salary settlements, but the cumulative effect of these increases on average teacher salary, overall budget size, and percent of budget devoted to teacher salaries has not yet been substantial in aggregate terms. Collective bargaining has also continued to result in an increase in the size and frequency of both service and educational increments—with obvious implications for the earnings potential of individual teachers, but far more limited implications for district salary costs until or unless turnover drops sharply (which it is beginning to do in many of the urban systems).

The pattern of salary increases over time and across the systems suggests that collective bargaining in public education has not produced dramatically different results than it has in the private sector. Overall, negotiated increases in the nine systems slightly exceeded increases in the cost of living in the late 1960s when the labor market for teachers was tight, and increases fell slightly short of cost-of-living increases in the 1970s when the labor market for teachers was loose,[12] suggesting only the same limited degree of isolation of wage determination from market conditions as that found in the private sector. At the same time, overall percentage salary increases over the period were larger in the small than in the large systems, suggesting the possible existence of a pattern effect in which large and small districts tended to receive the same dollar increases during this period. This tendency is probably consistent with an explanation based on differences in ability to pay, but not, however, with differences in need to pay as reflected in rates of turnover. Finally, there can be little doubt that collective bargaining has served to enhance the salaries of long-service teachers who lack mobility alternatives in either a tight or loose labor market, which suggests the operation of an egalitarian wage policy not unlike that encountered in unions elsewhere.

Effort Bargains

A second set of bargaining issues that were the subject of considerable attention, if not action, in the early stages of collective bargaining in public school systems encompassed hours of work, work loads, and work responsibilities. Specifically, the original study suggested that collective bargaining could or would have an impact on one or more of the following: (1) length of the school year and school day; (2) student contact time during the school day; (3) non-teaching responsibilities; and (4) class size.

The original study found that collective bargaining had resulted in a shortening of the effective school year or day in a few systems. This thrust of bargaining appears to have continued and expanded, although systems in which a dramatic impact seemed evident remained limited in number. The school calendar was discussed in bargaining in all of the systems except one, which placed the responsibility for recommendations on the calendar on a committee of parents, teachers, and administrators; the school day was a subject of bargaining in all the systems. The length of the school year or school day, however, was specified in the contract in only five systems. In these five systems, which included the three largest, there was evidence that collective bargaining had contributed to a discernible reduction in hours. All five of these systems experienced a trend toward the minimum school year required by state law. In three of the five systems, collective bargaining was credited with producing a reduction in the length of the school day of between thirty and fifty-five minutes. In a fourth district, collective bargaining was instrumental in preventing a lengthening of the school day until it became evident that the system was failing to meet state standards on instruction time.

The issue of preparation periods was not a prominent one in 1965, but had become one at some point since then in all of the nine systems. The question of preparation time during the school day for secondary school teachers was resolved in their favor by 1970. Elementary school teachers, however, did not receive preparation periods in most of the systems until the early 1970s and, in at least three systems, still do not enjoy as much preparation time as their counterparts at the secondary level. Once preparation periods were established, a second issue arose over the permissible uses of such time. That issue also has now been universally resolved in favor of teachers in the nine systems through contract provisions that place control over such time in the hands of the teacher or severely limit any administrative infringement on such "free time."

The issue of relief from nonteaching duties received a limited amount of attention in bargaining in the early 1960s and has received continuing attention since then. In all of these nine systems, teachers had achieved a duty-free lunch period and some measure of relief from administrative duties by 1967. Since then, this thrust has carried into nonteaching activities such as faculty meetings, parent conferences, preparation of report cards, supervision of sporting events, and leadership of student activities. The goal of teachers in this area has been to make such activities voluntary or compensable. Teachers across the nine systems have been quite successful in this quest as a direct result of collective bargaining. Most systems now provide for faculty meetings, parent conferences, and report-card preparation on school time and require little or no teacher participation in after-school activities. Most systems now also provide far longer and far more pervasive pay premiums for teacher participation in student extracurricular activities, and some systems are beginning to face demands that teachers can be assigned to such activities only with their consent.

The class-size issue was the most contentious work-load issue in the mid-1960s, primarily because it was debated as a "policy" issue. That debate has now effectively been resolved and class size accepted as a working condition in the bargaining context in all nine of the systems. Despite that fact, unions in these systems have made relatively little concrete progress in achieving definite, enforceable limits on class size or in reducing those limits where they exist. Contracts in eight of the nine systems continued provisions governing class size in 1977, but only four of these eight established specified class size maxima by grade level. The remaining four contracts stated only goals or ranges for class size, although in two cases target average class sizes were stated and in one an amount of money to be expended each year to achieve the target was also stipulated. Contractual provisions for enforcement of class-size limits, targets, or goals were equally diverse. Three contracts were silent on the subject of enforcement, presumably leaving that matter to arbitration. Two other contracts required only that the superintendent inform the union and the affected teacher of the reasons for a class-size overage. One contract provided only that "prompt action" will be taken to eliminate classsize overages and another provided for a review of overage situations by a special union-management review board. Finally, one contract did call for extra pay for teachers with class-size overages.

The relative weakness of provisions governing class size in the nine systems reflects, at least in part, the substantial economic costs of reducing or even standardizing class size in any school system. These costs apparently have forced unions to accept the inevitability of a trade-off between wages and class size, particularly in the face of increasing fiscal stringency in the early 1970s. Class size does not appear to have fared well in this context. The union initiative on this issue across the nine districts reached its peak well before 1970, after which the issue was by-and-large dropped or increases tacitly accepted.

The experience in the nine districts c᾽ ᴉarly suggests that collective bargaining has had a discernible effect on teacher work loads, primarily in the areas of contact time and extracurricular responsibilities. The cost of these gains to the school systems has been subtle, but substantial—a fact that some are only now beginning to appreciate in the face of declining enrollments and increasing fiscal stringency. Such an appreciation has already led one of the systems in the sample to propose (unsuccessfully) a cutback in preparation periods and class-size limits. Most managements in the sample, however, would prefer to pursue a strategy of absorbing declining enrollments through smaller class sizes, as several have already begun to do in a quiet fashion. This strategy should not prove repugnant to teachers or their unions unless it requires unacceptable trade-offs between wages and job security, which it will most certainly do if communities perceive that declining enrollment should mean declining tax support as opposed to increasing quality as measured by class size or professional morale.

Rights Bargains

We found that the basic dimensions of the contractual system of teacher rights across the nine systems were fairly well set by 1967. The central elements in this system were provisions governing teacher personnel files, teacher evaluation procedures, and teacher assignments and transfers. The major additions to these systems since 1967 have been provisions regarding promotion and layoff. The net effect of these new provisions has been to expand significantly the importance of seniority in an "industry" in which both employees and employers have long stressed the importance of professional qualifications and ability.

Contractual provisions limiting management discretion in promotions were rare and weak in the early 1960s. By 1977, however, relatively strong provisions governing promotions existed in six of the nine systems, including one in which "peer ratings" were to be considered in decisions on promotions out of the bargaining unit into administration. The provisions on promotion within the bargaining unit were evenly divided on the relative weight to be given to seniority—half stipulated that promotions were to be made on the basis of seniority only when ability was equal and half specified that promotions were to be made on the basis of seniority unless one candidate was "substantially superior."

Contractual provisions regarding layoffs, which had been virtually nonexistent at the time of the original study, were found in eight of the nine systems by 1977. In six systems, layoff was to be strictly on the basis of seniority within area of past or present teaching certification and in one system the contract specified only that the procedures to be used to effectuate a reduction in staff would be worked out jointly should that contingency occur. In the remaining system, layoff was to be based on a point system under which teachers could earn fifteen points for seniority, twelve for advanced education, five for [evaluated] teaching performance, and one for participation in extra-curricular activities. This system had just been tested at the time of this study and was not expected to survive without serious challenge from the union in the next set of negotiations.

The contractual rights of teachers in many of the nine systems have been extended well beyond the specific substantive terms of the agreement to encompass the broad universe of past policy and practice that constitute the status quo. The first step in this process of institutionalizing the status quo was taken relatively early in a number of the systems in the negotiation of definitions of a "grievance" that went well beyond allegations of a violation of the contract to encompass, for example, "a complaint involving the work situation; that there is a lack of policy; that a policy or practice is improper or unfair; or that there has been a deviation from . . . a policy or practice." A next step taken in some of the systems was the negotiation of "maintenance of standards" clauses along the following lines: "all conditions of employment shall be maintained at not less than the minimum standards in effect at the time this agreement is signed. . . ." A third step recently taken in a few of the nine systems has been the extension of "just cause" clauses to protect teachers against the effects, among other things, of the type of "technological change" dealt with in the following clause:

> A teacher shall not be laid off because of curricular change unless such change would render him non-qualified under the State Certification Code, and he has refused other assignment opportunity or turned down training provided by the employer (at the employer's expense) to certify him for existing vacancies.

There is a discernible pattern in the incidence of these restrictive provisions. The contracts of the three largest systems contain some form of each. The contracts of the three next largest systems contain or have contained both broad definitions of a grievance and some form of maintenance of standards, although management in one of these systems has been successful in "ridding itself" of a maintenance-of-standards clause. The three smallest systems thus far have escaped all three types of clauses, although one has had to resist strong union demands for maintenance of standards and all have had to deal with repeated union proposals to expand the concept of a grievance in the contract.

There has been considerable speculation that collective bargaining can and will lead to the extension of teacher rights to the control of some or all matters of educational policy. The original study found little evidence of such an impact, despite the existence of contract clauses covering such policy issues as class size, teacher transfers, school integration, student discipline, and pupil grading and promotion. The more recent experience in the nine systems does not provide evidence to contradict this conclusion, despite the addition in some contracts of clauses dealing with academic freedom, "quality integrated education,"[13] and teacher accountability[14] to the historic list of what was and remains a sparse population of substantive "policy" provisions.

The fact that policy issues generally have not become part of the formal scope of bargaining does not mean that bargaining has not resulted in greater informal teacher participation in policy decisions. The original study pointed out significant potential for such participation through the basic bargaining process and the generalized consultative arrangements at all levels that have come to be part of that process in education. These avenues for participation have been used in all the systems; policy issues have often been raised and discussed in negotiations and consultation between administration and union representatives at both central and school levels.

Above and beyond this very basic avenue for participation and influence, the original study also suggested that bargaining might lead to expanded teacher participation through institutionalization and extension of the prebargaining "joint committees" approach to the "study of issues." The experience in the nine systems clearly suggests that this has been the case. The basic system of generalized consultation rights—regular meetings between union and administration at the central and school level to discuss matters of mutual concern—was fairly well in place in most of the systems by 1967 and has not changed significantly since then. What has changed is the number and variety of joint committees—both ad hoc and standing—that are recognized in contracts particularly, but not exclusively, in the larger systems. This large and constantly changing universe of special committees was assigned tasks ranging from reviewing the schedule of increments for extracurricular activities to evaluating a teacher-aid program and developing a teacher-evaluation program. The more stable and less diverse universe of standing committees typically dealt with such matters as sabbatical leaves, materials and supplies, textbook selection, and curriculum development.

The operational significance of this complex web of teacher rights is difficult to measure or assess. Spokesmen for teacher organizations have often pointed to the results of rights bargains as important evidence of the gains achieved through collective bargaining. Spokesmen for management, however, have equally often indicated that the expanding network of teacher rights has created only procedural as opposed to substantive barriers in the development or implementation of policy. The fact that in two of the systems studied management has felt compelled to seek a "rollback" of the concessions it made in rights bargains raises questions about the validity of this view but does not undermine it as a general statement of impact. At the same time, however, it was clear in many of the systems that the procedural or due-process requirements embodied in contracts had posed a serious if not insurmountable barrier for management in implementing some policy decisions and administrative actions.

There was a surprising consensus among union and management spokesmen that rights and policy issues were likely to receive far more intensive attention in the future than they have to date. The basis for this consensus is a shared perception that increasing fiscal stringency coupled with increasing barriers to mobility will turn teacher attention inward and to noneconomic issues. Only one system in the sample as yet appears to have reached this point. Its experience can only be regarded as idiosyncratic, but it is interesting, nonetheless. Management in that system has been forced to live within clear and stringent fiscal constraints. In order to secure the cooperation of the union in living within those constraints, it has given effective control over internal budget allocation decisions to the union, with clear implications for the control of "educational policy." The fact that the budget, per se, is within the "effective" scope of bargaining in this system clearly has not been reflected fully in the contractual definition of the "formal" scope of bargaining, which recognizes only that:

> The Union Fiscal Committee shall work directly with the Fiscal Department of the District in preparing budgets. All budgetary income and expenditures shall be discussed by the Fiscal Department with the Fiscal Committee and with the Superintendent before [being] submitted to the Board for approval.

Summary and Conclusions

The most fundamental conclusion that can be drawn from the long-term negotiation experiences of the nine systems is that collective bargaining in public education is not radically different in process and results from collective bargaining in the private sector. Bargaining relationships in both sectors have become highly diverse and have adapted to changing circumstances. Both the nature and magnitude of bargaining results also have been remarkably similar in the two sectors.

The fact that there appears to be little that is revolutionary about collective bargaining in the experience of these school systems does not mean that there is no basis for concern over the implications of bargaining for the distribution (or redistribution) of control over decisions and resources in the public sector in general, or in public education, in particular. The experience in this small sample of school systems suggests that political constraints on bargaining are, and tend to remain, relatively weak and diffuse.[15] Similarly, the experience in the nine systems indicates that institutional constraints on bargaining, such as formal community involvement in negotiations and fundamental managerial concern over long-run rights and fiscal responsibilities, are weak or difficult to implement, or both, particularly from the managerial standpoint. Thus, the primary burden of discipline in the bargaining context must fall on fiscal constraints, which appear to come into play only at or near a point of imminent crisis and then only with respect to issues with obvious short-run implications for the size of the system budget rather than the structure of that budget or of the educational effort it can sustain.

This lack of effective short-run constraints on the process and results of bargaining, absent an immediate and dramatic crisis, is not unique to public education or the public sector, nor are the bargaining outcomes that have flowed from this undisciplined system. Teachers have achieved real incremental, if not yet fundamental, gains in earnings through collective bargaining by forcing a redefinition of short-run ability to pay up to the limits of long-run willingness to support public education. They have not yet been successful, however, in producing a basic change in such willingness to pay. Teachers have also been able to achieve gains in the effort area through collective bargaining, as have unions in the private sector, but those apparently noneconomic gains are also beginning to encounter fiscal constraints, particularly since declining enrollments and employment must ultimately force both management and unions to choose between higher salaries and higher pupil/staff ratios in the allocation of available resources.

The most interesting and controversial aspect of teacher bargaining remains that involving employee and management rights. The past ten years have produced a substantial expansion in the contractual job rights of teachers in terms of both protection against arbitrary treatment and participation in decision making. Their protective rights are hardly revolutionary when contrasted to the rights of workers in the private sector; their participatory rights, however, appear to be far more substantial. The procedural implications of these participatory rights are clear; their substantive impact is not. Thus far, such impact appears to have been limited more by lack of teacher interest or consensus than by political or managerial constraints. Mounting economic constraints, however, may force teachers and teacher organizations to devote more attention and energy to their participatory rights and, if so, it will be interesting to see whether or when countervailing public or managerial interest emerges.

NOTES

1. Much of this literature is heir to the "disproportionate power" theory put forth by Wellington and Winter; see Harry H. Wellington and Ralph K. Winter, Jr., *The Unions and the Cities* (Washington, D.C.: The Brookings Institution, 1971), chap. 1. Some more recent thoughts on this subject by Wellington and Winter and others can be found in A. Lawrence Chickering, ed., *Public Employee Unions: A Study of the Crisis in Public Sector Labor Relations* (San Francisco: Institute for Contemporary Studies, 1976).

2. For example, see James I. Freund, "Market and Union Influences on Municipal Employee Wages," *Industrial and Labor Relations Review*, Vol. 27, No. 3 (April 1974), pp. 391-404; and David B. Lipsky and John E. Drotning, "The Influence of Collective Bargaining on Teachers' Salaries in New York State," *Industrial and Labor Relations Review*, Vol. 27, No. 1 (October 1973), pp. 18-35.

3. For example, see Thomas A. Kochan and Hoyt N. Wheeler, "Municipal Collective Bargaining: A Model and Analysis of Bargaining Outcomes," *Industrial and Labor Relations Review*, Vol. 29, No. 1 (October 1975), pp. 46-66; and Paul F. Gerhart, "Determinants of Bargaining Outcomes in Local Government Labor Negotiations," *Industrial and Labor Relations Review*, Vol. 29, No. 3 (April 1976), pp. 331-51.

4. Some attention has been given to the developmental aspects of bargaining relationships in the context of the New York City Fiscal crisis. For example, see Raymond D. Horton, "Economics, Politics and Collective Bargaining: The Case of New York City," and David Lewin, "Collective Bargaining and the Right to Strike," both in Chickering, *Public Employee Unions*.

5. Charles R. Perry and Wesley A. Wildman, *The Impact of Negotiations in Public Education: The Evidence from the Schools* (Worthington, Ohio: Charles A. Jones Publishing Co., 1970).

6. Kenneth McLennan and Michael H. Moskow, "Multilateral Bargaining in the Public Sector," *Proceedings of the Twenty-First Annual Winter Meeting, Industrial Relations Research Association* (Madison, Wisc.: IRRA, 1968), pp. 31-40.

7. This same phenomenon was noted in Lucian B. Gatewood, "Fact-Finding in Teacher Disputes: The Wisconsin Experience," *Monthly Labor Review*, Vol. 97, No. 10 (October 1974), pp. 47-51.

8. The potential advantages of such intervention to unions in the public sector may be significant. See Kochan and Wheeler, "Municipal Collective Bargaining," p. 59.

9. Charles R. Perry, *The Labor Relations Climate and Management Rights in Urban School Systems* (Philadelphia: Industrial Research Unit, Wharton School, University of Pennsylvania, 1974), pp. 21-27. For a more general treatment of these distinctions between real and formal scope of bargaining, see Paul F. Gerhart, "The Scope of Bargaining in Local Government Labor Negotiations," *Labor Law Journal*, Vol. 20, No. 8 (August 1969), pp. 545-52.

10. These findings subsequently have received support from empirical studies of broader samples of school systems. See, for example, Lipsky and Drotning, "The Influence of Collective Bargaining," pp. 33-35.

11. This finding is consistent with the results of other studies of the impact of bargaining on wage levels in the public sector.

12. In part, the weaker salary gains of teachers over this period may reflect the dramatic growth in fringe benefit costs experienced by most systems over this period, which amounted to almost $1200 per year per teacher.

13. This clause covers matters such as "Textbook and Curriculum Improvement," "Staff Integration," "Achievement and Intelligence Test Revision," and "Pupil Integration." The clause originally was proposed by the union with the encouragement of management.

14. This clause refers to a union statement of "Goals of Accountability," which is "not to be regarded as a compilation of conditions of employment or work standards but rather as goals of excellence which both the Board and the Union endorse." The clause and the statement it refers to were adopted in response to a management initiative linking pay to accountability in negotiations.

15. This conclusion appears to be at odds with that reached by Sanford Cohen in his article, "Does Public Employee Unionism Diminish Democracy?" *Industrial and Labor Relations Review*, Vol. 32, No. 2 (January 1979), p. 195. I do not dispute Professor Cohen's conclusion directly; indeed, my findings on substantive impact are consistent with his. I do, however, question whether those results are a product of "political" constraints independent of the "economic" constraints imposed by fiscal considerations. Thus far, this distinction has not been highly significant, primarily because unions have focused their attention on economic issues. If in the future the growing stringency of economic constraints should force unions to alter this focus of attention, political constraints per se may have to bear increasing responsibility for disciplining the bargaining process. There is little evidence yet in these nine systems that one can be optimistic that such constraints are or will quickly become operative.

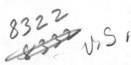

The Memphis Police and Firefighters Strikes of 1978: A Case Study

Herbert R. Northrup and J. Daniel Morgan[†]

During the summer of 1978, the city of Memphis suffered debilitating strikes by both the police and firefighters unions. Although public employee strikes are no longer unusual, there have been few case studies which analyze the strikes and the tactics employed by the strikers.[1] This study of the Memphis strikes will examine the issues involved in public protective service strikes, the impact of the strikers' tactics, including the use of violence as a coercive tool, and the unions' attempts to alter management's bargaining structure.

Tennessee has no comprehensive public employee bargaining statute. In 1957, two attempts to gain recognition and bargaining rights were rebuffed by the Tennessee appellate courts. In one case, a county successfully obtained a chancery court injunction against a strike, and the injunction was upheld by the state court of appeals. The court relied upon the traditional doctrine of forbidding public employee bargaining because such bargaining involves an illegal delegation of sovereign power.[2] In the only other case to reach the courts, union picketing of the city of Alcoa was enjoined because it was an attempt to coerce an unlawful delegation from a sovereign power.[3]

In 1978, the Tennessee legislature retreated from this position by enacting the Education Professional Negotiations Act,[4] which grants bargaining rights and union recognition to the teaching profession. Earlier, the Memphis garbage collectors strike of 1968 resulted in a complete abandonment of the sovereignty principle for Tennessee's largest city, proving again "that the *power* to strike . . . [is] of far greater relevance than the *right* to strike."[5]

Memphis began recognizing public employee unions as a result of the 1968 strike to obtain union recognition and end discrimination against blacks. Conducted by the all-black Local 1733 of the American Federation of State, County, and Municipal Workers, the strike ended in a complete union victory. The victory followed a police-union

---

[†] Herbert R. Northrup is Director of the Industrial Research Unit and Professor of Industry at the Wharton School, Philadelphia, Pennsylvania. J. Daniel Morgan is an Attorney with Young and Perl, P.C., in Memphis, Tennessee.

clash, the conversion of the dispute into a national civil rights cause
célèbre by AFSCME and the Rev. Dr. Martin Luther King, a black
community boycott of downtown stores, and riots spawned by the
assassination of Dr. King. Twelve days after Dr. King's death and
sixty-five days after the strike began, the city conceded, recognized
the union, and granted a checkoff of dues.[6]

After the strike ended, the city council passed a resolution authorizing the recognition of other unions of city employees upon a showing
of majority support within a unit. Local 1784 of the International
Association of Firefighters, AFL-CIO, petitioned Mayor Loeb for
recognition in early August 1971. The major reason for the firefighters' desire to unionize was the city's decision to break parity of pay
between police and firemen. The mayor withheld recognition for
several months, insisting that the union agree to a strict no-strike
clause. On December 16, 1971, the mayor and the union signed a
Memorandum of Understanding which granted official recognition
and contained the no-strike pledge.[7]

The Memphis Police Association obtained official recognition during July 1973.[8] The initial agreement with the city included a three-
page no-strike clause which narrowly defined the permissible range
of union activities.

The garbage strike of 1968 set the pattern for subsequent handling
of labor relations by the city of Memphis. The mayor was the city's
primary representative, bargaining agent, and decision maker. The
city council has generally played a secondary role in labor relations,
for the most part giving advice and support as requested by the
mayors.

Memphis has avoided problems of limiting the range of bargaining
by granting the mayor a good deal of flexibility in reallocating funds
between items. The only real constraints on the mayor's allocations of
funds are the overall budget figure, approval by the city council, and
the political process. When bargaining occurs after the approval of
the budget, the scope of bargaining on economic matters has not been
inflexibly and unilaterally determined.

1977 Negotiations

To appreciate the labor situation in Memphis during the summer of
1978, it is necessary first to look back to the 1977 bargaining sessions. During March 1977, Mayor Wyeth Chandler and other city
officials predicted a budget deficit of $12 million for the fiscal year
beginning July 1, 1977. The city unsuccessfully lobbied the state
legislature for a bill which would allow a sales tax increase without a

popular referendum. The city then began delaying projects, transferring funds from other sources, and utilizing other measures designed to ease the budget crisis. The city council approved a $1.00 increase in the monthly garbage fee.

During the negotiations with the police and firefighters' unions, Mayor Chandler was able to convince the union leaders that the city could afford only a 5 percent wage increase. After the much-publicized deficit predictions, the rank-and-file union members were also convinced, and they ratified the contracts. Contracts with the unions were executed in early July 1977.[9]

Then, on August 3, 1977, the city announced that it had been mistaken about the deficit predictions. After the books were closed on the preceding fiscal year, the city actually had a surplus of $1.5 million.[10] This amount would have been sufficient to meet the higher wage demands of the unions.

City administrators attributed the unexpected surplus to the austerity measures they had taken and to the overall complexity of the budget. Union members, however, were not convinced of the sincerity of these claims. The leaders of the unions were also discredited by the controversy and reportedly lost their leadership roles or did not seek reelection.[11]

Early 1978 Bargaining

When bargaining began in 1978, both unions had new leadership. There was a general feeling of distrust for the administration among the union members because of the 1977 surplus controversy. Other factors contributed to the restiveness of the members.

The firefighters had lived with the lack of parity with police pay for seven years and were concerned that the present system of percentage increases was widening the gap. Younger members of both protective forces were expressing dissatisfaction with the quasi-military nature of their departments and with what they termed the paternalistic attitude of city officials.

The firefighters' negotiations were the first to present problems for the city. On June 30, 1978, the union rejected a final offer which called for 6 percent increase in wages immediately, followed by a $30 across-the-board increase on April 1, 1978, and a 7.5 percent increase on October 2, 1979. This was the same final offer that had been made to the city's other unions, but the firefighters were holding out for a shift differential similar to that paid to other city employees. The issue had not been discussed until the "eleventh hour" of the negotiations and probably was a device used by the union to regain its loss of parity.

The First Strike: Violence

On July 1, 1978, 1,400 Memphis firemen walked out, leaving only 150 nonunion firemen to assist supervisory personnel in fighting fires. The mayor immediately called for and received National Guard troops. The city also received the assistance of federal firefighters from the National Parks Service.

A temporary restraining order was issued by the chancery court against mass picketing and blocking the driveways at fire stations. During the first night of the strike, numerous instances of misconduct by striking firemen were reported. Police reports indicated that the tires had been slashed on seven fire department vehicles.[12]

Only three of the fire department's fourteen ambulances were still in operating condition. The tires on the ambulances had been slashed, engines tampered with, and medical equipment damaged. Headlamps on several vehicles were smashed. Pickets reportedly kicked the sides of automobiles as National Guardsmen reported for duty at the Armory.

Over the weekend of July 2 and 3, more than 300 fires were reported in the city. Extensive damage occurred in at least twelve of these fires. During this period, the fire hoses were manned by the few nonstriking firefighters, supervisory personnel, and volunteers at the scenes of fires. At several fires, strikers were on hand to taunt the undermanned fire crews.[13]

There were also instances in which striking firemen actively hindered efforts to control fires. One striker allegedly parked his pickup truck on the hoses at the scene of a fire. When the police ordered him to remove the truck, he came dangerously close to striking a police officer with the truck. He was arrested and charged with aggravated assault.[14]

At yet another fire, one National Guardsman reported that the undermanned fire crews needed assistance in bringing the fire under control. When guardsmen were called upon to aid the crews, the strikers at the scene angrily objected. "After near physical confrontation [the] district chief decided that to avoid trouble he would not use guardsmen as fire fighters."[15]

At several fire stations, pickets obstructed the efforts of nonstriking firemen to report for work. One captain was reportedly forced into an automobile when he attempted to cross the picket line.[16] At the central fire station, a small group of strikers broke into the building by smashing a glass door and physically removed some nonstriking firemen from the building.[17]

Arson

The unusually large number of fires during the firefighters' three-day strike prompted charges by city officials that strikers were primarily responsible for the fires. Police Director Winslow Chapman told a news conference that he believed that firemen were responsible for setting 90 to 95 percent of the fires.[18]

Mayor Chandler also placed the blame for the large number of fires on the strikers. "The blame for these open and notorious acts of violence and threats against their fellow firefighters and the holocaust (which has followed) rests with those members of the firefighters' union—hopefully small in number—who believed that such actions would intimidate this government and its citizens into doing whatever was decided."[19]

City officials supported their theory that strikers were responsible by referring to the "definite pattern" in which the fires occurred.[20] A number occurred in areas served by fire companies which were already engaged in fighting fires at other locations within their area of responsibility. Officials implied that only persons with knowledge of the internal organization of the fire department could set fires in such a strategic manner.[21] Police Director Chapman stated that: "If you saw from the air, you'd see there was a very definite pattern. Last night (Saturday) was one of the most unreal scenes I've ever seen. It was like a World War II newsreel."[22]

A logbook of the weekend activities made by a National Guardsman tends to support the theory that some of the fires were set by those with inside information. While the crew from a fire station was out on another call, a half-completed house directly across the street from the station suddenly burst into flames. Because the firefighters and equipment were at another fire, nothing could be done to save the house. The fire was caused by arson.[23]

Other incidents also tended to indicate the involvement of striking firemen. One building site inspected during the strike by a person claiming to be a fire marshal was completely destroyed by arson the same night. From the placement of the incendiary devices in the building, the inference was drawn that the arsonist had knowledge of how the most damage could be inflicted. The building contractor asserts that the spurious fire inspector was "casing" the building.[24] Nonetheless, state investigators have failed to identify the culprit.

Two striking firemen were arrested on arson charges during the strike. Acting on a tip, the police had set up a still-watch near a vacant apartment building. The police observed one man pouring liquid on the building and the other then throwing a match. The building burst into flames and the two men fled. The police apprehended the arsonists after a short chase.[25] The firefighters union posted bond for the two suspects. They have pleaded guilty to charges of arson and have been sentenced to serve two to three years in prison.[26]

Another firefighter was arrested on arson charges when he allegedly set fire to his mother-in-law's home, causing $13,000 in damages. Fire Director Robert Walker described this incident as "a family affair."[27]

Union officials continued to place the blame for the rash of fires on "energetic arsonists who know the firemen will be accused of setting the blazes."[28] They have never been able to support this charge, however, City officials remain firm that the strikers were to blame, and, as noted, some were in fact caught and convicted.

The first firefighters' strike ended after three days. A chancery court injunction against the strike was granted on July 3, and the firemen voted to return to work in compliance. The city had been ravaged by over 300 fires, causing an estimated three million dollars in property damage. Damage to fire equipment and station houses was estimated at between $50,000 and $100,000.[29]

During the three-day strike, the firefighters had received little assistance from the police union. Memphis Police Association officers had instructed their members not to make arrests of pickets, but more substantial support was not forthcoming. To avoid problems of crossing picket lines, roll calls for police were held in parking lots away from the precinct houses.

More tangible support for the firefighters was given by the members of AFSCME. Although sanitation workers had ratified a contract with the city on July 1, members refused to cross picket lines on July 3. Only 12 of the city's 248 garbage trucks were operated on the third day of the strike.

Police and Fire Negotiations

On July 3, as the firefighters were voting to return to work, the 1100-member Memphis Police Association was voting to reject the city's final offer. The members also voted to give their president the authority to call for a "job action."

Negotiations with both unions continued until July 13, when tentative agreements with the leaders of the unions were reached. A federal mediator had joined the negotiations on July 8 and was credited with aiding in the rapprochement.

This tentative agreement with the police leaders involved a slight variation from the city's original final offer. The city agreed to pay $25.44 per month in insurance premiums in lieu of the $30 across-the-board increase which was to come in April 1979 under the final offer. The police leaders agreed to this change because of the income tax savings which would be produced for the members.

The firefighters' tentative accord left the basic wage terms of the city's final offer untouched. The major changes involved longevity pay and bonus day compensation. No mention was made of the shift differential over which the union had struck.

The firefighters' union did not hold a formal ratification vote on the tentative accord. Dissatisfaction with the package was evident among the members at a meeting held to explain the terms. The leaders decided not to put the issue to a vote, which would probably have resulted in another strike. Instead, the firefighters decided to wait and see what action the police union would take.

The membership of the police union rejected the tentative package on July 15 by a nine-to-one margin. The leaders announced that they would appeal to the city council before calling for any job action and request that the council compel the mayor to submit to binding arbitration.

On July 18, the city council chambers were packed with police and firefighters. The council listened to the unions' complaints about the negotiation process but refused to interfere with the mayor's exercise of his discretion.

At this meeting, a new union tactic was unveiled. A representative of the Memphis Education Association announced plans to begin a petition to recall the mayor. The police and firefighters in the audience cheered this new idea.

The Memphis Education Association had been secretly planning the recall campaign because of its dissatisfaction with the school board budget. Both unions immediately joined in the campaign. In order to get the recall issue on the November ballot, signatures of 19,396 registered voters (10 percent of those voting in the last election) would be required. Members of the unions began soliciting signatures for the petition without, however, much success.

On July 28, David Baker, president of the police association, and Mayor Chandler debated the issue on television. The mayor made an unexpected offer to Baker for a 32-month contract with a 7.5 percent increase, plus an additional 8 percent in the nineteenth month. The publicly owned Memphis Light, Gas, and Water Utility employees had accepted a contract on this basis earlier in the year.

Baker agreed to discuss the offer with the union leadership council, which rejected it and set August 13 as the date for a job action. The union also made a counterproposal to the mayor, which he rejected. The mayor then altered his original proposal by offering more at the beginning of the contract: a 6.653 percent increase retroactive to July 1, 1978, and $22.50 per month on July 1, 1979, and October 1, 1979. This was rejected, and the police struck on August 9.

Police Strike: More Violence

Police supervisory personnel and county deputies patrolled the city under curfew a second time, while the National Guard remained on call. The city obtained a temporary restraining order against the strike, but the court order was ignored by the striking police.

The police strike also involved numerous instances of violence and vandalism. During the first night of the strike, 25 police vehicles were disabled. Roofing nails were placed in the driveways of precinct houses to prevent entry or exit. A tear-gas bomb was detonated in the Shelby County Administration Building, which faces City Hall.

At the North Precinct, strikers turned on a fire hydrant, which spewed a strong stream of water into the street, and cut a tire on a water works truck which had been sent to turn off the hydrant. As the strike progressed, more vandalism and violence by strikers were to occur.

Several other city unions supported the police with sympathy strikes. The city court system was closed down because clerks refused to cross the picket lines. During the first days of the strike, firefighters continued to work but refused to cross picket lines. The fire equipment was moved onto the streets so that station house picket lines need not be crossed. The AFSCME sanitation workers offered financial assistance to the striking police but promised to observe the no-strike clause of their contract.

On Saturday night, August 12, Mayor Chandler ordered all striking policemen removed from the city payroll. The mayor gave the strikers a 24-hour grace period in which to report for duty. After the grace period, strikers would be rehired only as new employees on probationary status. The city had obtained a chancery court order which directed the strikers to return to work or to resign from the force.

Late that night, Police Association President Baker read the court order to a group of approximately 500 strikers who had assembled outside central police headquarters. Baker urged the strikers to comply with the order and was jeered by the strikers. A more radical member of the executive board, Chris Cothran, pushed Baker aside and announced that he had taken over the leadership of the union. The crowd of strikers began chanting "We want Chris," and Baker left the platform in apparent disgust.

Cothran then addressed the striking police. Along with urging a return to the picket lines, Cothran threatened violence if strikers were arrested by county police or National Guardsmen.

"If we are going to be arrested, we're going to be arrested by Memphis Police Officers. We're not going to be arrested by reserves. We're not going to be arrested by deputy sheriffs, I'm telling you right now if the National Guard wants another war."[30] Cothran was interrupted at this point by loud cheers from the crowd.

Cothran apparently expressed the sentiments of the majority of strikers. The strikers were not prepared to return to work in compliance with the court order or in the face of the mayor's threat of discharge.

This change in leadership lasted only a few hours. On Sunday morning, the attorney for the Police Association arranged a reconciliation between Baker and Cothran. Cothran was convinced that he would be unable to deal with City Hall because he had been involved in several disciplinary proceedings in previous years and was not well-respected by the city leaders.[31] His ultraradicalism would also have been a hindrance in negotiations.

Baker agreed to abandon his moderate stance and to comply with the wishes of the membership. He announced that he would fully support the continuance of the strike.

During the fourth day, more vandalism was reported. Windows and glass doors were broken by rocks and bricks thrown by large groups of strikers at three precinct houses. Strikers marched around the police stations, many armed with ax handles or clubs. Pickets at several stations physically prevented officers from returning to work.[32] Numerous striking policemen were arrested on charges of curfew violations and breach of the peace. Strikers temporarily disabled three fire trucks.

To prevent further vandalism of fire equipment, many trucks were moved into the shelter of the National Guard armory. The National Guard was ordered onto the streets to serve as support for the county deputies and police supervisors.

By the end of the mayor's 24-hour grace period, approximately 75 to 100 strikers had returned to duty. These officers were allowed to return home after a large number of phone calls were received which threatened their safety and their families.[33] The threatening callers knew the officers who returned to work, their work assignments, and their families.[34] Although supervisory personnel also received threatening calls, they remained on the job.

Second Firefighters Strike

During the first days of the strike, the firefighters remained on the job. On August 14, however, the leaders of the union called for a formal vote on the tentative pact which had been reached on July 8. The membership refused to ratify the pact and joined the police in striking. The leaders of the union labelled the strike a wildcat strike primarily because the union was still subject to the July injunction.

By calling the strike unauthorized, the leaders hoped to avoid citation for contempt of court. There can be little doubt, however, that the call for a formal vote was but a signal to join the police in striking.

Mayor Chandler reacted to the firefighters' strike by discharging the strikers, subject to a short grace period. Few strikers returned to work under this threat, however. The city received over 2,000 applications for positions vacated by the striking police and firemen, but the city was not able to break the strike with replacements. State law requires a considerable period of training before replacements can be used in the protection services (for example, 240 hours for police replacements).

On August 15, the striking police and firefighters received the support of the Memphis AFL-CIO Labor Council. The president of the labor council called for the mayor to submit to binding arbitration and threatened to call a general strike if a settlement was not soon reached.

The labor council represents nearly 60,000 workers in the Memphis area. The threat of a general strike, therefore, increased the pressure on the mayor, although the unions involved could have been subject to severe financial penalties by employers if they struck in violation of a contract.

Garbage workers honored police and firefighters' picket lines which were set up at their stations on August 15. Only 23 of the 1,036 garbage workers reported for duty. The day before, pickets had chased three sanitation workers from their truck and then thrown away the keys to the vehicle.[35]

Additional support for the strikers came from the Memphis Education Association, whose executive board promised to honor picket lines. City schools were scheduled to open on August 18.

The combination of strike pressures and sympathy strikes prompted Mayor Chandler to make another offer, hoping to get negotiations started once again. The mayor offered to let the people decide the issue of wage increases directly through a tax increase referendum on the November ballot.

The unions rejected this proposal for three reasons. First, the offer did not contain a promise of continued recognition of the unions. Second, there was no mention of amnesty for strikers. Third, and most interestingly, the unions contended that it was unrealistic to expect the voters to increase taxes during a period of tax revolt.[36] The police union had apparently reassessed its earlier desire to "let the people make the decision."[37]

The Seventh Day

The seventh day of the strike was very eventful. Governor Ray Blanton, acting upon the urgings of the Memphis Labor Council and AFL-CIO President George Meany, proposed that the city submit to binding arbitration. To encourage the city toward this end, the governor presented the city with a bill for the services of the National Guard.

The bill amounted to over one million dollars, and the governor emphasized that each additional day would cost the city $65,000. The bill included a $630,000 charge for National Guard services during the garbage strike of 1968. To further impress his point, the governor threatened to withhold the city's share of gasoline tax revenues until the bill was paid.

Mayor Chandler stood firmly against the governor's proposal. He presented a counterproposal which called for an immediate end to the strikes and amnesty for all strikers who were not charged with felonies. The city and the unions would then submit their last best offers to the Federal Mediation and Conciliation Service. The mediators would determine the amount necessary to fund the difference in the two offers.

After this difference was determined, a tax increase referendum would be placed on the November 7 ballot. If the voters rejected the tax increase, the city's final offer would continue as the compensation rate. If the voters approved the tax increase, the additional revenues would be used exclusively to fund the unions' final offers.

There was no formal response by the unions to this offer. Negotiations with both unions were, however, resumed and joined by five members of the Memphis Chamber of Commerce and five members of the Memphis AFL-CIO Labor Council. Three federal mediators were also involved in the talks. The business and labor leaders were allowed to join in the discussions to aid in finding a settlement acceptable to the Memphis community.

After long hours of shuttle diplomacy, the impasses were finally broken. The business and labor leaders were credited with a major role in working out the final compromises.

Strike Settlement

The final settlement was basically the same wage package as contained in the city's original final offer. The settlement called for a 6 percent increase retroactive to July 5, a $30 increase on April 1, 1979, and a 7.5 percent increase on October 1, 1979. The major concession made by the mayor was an agreement to make the final 7.5 percent increase subject to renegotiation based on a factfinding committee's report.

The factfinding committee was to be composed of one member appointed by the city and one by the unions. The third member was to be selected by the appointed members. The report of the factfinders was not to be binding on the city.[38]

The mayor also agreed to rehire all strikers without loss of status, except for those charged with felonies. Strikers who were charged with curfew violations and breach of the peace would be fully reinstated.[39]

The unions ratified the settlement and the eight-day strike ended. The mayor had held the unions to his basic wage package. The unions succeeded in their quest for a one-year contract, since the 1979 wage renegotiation provision basically amounts to a one-year contract.

More importantly, the unions succeeded in their attempts to alter management's bargaining structure. Although the unions were not immediately successful in forcing the mayor to submit to binding arbitration or in involving the city council,[40] a broader representation of interests was brought into the negotiation sessions.

Union Tactics

The preceding account of the strikes presents an interesting case study of union tactics in the public sector. The strikers' tactics which warrant the most attention are the use of violence and the attempts to alter the structure of the bargaining relationship. Both were used by the strikers to increase political pressures on the city administrators or to force changes in the decision-making processes of the government relative to collective bargaining.

In any strike by public employees, the purpose is to disrupt the delivery of governmental services to the citizens of the community. "This deprivation of essential services is intended to increase public concern and create pressure upon the city's elected officials to take steps to restore the deprived services—that is, to accede to some or all of the . . . union's demands."[41] A higher level of violence during a strike could be expected to generate greater public concern and commensurately greater political pressure.

During both the July and August strikes, there were, as noted, numerous instances of violence and vandalism by members of both unions. The most serious threats to the health, safety, and property of the citizens arose during the three-day firefighters' strike in July. During this period, over 300 fires were reported, causing an estimated three million dollars in property loss, and three firefighters were arrested and charged with arson. Mayor Chandler stated that many of the fires had been set by union members in an attempt to increase the pressure on the administration to settle.[42]

Whether the union (or groups within the union) was directly responsible for setting the large number of fires, the responsibility for the property losses seems clear. By authorizing an illegal strike, the union deprived the citizens of effective protective services and thereby caused losses which would not have been incurred but for the illegal strike.[43]

The violence and vandalism which occurred during the strikes can be explained by several theories. The strikes and their attendant violence were motivated in part by the unions' desire to bring additional pressure to bear on Mayor Chandler. Vandalism of city equipment, breaking windows of city buildings, and other acts against city property increased the costs to the city of its refusal to concede to the unions' demands. This type of violence increased the economic costs of the city's disagreement.

Political Costs

The coercive acts may also be explained as attempts to increase the political costs of disagreement. Strikes by police and firemen, even without violence, bring to bear considerable political pressure "because strikes in public employment disrupt important services, [and] a large part of the mayor's political constituency will, in many cases, press for a quick end to the strike with little concern for the cost of settlement."[44]

Violence against the public emphasizes the lack of the essential protective services. For example, a larger number of fires will increase the public's awareness and fear, and more pressure to settle will likely be exerted on the city's negotiators.

A union or union member using violence against the public as a means of increasing the political costs of disagreement is, however, not only morally reprehensible but also risks defeating the strike's purpose if discovered or credibly blamed for the terrorist activity. In such a situation, public opinion will turn against the strikers, and little pressure to accede will be exerted on city management.

The arrests of two striking firemen and city officials' blaming the striking firefighters for the rash of fires during the July strike solidified public opinion against the union. The firefighters were put into a defensive position and decided to return to work after striking for three days. The firefighters had lost the public as a political ally.

One analyst of strike strategies in public employment has stated that, whenever coercive tactics are used, "it is made clear by the union that they are directed at an uncompromising individual or group [for example, the mayor or council] and *not* at the community at large. Although such activity, especially job action, will affect the public, the fire fighters try not to alienate the community any more than is necessary."[45] The Memphis firefighters failed to follow this advice and lost the support of the public.

Other acts of violence may be explained as attempts to make the strikes more completely successful in disrupting essential services. Vandalism of equipment was designed to assure that services could not be provided with that equipment by nonstrikers, replacements, or the National Guard. Blocking driveways to stations, placing nails in the driveways, and slashing tires on city vehicles also assured a more complete shutdown of services.

The level of services was further reduced by violence or threats of violence against nonstrikers. Several officers were physically prevented from crossing picket lines, and some nonstrikers were physically removed from their posts. There may also, of course, have been some violence which resulted from mob psychology.[46]

Whatever the explanations for the violence and vandalism which occurred during the strikes, the use of this type of tactic (whether or not it is sanctioned officially by the union) presents a strong argument for truly effective bans on strikes by public safety employees. Wellington and Winter have argued that essential service strikes, in and of themselves, give a "disproportionate share of effective power in the process of decision" to the unions. This disproportionate power may threaten the "normal American political process."[47] When violence is used as a tactic to increase the power of the unions, the strike becomes all the more intolerable, and the political process is distorted even further.

Altering the Bargaining Structure

The concept of collective bargaining structure and its relationship to the relative power of the parties have received considerable attention in the context of private sector bargaining.[48] Attempts by unions to increase their power through "coalition" bargaining is a notable development in this area.[49] "Disputes arising from attempts to change the structure of bargaining no doubt involve the most serious and longest work stoppages."[50]

"A structural change upsets both the existing power balance and the political status quo."[51] Therefore, management is frequently willing to endure a costly strike rather than acquiesce in a union-sought structural change that will weaken its position in all future negotiations.

Public sector unions may also attempt to enhance their power by altering the structure of bargaining. Once an impasse in negotiations is reached, the union may attempt to achieve its objectives by altering the decision-making process of the city's management. This is particularly true when no procedures for resolving impasses are available (as was the case in Memphis).

Tactics may include appeals to the legislative branch of government, to higher levels of government, and to the public to apply pressure on the decision makers. Calls for third-party arbitration, factfinding, or the involvement of "neutrals" in the bargaining are additional tactics. New York City lost whatever control it had of the bargaining relationship with its employees when former Mayor Robert Wagner agreed to submit a dispute to third parties.[52]

The Memphis police and firefighters unions appealed to the city council, to the governor, and to the state legislature. They requested arbitration and factfinding. They succeeded in obtaining support from the governor, whose threat (never implemented) of financial penalties surely put additional pressure on the mayor.

The unions appealed to the public through a recall petition and a televised debate. The petition failed to gain momentum, however, and quietly disappeared, and the debate failed to call forth a public outcry against the mayor. In fact, public opinion generally was favorable to the mayor.

When these tactics failed, the unions' desire for public involvement waned. The mayor's proposals for a direct referendum on wage increases were met with responses from the unions that it was unrealistic to expect the voters to approve a tax increase.

The unions also attempted to alter the structure of bargaining by involving other labor organizations in the disputes. The Memphis AFL-CIO Labor Council brought additional pressure to bear on the mayor by threatening to call a general strike in the city. The Memphis Education Association threatened to honor picket lines.

These pressures from labor organizations which were not directly involved in the disputes expanded the scope of the controversy beyond the units actually involved in the negotiations. Businessmen, anxious to avoid further adverse impacts on sales, joined the clamor. The addition of these third-party pressures was a structural change which enhanced the bargaining power of the police and firefighters unions. The impact of the mayor's refusal to come to terms would have spread far beyond the strikes of the two unions involved if he had refused this intervention.

At the end of the strikes, the structure of bargaining was ultimately changed. Five representatives of the Memphis Chamber of Commerce and five members of the Memphis AFL-CIO Labor Council were allowed to participate in the bargaining sessions.

These representatives of community interest groups were able to act as mediators between the mayor and the striking unions. A compromise settlement was finally reached, and the mediators were credited with finding the solution. The impasse was broken through the introduction of "community multilateral bargaining."

Thus, the mayor had won on the basic wage issues, but the unions had succeeded in altering the structure of bargaining in these negotiations and for the future. The mayor will never again have complete and unfettered discretion in formulating and presenting collective bargaining proposals.

The contract which was finally executed contained a later eliminated provision for recommendations of a factfinding board on 1979 wage increases. The record clearly indicates that factfinding proposals are likely to be binding upon employers, whether public or private, but are often either successfully rejected by unions or used by unions as a takeoff point for securing greater benefits.[53]

Outrageous Tactics

The Memphis police and firefighters' attempts to alter the structure of bargaining (or the decision-making process) were made during, or under the threat of, strikes and were compounded by the use of violence as a tactic. Strikes are by definition coercive tools. When attempts to alter the structure of governmental bargaining are viewed as attempts to alter the decision-making process of government, and when used in conjunction with a strike or strike threat, the inappropriateness of such tactics is apparent. When violence is added, the tactics become outrageous.

The unions were in effect attempting to alter the structure of government by coercive means and in a manner that certainly appears to be antithetical to the democratic process. Perhaps, as Wellington and Winter have suggested, strikes by public employee unions may truly endanger the "normal American political process."[54]

In addition to the political consequences, protective service strikes also have a great impact on the social and economic life of the community. Unlike most other public services, police and fire protection cannot easily be replaced during a strike. The lack of full fire and police protection jeopardizes the safety of the public, and curfews are often imposed which damage the economic and social life of the community. Strikes by police and firefighters are simply too devastating to be tolerated. The Memphis experience adds further evidence to this seemingly obvious fact.

Epilogue to the Strikes

Following the Memphis strikes, the city council decided that a more effective bargaining structure, along with a more effective deterrent to strikes, was needed. The council therefore approved placing a charter-change referendum on the November 1978 ballot.

The referendum contained a provision for the arbitration of impasses in bargaining and a provision for the mandatory disciplining of city employees who engage in strikes. The arbitration clause provides that: "The city council shall, by ordinance, set up procedures for arbitration of economic issues of municipal labor disputes by the council or a committee of the council, and establish rules and procedures therefore."[55]

The mandatory discipline provision provides, inter alia, that "Any municipal employee who participates in a strike as herein defined shall be conclusively deemed to have resigned his appointment or employment with the City . . . . No person exercising any authority, supervision or direction over any municipal employee shall have the power to authorize, approve, or consent to a strike by any one or more municipal employees, and such person shall not authorize, approve, or consent to such strike. No officer, board, commission, or committee of the City of Memphis shall have the power to grant amnesty to any person who has violated any of the provisions of this section."[56]

The change in the city charter was approved by the voters in the November 7, 1978, referendum. The unions had achieved the involvement of the council and the binding arbitration which they had sought so fervently during the strikes, but they received something more. Leaders of the unions opposed the charter-change provision as "punitive."

The new arbitration procedures will not be without problems. Mandatory discipline provisions have been notorious failures in other jurisdictions.[57] Furthermore, the advent of binding arbitration cannot be hailed as a cure-all. The big test arises when unfavorable binding awards are issued. The evidence of disregard for the law by engaging in illegal strikes has been known to occur in the event of unfavorable arbitral awards. The Montreal police strike was called to protest an arbitrator's final award.[58]

Whatever the potential flaws, the new system will offer some advantages. In terms of internal union politics, compulsory arbitration will allow "the union leader to duck the question of whether to engage in a job action. For the union leader with a militant, young membership anxious to press any advantage including the strike, compulsory arbitration offers a safe haven in a stormy sea."[59]

The new arbitration procedures will also provide a broader range of participation by elected officials in the bargaining process. The next chapter of the Memphis public employee collective bargaining story is thus being carried out under an entirely new structure.

NOTES

1. One exception is Keith Ocheltree, ed., *Six Strike Stories* (Chicago: Public Personnel Association, 1969); Frank H. Cassell and Jean J. Baron, *Collective Bargaining in the Public Sector* (Columbus, Ohio: Grid, 1975).

2. Weakley County Municipal Electric System v. Vick, 43 TennApp 524, 309 SW2d 792 (TennCtApp, 1957), 33 LC § 70,874, *cert denied* (TennCtApp, 1958), 34 LC § 71,273.

3. City of Alcoa v. IBEW Local 760, 203 Tenn 12, 308 SW2d 476 (TennSupCt. 1957), 33 LC § 71,125.

4. 49 Tennessee Code Annotated Section 55.01 et seq. (Supp. 1978).

5. Arnold M. Zack, "Impasses, Strikes, and Resolutions," ed. Sam Zagoria, *Public Workers and Unions* (Englewood Cliffs, N.J.: Prentice-Hall, Inc., 1972), p. 102.

6. See, e.g., J. Edwin Stanfield, "Memphis: More Than a Garbage Strike," *Current*, No. 95 (May 1968), p. 11 et seq.; *Wall Street Journal*, April 8, 1968, p. 1; *Business Week*, March 30, 1968, pp. 40-42; *Time*, August 16, 1968, p. 23.

7. *Commercial Appeal* (Memphis), August 13, 1971, p. 1, and December 17, 1971, p. 1.

8. *Ibid.*, July 8, 1973, p. 1.

9. *Memphis Press-Scimiter*, July 8, 1977, p. 1.

10. *Ibid.*, August 5, 1977, p. 1.

11. *Commercial Appeal* (Memphis), July 11, 1978, p. 10.

12. *Ibid.*, p. 1.

13. *Ibid.*

14. Shelby County Criminal Court, *Jail Book* (1978), p. 23.

15. *Commercial Appeal* (Memphis), July 9, 1978, p. 1.

16. *Memphis Press-Scimiter*, July 3, 1978, p. 3.

17. *Commercial Appeal* (Memphis), October 22, 1978, p. 3; *Memphis Press-Scimiter*, October 11, 1978, p. 4.

18. *Memphis Press-Scimiter*, July 3, 1978, p. 1; *Government Employee Relations Report*, No. 787 (July 10, 1978), p. 15.

19. *Memphis Press-Scimiter*, July 3, 1978, p. 3.

20. *Ibid.*

21. *Ibid.*

22. *Ibid.*

23. *Commercial Appeal* (Memphis), July 9, 1978, p. 6.

24. Interview, Memphis, January 24, 1979.

25. *Commercial Appeal* (Memphis), July 3, 1978, p. 5.

26. Shelby County Criminal Court, *Docket Book*, Entry No. 364661 (1978).

27. *Commercial Appeal* (Memphis), December 21, 1978, p. 23.

28. *Memphis Press-Scimiter*, July 3, 1978, p. 1.

29. *Ibid.*, July 5, 1978, p. 1.

30. *Commercial Appeal* (Memphis), August 13, 1978, p. 10.

31. *Ibid.*, August 14, 1978, p. 14.

32. *Ibid.*

33. *Ibid.*, August 8, 1978, p. 1.

34. *Ibid.*

35. *Ibid.*, August 15, 1978, p. 9.

36. *Ibid.*, August 16, 1978, p. 1.

37. *Government Employee Relations Report*, No. 774 (August 28, 1978), p. 18.

38. The factfinding provisions of the settlement were superseded by later action by the city council and the voters. (See below.)

39. A city court judge later dismissed charges against 130 police and firemen who had been arrested for curfew infractions.

40. The unions were ultimately successful in involving the council in negotiations and in winning an arbitration procedure. (See below.)

41. Hervey A. Juris and Peter Feuille, *Police Unionism: Power and Impact in Public-Sector Bargaining* (Lexington, Mass.: Lexington Books, 1973), p. 88.

42. See notes 15-21 and relevant text.

43. See Note, "Private Damage Actions against Public Sector Unions for Illegal Strikes," *Harvard Law Review*, Vol. 91 (April 1978), p. 1309.

44. Harry H. Wellington and Ralph K. Winter, *The Unions and the Cities* (Washington, D.C.: Brookings Institution, 1971), p. 25. See also Lee C. Shaw and R. Theodore Clark, "Public Sector Strikes: An Empirical Analysis," *Journal of Law and Education*, Vol. 2 (April 1973), p. 233.

45. James A. Craft, "Fire Fighter Strategy in Wage Negotiations," *Quarterly Review of Economics and Business,* Vol. 11 (Autumn 1971), p. 68 (emphasis in original).

46. See, e.g., Elias Canetti, *Crowds and Power* (New York: Viking Press, 1966), pp. 16-22, 485-495.

47. Wellington and Winter, cited at note 44, p. 25.

48. See, e.g., William N. Chernish, *Coalition Bargaining: A Study of Union Tactics and Public Policy* (Philadelphia: Industrial Research Unit, The Wharton School, University of Pennsylvania, 1969); George H. Hildebrand, "Bargaining Structure and Relative Power," ed. Richard L. Rowan, *Collective Bargaining: Survival in the '70s?* (Philadelphia: Industrial Research Unit, The Wharton School, University of Pennsylvania, 1972), p. 10; E. R. Livernash, "The Relation of Power to the Structure and Process of Collective Bargaining," *Journal of Law and Economics,* Vol. 6 (October 1963), p. 10; Herbert R. Northrup, "Reflections on Bargaining Structure Change," ed. Richard L. Rowan, *Readings in Labor Economics and Labor Relations,* 3rd ed. (Homewood, Ill.: Richard D. Irwin, 1976), p. 242.

49. See Chernish, cited at note 48, p. 109.

50. Derek C. Bok and John T. Dunlop, *Labor and the American Community* (New York: Simon & Schuster, 1970), p. 256.

51. Northrup, "Reflections on Bargaining Structure Change," p. 242.

52. See Raymond D. Horton, *Municipal Labor Relations in New York City: Lessons of the Lindsay-Wagner Years* (New York: Praeger Publishers, 1972).

53. For the factfinding experience under the Railway Labor Act, see Herbert R. Northrup, "The Railway Labor Act: A Critical Reappraisal," *Industrial and Labor Relations Review,* Vol. 25 (October 1971), pp. 3-31.

54. Wellington and Winter, p. 24. The late Professor George W. Taylor expressed a similar view on the impact of strikes by public employee unions. "Against employer inertia, state and local employees have discovered that strikes, or the threat of strikes, have enabled them suddenly to achieve long-desired but long-unattained objectives—and often more. In the headlines of this discovery, the obligation of public employees to work *within* the framework of the institutions of democratic government has been obscured." From "Public Employement: Strikes or Procedures?" *Industrial and Labor Relations Review,* Vol. 20 (July 1967), p. 617 (emphasis in original).

55. *Commercial Appeal* (Memphis), November 5, 1978, p. 12-H.

56. *Ibid.*

57. "[E]xperience in various jurisdictions has shown that in order to settle a strike the authorities have sometimes had to ignore or evade the penalty provisions in the law they have sworn to uphold." M. W. Aussicker, *Police Collective Bargaining* (Chicago: Public Personnel Association, 1969), p. 23.

58. Zack, cited at note 5, p. 118.

59. Juris and Feuille, cited at note 41, p. 93.

PART IV

C. Investing Pensions for Social or Union Purposes

409-38

Investing Pensions for Social or Union Purposes: A Legal Analysis

Roy A. Schotland[†]

I. Introduction

> Pension funds represent the largest single source of capital in the United States today, representing 27 percent of gross national product. About 500,000 private pension plans, 6,600 state and local government plans, and 38 special federal worker retirement plans collectively hold more than $550 billion in assets. The Department of Labor estimates that total assets of all plans could amount to $3 trillion by 1995.[1]

Thus opens a December 1980 study for the Northeast-Midwest Congressional Coalition, representing over 240 members of Congress. Senator Chafee (R-R.I.) and Congressman Edgar (D-Pa.), the coalition officers releasing the study, announced hearings in 1981 to investigate how pension assets are invested and to get "more of the pension funds directed to local investments."[2]

That study's approach to pension investment typifies many recent studies, articles, and speeches—including the Democratic National Convention spotlight talk on pension investing by Governor Brown of California. Typically, the first note is the sheer size of pension assets, and the reason for pointing to such size typically follows at once: some special objective is deemed worthy of an investment preference. Here the call is for more local investing; elsewhere it is for investing to promote reindustrialization, or unionization, or unionized building, or homebuilding whether or not unionized, or home financing for members of the pension plan, or exclusion of the securities of some companies, or etc.

Also typical is the exaggeration of the vastness of pension assets. "27 percent of gross national product" is misleading: it measures a fixed asset amount accumulated over decades against a single year's output.

---

* Reprinted by permission of the author and the *Journal of Labor Research* from Roy A. Schotland, "Have Pension Investment Managers Over-Emphasized the Needs of Retirees?," *Journal of Labor Research*, Vol. II, No. 2 (Fall 1981).

† Roy A. Schotland is Professor of Law at the Georgetown University Law Center.

In the less dramatic, but only proper, comparison, if we measure the $653 billion in pension assets as of end-1980[3] against the relevant figure—the total outstanding financial assets in the U.S. of $4,882 billion (the stock, the bonds, and the mortgages, not even counting such other assets as several trillion dollars in real estate equity)—we find that pension assets are not 27 percent but 13 percent.

Those aspects of typicality are minor, compared to one overriding aspect that typifies all calls to turn pension investing toward new directions: the utterly unqualified failure even to note why pension assets are there at all. Retirement security is simply ignored in these advocates' approach to pension investing.

The advocates' unconcern for retirees and the need for retirement income is not merely callous, it also gets around the major flaw in their discovery of pension assets as a huge sum available for new uses. Even $653 billion sounds small—and unavailable— when one recalls that these assets exist to honor the pension promise, or in less colorful terms, to meet legal obligations. Although we cannot measure the liabilities as precisely as the assets, fair estimates are that the $653 billion, plus new contributions and investment earnings, must meet merely *vested* pension liabilities of around $775 billion; or more realistically measured, total accrued obligations of around $955 billion.[4] Still further, since most people's pensions are not rich to begin with and, yet worse, are severely eroded in our inflationary era, the liabilities must be revised upward if the pension promise is to be honored actually, not merely nominally. In fact, as inflation has continued, pension benefits have been increased, even for people already retired. Although the increases are far too little to make up for inflation, they balloon liabilities. Just one example: in 1979 General Motors agreed upon improved pension benefits, which of course did not produce a leap upward in their massive pension assets of $11 billion, but did immediately raise their corresponding vested pension liabilities from $13.8 billion to about $17.6 billion, a rise in their *unfunded* vested liability from 22 percent of corporate net worth, to 32 percent.[5] The agreement provided not merely for that rise, but for two further ones in the contract's second and third years.

II. Terminology, Perspective, and Recent Events

The traditional goal of pension investment management has been to maximize returns while maintaining an appropriate level of risk in order to assure retirement income security. Advocates of "social investing" would divert pension assets from that traditional goal in order to pursue other, socially desirable objectives. The issue is not one of For vs. Against "social" or "socially responsible" investing, for few people would be open to a plea for antisocial or irresponsible investments. And the "social" label is too broad—everyone agrees that investing for retirement security is itself a socially responsible goal. The new advocacy would more accurately be labelled "divergent" investing, since the proposal is to tap pension assets for goals other than retirement security.

Perhaps the label should be "anti-retiree," since the advocates who anoint themselves with the more affirmative labels usually simply ignore retirement income security, sometimes assign it a new, low priority, and always recommend courses of action that are likely (to say the least) to impair retirement security.

Whatever the label, surely it sounds attractive to invest both to protect retirement security and to promote such other goals as equal employment opportunity, environmental quality, local jobs, or housing. If "investment double-whammy"—that is, investment with as high a return and as low a risk as other clearly appropriate investments—also promotes common concerns of the pension fund's beneficiaries, then the only investment manager who would not buy it would be a misanthrope, hating both his clients and his own firm's future. "Double-whammy" investments do exist, they are already actively pursued by any sober pension manager,[6] although (as I specify below) more should be done with certain investment vehicles. But few advocates of divergent investing will settle for double-whammy investments, since by definition such investments meet market levels of return, and most advocates' whole point is that there are worthy needs which cannot meet market tests and therefore should be subsidized by the deepest pocket available—pension assets. Of course, the market system leaves some worthy needs unsatisfied, and I agree that many of these needs warrant government intervention. I am not one of those true believers who views free markets as the best answer to all problems except the three obvious needs for collective action: traffic lights, an army, and subsidy to my own business.

But tapping pension assets for hidden subsidies to further other goals is an especially ineffective way to pursue those other goals, and cannot be implemented without overcoming substantial obstacles, as I shall show. Most importantly, I reject any divergence from protection of retirement security.

I wholly agree with any advocate who would in no event subordinate retirement security to other goals, but who merely wants investment managers to wear no blinders. But some advocates bow to retirement security as the primary or "paramount" or "cardinal" concern, then give so little attention to protecting that security and so much concern to other goals, even suggesting that those other goals are equal—for *pension* funds—that they show an unbalance which will, I fear, immediately produce unbalanced investment decisions.

The crux of the divergent investment issue is whether there should be any investment "concession," or hidden subsidy, to pursue other goals. Investment selections are not made in tangibly measurable, "all else being equal" settings, but rather with judgment calls and predictions as well as hard data. When I hear a pension investment justified on the basis that it will serve the long-term needs of the participants by promoting jobs or the local economy, I have this response: If it is clear that there is no hidden subsidy for those other goals, then full steam ahead. But if there is any reduction in return, or uncompensated rise in riskiness or illiquidity in comparison with other readily available and appropriate investments, then the proposed step is unwise and unlawful. It is unwise because: (1) the long-term benefit is "iffy," and the immediate investment handicap is definite; and (2) for all the other reasons developed in this paper. It is unlawful because the pursuit of any goal other than retirement security has produced patterns of abuse by corporate pension sponsors as well as by unions and state and local governments, which underlie the express requirements of the Employee Retirement Income Security Act (ERISA) and, since 1937, of the Tax Code.

This advocacy is not all new. In 1931, in Wisconsin, a state assemblyman proposed to have the State Teachers Retirement Fund emphasize investment in Wisconsin farm mortgages. He said that the fund's board had "more confidence in the Dominion of Canada, Puget Sound, and God knows where than in the State of Wisconsin." In 1932, the Democratic candidate for governor pledged "to wrest control of the state investment board from big business and replace it in the hands of the people to be operated for the public good." That candidate won, and soon a statute mandated that at least 70 percent of trust monies be invested within Wisconsin, with preference for small loans on improved farm property, loans to cooperative and mutual organizations, and town mutual insurance company mortgages, in that priority.

That statute was repealed in 1945. As admitted by a recent report advocating resurrection (!) of such local preference, "The performance level of the Wisconsin portfolio may have had a bearing on the [repeal]."

Despite that Wisconsin experience, and a panoply of fundamental flaws, divergent investing is very much a live issue. Governor

Brown's Democratic Convention speech was surely the major exposure in size of audience, but similar advocacy has rung out repeatedly over the past two years. Consider:

A. *At the Federal Level.* After the Northeast-Midwest Coalition's December announcement of their coming effort to encourage local investment, coalition leader Chafee became chairman of the Senate Finance Committee's newly entitled subcommittee on Savings, Pensions, and Investment Policy. (One would expect snowbelt supporters, in light of the November election and the forthcoming redistricting, to discourage rather than to excite congressional interest in Balkanizing the American economy.) On the other hand, the presidential campaign included an exchange which suggests that federal action is not imminent. During the campaign, Carter joined AFL-CIO leaders in calling for an industrial redevelopment authority for improving railbeds and modernizing manufacturing facilities by drawing upon investment by pension funds in particular. Reagan responded that Carter was "toying with American's pension funds."[7]

B. *Among the Unions.* The AFL-CIO Executive Council, in August 1980, adopted goals for "union participation in pension fund management" and recommended these steps:[8] (1) the AFL-CIO should move to establish a new federal reindustrialization institution, supported in part by pension funds; (2) unions should encourage pension fund investment designed to increase employment, such as pooled mortgage investment in union-built housing; (3) unions should explore the possibility of coordinating the exercise of voting rights associated with the stock in pension portfolios; (4) unions should gain a voice in collectively-bargained corporate pension plans if the union has no say in management; (5) the AFL-CIO should increase training about investment policy and other aspects of pension management for representatives of unions with or without direct roles in pension mangement.

A few months earlier, the AFL-CIO's Industrial Union Department (IUD) had also brought out a report and recommendations which included a call, modified by the AFL-CIO Executive Council, for pension investment in firms with domestic rather than foreign work forces and in firms with good labor relations records. Starting in January 1981, the IUD began a monthly publication on "Labor, Pension and Benefit Funds, and Investments."

The most publicized recent union action on pension investing is the UAW-Chrysler agreement to establish a joint advisory committee to recommend to the Chrysler Corporation's pension trustees, for up to 10 percent of annual net *new* contributions (thus, this has not yet

been implemented) to the pension plan, investments in debt securities of such nonprofit institutions as nursery schools and nursing
homes, or in residential mortgages (at prevailing rates and terms) on
low-cost housing for the general public, not merely for United Automobile, Aerospace and Agricultural Implement Workers of America
(UAW) members—all such investments to be in unspecified communities, presumably where active UAW members or retirees reside.
The UAW also was authorized to recommend against any *new* Chrysler pension investment in five companies each year that conduct
business with South Africa but have not supported the elimination
of racial discrimination there (presumably, companies that have
not signed the Sullivan Principles endorsed by almost all U.S.
multinationals).

Other notable union pension efforts in 1980[10] included the establishment (by 12 multi-employer funds with total annual net cash
inflow of $200 million) of the Southern California Construction In-
dustry Real Estate Development Financing Foundation, which since
August has invested over $60 million in union-built projects screened
by established mortgage companies and if taken on, administered by
the Crocker Bank. In striking contrast, one Florida Operating Engineers multi-employer fund began giving thirty-year mortgage
loans to its own members at 10 percent interest when market rates
were around 15 percent—that program was put on "hold" after the
pension trustees lost their fiduciary liability insurance. And the
Marine Engineers' pension fund decided to put $11 million (of its
$177 million) into a $20 million project to build two new ships to be
crewed by members. Is so large a proportion of one project prudent?
Will it produce a market-level investment return? If not (even if it
were somewhere deemed legal), how evaluate whether the project
produced enough jobs to make up for the higher risk and lower return
of the investment? (That Marine Engineers' action allows questions
more precise and fewer than the many raised by the other recent
efforts described above; it is the task of the bulk of this paper to raise
those further questions.)

C. The State and Local Funds. With the biggest such funds, California's governor started a Public Investment Task Force "to develop
plans for creating new investments 'that are both prudent and responsive to the needs which California faces in the areas of affordable
housing, small business development, alternative energy development and job creation.' "[11] But, when one of his cabinet agencies,
State and Consumer Services, commissioned a study of "ethical investing," it was limited to equal employment and South African

involvement, not on the governor's list of goals nor obvious "consumer" concerns like product safety or fair sales practices. The study, by an able New York City public interest organization, is discussed more fully below.

In March 1981, the California governor's task force issued an interim report, significant particularly for its time-after-time emphasis that:

> [P]rudence is the basis of all investment decisions. It is paramount that pension funds be managed prudently and in the best interests of beneficiaries so that retirement income is secure. The financial integrity of a retirement system must be the cardinal concern of any pension investment policy.

Despite that emphasis, a few times the wish to "have it both ways" peeps through, raising doubts about how and how much the task force would safeguard against divergence from "the cardinal concern." For example:

> Programs of less-than-market-rate investments that may directly benefit the pension plan members should be a matter jointly determined by the trustees, fund managers and the beneficiaries themselves so as to prudently balance cost and benefits.[12]

Particularly useful is that report's repeated focus on how much more is needed than hip-shooting redirection of pension fund assets. The report calls for numerous new state government agencies, lending and guarantee programs, etc. (as if California were not the home of the "tax revolt" and shrinking government), as well as for new mortgage-related instruments to join the current federal family of Fanny Mae, Ginny Mae, Freddy Mac—new state-sponsored siblings—Cali Mae, her quite different sister Callie Mae, and their cousin Sunny Mac, this last a solar and energy conservation mortgage program with the interesting feature that "if a [solar] device didn't work, consumers would have recourse and protection." One of the task force's most troubling proposals is that the managers of the $60 billion in California's private, state, and local pension funds should coordinate their information and local investing. Is the new passion for localism, a near-resurrection of the Articles of Confederacy, really worth obliterating the older fear of concentration among centers of economic power and conspiracy in restraint of free-market choices?

For all the enormity of the California state pension funds, the proposed new investment goals may be an over-ambitious overload. In addition to the *six* goals noted above (and "job creation" is read broadly, i.e., overall local economic development), a 1980 statute directed the public employees' fund to provide home mortgages for participants, and the task force broadened the "ethical investing goals." Unsurprisingly, substantially larger staffing for the funds is also proposed.

In New York as in several other states, a legislator has been in the press repeatedly attacking the state funds' investment practices, and a city official called for city fund investments in local federally-guaranteed residential mortgages. Texas and Massachusetts are increasing mortgage-related investing (although whether this is to involve market rates or a preference is unclear, depending upon who is quoted[13]); the governor of Illinois has appointed a task force; a border state's fund is under seige by the home builders; Kansas purports to help its state economy by keeping its liquid assets in Kansas bank certificates of deposit; and in short, the scene generally is best summed up by two high officials of major states:

—A state treasurer, responding to another cabinet officer's proposal for divergent investing:

> We have reviewed this type of proposal over and over again, and we must resist any ill-conceived generalities which would open the investment of pension funds to political and special interest influences, or to the passing fancies of the day.

— James Sublett, executive director of the Ohio State Teachers Retirement System, opening his 1979 annual report to 250,000 participants:

> Dear Member:
>
> Sometime before the next annual report is issued we will pass another milestone—the assets of your retirement program will exceed $5 billion. These are the funds which provide benefits for 45,000 current retirees and are being accumulated to pay benefits to active members as they reach retirement age.
>
> Unfortunately, there are constant demands by pressure groups to utilize these funds for "pet" projects of one kind or another. Other groups wish to impose artificial restrictions on the investment of your funds, generally in a manner which will reduce the return therefrom.
>
> Investment income continues to be the largest single contributor to our assets. In the year ended June 30 this source produced nearly 40% of the total annual income of the System, in excess of $333 million. Any reduction in that income brought about by unwise restrictions must be made up by increasing either the cost to the member or to the taxpayer, or both.
>
> We urge you to maintain a close watch on your money and help us protect it from any and all attempts to divert it to causes and for purposes not in the best interest of the participants.

Fittingly, the last action in the state scene is probably the opening of the rollback of divergent proposals. A major state fund is considering adopting a policy on "non-economic investment considerations," endorsing investments if they are wholly sound financially and also have some special attraction for that state, but closing as follows:

> In cases where there is an apparent investment handicap, the nature and estimated amount of the difference in expected return and risk shall also be publicly announced to inform and protect the interests of our plan participants before any material investments are made.

How would you expect the participants of that State's plan to respond to any such notice?

III. Forces Fueling Advocacy of Divergent Investing

The main force fueling the efforts aimed at new uses for pension assets is the idea that these assets offer the most promising bridge between our society's problems and the limited resources available to meet them. At least since 1973, when the sheiks of Araby took revenge for the nineteenth century (to use Giscard d'Estaing's immortal phrase), our economy has not been growing as it had, but private pension assets are growing at an annual rate of 10 percent, state and local funds at 12 to 15 percent.

Under most pressure for divergent investing are the state and local funds, which combine political vulnerability with unusually large assets, $203 billion at end-1980, $170 billion at end-1979. Of that $170 billion, New York and California alone held—

New York State Funds:	$27 billion
California State Funds:	21 billion
New York City Funds:	13 billion
California Local Funds:	8 billion
	$69 billion

The top twenty-five state and local funds held $126 to $130 billion, while the twenty-five largest multi-employer or Taft-Hartley funds, the other vulnerable group, held only $12 billion. (For perspective: the top twenty-five corporate funds held $120 billion.)[14]

Pension assets draw attention because they look so large, but attention turns into clamor for change because prudent pension investing has done poorly at winning the financial returns which, it is argued, must be the exclusive concern if retirement security is to be protected. Everybody knows that our economy, and therefore our securities markets, have done poorly in recent years. But the mediocrity of pension investment performance cannot be so easily excused.

I have shown elsewhere that pension funds' equity performances have been strikingly inferior to the performance of a comparable set of portfolios, equity mutual funds (either with or without risk adjustment), over seventeen years, ten years, five years, three years and one year. Over seventeen years (to end-1978), equity mutual funds outperformed the equity performance of pension funds by almost 40 percent; over ten years and five years (to 9/30/79), equity mutual funds again outperformed the others by 22 percent and over 5 percent, respectively.[15] Other studies produced the same sad result. While various *caveats* about the data are in order (and are set forth there at length), no explanation of the data nor speculation about the causes of such relative weakness can obscure the appalling fact that pension investment professionals have not produced even tolerably well.

Mediocre investment performance by the private pension system exposes it not only to arguments against traditional prudent investing, but even calls into question the justification for having a private pension system.

Such weak pension investment performance looms up like a loud litany in the advocates' call for divergent investing. Thus, President Carter's 1980 call for pulling pension assets into a reindustrialization fund—with curious silence about what returns such investment would produce for the pension investors—pointed with justifiable alarm to the ten-year median pension fund investment annualized return, 4.3 percent, the figure from the Becker evaluation service. That figure also appeared prominently in the AFL-CIO IUD's report, and in the Northeast-Midwest Coalitions.[16] In fact, if we use more current data, shifting the ten-year period forward merely from end-1979 to end-1980, the 4.3 percent annualized return rises by almost one-half, to 6.3 percent. Even though second-guessing about investing is even easier than about football, can one abandon traditional investing with confidence that the poor 1970s' markets will continue? Or alternatively, might we see markets yielding returns more like those from prudent equity investing (using the S.&P. 500 as a proxy) in other periods:[17]

1959-68:	9.8 percent	annualized
1958-67:	12.6 percent	annualized
1954-63:	15.7 percent	annualized
1949-58:	19.5 percent	annualized!

IV. Who Would Lose from Divergent Investing?

If a proposed divergent investment offers market-equivalent likelihood of returns, liquidity, and riskiness, then as noted at the outset, Viva!—there is no problem. But since advocacy of divergence is precisely a call for some degree of *hidden* subsidy, i.e., some sacrifice of investment earnings, remember just how much investment earnings matter. As the Ohio State Teachers' director noted, that fund relies on investment income for almost 40 percent of the system's total annual income, a figure almost exactly the same as the finding—38.3 percent—from the latest study of state and local funds.[18] If pension costs as a percent of payroll run about 10 percent of state and local payrolls and investment returns run about 7 percent of assets—both figures from that study—and if divergent investing lowered returns to 6 percent of assets, then employer contributions would have to make up for the lost inflow, which translates to boosting total payroll costs just about 1 percent, small as a percentage, but not small in tax dollars. And that calculation may be too conservative; many systems use a rule of thumb that a 1 percent (100 basis points) lower investment return means a 20 to 25 percent higher contribution burden. Perhaps the advocates of divergent investing live in communities that, even these days, are inviting tax boosts?

Lower investment earnings not only mean higher taxes for governmental employers, or a profit squeeze for private employers, they also jeopardize retirees. For one thing, benefits must be moved up in an inflationary era, or the retirees moved down, as shown in precise figures below; but raising benefits, of course, raises costs, which are far harder to bear if investment earnings are weak. Even without the retirees' need to keep real purchasing power, the retiree is at risk if pension earnings suffer. First, the law is not settled that the participant can look beyond the pension fund to satisfy his claim (and most pension lawyers would disagree with my view that this question should be settled in favor of participants at the expense of sponsors). To the extent that pension claims must be settled out of pension assets, without recourse to the employer, then obviously the participant has quite a stake in strong pension earnings. Second, the pension claim is not fully insured. Under the 1980 ERISA amendments for multi-employer plans, which unfortunately may be followed soon for all plans, there are very low limits on the federal guarantees, so the participant who wants to enjoy not a guaranteed pittance, but a pension as promised, needs strong pension earnings. (Of course, lower investment earnings are "smoothed out" by actuarial spreading over a longer period, and there is no immediate, provable tie between investment earnings and benefits.)

George Lingua put it best: if divergent investing jeopardizes investment returns, then "everyone, all the major parties, bear the risk."[19]

V. The Prime Objection to Divergent Investing

The prime objection to divergent investing is that any interference with pension funds' maximizing investment returns (at acceptable levels of risk) undeniably interferes with retirement security. Protection of retirement security is itself so socially responsible a goal that it is not only agreed to by ever-increasing numbers of employers and employees, but is underwritten by favorable tax treatment for contributions into pension funds, for the funds' earnings, and even for the benefits paid out. Nor is this one of those tax subsidies which is mainly loophole: for four decades the Internal Revenue Code required that pension funds be used for the "exclusive benefit" of participants' retirement security. The commitment to retirement security as the "exclusive benefit" was repeated in the Taft-Hartley Act in 1947, and in 1974, it was greatly reinforced by the ERISA with its panoply of bans against divergent uses of pension funds. Could it be any clearer that Congress deems retirement security, in its legislative litany, the *"exclusive* benefit"?

Insistence on *"exclusive* benefit" is explained by the same reason that pension assets look so huge: the cost of retirement security. State and local pension funds, now over $203 billion of assets, have an unfunded liability so vast—and involving such uncertainties and data gaps—that in 1975,[20] estimates ranged from 150 percent to 270 percent of the then assets. According to the most recent study, the unfunded obligations are 27 percent of current assets by the most sanguine measure, and 79 percent of current assets by the plans' own measurements.[21] The current $203 billion of assets is so inadequate that a 1979 Government Accounting Office (GAO) study of representative state and local funds, including such strong ones as California state funds, found ¾ of the funds so underfunded that they were not even up to ERISA *minima* for private plans. As for the obligations of private pension plans, estimates of unfunded *vested* liabilities are 19 percent or 20 percent of current pension assets, looking only at major corporations. More realistic unfunded obligations (past service liability) are estimated to range from 42 percent to 82 percent of the major corporation's current pension assets.[22]

Yet even these obligations, so massive as to make pension assets look modest, plus the additional annual pension contributions of about 10 percent of state and local government payrolls and over 7 percent of large company payrolls, are understated— they fail to honor the pension promise. We all know inflation, but only economists and retirees see fully who suffers most: retirees.

What has inflation meant to a person who retired ten years ago, or five years ago? We need not worry about the consumer price index's (CPI) drawbacks, in light of how far behind the pensioners of even America's strongest companies, the Fortune 500, have been.[23]

Fortune 500 Average Retiree Retired for—

CPI rise:	—15 yrs.	—10 yrs.	—5 yrs.
	Benefit increases since:		
1970-75	37.6%	28%	22%	11%
1975-80	47.9%	20%	17%	8%

The only similar data—and no other data are usable[24]—are from one of the strongest state systems, Ohio Teachers.[25] Their retirees are *not* covered by Social Security.

Ohio Teacher, Retired—

CPI rise since:	—15 yrs.	—10 yrs.	—5 yrs.
	Benefit increases since:		
1965	162.1	76.3%		
1970	111.8		32.3%	
1975	52.1			14.7%

For persons receiving Social Security, with its full indexing, the picture must be adjusted. But Social Security benefits are not lavish and, sadly, are decreasing. And it has not been the purpose of the private pension system to leave pensioners little or no better off than Social Security recipients. The pension promise was stated perfectly by Ford Motor's Theodore Yntema in 1950:

> Our pension obligation cannot be considered a dollar obligation, such as that of an insurance company. We must consider it as an obligation to provide future purchasing power and, if possible, take action to offset the inflationary trend.[26]

And the favorable tax treatment for the private pension system is not extended merely to aid upper-income participants while lower-income participants are left to rely mainly—or, if "integrated out," then wholly—on Social Security. In saying this, by no means do I fault private (or state and local) pension sponsors— inflation has also rendered them less able to meet retirement needs. I mean to say only that in the current economic era, protecting retirement security requires *increasing* emphasis on the needs of retirees, not diverging to other goals.

If the day comes when retirees are well off, relative to the rest of society, we can reopen the question whether the "exclusive benefit" of retirement security should be relaxed for divergent goals. Until then, pension assets are needed for a social task far bigger than the assets themselves—paying adequate retirement benefits. Until then, advocacy of divergent investing is an unconscious—or if conscious, a contemptible—effort to take money from the elderly, who themselves need financial aid at least as much as any other group.

VI. The Six Problems of Implementing Divergent Investing

Which divergent goals should be pursued? Consider: (1) equal employment opportunity—in terms of race, sex, age, *et al.*; (2) occupational safety and health; (3) consumer protection—product safety, fair advertising, etc.; (4) unionization; (5) environmental protection; (6) energy conservation; (7) discouraging involvement in countries violating human rights—South Africa—what about all the others? (8) inner-city redevelopment; (9) housing generally; (10) small business generally; (11) local or regional development; (12) discouraging production of alcohol and tobacco; and (13) discouraging production of war material.

Then came the goals that would emerge as soon as divergent investing took hold. An example we all should have thought of, but probably did not, emerges from a survey of corporate pension investment professionals conducted in 1978 by *Institutional Investor* magazine. After asking whether the respondents had engaged in "socially responsible" investing—none were so engaged—the survey asked what "social" goals would be followed, if any. The response, the clear top priority of the corporate pension funds: "setting limits on how much your fund should invest in companies or industries in competition with your own company."

Second implementation problem: what priorities should rank the divergent goals, if more than one is to be pursued? This is not merely a matter of the finitude of resources, meaning the pension fund can no more pursue all the goals than the child in the candy shop can buy all the goodies. Worse, what happens if a pension system wants both to promote equal employment opportunity and to discourage involvement in South Africa, and finds that a firm at the forefront of equal employment hiring is also involved in South Africa?

Third, who decides what should be the goals and priorities? The *sole* goal on which all pension plan participants will agree, is protection of retirement security. Divergence involves the participants and their trustees in a decision process that will be political at best or subjective and divisive at worst. The decisions are likely to be unacceptable unless they result from a truly political process, i.e., a representative and accountable group making the decisions. Simple and uncontroversial as it may seem to install such a process, it is not.

It is intolerable for a fund to diverge from the exclusive benefit of retirement security without any retiree role in the decision about such divergence. In Taft-Hartley funds, by statutory requirement, the employees have as many representatives as employers—but retirees have none. Retirees do not need separate pension board representation if they are entitled to vote, just like active union members, for the union officials generally. But such democratic and fraternal treatment of the franchise is found only in a small minority of unions—e.g., Mine Workers, Auto Workers, Machinists, and a few others.

I have long argued for representation of employees, and of retirees, in pension plan governance.[27] Only in state and local pension systems is such representation frequent. But even in most state and local systems with employee representation, there is none for retirees. The difference between actives and retirees becomes a conflict of interest as the assets are exploited for goals other than retirement security.

Consider New York City. The police pension fund, with 25,911 actives and 18,212 retirees, includes on its board three PBA officers representing active patrolmen, one representative of the sergeants, one the lieutenants, one the captains and one of the detectives. But for the retired members of New York's Finest—no representative at all. While it was necessary to use the five New York City pension funds as a temporary bridge to get the city through its financial crisis, the funds are being put at risk to render long-term aid that only a captive source would render. This was done largely to protect current job security and pay, thereby favoring the actives although the several billion dollars of assets so gambled could still turn sour and cause untold harm to retirees.

As for corporate pension funds, there has been only one exception to the flat statement that employees, both active and retired, have no role at all in pension governance. (That one exception, Citicorp's pension plan for its own employees, was recently joined by new joint administrations at Heileman Brewing in Milwaukee and PF Laboratories in New Jersey.[28]) Such paternalism is perfectly appropriate at, say, U.S. Steel, where the company itself stands liable for the pension promises. But since the great majority of corporate pension sponsors insert a dubious provision that only the pension fund, not the employer, is liable for payment of the promised benefits, either such disclaimers should be scrapped (as there are other good reasons for doing) or the pension trustees must include representatives of both active and retired employees.

How revealing that in the 1980 AFL-CIO and IUD reports and recommendations, for all their focus on getting more voice in corporate pension management for the union, there is not a word about getting any voice—let alone voting rights—for retirees in the great majority of unions which emasculate their members as soon as they retire. Those unions are no less paternalistic about their retirees than employers were paternalistic about employees before the Wagner Act.

The fourth implementation problem is the severe lack of information on which to base investment decisions aimed at furthering divergent goals. If the goal of divergent investing is to promote investment in local mortgages, then defining proper investments is easy. But when divergent investing goes beyond simple local chauvinism (a nostalgia, perhaps, for the medieval Italian or ancient Greek city-states—glorious eras, but hard to reconcile with steel mills and computers), real difficulties arise.

If a pension fund decides it wants to pursue divergent investing in its equity portfolio, how does it select the companies to buy or to avoid? The fact that "there is no systematic method for obtaining and evaluating information about the activities and practices of companies in which the funds invest" is deemed one of the prime reasons that "the current decision-making framework [for divergent investing] appears inadequate," according to one of the best studies advocating divergent investing.[29] The latest similar study, done by an able organization for a California agency, also emphasizes "the incomplete and preliminary nature of much of the data available—a prerequisite for development of a coherent ethical investment policy for just these two issues [Equal Employment Opportunity (EEP) and involvement with South Africa] requires the gathering of sufficient data upon which informed judgment can be based."[30]

The data gap does not mean that pension fund managers cannot find out about General Electric's (GE) relations with the Equal Employment Opportunity Commission (EEOC), or General Motors' (GM) relations with the Occupational Safety and Health Administration (OSHA). But how can it be decided whether GE or GM is notably good, or notably bad, without employing some standard of comparison? Without comparable data, investment decisions on non-financial grounds risk being inaccurate (and therefore unfair) and ineffective; Company A might look good or bad on, say, equal employment, only as long as one does not know how others in its industry or its geographic area are performing. Producing responsible analyses in this area is a considerable task involving substantial costs: the Council on Economic Priorities' (CEP) study of political influence and lobbying by military contractors cost $75,000; its study of nuclear power's impact on job creation (in one locale!) cost $292,000; its much-praised study of paper companies' pollution practices cost $50,000 (and that was back in 1969-1970).

The problem of timely data is pointed up by the fact that months before release of the CEP's report for California, which listed Coca-Cola as a "bad" investment because it was active in South Africa but had not agreed to the Sullivan Principles, Coca-Cola switched its position—in response to a shareholder proposal—and signed the Sullivan Principles.[31]

Although responsible "social performance" data are costly, they can be developed, and certainly, I join in believing that they should be. But this will occur only if groups, instead of seeking publicity about being "socially responsible," try to implement that goal by joining with major companies and major institutional investors to bring us usable social performance data. We need the economies of scale if such data are to be sound and routinely available, the *only* way such data will make a difference.

I would like to see such data available because I personally sympathize with most of the social goals in question. I would also like to see it because I believe that poor social performance is a forerunner of poor financial performance.

Still more implementation problems: to the extent that the divergent investments are aimed to benefit—or bring pressure on—firms or ventures situated in the same locality or industry as the pension fund, consider what kinds of investments are likely to occur: those with political appeal, and often those that raise acute conflicts of interest. If a construction union invests in mortgages to finance a construction project on which its members will have jobs, can we be confident that the projects will be selected by neutral criteria? If state and local pension funds are to invest in local projects, then (once we abandon the discipline of seeking market returns) will there not be enormous competition for the pension fund dollars, with politics replacing market return as the determinant?

Politics are the right measure of who gets into office and how public policy issues are resolved. Contrast the safeguards surrounding political decisions (pork-barrel or not) as against what will happen when the bees gather around the pension fund honey pot. Not even the strongest and most representative pension board will have as much independence, as much political balance of countervailing forces, as a legislature. Not even the most major pension fund investment decisions will have as much public visibility and relative comprehensibility as decisions being forged in the legislature. Last, how do we evaluate the portfolio managers' performance if we diverge from traditional prudent investing with its sole focus on investment return? How evaluate success or failure in furthering the divergent goals? In short, a pension fund being engaged in divergent investing is likely to become captive to whatever interests have muscle—whatever form their strength may take—to shape the choice of divergent goals and the selection of specific investments.

VII. Three Reasons Why Divergent Investing, Even If Implemented, Will Not Work

Even if the implementation hurdles are overcome, still to be faced are three easily described "impact hurdles," obstacles standing in the way of the divergent investments having any impact on the divergent goal.

First, the "displacement" problem: if, for example, a pension fund buys stock in a firm because of its admirable EEO record, or sells or avoids some other firm because of its awful record, what reason is there to believe the fund's purchase or sale will have *any* impact on the company in question? Massive liquidation or accumulation of a security will move its price, but the bigger the company—and by definition it is the bigger companies' conduct that must be the focus in corporate "social performance"—the harder to affect the stock price.

The second "impact problem" involves "leakage" and "multipliers." Will an investment in a firm because it has a fine EEO record actually do anything to promote equal employment, or will it go into uses having no relationship to the conduct motivating the investment? "Leakage" is most obvious when it comes to trying to make "local" investments.[32] Even if a target company is local, unless all its activity is local, how to be sure the local community benefits from the investment? Or even if the company is wholly local, what if the funds are used to purchase new equipment to make the firm more profitable by reducing labor costs?

The last impact problem—and the last hurdle I will note[33]—is "interference": the investment impact of the pension fund may run into forces running in the opposite direction. For example: the Wisconsin State Investment Board had made a $1,700,000 private-placement loan to Kearney & Trecker, a Milwaukee-based manufacturer of machine tools. Upon Kearney's merger with The Cross Company, a Michigan-based machine tool firm of about the same size, the new combined headquarters were located in Detroit. The choice went against Wisconsin because of what the firm's chief executive called Wisconsin's "adverse tax structure related to capital gains, inheritance and personal income taxes."

Divergent investors not only face insurmountable obstacles in deciding what to do, how to do it, and whether doing it will matter—but other parts of their own team may be running inconsistent plays.

VIII. The Advocacy

With the case for divergent investing clearly so poor, what do the advocates say? Talks and articles follow the lines shown at the outset of this paper: (1) pension funds have big bucks; (2) Area A or Project B or Cause C is worthy and needs big bucks; (3) everyone in Area A or all employees in a B-type pension fund, benefit from aid to A or B; (4) Q.E.D. . . . add some quasi-facts, like pointing to the experience of small university endowments or mutual funds with no recognition that what may be feasible in a $20-million portfolio is unfeasible or unduly risky with $100 million, let alone with the billion-dollar funds the advocates look upon as if more were only merrier. Then add rhetoric with proper proportions of compassion and anger, and so: Have talk, Will travel.

The "studies" must go beyond that. I recognize the limits of lumping together various people and statements calling for substantially similar new directions; brevity forces compression at the price of noting subtle or arguably larger differences. But the acid test is action. If sound action is taken, we can forget about any inadequacies in preliminary studies—and so far, going by public information, I deem the Chrysler-UAW agreement and the Southern California Construction Industry mortgage program impressively sound, "double-whammy" efforts. I would rather err by calling attention to weaknesses in studies put forward by groups who matter and who call for action, however, then see silence allow the weaknesses of such studies to infect the action when it is taken. Better my skepticism proven unwarranted, than misguided investment policies proven costly. Nor is this academic piddling: the inadequacies in these studies suggest—

strongly—not merely a lack of familiarity, but a cavalier lack of caring about financial *facts*, so much so as to compel skepticism about much of the claimed concern for optimizing investment returns and protecting retirement security.

For example, both the first "social audit" of pension performance and the AFL-CIO IUD's 1980 pension investment study (the former study by, and the latter substantially researched by, the same organization) rest on faith that while George Orwell and the totalitarians may have taught us how totally language can be distorted, there is still trust in numbers, still a willingness to be impressed by well-arranged tables. After I analyzed the "social audit" in detail,[34] showing for example that its most prominent table rested on plain double-counting, its authors responded that I had made two major errors: they had not erred by 100 percent overstatement, merely by 66 percent, and I had overlooked their caveats that the "audit" was not for use but only to exemplify that such audits could be done.[35] Since there is little utility in endless analysis of distortion, I will settle for their concession of 66 percent overstatement. As for my other "error," the authors did not cite and one cannot find any caveats in the "audit" or their press release. The authors are the polar opposite of the Emperor Gordian who, Gibbon told us, had a library of 69,000 volumes and a harem of 22, both for use and not for ostentation.[36]

I need spend only a moment on the IUD's 1980 study. Earlier I noted its unawareness of the difference between *total* and *equity* investment returns. The unfamiliarity with finance, which after all is the subject, is disturbing (e.g., they give top priority to getting information on funds' investments, but there is no awareness that for a decade, pension investors have used more than prices and yields: data on relative riskiness, and on comparison with other accounts). Surely astonishing is the ignorance of their own sphere—Taft-Hartley pension funds. Leaving aside the irony in their calling for more union voice in corporate pension management without a bow to the historic Walter Reuther-UAW and Steelworkers' insistence on keeping pension management a corporate responsibility, when they do get to the Taft-Hartleys, in which unions already have at least half the management role, they show how little attention they have given their role. For one thing, the report's first recommendation is to "attain a voice in fund management." (With which I wholly agree. If I may be forgiven for quoting myself, the Twentieth Century Fund's 1980 project on conflicts of interest in securities markets called for representative pension fund *boards* because "the proposition that certain funds shall be managed for the 'exclusive benefit' of a defined group whose members are excluded from representation in the fund's management is absurd."[37]) The IUD study's first "finding" supporting their call for a voice, is the poor rate of return of "company-controlled" pension investments. Not a peep about the rates of return of jointly-administered funds! That gap might be due to embarrassment, but more likely is simple unawareness stemming from sheer inattention to the many funds in which unions already have not mere voice, but fiduciary responsibility. They do not know even the rough magnitude of their Taft-Hartley assets. "Estimates range from 10 percent to 15 percent" of private pension assets, or by their figures, from *$36* to *$54* billion. As they could have learned from several sources, even by 1980 Taft-Hartleys aggregated little more than *$34* billion. The ten largest hold $10.039 billion, the top 25 hold $12.267 billion, and virtually all—1,117 Taft-Hartleys—aggregate *$34* billion.[38] Almost as astonishing, since they concentrated on only a ten-company sample (too low for reliability, though not for publicity), and since the AFL-CIO just might be able to get *public* information from the kind of companies selected—e.g., GE, the National Cash Register Company (NCR), Tenneco, Texas Instruments—why did they use 1976(!) public reports on those companies' funds? Because they could not secure anything more recent from the Labor Department.[39] (Since the ten were selected "largely at random"— surely an odd method of selecting so few as ten—one could easily have replaced companies on whom the data were antique.) Small as is their sample, obsolete as are their data, consider their sense of fairness: they criticize NCR for a conflict-of-interest relationship with Citibank, oblivious of Citibank's unique steps to protect against abuse in such situations[40] and oblivious that their own appendix reveals Citibank was merely one of NCR's *ten* fund managers, all other nine being unconflicted.[41] While the report purports to point up these conflicts merely to "raise the question, which bears further investigation,"[42] the only natural reading of this hit-and-run "you're associated so there must be guilt in the association," is suggestion of improper conduct. Why else call the existence of conflicts "one of the study's most intriguing revelations"?[43] (Is it an "intriguing revelation" that UAW head Fraser is also on the board of Chrysler?) The revealed intent of this slap-dash tar-brushing is precisely to leave "a suspicion of serious conflicts of interest,"[44] to quote the very first finding at the very opening of the press release for this "study." Gappy as are their facts, questionable as is their fairness, how implementable is their ambitious goal of emphasizing "investments that generally tend to promote the ready availability of food, shelter, and energy for fund beneficiaries?"[45]

The AFL Executive Council study is much better and I concur in most of its recommendations.[46] Yet, again our AFL-CIO seems more interested in practices in Western Europe and Israel, which were visited for this study, than in their own Taft-Hartleys, which in this report are said to hold $92 [*sic*] billion, a bit off the IUD's range—released only two months earlier—of $36 to $54 billion. "This [$92 billion] estimate—made by independent experts [unidentified]—could be on the high side."[47] And: "The exact . . . numbers of members covered under jointly trustee plans is unavailable . . . further research is needed."[48] The number is 8,422,155, according to a December 1979 study for the Labor Department.[49]

It is good that the unions are beginning to care about pension management, and I say that sincerely.[50] But more knowledge, understanding, and care are in order before trumpeting major changes in direction.

In this league of weak studies, the best is by the Council on Economic Priorities for a California agency. Despite such typical flaws as suggesting that efforts at small endowments and mutual funds are illuminative for California's $21-billion funds, the report is honest. Noted earlier was its emphasis on the implementation problem of inadequate data. The CEP commends California's funds for "commendable sensitivity" regarding proxy voting;[51] they bring out the potential of shareholder activism,[52] make the South African involvement problem turn on whether a company is a Sullivan signatory and how well it complies with the Sullivan Principles, and recognize that "ascertaining the correct corporate course of action with respect to South Africa is difficult."[53] They even recognize that their assigned focus on South Africa and equal employment cover

> but two of many issues which could properly be addressed. A coherent overall vision of corporate responsibility would assist [the California funds] in placing these two issues in perspective. This will involve the weighing of many issues.[54]

They admit, "we, too, are uncertain about the effectiveness of divestment and/or exclusion as a means to influence corporate behavior."[55] But I part from CEP in not seeing how it helps to say, "at the heart of the South African investment issue, however, are the moral considerations."[56] My heart, my view of the morality and of the goals, are wholly with the CEP, but for me the real heart of the issues before us lies in deciding what the effective means are. Divergent investing is no more effective a means to the many well-meant ends, than a hammer or screwdriver is an effective tool for cutting roast beef.

IX. Alternatives Superior to Divergent Investing

If divergent investing is not merely ineffective, but also injurious to retirement security, and therefore quite rightly illegal, does it follow that persons who want pension funds to pay more heed to non-financial goals should give up? No, there are at least five routes worthy of attention: (1) increased mortgage-related holdings; (2) increased joint participation in local or other special investments; (3) free choice for plan participants between retirement-devoted funds and funds pursuing other goals as well; (4) pass-through of stock proxies; and (5) shareholder activism.

(1) Increased Mortgage-related Holdings. "Too much pension investment in corporate securities" is one attack advocates of divergent investing make. Might they not be right?

Outstanding mortgages in America total $1,450 billion, in contrast to the strikingly small total of corporate bonds (and foreign bonds held here) of $490 billion. Yet private noninsured pension funds, with aggregate assets of $286 billion, hold $60 billion in corporate bonds, but an amazingly small $4 billion in mortgages. State and local pension funds, with aggregate assets of $203 billion, hold $91 billion in bonds, and $10 billion in mortgages.[57]

Direct mortgages have been understandably unattractive to pension funds because of administrative difficulties. Even most of the funds most sympathetic to mortgage investment, the building and construction trades union pension funds, held only minuscule amounts of direct mortgages, as I have shown.[58] I am delighted that the AFL-CIO, going by its recommendations of August 1980, is beginning to take seriously the sorely neglected pooled mortgage accounts run by the Union Labor Life Insurance Company and by the AFL-CIO's Mortgage Investment Trust, which I tried to highlight in EBRI's December 1979 forum and later talks.[59]

In fact, pension funds do hold substantial amounts of the approximately $150 billion of mortgage-related securities, but our statisticians lump these relatively new instruments in with "U.S. Governments and Agencies." We are just beginning to uncover the amounts of mortgage-related securities in pension accounts. Over a year ago, examining a sample of nineteen state funds, each over $500 million in assets—almost one-third of all state and local funds that large—I found eight with mortgage-related securities at over 50 percent of their holdings of all U.S. governments; four of the eight were over 80 percent.[60] A forthcoming study of ninety-three state and local pension portfolios with $81 billion in assets, shows steadily rising proportions in mortgage-related holdings, although direct mortgage holdings have been static. The most recent data in this 1981 study, which are from 1978, the average portfolio held—

		Entire Sample	State Sample
1.	Corp. Debt	41.47%	41.04%
2.	Equities	20.26%	22.83%
3.	Federal Agency, Mortgage-related, long-term	8.68%	10.53%
4.	All other U.S. Govt./Agency, long term	8.22%	9.33%
5.	Direct Mortgages	4.87%	5.09%

In sad contrast, private pension plans, going by the only available data,[62] have moved gingerly into mortgage-related holdings, despite the explosion of such instruments with total liquidity, with slightly lower riskiness—even apart from the federal guarantees—and with strikingly higher yields than high-grade corporate bonds.

Why are private pension funds much less inclined than public funds to hold these investments? One view is that private pension managers, particularly in trust departments, are simply not familiar with much other than corporate securities and traditional governments. The time is ripe for more mortgage investing, especially when other sources of mortgages are illiquid and yields are unusually high, so that pension fund entry at such times is both particularly needed by the community and particularly rewarding to the entering funds.

(2) Joint Participation. If a pension fund wants some divergent investing, one of the surest safeguards against the implementation problems and at the same time one of the likeliest methods to make the pension fund's action matter, is joint participation with other financial institutions on the same terms. For example, it is the rare bank, thrift, insurer, or private or public pension fund that cares no more about its own geographic community than it does about other places. If a pension fund were to try local development on its own, it is too likely to make unprofessional judgments as a result of lack of expertise, too likely to suffer severe reactions if the investment is unsuccessful, and too likely—if a public fund—to be a closed-door captive subjected to poor terms. Problems fall away if the pension fund takes, say, 10 to 30 percent of a local venture shared, on the same terms, with local financial institutions.

(3) Participant choice of funds. Several writers have suggested re-

cently that plan sponsors establish, if interest warrants, a separate pension fund for any plan participants who choose to have their pension assets invested for pursuit of various goals.[63] Assuming there is enough participant interest to warrant such separate funds, the suggestion seems sound to me. But, in light of the extremely low response to the mutual funds which pursue "social" as well as investment goals[64]—so low that the largest such fund, Dreyfus Third Century, has just abandoned its "social" goals because there was too little support—I expect this route will be a dead-end.

(4) Proxy Pass-Through. Citibank has undertaken to increase the "socially responsible" handling of pension assets through proxy pass-through. Starting about four years ago, Citibank's trust department began revising its pension management agreements with many sponsors to have proxy votes exercised not by the trust department but by the pension account principals (e.g., in the case of Taft-Hartley funds, the plan sponsors; in the case of profit-sharing plans, a committee of participants). As of 1978, 74 percent of the $863 million in profit-sharing and thrift plans, and 46 percent of the $5.1 billion in defined benefits, were passed through. While most of Citibank's Taft-Hartley plans accepted pass-throughs, four such plans surprisingly refused, preferring to have Citibank handle the voting as well as the investment decisions.

No plan with pooled assets should be required to send proxies to all participants; the simple costs of doing so would be preclusive. If participants in pension plans care about how their plans are voted, they can at least form an advisory committee furnishing policy guidelines or specific suggestions. If they do not choose that route, surely they cannot handle the incomparably tougher tasks of divergent investing.

(5) Shareholder Activism. Responsible proxy voting or offering shareholder proposals are as different from divergent investing as speaking out is different from pouting in silence. "We aren't out to nail corporations, we are out to influence them," is the perfect explanation the Sisters of Loretto give for holding stock in J.P. Stevens and conducting a shareholder campaign against Blue Diamond Coal, a firm that has been indicted for violating federal mine safety law, sued civilly because of an explosion killing twenty-six men, and involved in violence surrounding an unsuccessful United Mine Workers' (UMW) strike.

Pension funds have been heard from on stockholder proposals and similar matters. Ohio Public Employees, holding 280,000 shares of McGraw-Hill, was one of the few stockholders to protest openly against that management's being the final arbiter of whether to accept American Express's tender offer. That same system and Minnesota's State Board of Investment voted against reelection of Northwest Airlines' directors because of poor labor and customer relations. And near the end of the successful struggle to stop J.P. Stevens' outlawry, Ohio State Teachers, New York State and City funds, and various Taft-Hartley funds voted against the Stevens' chairman's continuance on the board of Sperry Corp.[65] A number of state boards have exemplary statements of policy, and practices, on voting. (Uniquely commendable is the California State Teachers' detailed annual report on how it voted its shares.)

Perspective must be retained lest involvement in shareholder activism exceed its worth. Nevertheless, every vote, let alone every shareholder proposal, is an explicit, open communication of a fund's views, to the company in question, and to the community in general. How can divergent investing compete? Divergent investing is unproductive investing and unproductive social action. Worse, it distracts us from productive efforts. It has been said that it is God's work to care for the elderly. Let us get back to work.

NOTES

1. Northeast-Midwest Institute, *Pension Power for Economic Development* (December 1980), i. 1.

2. Northeast-Midwest Congressional Coalition Press Release, December 22, 1980.

3. Federal Reserve Board, Flow of Funds Outstanding (Feb. 1981). Private funds hold $450.7. State and locals report $202.7, but note that virtually all of them have substantial bond holding and some use book value.

4. For example, the California state pension funds have $21 billion in assets and Governor Brown's recent Public Investment Task Force report opened as did the Northeast-Midwest Congressional Coalition with expressions of wonder over the current size and 1995 projection for pension assets—$3 trillion according to the Northeast-Midwest statement, $4 trillion according to California. But the California report utterly overlooks that their $21 billion in assets must help meet over $40 billion in liabilities. See *Interim Report* (March 1981), at 4. For data underlying my aggregate estimates, see *infra*, and n.22.

5. "Unfunded Liabilities Continue to Grow," *Business Week*, August 25, 1980, pp. 94-95.

6. For example, New York's Common Retirement Fund included equities of 228 corporations, 49 of them headquartered in New York, 87 manufacturing there,

and 28 with retail or other sales outlets there. Alabama made private placements to local banks and such "Alabama corporations" as PPG and International Paper, with facilities there, as well as heavy holdings in Alabama-originated GNMAs.

Here and at other uncited references, the full citations appear in my "Should Pension Funds be Managed for Social Purposes," *Trusts & Estates*, September, October and November, 1980.

7. *Pensions & Investments*, October 27, 1980, at 1.

8. AFL-CIO, "Investment of Union Pension Funds," (undated; 1980); and AFL-CIO Executive Council, "Recommendations" (adopted as proposed, August 1980, see BNA Pension Reporter August 25, 1980, R-16 and R-17).

9. AFL-CIO Industrial Union Department, "Pensions: A Study of Benefit Fund Investment Policies," June 1980.

10. Far more important than divergent investing in the union pension scene is the 1980 enactment of massive and massively complex amendments to ERISA, changing the treatment of liability for jointly-administered pension benefits, with many related changes.

11. Office of the Governor, Press Release, March 26, 1980; *Los Angeles Times*, July 31, 1980, reporting on first Task Force meeting.

12. *Interim Report, supra* n. 4.

13. See "Massachusetts and Texas pension funds plan to invest in home mortgage markets," *Wall Street Journal*, January 12, 1981; "Public Funds Eye Mortgages," *Pensions & Investments*, February 2, 1981, p. 3.

14. The "top 25" data are from *Pensions & Investments*, January 19, 1981.

15. See my "Should Pension Funds be Managed for Social Purposes," *Trusts & Estates*, September 1980, pp. 14-15; and November 1980, pp. 37-38.

16. While the Northeast-Midwest Coalition's report used a figure of 4.1 percent, a minor typo but otherwise correctly used figure (see Northeast-Midwest Institute, "Pension Power for Economic Development," December 1980, at 8), the IUD misused the correct 4.3 percent figure in a way illustrative of their report's unfamiliarity with even the simplest aspects of investment. The IUD report tried to make the 4.3 percent look worse by noting that it was below the annualized S. & P. 500 return for the same decade, 5.9 percent. (See IUD, *supra*, n. 4b, at 8.) Not only was that an erroneous comparison of *total* return—i.e., on stocks, bonds, and any other investments—with an *equity* index, but the IUD's error kept them from making their argument more forceful. The median pension fund *equity* return for that period was 3.6 percent, even further below the S. & P.

17. For data on returns in all the ten-year periods from 1900-1909 and 1901-10 to 1969-78, see my Table 1 in *Trusts & Estates*, September 1980, at 14.

18. Urban Institute (HUD *et al.* Grant), "The Future of State and Local Pensions" (Draft Final Report, November 1980), Table 18-5.

19. Senior vice president of Citibank Investment Management Group, at the EBRI Forum on December 6, 1979. See Employee Benefit Research Institute, "Should Pension Assets be Managed for Social/ Political Purposes?" 1980, at 138.

20. House Committee on Education & Labor, Pension Task Force Report on Public Employee Retirement Systems, March 1978, at 165.

21. Urban Institute, *supra* n. 18.

22. Three important *caveats* about the use of pension liability figures. *First,* different
     employers are, of course, in quite different circumstances, and even similarly
     situated employers may use different actuarial methods or assumptions, so that
     aggregate liabilities are a much rougher figure than the far firmer asset figures.
     Second caveat: Some people believe state and local funds' liabilities are less sig-
     nificant than private plan liabilities; but see my response, *Trusts & Estates,*
     October 1980, at 37, n. 19. The last *caveat* involves the fact that aggregate pension
     asset figures lump all kinds of pension plans, both defined benefit and the far
     smaller categories with no more liabilities than assets, defined contribution
     plans and profit-sharing plans.

23. Bankers Trust Company, "Corporate Pension Plan Study," 1980, at 53. The
     length of the retirement period is measured from the end of the years stated; e.g.,
     the person retired 15 years began retirement in 1960 for the 1970-75 data, in 1965
     for the 1975-80.

24. See my treatment in *Trusts & Estates,* October 1980, at 28, 37-8, n. 29.

25. State Teachers Retirement System, "Annual Benefits Summary 1980," at 33. The
     CPI figures differ slightly from the Bankers Trust data because these use a
     June-June fiscal year.

26. A typical recent statement is California legislation "designed to restore a part of
     the purchasing power of the current retirement allowance to at least 72% of the
     original allowance." 66th California State Teachers Retirement System Annual
     Report, 35 (1979).

27. See my testimony in Hearings on PERISA of 1975, House Committee on Educa-
     tion & Labor, Subcommittee on Labor Standards, 94th Congress, 1st Session,
     1975, pp. 115, 125.
         See also my Conclusions and Recommendations of the Steering Committee,
     Twentieth Century Fund Report on Conflicts of Interest in Securities Markets,
     Abuse on Wall Street (1980).

28. *BNA Pension Reporter,* March 30, 1981, at A-19; AFL-CIO IUD Labor & Invest-
     ments, January 1981, at 7.

29. Coltman & Metzenbaum, *Investing in Ourselves* (Massachusetts Social & Econo-
     mic Opportunity Council Task Force), June 1979, at 29.

30. Council on Economic Prioroites, "A Study of Investment Practices and Opportu-
     nities," 1980, at 68, 144, and 159-60.

31. "Coca-Cola, at unusual annual meeting, reports 8.% profit rise for 1st quarter,"
     Wall Street Journal, May 6, 1980.

32. The new California Pension Task Force report, with its emphasis on localism—
     even for municipal and county pension fund investing—almost ignores this
     problem, but "is exploring the feasibility of commissioning a study on the multi-
     plier effects and other impacts of in-state pension investments." Task Force
     Interim Report, supra n. 4.
         Study should *precede* any newly directed investing, and after such study only
     modest amounts of newly directed investing should occur so as to secure the best
     study of all, *experience.*

33. This paper concentrates on the pragmatics of divergent investing. The legal
     problems were thoroughly presented (at the December 1979 Employee Benefit
     Research Institute Forum at which I presented the lengthy treatment later
     republished in *Trusts & Estates)* by Hutchinson & Cole, Legal Standards Gov-
     erning Investment of Pension Assets for Social and Political Goals, republished in
     128 *U. Penn. L. Rev.* 1291 (1980).

34. *Trusts & Estates*, October 1980, at 32-35. For details on the liveliest fiction in this field, *The North Will Rise Again*, see my n. 8 in *Trust & Estates*, September 1980, at 22.

35. Taylor & Locker, "CDE Directors Rebut Schotland," *Pensions & Investments*, February 4, 1980, at 24.

36. *The Decline and Fall of the Roman Empire* (Modern Library), *I*:153.

37. Twentieth Century Fund, *supra* n. 27.

38. Data on top 10 and 25 from latest annual listing in *Pensions & Investments*, January 19, 1981, pp. 1 *et seq.* Data on the 1,117 from Money Market Directory, June 1980.

39. IUD, *supra* n. 9.

40. See annual report of Investment of Management Division, listing all transactions by Citibank in shares of interlocked companies.

41. Compare IUD, at 30 and Table 5, at 46.

42. *Id.*, at 9.

43. *Id.*, at 17.

44. IUD News Release, June 5, 1980, at 1.

45. *Id.*, at 6.

46. Compare my Conclusions and Recommendations in Twentieth Century Fund, *supra*, n. 27.

47. AFL-CIO, *supra* n. 8.

48. *Id.*

49. Towers, Perrin, Forster & Crosby, Study of Multi-Employer Plans, at III-5A. See also PBGC, Multi-employer Study Required by P.L. 95-214, at 1, 20 (July 1978).

50. See my "Picking Investment Managers," *Pensions & Investments*, April 24, 1978, pp. 61-2; and Twentieth Century Fund, *supra*, n. 27, at 572, 574, 575-6.

51. CEP, *supra* n. 30, at 152.

52. *Id.*, at 91-2 and 147-50.

53. *Id.*, at 5, 23-6, and 152-4.

54. *Id.*, "Afterword," p. 163.

55. *Id.*, at 145.

56. *Id.*, at 50. In response to request by the California Teachers' Retirement Fund, I have written a full analysis of the CEP report in a letter to that Fund.

57. Federal Reserve Bank Flow of Funds data, end-1979.

58. See *Trust & Estates*, November 1980, at 28; and my Table 3 in EBRI, *supra*, n. 19, at 193.

59. See talk to Ass'n. Pvt. Pens. and Welf. Plans, "The pension funds answer: increase mortgage-related investments," *Washington Post*, May 5, 1980, p. 20; and talk to Int'l. Found. Emp. Ben. Plans, *Pensions & Investments*, May 26, 1980, p. 42.

60. Mostly 1978 data; see my Table 4, EBRI, *supra* n. 19.

61. Petersen, Summary of State & Local Government Public Employee Retirement System Investment Practices and Policies, MFOA/HUD Grant (Final Draft November 1980), Tables 1.14-1.16.

62. See EBRI, *supra* n. 19, at 167; for 1979 data, showing a modest proportionate increase in mortgage-related holdings, see FRB/FDIC/OCC, Trust Assets of Banks and Trust Companies—1979, Table 1, p. 10.

63. Langbein & Posner, *supra*, n. 33; and Letter to Editor, *Pensions & Investment Age*, February _____, 1981, p._____.

64. See *Trusts & Estates*, October 1980, at 31 and 40, n. 63.

65. *Pensions & Investments*, August 4, 1980, p. 2.

439-57

3140
8310
$ U.S.

Investing Pension Assets For Social Or Union Purposes: Management Analysis

James P. Northrup[†]

Introduction

The current debate on the issue of investing pension assets for social or union purposes is one aspect of a larger political debate involving fundamental differences of opinion about the future of the market economy in our society. Various interest groups that advocate so-called "social" investing of pension assets believe that the use of these assets, the primary purpose of which is to provide for retirement income security, can be linked successfully with other goals—goals that they conveniently find capable of being furthered by *diverting* pension assets into unconventional or high risk investment vehicles chosen by them.

Because there are a number of groups that advocate diverting pension assets and not all can be thoroughly examined, I shall limit my remarks to an examination of social investing as advocated by organized labor in the United States.

Historical Background

Organized labor's interest in control of financial resources, or use of such resources for the attainment of union goals, is not new. In the 1920s, for example, the labor movement established approximately thirty-five banking institutions with resources in excess of $125 million—a major sum at that time. The avowed purposes included the protection and advancement of the labor movement by ensuring a flow of funds for organizing and strikes, the use of workers' savings to control and channel investment into industry in order to counter the open-shop movement of that period, and ultimately, control of the basic industry of the country.[1] Mismanagement and then the Great Depression wiped out all the banks except those of the Amalgamated

---

† James P. Northrup is Director of Human Resources at Bowater Incorporated.

Clothing Workers. The Union Labor Life Insurance Company, founded by union officials during that period, still survives and could play a role in the current union drive.[2]

During the Great Depression era, the state of Wisconsin enacted legislation mandating investment of pension funds to support in-state activities, obviously a use other than maximizing safe return for beneficiaries. A state commission found that the policy produced inferior returns, and it was therefore abandoned in 1945. These results did not restrain the Wisconsin advocates of social investing who, in 1979, recommended "socially responsible" investment criteria for state pension funds.[3]

Thus the issue of social—or "divergent"[4]—investing is inexorably linked to organized labor's examination of possible vehicles that might be used to further its goals. Serious questions should be asked, however, about the propriety of divergent investing and about the potentially negative impact such investing would have on retiree income security. In fact, for labor organizations as institutions, the issue strongly resembles certain aspects of the drive for codetermination of management and control of corporations through "asset formation" plans by labor organizations in Europe.[5]

I shall first examine what proponents advocate as divergent investing; second, I shall provide a brief summary of what the law allows in regard to divergent investing; then I shall analyze the implications of divergent investing proposals and summarize my conclusions.

Divergent Investing: Definition and Law

Advocates of divergent investing (among whom unions are but one, albeit the numerically largest, group) generally claim that it is possible to pursue their divergent investment goals and, at the same time, maximize investment returns for pension plan assets at an acceptable level of risk. These advocates often point to rates of return for professionally managed funds where a majority of those funds in recent years have not done so well as major stock market indices. Their advice, however, was not available for all to see some years ago as guidance for the rest of us in choosing investment vehicles that would have outperformed those major market indices. Such perfect hindsight adds nothing to our understanding of the market, nor does it lend support to the concept of divergent investing.

Divergent investment advocates believe that two or more goals can be simultaneously pursued without endangering the retirement security of existing and prospective pensioners. In the case of unions, the AFL-CIO Industrial Union Department (IUD) study offers the best summary of union goals for divergent investing.[6] These include: (1) denying capital to nonunion employers; (2) denying capital to employers with large overseas work forces; (3) making capital available for prounion employers; (4) making capital available for such "social" purposes as subsidized housing, health care, etc., particularly if jobs are created for unionized employees; and (5) using capital to further such union goals as organizing and gaining control over managerial prerogatives to influence such actions as plant closings. As I shall note, examples can be found to demonstrate that some of these policies have already been effectuated in a small way.

Divergent Investing and ERISA

Public policy governing divergent investing is found in section 404(a) of the Employee Retirement Income Security Act of 1974 (ERISA). Basically, ERISA requires a fiduciary to: (1) determine whether the financial characteristics of a given investment will satisfy the prudence and diversification requirements of the law, and (2) determine whether the purpose of the investment is consistent with the requirement that such investment be undertaken *solely* in the interest of the participants and beneficiaries of the plan. Further, the investment objectives must be formulated with due regard for the plan's size and structure, funding patterns, liquidity needs, and other individual characteristics. Thus, the prudence of the proposed divergent investment cannot be evaluated in the abstract but must be measured against investment objectives that are based on the plan's characteristics and needs.[7] Moreover, when Congress considered ERISA in 1974 after nearly ten years of debate, it had been presented with—and had rejected—various proposals for broadening the fiduciary standards of the bill in order to allow for the ramifications of divergent investing.[8] It would therefore seem that, if a divergent investment policy is adopted, the legal framework would appear "to require that every plan investment be subjected to a three-part analysis":

> In the first part, the responsible fiduciary must determine whether the financial characteristics of the investment will satisfy the prudence and diversification requirements of the statute . . . . While a fiduciary may be able to invoke a socially sensitive investment policy in order to select among these alternative investments, a socially dictated investment policy, in which financial comparability is sacrificed in order to achieve some social purpose, will not withstand scrutiny under this part of the statutory analysis.

> In the second part of the analysis, the fiduciary's actions in selecting

particular strategies or investments must be reconciled with the purposes declared permissible by choice of investments, whether that interest is financial or ideological, then the statute may well prohibit such conduct. Even where the fiduciary acts without regard to his own interests, it is nevertheless essential that the investment program be designed primarily to further the interests of participants and beneficiaries. If the fiduciary faces a choice between investments whose financial characteristics are identical, it may be possible to choose an alternative which offers indirect benefits to plan participants as members of some larger community. But in light of the difficulty in proving both a pure motive and financial equivalence, it may be more sensible to develop an investment policy which is designed to permit only those investments which aid the interests of the plan participants as participants. Under this criterion, then, even some socially sensitive investment policies could be rejected as inconsistent with the objectives of the statute.

Finally, each transaction must be consistent with the structural standards of ERISA. If the investment will benefit a party in interest such as the employer or union, the plan may find it necessary to obtain an exemption from the "prohibited transactions" rules of the statute. In all events, the investment decision must be made in accordance with the plan documents.[9]

Finally, it should be pointed out that section 409 (a) of ERISA gives interested parties the right to challenge a divergent investment program, and that a fiduciary may be held personally liable in damages not only for an investment that a court finds imprudent, but also for any violation of other fiduciary standards of the statute. "Thus if a loss ensues from a program of social investing which is not 'solely in the interest of the participants and beneficiaries,' the responsible fiduciaries might be required to restore the lost assets to the fund."[10]

The IUD Approach and Program

Assuming that the IUD program for divergent investing can meet the tests of ERISA as previously summarized, which may be doubtful, the IUD proposed that unions follow these four steps:

1. Obtain a voice in benefit fund management;

2. Obtain full information with respect to the operation of any fund covering its members;

3. Implement the study's recommended general investment guidelines; and

4. Assist in the development and passage of new legislation that would "actually require that [benefit plan fund] investments

be consistent with the broader interests of fund beneficiaries as well as financially prudent."[11]

Attaining a Voice in Benefit Fund Management

The IUD proposes that, through collective bargaining or other means, unions should gain an equal voice, hence veto power, over fund investment practices and choice of investment managers, and in addition gain control of stock voting rights for fund investments. The rationale here is that fund managers have been poor investors; that pension funds are deferred wages that really belong to employees; that "employers and institutions that manage assets of company-controlled funds suggest the possibility of conflicts of interest that may work to the detriment of fund beneficiaries"; and that "investment practices of the benefit funds . . . surveyed were often inconsistent with the long-term interests of fund beneficiaries."[12]

Fund Return. I would certainly not defend the record of some fund investors—or the record of some union-controlled plans, either. The comparisons used in the IUD report, however, are less than scholarly. As I mentioned before, criticizing past performance on the basis of hindsight while advocating that pension assets subsidize various union goals does disservice to a difficult and complex problem. Certainly the use of very limited comparisons for the purposes of investment return analysis as was done in the IUD report[12] is no basis for turning over control of pension assets to unions.[13]

Deferred Wages. The IUD report uses the term "benefit fund" while I am primarily concerned with the use of pension assets. This nomenclature is important in assessing the problem at hand. Some benefit funds, such as those under the jurisdiction of section 302(c) of the Taft-Hartley Act, already require employee and/or union representations. Many such funds involve health and welfare programs as well as pensions.

In addition, one could make a case for employee representation in benefit fund management when the employer merely agrees to a stated rate of contribution to a fund, but no stated benefit. The claim that pension assets are merely deferred wages, and as such belong to workers, is to some extent valid for contribution plans defined in this way. Because the level of retirement benefits is dependent upon the proceeds from plan investments, it is the employee and not the employer who directly bears the brunt of lower investment return. It is the safety of the plan's principal and the returns generated by its assets that are the sole determinants of the retiring employee's adequacy of benefit.

Of course, this assumes that the employees, both retired and active, would benefit from employee participation in fund management. This could only be true if such employee representation actually improved fund performance and/or employee and retired employee morale or well-being. This, however, is problematical at best.

In fact, many defined contribution plans are profit-sharing or savings plans, and most of these are found in nonunion companies. Moreover, in such plans it is typical for the employee to have some control over fund investment. Thus, generally, the employee can decide whether to have the contributions made in his name invested in company stock, government bonds, a mutual fund, a money fund, or some combination thereof. Such investment options have tended to be expanded in recent years.[14]

For defined benefit plans, the claim that retirement benefits are deferred wages is true, but only in a highly restricted sense. In this situation, the employer has promised to pay employees a certain amount of retirement benefits, the amount of which is to be determined at the date of actual retirement or vested termination. In addition, most plans provide for a waiting period during which employees are entitled to no benefits whatsoever. While this period can vary from ten years on down, it generally takes at least twenty years of participating service under a defined benefit plan to accumulate a substantial amount of credited retirement income. It should also be remembered that a promise to pay wages does not necessarily create an ownership right in the capital that generates those wages. Wages, whether current or deferred, are paid in *exchange* for labor and services rendered. Improvements in pension benefits are granted in exchange for improvements in future employee productivity and morale.

Because a pension provides for a deferred benefit at retirement, the employer is held liable by ERISA to deliver that benefit or some portion thereof to the participant regardless of how well the pension trust investments have performed, while unions have no corresponding obligation.

Thus a defined benefit plan requires the employer to make annual contributions to the pension plan trust on the basis of an actuarial determination of payments to future beneficiaries and an amortization of expected payments to current retirees. To the extent that the amounts set aside for the future—the pension capital—prove inadequate, the economic impact is on the employer: he must pay the difference. Moreover, to the extent that the pension capital is not maximizing earnings, the employer must make up the shortfall, which can put a marked strain on a company's financial well-being.[15] A company that permits anyone to gain veto power over pension fund investment and management can therefore risk both the viability of its pension fund and of the company itself.

A serious employee relations problem involved in unions obtaining control of fund management is the potential for a conflict of interests to develop between the active participants and the retired participants and their beneficiaries. It is obvious that these two groups have varied interests, the former in maintaining employment security, the latter in the safety and financial soundness of the plan trust. The national labor policy recognizes this divergency of interests. The Taft-Hartley Act excludes retirees in its definition of employees within the meaning of the act. Thus, although management may deal with unions concerning pension payments to former employees who have retired, management is under no obligation to do so.[16] On the other hand, when a union is the legal bargaining party, it is well settled that pension matters must be bargained when they pertain to active employees.[17]

For those who doubt that such a conflict of interests exists between active and retired employees, the problems of New York City illustrate with great clarity the ease with which pension funds can be held hostage to the needs of active employees at the expense of retired employees. Union-controlled pension fund assets were used to bail out the city from bankruptcy. They were invested in long-term bonds, certainly a risky investment given the city's precarious financial standing and prospects. The purpose, of course, was to secure the jobs of the current city employees. Undoubtedly, therefore, this divergent investment aided employee morale. What it did to pensioner morale is something else again.[18]

Obtaining Full Information

The second recommendation of the IUD study states that "in order to facilitate bargaining with respect to employee participation in fund management, each union that does not already have full information with respect to the operation of any fund covering its members should request that the employer furnish it with such information . . . . " The report goes on to list various items that unions should consider relevant to their participation in fund management. In effect, this should be read in conjunction with recommendation one because attaining a "voice" in fund management requires that union members become knowledgeable about the various aspects of pension fund management.

In some cases, the information that unions would need is available through various government agencies, especially the Department of Labor and the Internal Revenue Service. Up-to-date information, however, is generally not available except via fund trustees and investment managers.

The IUD method of obtaining additional information, use of an organization called Corporate Data Exchange, is hardly to be recommended on the basis of performance thus far. Professor Roy Schotland examined in detail this organization's social audit of pension investing[19] and found it severely flawed and "propaganda rather than an 'audit,'" which disregarded investment return as a criterion.[20] Relying for policy on documents that lack an objective research basis could certainly affect pension investments adversely and therefore would not be conducive to improved employee relations or enhancement of individual employee welfare.

Implementing the IUD's Guidelines

The IUD advocates two principles for implementing its guidelines: (1) assuring that employers and pension fund managers avoid "potential conflicts of interest"; and (2) "generally promoting fund management sensitivity to enhancing returns on sound and secure fund investments."

Avoiding Conflicts of Interest. The inference that conflicts of interest abound among employer-managed pension funds and their designated trustees and investment managers should not be taken seriously, and is obviously designed to direct member unions to suggest to employers that investments cannot be properly handled unless the union assists in or manages the selection of such parties. ERISA, however, is quite clear about the role of the trustee as fiduciary.

A fiduciary must refrain from dealing as an individual with the trust assets; from acting in his individual capacity or any other capacity in any transaction involving the plan on behalf of a party whose interests are adverse to the interests of the plan or its participants or beneficiaries; and from deriving personal gain from his position other than a reasonable fee for his services. It should be obvious, in light of the aforementioned, that conflicts of interest among employers and named fiduciaries have been sufficiently safeguarded by the laws governing such activity. More vigilance on the part of union officials in reporting any alleged violations of employer-managed plans would, of course, be all to the good, as would greater interest on the part of employers in reporting union official malfeasance in handling union-run plans. The claim that the former is widespread and can be aborted by union comanagement of pension funds seems to be on the record false; but even if it were true, the remedy could be worse than the disease. Unions are not generally thought of as guardians of public morals. In any case, except when illegal or immoral conduct is found and thwarted, and pension assets and earnings are thereby saved, the individual employee and retiree will certainly neither be uplifted nor have his income necessarily enhanced by such union representation.

Actually, the most serious conflict of interest problem today must be the Central States Pension Fund of the Teamsters' Union. The actions of this fund's management, as highlighted by several governmental investigative proceedings,[21] have done little to further the cause of union divergent investing of pension assets.

Generally Promoting Fund Management. No one can quarrel with the IUD's call for "promoting fund management sensitivity to enhancing returns on sound and secure fund investments." Unfortunately, the IUD would have this worthy objective accomplished by a policy of divergent investing, a seemingly fundamental conflict of goals. Certainly there is nothing in the record thus far that would permit the belief that union administration of pension funds would, per se, increase the return therefrom and improve the safety of the investment. The record of union participation is, of course, not all bad; but even ignoring the Central States Fund, neither is it all good.

Union Pension Fund Criteria

What types of divergent uses unions would promote for pension funds, and what the employee relations implications thereof are can be analyzed not only from the proposal of the IUD report, but also from some actions taken by unions during the past several years. It will be convenient to discuss the union approach by following the IUD's suggested guidelines.

Promoting Domestic Employment

According to the IUD, its "study of certain representative pension plans indicates . . . that investments are frequently made with indifference to whether the companies whose stocks are purchased promote employment in this country rather than overseas."[22] One can sympathize with union concern for the promotion of employment of its members. Indeed, if such unions as the United Automobile Workers (UAW), the United Steelworkers, the United Mine Workers, and the United Rubber Workers, to name just a few, had over the years been more concerned with the employment of the many and less concerned with high wages for the few, these industries today would no doubt be employing far more workers.

Even if it were legitimate to invest pension funds to stimulate employment of existing union members instead of providing for pensions of retired ones, the criterion of domestic versus foreign employment is a simplistic one that would not necessarily enhance the employment of union members. For example, the Ford Motor Company is literally being saved from a fate worse than Chrysler's by having a viable income-producing and people-employing set of businesses overseas. These foreign operations are keeping Ford employees on the job in the United States. Similarly, if General Electric did not produce radios and audio equipment abroad, it would not be producing and selling that equipment at all, and therefore not providing any jobs in these businesses for Americans. One could add numerous examples to demonstrate that investment of pension funds to spur domestic employment and to discourage foreign employment could easily backfire and have the opposite impact.

Finally, of course, the IUD guidelines fail to distinguish the obvious difference of interests between active employees and retired employees. This is not surprising, because unions are the servants of their members, and retirees are former members. The already noted New York City situation provides clear evidence of this dichotomy.

Investing in Housing

A number of unions and church organizations have invested in housing developments for retired members or others, sometimes using pension funds for this social purpose. Some of this investment may well have been to the general good; it would seem both to provide income and a home for the retirees and to provide work for union members, especially in the building trades. In other cases financial difficulties have offset any benefits.[23]

Particularly in times of inflation, housing projects for the elderly can be quite speculative. Consider the following:

> In Northwestern Ohio during 1977, a developer proposed a low-cost apartment housing project for the elderly. Assuming 80% conventional financing is granted by the pension trust of a large construction trade union, it would meet the exact requirements of the AFL-CIO . . . local investment policy criteria.

The total cost of the actual project was $2,375,292; thus, the mortgage would be approximately $1,900,000. Of the $2,375,292 total project costs, $2,130,292 is the construction cost. But of this amount, $1,032,835 will go for materials, leaving only $1,097,457 for labor. The subcontract for the trade of the union on this project was $153,000 of which $93,090 is for materials and $60,000 was for labor. The current collective bargaining agreement between the union and the employer association set a wage rate of $13.80 per hour for this union's craft. The project would generate 4,348 hours of work. Assuming a crew of 20 men, an investment of $1,900,000, or 15.8% of the trust, or more than 6 months of contributions, would provide a crew of 20, which is 1.6% of the membership of the local, with work for 5½ weeks. I submit that an investment of the $1,900,000 in a recognized investment, with a higher rate of return, with greater liquidity and marketability, with an established credit rating, would be a more responsible investment of 15% of the trust for 98.4% of the participants.[24]

Here, too, even assuming that retirees would desire to live in the low-cost apartment housing, what percentage of retirees would actually be available? Would many be living in Florida or some other climatic region more inviting than northwest Ohio? This example illustrates the difficulty of finding truly worthwhile divergent investments that do not create conflicts between the active and retired employee groups, or that do not entail other difficulties.

The construction unions are understandably anxious to spur investment in their field, not only because it might increase jobs, but also because if they control the investment, they can insist on union jobs. Union construction is now a minority of the industry, and a declining one. Housing, including garden apartments, is presently built overwhelmingly—about 85 percent—by open-shop firms. Apartment construction is no more than 50 percent union. The reason is, of course, that union wages, strikes, and restrictive practices have priced union firms out of the market.[25] Hence, a union pension-financed project will often be high-cost and more likely to carry a higher risk factor than one built under open-shop conditions. Again the pension income of retirees could easily be sacrificed for the jobs of active members.

Nonunion Investments

The IUD investment strategy proposes that pension funds avoid investment in nonunion firms "in order to encourage positive labor relations." This poses several practical difficulties stemming from the fact that unions represent at most only 20 percent of the United

States labor force, and for the most part are concentrated in older manufacturing, public utility, and transportation companies within the private sector. Thus, this IUD criterion would put the high technology companies, which are almost all nonunion, outside the union pension fund investment area, and concentrate such fund investment opportunities in areas of the economy that often exhibit considerably less investment potential. It is therefore difficult to see how this criterion will enhance retirement income security or acceptable pension asset returns.

Another practical problem for this criterion is that many companies in the United States are partially, but far from wholly, unionized. The salaried employees—clerical, professional, and managerial—throughout the private sector are overwhelmingly nonunion; and many, if not most, new plants also operate union-free. Should, for example, General Electric stock be barred as a union pension fund investment because its employees are about two-thirds nonunion, and because unions have won only one of approximately twenty-five National Labor Relations Board (NLRB) elections at General Electric during the last several years? If the answer is affirmative, what effect will that have on the 60,000 unionized General Electric employees? Putting General Electric and other nonunion firms off-limits to union pension funds, or doing the same to the high technology companies, is unlikely to serve the interests of retirement income security. The employees of such companies have determined in secret ballot elections, carefully supervised by the NLRB, that they do not desire to be represented by unions. I therefore conclude that, contrary to other claims, investment criteria based upon a union-nonunion dichotomy is in general unlikely to improve employee or retiree welfare.

There is another aspect to the IUD interest in withdrawing investment of pension trusts from nonunion firms. The real purpose, of course, is to aid union organizing. It is an avenue of pressure open to unions, although in most cases, as noted, it is not likely to be effective because so many of the nonunion companies are likely to be those with excellent records and/or prospects that easily attract investment.[26] Nevertheless, the union purpose is clearly to pressure companies to assist in organizing employees whom the unions have been unable to persuade to organize. This violates at least the spirit of the Taft-Hartley Act, which guarantees employees the right to join, or not to join, unions and provides that the decision shall be their's alone.

Finally, unions should realize that they are not the only institutions capable of applying policies that are divergent. What is to prevent, for example, major corporations with far more economic muscle from applying counterpressure? If banks and fiduciary institutions are caught in a squeeze between union and corporate pressures, what happens to retiree interests? Pressuring fiduciary institutions to apply pressure on a company in turn or a union involved in a complicated labor dispute is a divergency that could be dangerous to pensioners' financial health.

ERISA and the Union-Nonunion Dichotomy

A final aspect of the divergent use of pension fund investments for union organizing purposes is the question of legality. The standards to which a fiduciary must adhere proscribe any form of social investing that is intended to benefit any fiduciary of a plan trust. This could be interpreted to preclude a union from formulating a program of divergent investing intended to facilitate the organizing activities of that union. Even though it might be claimed that the participating active employees might benefit indirectly from a stronger union, a court could find that the primary purpose of the investment was an impermissible one.[27]

Other Unions' Actions

The IUD report was adopted as official AFL-CIO policy at the federation's executive council meeting in August 1980. The IUD is apparently charged with the official dissemination of this policy and has instituted an attractive, well-written newsletter, *Labor & Investments*, to report on actions in this field. The first issue, which appeared in January 1981, contains a good compilation of actions designed to further the union goals. These are summarized below.

Ship Financing

The Marine Engineers Beneficial Association (MEBA) has invested $11 million of its pension fund to help underwrite the construction of two ships that will be operated by American crews. For this, the MEBA fund will obtain a majority interest in a joint venture company, and expects an annual return on investment of 15 percent.

Such ships carry a complement of about four engineers, but of course other United States maritime employment has dwindled to a negligible portion of the world's seamen, and these ships will be built by unionized shipbuilders in the United States. The return on investment appears to be good, but shipping is a volatile industry. These ships will be bulk carriers, which are now in high demand; that such demand can change dramatically is illustrated by the huge fleet of tankers that are now laid up with no cargo to carry. Whether this will be a good investment for pensioners remains to be determined.

Building Financing

The first issue of *Labor & Investments* reported on construction union funds that have financed construction, and particularly a foundation established for that purpose by the construction unions in southern California. I have previously pointed out some of the pitfalls pertaining to such financing. Professor Schotland has noted that the construction union funds in fact have invested only a small fraction of their pension funds in such ventures, and that the Union Labor Life Insurance Company likewise has been very conservative in this regard.[28] Given the current union pension-fund push, and the tremendous inroads being made by open-shop construction, it may well be that there will be a greater union utilization of pension funds for such purposes. Given the risks involved, this again could put the needs of current employees above those for whom the pension trust funds exist.

In a companion move, the Washington, D.C., AFL-CIO Building Trades Council discharged the Prudential Insurance Company as a fund manager on the grounds that this company was investing in nonunion construction.[29] The problem, of course, is that union construction is losing its share of work and costing so much that the open-shop offers both greater opportunity and a greater return. Again, the conflict between present employees' interests and those of retirees is apparent.

State Funds

Unions are likely to have their greatest success in gaining divergent investments from state or municipal funds. These are also the funds that are in the most serious difficulties in that they tend to be underfunded, and their pension benefits are often over-liberal. Divergent investing, therefore, adds an additional risk and additional potential burdens on the public. Nevertheless, under union pressure, the state of New York has already provided that $100 million in New York-leased mortgages for housing, commercial facilities, and industrial sites be invested from the State Common Retirement Fund, and unions are demanding an "effective voice" in the fund's administration. The fund has now established a stock proxy voting committee that has cast the fund's votes for anti-doing business in South Africa resolutions, against J.P. Stevens officials as other company board members, and against slates of candidates in nonunion companies.[30]

The New York state fund is a good illustration of how adopting union goals as public policy can contribute to making a questionable business climate even less attractive. For company site selection studies, New York state is likely to end near the bottom of the list. High taxes, poor police protection in labor disputes, excessive workers' compensation awards, payments of unemployment compensation during strikes, and above-average union political power all make the state a very difficult area when establishing a business. The gains of union labor toward influencing excessively the state pension funds could well worsen the business climate and thus reduce employment opportunities while utilizing money set aside for retirees to benefit active employees and to enhance the power of union officials.

ICWU Self-Management

The small International Chemical Workers' Union (ICWU) has followed the lead of many companies by taking control of its staff pension trust fund management away from a financial institution and handling the investment of the funds itself. Companies are doing this because they have found that the rate of return produced by fund managers is less than they can obtain themselves through prudent investing.[31] The ICWU acted because "the insurance company refused to agree to our demand for assurances that the monies would not be invested against our own or other workers' interests."[32]

If one is aware of statistics relative to the ICWU, this action gives pause. The union has been in a steady decline since 1975, having lost about 25 percent of its membership, which now may be below 50,000. Its finances have been in a precarious state, and its activities had been directly and indirectly supported by generous grants from the former assistant secretary for the Occupational Safety and Health Administration in the Carter administration—grants not likely to continue.[33] I wonder, therefore, whether current and retired ICWU staff members will be pleased by this action, which the ICWU president says "is integrally tied to the vision we in the Chemical Workers' Union have of a more just society."[34]

The UAW-Chrysler Agreement

In its difficult struggle to survive, the Chrysler Corporation has agreed to codetermination of many managerial decisions with the UAW. According to A.H. Raskin,

> Chrysler was so desperate that it agreed to. . . a payoff for the union's agreement that deposit of the pension-fund contribution could be delayed. The payoff came in the form of a joint advisory board—with three representatives from the U.A.W. and three from Chrysler—that will be set up to invest 10 percent of each year's net increase in pension money in "socially desirable" areas. Money will be steered into investments in low-and middle-income housing, nursing homes, child care centers, and similar projects in communities where Chrysler employees work and live. As part of the deal, union representatives also will be authorized to "shut out" as many as five companies annually because they have investments in South Africa.
>
> The union failed, however, in its attempt to set up a third pension-investment yardstick—one that would permit it to blacklist corporations that engage in "'anti-union' activities." Fraser confessed that the criteria for debarment "got too sticky to define," and postponed that phase of investment policy until the negotiating sessions in 1982.[35]

Just how Chrysler retirees or workers will benefit from the UAW's successful launching of a divergent investing program with pension assets so alarmingly short of fulfilling promised benefits that Ford Motor Company declined a merger proposal with Chrysler remains to be demonstrated. It is of interest to note, however, that Chrysler had an operation in South Africa until it was forced by its current financial state to sell it. Automobile workers in the United States have more jobs because automobile parts are made here for assembly in South Africa. Interestingly, there is no mention in the Chrysler pension agreement about companies that invest in communist dictatorships. These points indicate some of the problems of divergent investments based upon "social" considerations.

PBGC to the Rescue?

Suppose as a result of divergent investing, a pension trust fails. Does the Pension Benefit Guarantee Corporation (PBGC) come to the rescue? For private funds, the answer is undoubtedly positive. Does this give a free hand for divergent investors to have their fling? Here the answer would appear to be negative. In theory, the PBGC machinery is insurance that prevents the retirees and those vested from having their pensions wiped out. It does not protect a company from being bankrupted by excessive pension contributions required to make up for losses suffered by a pension trust. And it does not help retirees under a defined contribution plan that guarantees no specific benefits. If a company with a large plan were to fail, the PBGC program might be compelled to shift some of the burden that could result from divergent investing to the general taxpaying public. It does not, however, relieve pension managers of their obligations, nor does it protect employees whose jobs or future pensions disappear because of uneconomic investing practices.

Conclusion

Union goals for divergent investing of pension assets, namely, (1) the enhancement of union-member employment; (2) the attainment of ideologically compatible social goals; (3) the exercise of shareholder rights on behalf of union objectives; and (4) the use of investment funds to influence organizing objectives, will prove to be unproductive from a return-on-investment perspective and inadequate, or possibly illegal, from a "social" action orientation. These goals represent a divergent attempt to decrease retirement income security for objectives that should be undertaken pursuant to laws and regulations already on the books.

It must be remembered that providing retirement security is the *exclusive* purpose of pension assets. This is true as a matter of law and as a matter of conscience.

In spite of the fact that pension assets are large when listed in the abstract, those assets are inadequate to fully cover the pension promises that have been made to date, and become grossly inadequate should benefit levels be adjusted upward to offset the effects of inflation. Honoring the pension promise to retirees requires that pension assets be invested as prudently as possible with a goal of maximizing investment returns at an acceptable level of risk—a level of risk, I might add, that can be measured.

Finally, the question should be asked: if acceptable divergent investing goals exist—investments that provide for retirement income security while at the same time accomplishing the objectives of unions and other divergent investment advocates—why all the fuss? Such investments obviously have every desirable characteristic and could be employed without debate.

The fact of the matter is that there are very, very few of these investments available. What divergent investment advocates really desire is to subsidize their favorite cause with pension assets. Subsidies cost money, however. Subsidizing other goals, no matter how laudable, will penalize retirement income security. In addition, moving away from market-based investment criteria produces the alternative of political selection of investment vehicles. Political pressure is not the answer for determining how pension assets should be invested, yet this is the logical result of divergent investing advocacy. Let us hope that such a result never comes to pass.

NOTES

1. For details on this period, see *The Labor Banking Movement in the United States* (Princeton, N.J.: Industrial Relations Section, Princeton University, 1929).

2. This company was founded in 1925 and began business in 1927. It was long led by Matthew Woll, one-time heir apparent to Samuel Gompers. It is a well-managed viable company, the stock of which is owned principally by unions and unionists. Present and past union officials comprise its board, and the son of Matthew Woll, a prominent union attorney, is chairman. Best's rates it B + (very good). Its portfolio shows no sign of divergent investing.

3. Roy A. Schotland, "Divergent Investing for Pension Funds," in Dallas L. Salisbury, ed., *Should Pension Assets Be Managed for Social/Political Purposes?* (Washington, D.C.: Employee Benefit Research Institute, 1980), pp. 114-15.

4. *Ibid.*, p. 112.

5. For an analysis of defined contribution profit-sharing and savings plans in the United States and asset formation plans in Western Europe, see Geoffrey W. Latta, *Profit Sharing, Employee Stock Ownership, Savings and Asset Formation Plans in the Western World*, Multinational Industrial Relations Series, No. 5 (Philadelphia: Industrial Research Unit, The Wharton School, University of Pennsylvania, 1979).

6. *Pensions: A Study of Benefit Fund Investment Policies* (Washington, D.C.: Industrial Union Department, AFL-CIO, 1980) (referred to hereinafter as *IUD Report*).

7. Dan M. McGill, *Fundamentals of Private Pensions,* 3rd ed. (Homewood, Ill.: Richard D. Irwin, Inc., 1975), pp. 49-57.

8. Testimony of James D. Hutchinson before the President's Commission on Pension Policy, December 10, 1980, processed copy, p. 2.

9. James D. Hutchinson and Charles G. Cole, "Legal Standards Governing the Investment of Private Pension Capital," in Salisbury, *Should Pension Assets Be Managed for Social/Political Purposes?*, pp. 87-88.

10. *Ibid.*, p. 83.

11. *IUD Report*, pp. 5-6.

12. *Ibid.*, pp. 2-3.

13. See, e.g., Peat, Marwick, Mitchell & Co., *1980 Survey of Investment Performance*, in which the great variety of indices giving different investment performance ratings is demonstrated. The study emphasizes the need to select indices that are compatible with a fund's investment policy and which cover an appropriate time and cyclical period.

14. Latta, *Profit Sharing.*

15. Testimony of Richard O'Brien, ERISA Industry Committee, before the President's Commission on Pension Policy, December 10, 1980, p. 3.

16. Allied Chemical & Alkali Workers v. Pittsburgh Plate Glass Co., 404 U.S. 157 (1971).

17. Inland Steel Company, 77 N.L.R.B. 1; *enf'd*, 170 F.2d 247 (7th Cir., 1948), *cert. denied*, 336 U.S. 960 (1949).

18. On this point see the testimony of James Hacking, American Association of Retired Persons, before the President's Commission on Pension Policy, p. 10.

19. Corporate Data Exchange, Inc., *Pension Investments: A Social Audit* (New York: Corporate Data Exchange, Inc., n.d.).

20. Schotland, "Divergent Investing," pp. 148-57.

21. See the *Daily Labor Report*, No. 166 (August 25, 1980), pp. F-1-3; No. 172 (September 3, 1980), pp. A-3-4; No. 190 (September 29, 1980), pp. A-15-18, E-1-6; and No. 191 (September 30, 1980), pp. A-12-15.

22. *IUD Report*, p. 9.

23. See the *Presbyterian Layman*, January/February 1981, p. 7, for accounts of a $21 million settlement of a class action suit against the United Methodist Church and its agencies over the failure of a retirement building complex and the defrauding of elderly persons by the sale of life care contracts for current operating expenses.

24. Quoted by Schotland, "Divergent Investing," pp. 161-62.

25. For background, see Herbert R. Northrup and Howard G. Foster, *Open Shop Construction*, Major Study No. 54 (Philadelphia: Industrial Research Unit, The Wharton School, University of Pennsylvania, 1975).

26. The small size of many new companies, their highly professional ratio of employment, and probably their caliber of management makes union organization difficult.

27. Hutchinson's testimony, President's Commission on Pension Policy, p. 6.

28. Schotland, "Divergent Investing," pp. 164-65.

29. *Daily Labor Report*, No. 226 (November 20, 1980), pp. A-1-2.

30. There is a tremendous amount of literature on the problems of state and municipal pension plans. A good summary is found in Robert P. Inman, "Paying for Public Pensions: Now or Later?" *Business Review*, November/December 1980 (publication released by Federal Reserve Bank of Philadelphia), pp. 3-12.

31. Tim Metz, "Companies Taking Back Pension Funds Control," *Wall Street Journal*, November 26, 1980, p. 29.

32. IUD, *Labor & Investments*, January 1981, p. 3.

33. This information is based upon a regular reading of the ICWU's publication, *The Chemical Worker*, in which is annually published the union's financial information.

34. IUD, *Labor & Investments*, January 1981, p. 3.

35. A.H. Raskin, "Pension Funds Could be the Unions' Secret Weapon," *Fortune*, Vol. 100 (December 31, 1979), pp. 65-66.

459-64

8310
3140 U.S.

Investing Pensions for Social or Union Purposes: Union Viewpoint

Jacob Sheinkman[†]

With all due respect to the sponsors of this conference, I suggest that the title of this portion of the conference is inappropriate insofar as we are considering the investments of union pension funds. The issue on which I, as a union leader, should be expected to comment is not whether union pension funds are to be invested for "social or union purposes." Rather, the issue on which I believe I should comment is whether or not, and through what mechanisms, a union may protect the immediate and long-term interests of its members by attempting to influence the administration of union pension funds—pension funds which have been built up solely by contributions obtained as a result of the efforts of unions to obtain benefits for their members through collective bargaining—contributions which are pledged, as a matter of law, for the exclusive benefit of such members.

The real issue facing those interested in union pension funds is not whether a union should have the option of somehow influencing and directing the investment of pension funds for social or union purposes. The real question with which I and every union leader, and those in the investment community administering such funds, must grapple is *first*, what fiduciary responsibility does the union leader have to protect the immediate and long-term interests of the members of his union who are the direct beneficiaries of these funds; and *second*, what right does anyone, whether in the investment community or otherwise, have to oppose the lawful attempts of union leaders to exert a level of supervision and direction consistent with their fiduciary obligations to their members over the investment of such funds.

Recent studies, including a 1980 study by the Industrial Union Department (IUD) of the AFL-CIO, have disclosed that union leaders have been derelict in making certain that their members' money in pension funds has been invested so as to maximize, with prudence, the earnings and growth of such funds.

[†] Jacob Sheinkman is Secretary-Treasurer, Amalgamated Clothing & Textile Workers Union of America.

459

The IUD study also indicated that not only did the investment community, operating without any real supervision from union leadership, earn a lamentable return (less than 5 percent between 1970 and 1980) on the monies of union members in these funds, but that it also invested substantial portions of these funds in enterprises that were at odds with the long-term interests of the union members covered by the funds.

If a union leader is to satisfy his obligations to the union members he represents, he must make certain that the pension funds created for the benefit of union members earn an appropriate return. For the same reason, he must attempt to avoid pension fund investments inimical to the immediate or long-term interests of union members. The union leader has a fiduciary responsibility even more extensive than the fiduciary responsibility of those professionals and institutions that actually manage these pension funds. Union leaders are not intruding on the prerogatives of such professionals and institutions when they now, at long last, demand that their members' pension funds be handled so as to yield optimum returns without sacrificing safety. Nor are they intruding on such prerogatives by insisting that pension fund investments do not result in immediate or long-term injury to their members. With their new active approach to their members' pension funds, union leaders are merely satisfying their fiduciary duty to protect the interests of their members. Responsible union leaders like those who subscribed to the IUD study are fully aware that the exercise of these fiduciary obligations requires, rather than minimizes, strict adherence to the principle that pension funds be invested prudently in the interest of their members.

How will this new approach by union leaders affect existing patterns of pension fund investment? The union leader recognizes that he has as much responsibility as fund managers to make certain that funds remain secure and afford a reasonable return on their investments. Nevertheless, the union leader, who must protect his members' interests, should seek to replace any investment, no matter how sound, that injures the long-term interest of members with another prudent investment that does not create such injury. For example, if a pension fund for American Auto Workers was invested in a Japanese auto firm or any firm participating in the Japanese automobile industry, union leadership would be obligated to attempt to eliminate it, since such an investment contributes to the loss of jobs of members whom the pension fund was designed to protect. In such a situation there certainly would be alternate, prudent investments that would not injure the American Auto Workers constituting the plan beneficiaries.

Many of the unions with the largest pension funds have their major concentration of members in large urban centers such as Detroit, New York, Philadelphia, and Boston. The investment managers of such union pension funds have often invested large portions of the funds in industries located in other parts of the country, and/or have ignored suitable investments in these urban centers, thereby contributing to the deterioration of the economies of the urban centers in which these union members live. Such decline may ultimately result in the loss of jobs for union members in these urban centers and also helps destroy the environment in which these union members and their familes live. Witness the deterioration of mass transit and housing, and all public services in the established urban centers whose economies have been deprived, in large measure, of union pension fund investments.

Similarly, any investment in overseas industries may damage the American economy and thereby damage the prosperity of many American industries, including those in which union members are employed and have pension funds.

If the pattern of pension investment can be altered so as to bring economic life back to areas of the United States with deteriorating economies, without sacrificing the requirements of safety and a reasonable return, union leaders have an obligation to attempt such an alteration and thereby serve the interests of their members.

Lastly, there are investments in business firms that operate so far outside the pale of human decency that union leaders may believe it their ethical and moral obligation to avoid investment of their members' pension funds in such firms. A suitable hypothetical example would be an investment of union pension funds in I.G. Farben in 1938, a time when I.G. Farben was using slave labor drawn from concentration camps to produce its goods and, at the same time, make a very handsome profit for its investors. Another example is union funds invested in industries in South Africa, which continues to conduct an economy and a society at the core of which is the racist doctrine of apartheid.

The elimination of investments in corporations engaging in morally repugnant activities will violate no legal rule if alternative suitable investments are available, as they always are. There is no legal obligation on the part of those managing the fund to search out investments in entities that are so tainted morally that they may yield an extraordinarily high return. Indeed, the little law that exists on the subject is set forth in Scott's Law of Trusts (1978 Supplement) as follows:

Trustees in deciding whether to invest in, or to retain, the securities of a corporation may properly consider the social performance of the corporation. They may decline to invest in, or to retain, the securities of corporations whose activities or some of them are contrary to fundamental or generally acceptable ethical principles. They may consider such matters as pollution, race discrimination, fair employment and consumer responsibility. (III Scott §227.13)

When unions, through their associations such as the Industrial Union Department of the AFL-CIO, began to realize that professional pension management organizations, whether they be banks, investment counselors, investment bankers, insurance companies, or the like (which I shall refer to collectively as "the investment community") often were managing union pension funds in a manner inconsistent with the immediate and long-range interests of the union members covered by such funds, the investment community began to react strongly in opposition to the budding efforts of union leadership to ensure that pension funds established for their members were really being used for the immediate and long-term benefit of their members. Significantly, in the one area in which the investment community claims a first-class level of expertise—financial performance of the funds—the investment community has been discredited. As the IUD study indicated, the average return achieved by the investment community for union pension funds between 1970 and 1980 was less than 5 percent per year; a rate which hardly demonstrates that the investment community has the expertise it claims.

The investment community and others allied with them in the business world were all so quick to warn that any supervision of or interference with their activities over union pension funds constituted unwarranted arrogation of union power in a field in which only those with financial expertise should operate. This argument is a proverbial red herring. Union leaders have an even greater fiduciary obligation than the investment community has to make certain that pension funds established and maintained for the benefit of their union members are managed in a way that will secure and optimize the plan benefits for union members and best serve their interests. The attempt of union leadership to comply with their fiduciary obligation to their members' pension funds is not an arbitrary arrogation of union power in the pension field but rather a rightful exercise of the responsibility to ensure that the pension experts are managing the fund in a manner which best benefits their union members. This responsibility is not eliminated legally, or otherwise, by handing over the management of union pension funds to the investment community. Not only is the union leader legally responsible for the maintenance of a fund that protects the interests of his members, but he is also accountable to the members who vote to keep him in office for poor fund performance or fund investments injurious to union members.

Had union leadership such as the IUD not pointed out the deplorable performance of the investment experts in managing pension funds covering union members, it is likely that such performance would have continued indefinitely, and that union pension funds would thereby have less earnings and assets with which to provide the benefits for which they were created.

To imply that union leaders are totally ignorant of the intricacies of investment practice is to ignore the fact that almost every major union has millions of dollars of its own funds to invest and does so generally with its own expert personnel cooperating with investment counselors or financial institutions such as the Amalgamated Bank. Indeed, unions such as the Amalgamated Clothing and Textile Workers' Union (ACTWU), the United Federation of Teachers (UFT), the International Leather and Garment Workers' Union (ILGWU), who have secured much higher returns on their investments than the returns secured on the pension fund investments managed by the investment community may be able to educate the investment community on intricacies of investment practice that will yield much better results than the 5 percent return the investment community has thus far managed for most union pension funds during the last ten years.

There is one final major attack that employers and the investment community have mounted against the attempt by union leadership to influence the investment practices used thus far by the investment community for union pension funds. They argue that if union leadership interferes in fund investment, it will be guided by socially-motivated investments that will undercut the standard of financially-responsible investments which a prudent investment manager would otherwise undertake.

A close reading of the IUD study belies the assertion that union leadership wishes to substitute the standard of "socially responsible" investment for prudent financially responsible investment. When an investment deemed injurious to union members is eliminated, there is no desire by responsible union leadership to substitute any investment, whether or not it serves some social objective, with an investment that is not financially sound. Similarly, investments that improve the economy, job opportunities, and public services available for union members in urban centers need not and should not be made with pension funds unless they are financially sound. The recent experience of public pension fund investment in New York City, with special safeguards at a time when New York City was in financial distress, indicates that innovative investment in such areas possibly may be prudently made.

Similarly, if pension fund investments are used to provide essential mortgage financing, which would be otherwise unavailable, for housing for union members, this investment of pension funds would be responsible and would endure to the benefit of union members, probably at little or no loss of investment return (current mortgage interest rates are 15 percent to 16 percent), and housing for moderate income persons has proven to be a good investment over the last fifty years.

I suggest that the investment community, allied with certain others in the business world, has attempted to put the shoe on the wrong foot. Union leadership is not unlawfully or irresponsibly invading its private preserve and has no intention of unlawfully dissipating the assets thus far entrusted to them. In contrast, the investment community is asserting a prerogative equivalent to ownership of assets which are in no sense owned by the investment community. The real owners are the members of the unions for whose benefit billions of dollars of assets have been placed in the hands of the investment community, which derives substantial fees from the investment of such assets.

It is inaccurate and unfair to label the recent effort of union leaders to satisfy their fiduciary responsibilities with respect to union pension funds as an attempt to ursurp power that belongs elsewhere. To the extent that they use their power over the pension funds they have created to benefit their own members,they are exerting their lawful power only to satisfy their legal obligations to their members. They do not seek to deprive others of any asset or power belonging to them. If the investment community now demands complete freedom from any supervision or influence by union leaders over the pension funds that the investment community manages solely for the benefit of union members, it is demanding an unwarranted arrogation of the power in the union pension field. Such a demand can be satisfied only at the expense of the legitimate interests of the union members who the investment community has been hired to serve.

Appendix A

University of Pennsylvania
The Wharton School Centennial, 1881–1981

Conference

EMPLOYEE RELATIONS AND REGULATION IN THE '80s

Thursday and Friday, June 11–12, 1981

The Hilton Hotel
34th Street and Civic Center Boulevard
(on the University of Pennsylvania Campus)
Philadelphia

Sponsored by
The INDUSTRIAL RESEARCH UNIT, 1921–1981
and
The LABOR RELATIONS COUNCIL, 1946–1981
of
THE WHARTON SCHOOL
IN ITS 100TH ANNIVERSARY YEAR

This Wharton School Conference marks the sixtieth anniversary of the Industrial Research Unit and the thirty-fifth anniversary of the Labor Relations Council. It is also one of a series of activities commemorating the centennial of The Wharton School, the world's first school of business.

The Industrial Research Unit has a proud sixty-year record of relevant research and publication in industrial relations, manpower, personnel, and international employee relations. It is the world's largest academic publisher in these fields. A list of the Unit's current publications is included with this Conference announcement.

The Labor Relations Council was established in 1946. The Council's main purpose is to facilitate the exchange of ideas about major problems in the employee relations area. This Conference is designed to fulfill that objective, bringing together a group of outstanding persons whose experience makes them eminently qualified to discuss the critical issues before us. We extend to all a cordial invitation to attend.

HERBERT R. NORTHRUP   RICHARD L. ROWAN
Chairman, Labor Relations Council   Codirector, Industrial
Director, Industrial Research Unit   Research Unit

Registration Information

The registration fee for the Conference (including two luncheons, dinner, and refreshments) is $200, and for spouses, $75. Each participant will also be mailed a copy of the proceedings when printed. For registration by mail, please fill out enclosed registration form and return with check. Registrations will be accepted in the order received. (Please register as early as possible.) Checks should be made payable to the Labor Relations Council, University of Pennsylvania. Any questions relating to the Conference may be directed to Mrs. Margaret E. Doyle, Office Manager, at the Industrial Research Unit, 308 Vance Hall/CS, University of Pennsylvania (215 243-5605 or 5606). The registration desk located in the lobby of the Hilton Hotel will be open at 8:30 a.m., June 11. Ample parking will be available in the Hilton garage and in nearby parking facilities.

The Hilton Hotel is holding a number of rooms for Conference participants. In making reservations, please advise the Hilton that you are a Conference attendee.

Thursday, June 11, 1981

Morning Session

9:15 Welcome

DONALD C. CARROLL, Dean, The Wharton School

9:30–12:15 Employee Relations and Regulation— An Overview

Chaired by: HERBERT R. NORTHRUP, Director, Industrial Research Unit and Chairman, Labor Relations Council

Employee Relations Innovations for the 1980s—HOWARD H. KEHRL, Vice Chairman, General Motors Corporation

The Beginning of the Industrial Relations Renaissance—VIRGIL B. DAY, Vedder, Price, Kaufman, Kammholz & Day

Employee Relations and Regulation: A Union Viewpoint—ELMER CHATAK, Secretary-Treasurer, Industrial Union Department, AFL-CIO

Managerial Control of Regulation—DOUGLAS SOUTAR, Vice President, Industrial Relations and Personnel, ASARCO, Inc.

Questions and Discussion

12:30–2:15 Refreshments and Luncheon

Chaired by: PAUL F. MILLER, Chairman, Trustees of the University of Pennsylvania

Employee Relations and World Competition—The View of a Chief Executive—DAVID M. RODERICK, Chairman and Chief Executive Officer, United States Steel Corporation

---

All sessions of the Conference will take place in the salons and ballroom located on the mezzanine floor of the Hilton Hotel.

Thursday, June 11, 1981

Afternoon Session

2:30–4:00   Federal Agency Regulation in the '80s

Chaired by: JANICE R. BELLACE, Assistant Professor, Legal Studies and Management, The Wharton School, and Senior Faculty Research Associate, Legal, Industrial Research Unit

The National Labor Relations Board: Two Views

JOHN H. FANNING, Member, National Labor Relations Board (1957—   ); Chairman, NLRB (1977–1981)

EDWARD B. MILLER, Pope, Ballard, Shepard & Fowle; Chairman, NLRB (1970–1975)

Occupational Safety and Health Administration—BRUCE W. KARRH, Corporate Medical Director, E.I. duPont de Nemours & Company, Inc.

Equal Employment Agencies—KENNETH C. MCGUINESS, McGuiness and Williams; President, Equal Employment Advisory Council

Questions and Discussion

4:00–4:15   Break

4:15–5:30   Investing Pensions for Social or Union Purposes: Two Views

Chaired by: LOUIS R. BAUER, Vice President, Human Resources, Hercules Incorporated

Management Viewpoint—JAMES P. NORTHRUP, Director of Human Resources, Bowater Incorporated

Union Viewpoint—JACOB SHEINKMAN, Secretary-Treasurer, Amalgamated Clothing and Textile Workers Union of America

Questions and Discussion

Evening Session

6:30–7:30   Reception

7:30   Dinner

Chaired by: SHELDON HACKNEY, President, University of Pennsylvania

Transportation Regulation—HON. DREW LEWIS, Secretary of Transportation

Friday, June 12, 1981

Morning Session

9:00–11:00   International Regulation of Employee Relations

Chaired by: RICHARD L. ROWAN, Professor of Industry and Codirector, Industrial Research Unit

Regulation and Employee Relations: The Japanese Experience— JAMES D. HODGSON, former Secretary of Labor; Ambassador to Japan

International Codes of Conduct and Corporate Behavior— GEORGE B. MCCULLOUGH, Vice President, Exxon Corporation

*Codetermination: Wave of the Future?—*HARRY R. GUDENBERG, Vice President, International Telephone and Telegraph Corporation

*Responding Effectively to International Pressures—*ROBERT W. COPP, Overseas Liaison Manager, Labor Relations Staff, Ford Motor Company

Questions and Discussion

11:00–11:15   Break

11:15–12:30   New Union and Management Tactics

Chaired by: JAMES H. JORDAN, Vice President, Employee Relations, ICI Americas, Inc.

*Operating during Strikes—*CHARLES R. PERRY, Associate Professor, Industrial Relations, and Senior Faculty Research Associate, Industrial Research Unit

*Neutrality Agreements—*ANDREW M. KRAMER, Seyfarth, Shaw, Fairweather & Geraldson

Questions and Discussion

12:30   Refreshments and Luncheon

Chaired by: LOUIS J. BIBRI, Vice President and Director of Employee Relations, Armstrong World Industries, Inc.

*Congressional Oversight in Employee Relations—*HON. ORRIN G. HATCH, Senator from Utah, Chairman, Senate Committee on Labor and Human Resources

2:45   Adjournment

The Industrial Research Unit, 1921–1981
Sixty Years of Relevant Research

The Labor Relations Council, 1946–1981
*Thirty-five Years of Faculty–
Industry Cooperation*

Racial Policies of American Industry Series

Order from: Kraus Reprint Co., Route 100, Millwood, New York 10546

STUDIES OF NEGRO EMPLOYMENT

Order from the Industrial Research Unit
The Wharton School, University of Pennsylvania
Philadelphia, Pennsylvania 19104

* Order these books from University Microfilms, Inc., Attn: Books Editorial Department, 300 North Zeeb Road, Ann Arbor, Michigan 48106.

6381